D1736661

Animal City

ANIMAL CITY

The Domestication of America

ANDREW A. ROBICHAUD

Harvard University Press

Cambridge, Massachusetts
London, England

2019

Publication of this book has been supported through the generous provisions
of the Maurice and Lula Bradley Smith Memorial Fund.

First printing

Library of Congress Cataloging-in-Publication Data

Names: Robichaud, Andrew A., 1981– author.
Title: Animal city : the domestication of America / Andrew A. Robichaud.
Description: First. | Cambridge, Massachusetts : Harvard University Press, 2019.
Identifiers: LCCN 2019018789 | ISBN 9780674919365 (hardcover)
Subjects: LCSH: Human-animal relationships—United States—
History—19th century. | Urban animals—United States—History—
19th century. | Animal culture—United States—History—19th century. |
Urban policy—United States—History—19th century.
Classification: LCC QL85 .R63 2019 | DDC 591.75/6—dc23
LC record available at https://lccn.loc.gov/2019018789

For my parents
And for Liz

CONTENTS

Animal City

Introduction

Gentlemen Hogs

CHARLES DICKENS was relieved to finally set foot on dry land in January 1842. The last leg of his trip to North America had been "squally," and the ship "tumbled and rolled about" in the sharp winds and biting cold. "I strained my eyes as the first patches of American soil peeped like molehills from the green sea," he wrote on his final approach into the Boston Harbor. Over the next several months, Dickens would embark on an extensive tour of North America, which he recorded for his faithful readers in England. After a few days in Boston, he made his way to New York City—which he called that "beautiful metropolis of America." Boston was older and smaller, and in some ways more "refined," but New York was the booming commercial city that seemed to embody the new American experiment that captivated Old World observers. Compared to Boston, New York was not quite so clean, wrote Dickens, "the bricks not quite so red" and "the stone not quite so white." But the colors and textures of New York nevertheless dazzled the English writer: the pavement stones "polished with the tread of feet until they shine;" in one part of town a "deep green leafy square," in another the "glittering shops." The women dressed in clothes so bright and varied that Dickens said he had "seen more colours in these ten minutes, than we should have seen elsewhere, in as many days." He toured many parts of New York City, from that "narrow thoroughfare" known as Wall Street, to the Five Points in all its "filth and wretchedness."[1]

But Dickens's interest in New York was not limited to its human inhabitants. In 1842, Dickens was setting foot in a city teeming with animal life—and a city on the cusp of extraordinary ecological and population changes, including the transformation of its nonhuman inhabitants. Dickens was seeing the antebellum animal city in full—a city that would not last as he experienced it for much longer.[2] He was surprised by the abundance of horses and carriages. "No stint of omnibuses here!" he wrote, adding that there were "plenty of hackney cabs and coaches too, gigs, phaetons, [and] large-wheeled tilburies," he wrote, employing a lost lexicon to describe the nuance and variety of horse conveyances once common in everyday life. Near the Bowery he saw two "stout horses" pulling "a great wooden ark" filled with "a score or two of people." Elsewhere he would have seen more refined breeds pulling the decorated carriages of the city's wealthiest residents.

But it was crossing Broadway that Dickens had his most memorable animal encounter in New York. Broadway, he wrote, was "the great promenade and thoroughfare," of the city—the crowded artery that started in the Battery and sliced through downtown, before it gradually became "a country road" that connected the city and its northern hinterlands. Where Dickens was crossing, Broadway was a "wide and bustling street," with shops and hotels. The fashionable and well-to-do strolled up and down the wide sidewalks: "ladies in bright colors walking to and fro, in pair and singly," one with a light blue parasol who "passed and repassed the hotel-window twenty times while we were sitting there."[3]

As Dickens prepared to cross Broadway he watched for carriages and omnibuses that jockeyed for space on the busy street, and whose presence filled the air with a constant clatter of hooves and wheels on uneven roads. But Dickens had to keep watch for another type of street traffic. Mixing with the ladies in bright clothes and parasols were "two portly sows," Dickens observed, and around the corner came a "half-a dozen gentlemen hogs." Dickens spent two pages reflecting on New York City's pigs—the independent "republican hogs" who scavenged streets by day and returned home each night, spending their lives transforming the city's trash into meat. Dickens reflected on the life of another "solitary swine, lounging homeward by himself," with one good ear, "having parted with the other to vagrant dogs."[4] And in the "rotten" and "debaucherous" Five Points, Dickens again noted the numerous porcine residents. "Do they ever wonder," he asked, "why their masters walk upright in lieu of going on all-fours?" Here, in the center of the largest American city—in what seemed like all parts of town—were swine.[5]

Although Dickens seemed especially enamored with New York's "gentlemen-hogs," pigs were not the only animals that inhabited nineteenth-century American cities—nor was New York all that exceptional for its pervasive and unruly population of urban livestock. For much of the nineteenth century, American cities were ecologically diverse places, invariably made up of a multitude of domesticated, semidomesticated, and undomesticated species. Indeed, animals were

FIGURE O.I Anne Marguerite Hyde de Neuville, "Bridewell, and Charity-School, Broadway, opposite Chamber Street—February 1808." The Miriam and Ira D. Wallach Division of Art, Prints and Photographs, The New York Public Library.

so commonplace in American cities that, at times, their presence seemed not worth mentioning at all. Observations of the "animal city" were often left to visitors and tourists from places where urban livestock had already been largely regulated or excluded. For Dickens and others, the sight of swine was perhaps rustic and quaint—a symbol of the unrefined and unwieldy American metropolis, a New World riff on the urbane. Other writers and artists echoed Dickens's astonishment at the animal life of American cities. When visiting San Francisco in the 1850s, a French journalist thought it noteworthy that the city's domesticated animals lived "in freedom" in many parts of the city, and went on to describe "all the inconveniences such a population [of animals] brings in its train."[6] Countless drawings and paintings of nineteenth-century American cities included depictions of these urban animal populations.

By the turn of the twentieth century, however, many of these domesticated animal species had vanished from American cities. Cattle, dairy cows, sheep, and pigs were increasingly absent from downtown landscapes—as were the workers and physical structures that contained animal lives: corrals, feedlots, hog ranches, dairy barns, and slaughterhouses. As domesticated animals used for food and clothing became increasingly invisible to urban residents, other forms of animal life remained and flourished in the Gilded Age city. Urban horse populations swelled, creating new problems and challenges.[7] Increasingly, urban residents experienced and understood animals through zoos, popular media and performances, and as pets. Taken together, this set of transformations in the way that an emerging majority of Americans related to animals was nothing short of a radical remaking of human and animal life in America. This book is about how and why that transformation happened, and why it mattered—and continues to matter. Tracing the specific histories of human and animal interactions in cities offers a powerful new lens in understanding the history of American culture, law, commerce, politics, and urban development. Dickens's pigs reveal even more than the novelist knew.

Animals were central to the way Americans understood the world. Americans thought with animals. They used animals to debate some of the most central and important questions of their day. Through animals, Americans contemplated their place in nature and in God's creation. Through animals, they considered the morality of new economic relationships. Through animals, they planned and imagined ideal environments for human and animal life. Through animals, they worked out key political questions of who counted, and in what ways. Through animals, local, state, and national governments tested and expanded legal and law-enforcement powers. Through animals, Americans debated what it was to be human.

Environmentally, animals posed significant challenges to urbanization. As population densities increased, the question of what to do with animals—in both life and death—became a central concern of urban residents, politicians, and reformers. Socially and culturally, remaking animal life held immense promise as a way of reforming and improving human life, with the capacity to shape politics and society. Remaking human-animal relationships in cities required new laws, new means of enforcement, and new forms of activism—pushing boundaries of governance and politics. By the last decades of the nineteenth century, laws across the United States dictated where urban residents could keep and kill animals, how many and what types of animals they could have, and even the intricate rules of how they were allowed to treat their animals. A growing number of public and private police forces emerged to enforce these laws, which they did unevenly across class and space.

Without a history of the nineteenth-century animal city, we cannot fully explain why modern cities look the way they do. The decisions city and state authorities made in the nineteenth century to organize animal life and animal industries created deep historical pathways of development that are often still active, though invisible or missing from the stories we tell about our cities. The places set aside for concentrated animal industries in the late nineteenth century have a legacy that has shaped neighborhoods for more than a century: relentlessly polluted in the nineteenth century, redlined in the 1930s, rusted out in the 1950s, and made susceptible to redevelopment schemes in the decades that followed. Boston's slaughterhouse district remains visible today in the worn-down triple-deckers and windowless warehouses that stand in the cold shadows of towering new buildings of glass and steel.

=

The disappearance of livestock from cities would have surprised past generations. For millennia, people lived—and expected to live—alongside livestock out of necessity or convenience.[8] As Europeans colonized North America, they nearly always did so with herds of domesticated animals. Most European colonists and enslaved Africans were farmers in one way or another—and even those who were not full-time farmers dabbled in raising animals as a side business, or to provide milk and meat for their families. Even as American cities developed in the early nineteenth century, many urban residents continued to expect that they would be able to maintain farm animals despite the increasingly crowded conditions of urban life.[9] Urban residents not only kept livestock in antebellum cities, but businesses that relied on animals—dairy farms, horse stables, hog ranches, wholesale butchers, tanners, and others—formed essential parts of the urban landscape. The segregating and sorting of animal lives and animal industries became a central part of the business and politics of the nineteenth century.[10]

To follow the changes in human relations with animals amid urbanization is to follow changes in urban economy and politics. Many cities and towns were at first accommodating or at least tolerant of residents who wished to keep domesticated species, even in the face of growing population density. Boston instituted stricter rules to prevent overgrazing of the Boston Common in the eighteenth and early nineteenth centuries, which helped maintain the vestiges of animal husbandry in the city.[11] Some of these rules persisted into the late nineteenth century. In San Francisco, lawmakers sought to exclude dense concentrations of livestock, but continued to allow residents to keep as many as two cows (with some restrictions) into the twentieth century, implicitly maintaining a romantic ideal of independent yeomanry within the industrial metropolis.[12] Livestock removal was not an inevitable outcome, but was gradually built over time through evolving political, economic, social, and cultural developments.

But the story of urban livestock policy in the nineteenth century is largely one of regulation and restriction. Boston ultimately banned grazing on the Common as part of a larger movement to transform working landscapes into places of refined leisure, complete with planted trees and walking paths.[13] Leaders in other

FIGURE 0.2 James Kidder's 1829 lithograph of the Boston Common shows a landscape in transition from a cow pasture and multiuse space into an urban park and place of leisure. James Kidder and Senefelder Lith. Co., "Boston Common." Print. 1829. Boston Public Library.

cities instituted similar policies that favored certain environmental and social characteristics over others. Lawmakers in New York sought to impose order on city streets and on the fringes of urban development by waging war on hog ranches and swill-milk dairies in the 1850s and 1860s.[14] Around the same time, officials in San Francisco created and effectively enforced new rules to prevent cattle drives and the operation of slaughterhouses downtown. This wave of new and forceful animal regulation and law enforcement swept across cities in the United States. In countless cases, city and state governments exercised notable levels of power and authority in making animal policy and remaking urban life.[15]

These new restrictions on animals did not go unchallenged. New Yorkers famously rioted in the 1820s and 1830s in response to city efforts to impound their free-roaming pigs. Urban dairymen in New York pushed back at every attempt to regulate and relocate the city's dairy stables, with some success. The continued presence of "gentlemen hogs" when Dickens visited in 1842 suggests that efforts to control animals in antebellum cities often failed or faltered in the face of popular

6

resistance. But after the Civil War, many cities found ways to more forcefully and effectively implement animal policy to remake urban landscapes. In San Francisco, the city's "War on Butchers" in the late 1860s marked a more energetic and effective governmental intervention in removing cattle, pigs, slaughterhouses, and other nuisances from downtown. Other cities across the United States participated in this wave of urban animal reform, which required the creation of new city and state departments with greater levels of police powers and funding and led to years of policing and litigation.

It is tempting to ascribe such changes to technology—namely, the new spatial and economic possibilities of railroads and growing scales of production. But technology alone was not enough to displace livestock from cities.[16] Railroads, for example, did not so much displace animals as expand the imagination of reformers in rethinking the spatial possibilities of animal life in cities. Railroads revealed the possibility of removing "noxious trades" to the urban fringe, while also enabling the possibilities of healthy rural production of meat and milk for urban consumers. In New York, San Francisco, Boston, and other cities, railroads opened up new possibilities for relocating slaughterhouses and certain animal businesses. But, as the following pages reveal, the *idea* of the railroad shaped landscapes in ways that often preceded material reality: railroad lines connecting the new Butchertown to downtown San Francisco, for example, were promised but not built until decades after the city forced butchers to relocate to the new slaughterhouse "reservation." In New York, railroads promised residents and lawmakers more than they could actually deliver in providing the city a clean and healthy supply of milk. Railroads may have activated the impulse and scale of regulation, but these were ultimately policy choices, and not merely part of a story of linear progress and technological determinism.[17]

Livestock exclusion marks only half of the consequential transformation in urban animal life in the nineteenth century. The urban menagerie changed by both addition and subtraction—in both quality and in quantity. Amid growing restrictions on urban livestock populations, city residents and reformers also actively made a new world of human and animal relationships. Beginning in the late 1860s, Societies for the Prevention of Cruelty to Animals (SPCAs) and Humane Societies spread across the continent with an evangelical fervor. These anticruelty organizations and campaigns began largely as urban movements, but gradually expanded into rural areas by the 1890s. Anticruelty took various forms—from the soft power of cultural production (lectures, books, stories, children's groups, teaching curricula), to the hard power of lawmaking and law enforcement. In all, the humane movement sought to improve the lives of animals, and in turn to improve human society by eliminating displays of violence toward animals, while also cultivating a culture of kindness toward animals. Anticruelty campaigns shaped both culture and law, developing innovative and distinctive uses of state power to remake urban life. SPCAs were part of a growing legal and cultural movement that regulated and redefined animal life and human-animal relations, beginning in the nineteenth century.[18]

The addition of various forms of animal entertainments also marked a profound cultural transformation during the late nineteenth century. As slaughterhouses and livestock lost visibility in the late 1800s, zoos and naturalistic animal displays became more prominent. Between 1860 and 1910, urban zoos developed and spread at an exceptional pace and began to emphasize passive, educational, leisurely, and contemplative observation. A distinct and powerful culture of pet ownership also flourished in the last decades of the nineteenth century, marked by the rise of kennel clubs and SPCAs and fueled by a thriving popular culture of cultivating kindness toward animals in childhood.[19] These changes increasingly turned urban animals into objects of human curiosity, kindness, and amusement: new forms of human consumption. Horses remained in cities as working animals into the twentieth century—their bodily presence indispensable to the workings of the urban economy. But horses, too, became highly regulated and increasingly protected by police and SPCA officers before losing their place in cities to electric streetcars, automobiles, and trains.[20] Collectively, these changes meant that, by the early twentieth century, the landscape of human-animal relations in cities was, in many ways, more familiar to modern American life than it was to urban residents only decades before.

In political and legal terms, animal laws were at the forefront of testing new regulatory powers of state and city governments. Through animals, lawmakers experimented with new spatial restrictions, pushed the boundaries of governmental intervention into work and home, and tested the reaches of police and regulatory powers. These experiments were largely reinforced and upheld in courts, ushering in an era of greater regulatory intervention historians have often attributed to the later Progressive Era.[21] This shift in augmenting municipal and state power had consequences far beyond the control of animals alone.

=====

This book is divided roughly into three parts. The first part (Chapters 1 to 3) focuses on the development of the animal city and key changes that led to livestock exclusion and reform. Chapter 1 examines the formation of the animal city through the development of urban feedlot dairies in New York City in the 1820s and 1830s, and the political, social, and moral tensions surrounding their emergence.

As the case in New York demonstrates, cities experienced not only human urbanization in the early nineteenth century but also animal urbanization—human industrial labor, along with animal forms as well. The development of new systems of large-scale animal production emerged in a world of evolving urban industrial capitalism. New Yorkers struggled to understand their place in this new economy, and their moral obligations to animals and to one another.

Chapters 2 and 3 focus in large part on San Francisco—a city that yielded rich and new historical sources—with an eye toward comparative analysis of urban animal policy. Here we see the centrality of animal policy in the transformation of nuisance law from reactive and court-based, to preemptive and bureaucratic. Although historians identify zoning as a twentieth-century concept of the Progressive Era—reinforced in the Supreme Court's decision in *Euclid v. Ambler* (1926)—nineteenth-century urban animal policy reveals thick layers of regulations designed to limit where people were allowed to own and maintain certain animals, how many they could have, and how they were allowed to treat those animals. Many nineteenth-century animal laws were zoning in all but name.[22] Chapter 3 reveals some of the immediate and long-term consequences of livestock and slaughterhouse reform in San Francisco. Nineteenth-century urban animal policy caused one of the most profound environmental transformations of its time—so profound that its effects continue to shape urban landscapes today.[23]

The second part of this book (Chapters 4 and 5) explores the ways in which urban residents simultaneously rebuilt animal relationships in the last decades of the nineteenth century, particularly through the development of SPCAs armed with police powers. Distant progenitors of the organizations they are today, SPCAs were, in most cases, semiprivate police forces incorporated by state legislatures to enforce a growing set of animal welfare laws. Regional societies set ambitious cultural and social agendas, published works of fiction and nonfiction advocating kindness to animals, lobbied for new legislation, promoted practices that contributed to a culture of kindness, and, in most cases, served as private police and prosecutorial agencies. SPCAs were part of a larger public-private law-enforcement apparatus that received bounties for convictions and sought to impose a vast social and legal order on nineteenth-century American life—particularly in cities.[24] Ironically, the two massive forces of urban animal reform—livestock exclusion and humane reform—came to work, unintentionally, at cross-purposes. New geographic restrictions on livestock in cities effectively limited the SPCAs' capacity to enforce laws on these increasingly distant animal populations and shaped the very work of these societies.

In the third part (Chapter 6 and 7), I conclude with an examination of the evolution of animal entertainment in American cities, focusing on developments in the mid- and late nineteenth century. Although animal entertainments were not entirely new to late nineteenth-century cities, the period marked a notable shift in the numbers and types of popular animal entertainments in cities. With those changes came new debates over what forms of animal entertainment were appropriate for public consumption and whether certain forms of entertainment were themselves cruel. In Chapter 6, I trace a long history of animal entertainments over the course of the nineteenth century, from Charles Willson Peale's republican museum of natural history to P. T. Barnum's American Museum in New York. In Chapter 7, I turn to Robert Woodward's zoo and gardens in Gilded Age San Francisco. Across time, Americans used animals to access changing intellectual, emotional, and cultural ideals. Many believed that proper relationships with animals would cultivate proper states of mind, and thereby improve society. Whereas older animal displays exhibited "freaks of nature" or "curiosities," new exhibits of the late nineteenth century increasingly sought to bring urban residents into contact with what they imagined were "representative species" of "nature."

This story begins in New York, ends in San Francisco, and explores other American cities across time and space. Each chapter offers a sort of case study, but the sum of each story is ultimately bigger than its parts. I have sought to make connections across cities whenever possible. Urban animal reform contained a set of ideas and organizations that linked cities across the United States—and even internationally—creating a remarkable degree of simultaneous policymaking across the nation. In some cases, city and state authorities intentionally shared and borrowed ideas and regulatory methods to handle animal nuisances and to remake human-animal relationships. It was no mere coincidence that San Francisco and Boston's slaughterhouse relocation laws happened within months of each other—and came in the wake of the creation of La Villette in Paris. Nor was it mere coincidence that New Orleans' slaughterhouse regulation—made famous in the Slaughterhouse Cases of 1873—followed those in San Francisco and Boston.[25] Ideas of public health and law kept pace across American cities, as city and state governments struggled with similar problems and borrowed ideas and practices from one another.

Taken together, the changes described in the chapters that follow marked a massive shift in how most Americans experienced and interacted with animals, with one another, and with their governing institutions. By the end of the nineteenth century, cities were knee-deep in animal regulations, with legislative and bureaucratic rules and enforcement from various levels of government and various departments: police officers, market inspectors, poundmasters, public health officials, and SPCA agents. New agencies and organizations together created a multi-layered police power that enforced laws dictating where people could own animals, how many animals they could possess, and how they were permitted to treat certain species. Once considered forms of private property largely beyond the reach of public intervention, animals were increasingly the prerogative of local and state governments. Animals trace the changing contours of American governance. Through this wide range of urban animal changes, we see animals as central players in an unfolding story of popular entertainment, urban reform, changing urban and suburban environments, and growing regulatory power in America. Without animals, we cannot fully understand the changing environmental relations of city and country, and the ways in which people came to define what it was to be human.

＝＝

The stories presented in the pages that follow trace large-scale human developments central to the *process* of creating modern American society. Our changing relations with animals have shaped and reflected changes in how we think of ourselves. In his 1980 essay, "Why Look at Animals?" John Berger argued that the nineteenth century marked the "beginning of a process, today being completed by 20th century corporate capitalism, by which every tradition that has previously mediated between man and nature was broken." Before this rupture, he said, "animals constituted the first circle of what surrounded man."[26] In highlighting this rupture between humans and the living animals they consume, Berger touched on an essential and vexing feature of modern life. Richard Bulliet has called the features of modern and western human-animal relationships "post-domesticity": a form of alienation that separates people from the animals they consume, which in turn has distorted human sensitivity to suffering, sex, and death, which had once been processed in human relationships with animals.[27]

Rather than having a successional relationship, livestock separation and ideas about animal welfare coexisted and were cocreated. In many cases, the public health leaders who advocated livestock exclusion were also active members of SPCAs. Both efforts fell under the larger umbrella of reforms associated with contemporary concepts of "progress" and "civilization." The sensibilities of a post-domesticity society were in constant dialogue with material conditions on the ground. Seeing these movements as co-constructed—rather than merely successional—offers a more complicated and nuanced understanding of the process of creating our modern landscape of human-animal interactions.

This project, like most histories, takes us back to a world of uncertain change and the unknown future that lay ahead of animal reformers of the late nineteenth century. In looking closely at the specific dimensions of human and animal interactions, this book begins to trace the cracks and fissures of that emerging chasm between modern human life and animal life. How and why did this growing chasm emerge between consumers and the living animals they consumed? How did many animals—particularly livestock—move so quickly from our "first circle" to a virtually invisible outer ring? What have these changes meant for the way modern Americans think about animals and our collective relationships with them and to each other? And what has it meant for animals themselves?

Though it bleeds into the present, this project is primarily history. It centers on questions of urban development, politics, law, and social change, and does so in the hopes of understanding events in their unique time and place. But it is also, in part, the story of the origins of our modern spatial and social relationships with animals. It contains stories of well-intentioned reformers who remade the world in ways they could never have imagined. In rethinking our own ideas and landscapes of animal interactions, we might do well to return to the beginnings of the changes that have created our world, to the "gentlemen hogs," "stumptail cows," and dog-powered machines that were once part of everyday life for millions of Americans.

Animals are appearing more often in the stories we tell of the past. They have always been there, but only more recently have we recognized their ubiquity and centrality. Animals deserve a place in our scholarship not only because animal lives and perspectives have inherent value, but because understanding changes to human-animal relationships yields insights into questions that have long interested historians, while raising new questions of our past and present.[28]

At the very least, animals also deserve a place in the stories we tell because their ghosts still haunt the places in which we live. Our cities still bear the scars and legacies of an urban world where animals once lived and died by the millions. New animal zones established in the 1860s and 1870s set certain parts of cities on new and distinct developmental paths, first characterized by pollution, neglect, and politically sanctioned degradation. Nineteenth-century animal ghosts are invisible at first glance, but they live on as active agents in urban development today. They are in the Home Owners' Loan Corporation Redlining maps from the 1930s, the siting of sewage treatment facilities and power generators in the twentieth century, the blocks of warehouses and rail lines that still lie at the urban fringe, and in public housing and redevelopment projects of the past half century. There are animal ghosts on desolate streets on the fringe of urban life, in the empty lots overrun with weeds where animal blood and bones still mix with the soil. As reformers remade animal landscapes in the late nineteenth century, they created pathways for development that still actively shape the urban world today. We cannot understand the modern city without understanding this deeper, invisible animal past.

CHAPTER ONE

Cow Town

New York City and the
Urban Dairy Crisis,
1830–1860

W ITHIN THE PAGES of the 1858 report produced by the New York Committee on City Milk is a short paragraph about an infant named "Martha Mc—." Martha lived on Mulberry Street in the poor and working-class Bowery of lower Manhattan. Her family was among the large and growing population of poor Irish residents in New York City, most likely scraping by and desperate for money. So when Martha's mother found work as a wet nurse for another family, she probably thought hard about her options and what the extra income would mean for her family's life.

We do not know the dimensions of her decision to become a wet nurse—whether her husband or extended family, if they were around, had any input or final say—or whether there was much of a decision for Martha's mother at all. Her daughter was, it seemed, old enough to be weaned from her mother's breast, and cow's milk was an inexpensive, plentiful, and widely accepted food for infants. Martha's mother decided to wean her daughter, to "put her out" on a diet of cow's milk, in hopes that the money she would earn and save would improve their lives. As one of the many milkmen made his pass on Mulberry Street, she probably walked out her door and purchased some milk from a cart, its exterior adorned with images and words that reassured her that the milk she was buying for her baby was fresh and pure and from the "country."

But problems soon emerged for baby Martha. She became sick, and her condition worsened. According to the city report, her symptoms were similar to

another child in the same neighborhood, on Elizabeth Street, named "Susan C."
Susan was "craving nourishment," and voraciously drinking large quantities of
cow's milk. But something was wrong with her digestion. Even though the child
was "filling itself to its utmost distension," she was quickly losing weight and
"gradually starving to death." Martha's condition was no better. When the doctor
arrived at Martha's house, he found her "suffering with enormously distended ab-
domen, and all the symptoms of what is usually called consumption of the
bowels" (referring to common symptoms of what was understood at the time as
an intestinal form of tuberculosis). Susan recovered, but Martha continued her
decline. Within a week of the doctor's first visit, Martha was dead in her mother's
arms.[1]

=====

Martha's story was not unusual. The death of a child was a tragedy that many
families experienced. But by 1858—the year in which Martha's death was noteworthy enough to be recorded in a city report—many Americans living in cities
believed they were seeing something entirely new. Infant mortality rates in
American cities had been rising sharply since the 1820s, and new studies based
on statistical evidence showed that rates in cities vastly exceeded those of the
country—reinforcing many existing ideas of the city as a place of poor health.[2]
In the late 1840s and early 1850s, children under five comprised almost half of the
deaths in New York City, according to the physician Russell Thacher Trall. "So
long as the present order of things continues," he said in 1853, the city would see
the deaths of *eight or nine thousand children annually*."[3] Reformers watched as
the great American cities of Boston, Philadelphia, and New York began seeing
larger percentages of their infants die. To reformers, the infant mortality trends
in American cities stood in sharp contrast to those in Europe at the same time:
the New York reformer Robert Hartley called the phenomenon "peculiar to our
own country, and therefore not inseparable from the conditions of city life."[4] Despite many markers of American progress, life in antebellum American cities
was getting worse, not better, and reformers sought to understand and stop what
they saw as the downward slide of the city, the nation, and the whole of God's
creation.

For many reformers, the cause of rising infant mortality, and a variety of other
social ills, could be traced back through city streets—along the routes of milk
carts—to the city's growing urban dairy stables. These stables epitomized a new,
highly competitive urban economy built on efficiency and a greater degree of anonymity of producers. Critics saw the new relationship with cows as one that

was driven by greed, riddled with sin, and a central node in a larger network of vice. To these reformers, the city dairies caused suffering and sickness in cows, which resulted in impurities in milk and spread illness and death across the city. If unhealthy city cows were "poisoning" the infants of the city, they argued, then members of society needed to remake their relationship with cows to bring them into greater alignment with what they called "nature," a word used to describe an ideal human interaction with the environment that mirrored what they believed were God's designs.

This possibility of natural perfection and its promise for urban reform was one that flourished in the age of radically new technologies that promised to connect the city and the country in ways previously unimaginable. The new economic and environmental dialogue that emerged between the city and the countryside— increasingly bound, as they were, by advancing roads, canals, and railroads— enlarged the spatial imaginations of urban consumers and reformers alike.[5] For reformers, new relationships with the hinterlands offered potential for the vast health of the country to remake and improve the city.[6] Through new technologies, an ideal relationship between people, cows, and nature could be restored—and with it would flourish the health of animals, the milk they produced, and, by transference, the lives of people living in cities. Machines allowed new possibilities of bringing urban society closer to nature and God. Better milk and healthier country cows—connected by advancing railroads—could inject natural health into urban environments and mend the cracks, sores, and fissures that threatened the physical and social health of cities. There was a lot riding on milk cows.[7]

Urban Herds

The presence of cows in cities was, for years, an unremarkable thing. For most colonial Americans, life invariably meant management and interaction with working animals—particularly animals used to produce milk and meat for human consumption. Most English colonists and early Americans structured their lives around the daily and seasonal needs of their relationships with domesticated animals. Days were marked by the morning and evening milking of cows, and seasons passed with cycles of calving, weaning, and slaughtering.[8] In New England, colonial records suggest that the most common item bequeathed to a widow was a milk cow. By the eighteenth century, even the smallest New England farms typically had at least one cow.[9]

As Americans made their way into burgeoning cities in the early nineteenth century, many brought with them the cows, horses, and other animals that had previously defined their ways of life. The idea of a city cow, and the oddity of it, was one that emerged over time. When Americans took up new types of urban work, many did not completely disavow agricultural relationships with animals. There was no clean break between agriculture and industry, between country labor and city labor. A worker might have labored all day in a shop before returning home to milk and feed a family cow. (Quite often women were responsible for the work of milking.) For the city's working poor, there were obvious economic incentives to raising animals for market or for personal consumption. Raising animals provided an inexpensive form of labor that effectively turned materials of little human value into flesh, milk, and leather. As cities emerged, the transition to a life without animals was never obvious or inevitable: Over the long course of human history, people lived—and expected to live—with and by the products of animals. Why would new city environments be any different?

As the urban market economy emerged in the nineteenth century, however, urban residents increasingly relied on markets to obtain animal products. The new economy of specialized labor and production left less time for average families to manage animals as intensively as their parents once had on farms. Some urban residents continued to keep animals for food as part of their way of life; others turned almost entirely to the market to purchase animal products. As larger numbers of families came to the marketplace to get their milk and meat, others turned to specializing in dairy and cattle production. Still, urban dairy cows, sheep, chickens, and roaming pigs were all part of a vital urban workforce and essential actors in the urban environment. Increasingly, dairy producers in cities treated cows as units of production, raising them in dense feedlots. Like their human counterparts in the early industrial city, the labor of animals happened in environments that resembled factories and increasingly structured, confined, and simplified to yield profits. The milk these confined cows produced was transported and sold to strangers on city streets and in busy urban markets.[10]

At first, most major cities sought to accommodate residents' desires to keep cows and other animals in densely populated areas. But as cities like New York and Boston grew at extraordinary rates in the early to mid-nineteenth century, new social and environmental pressures shaped the way people related to animals in cities. Since its inception, the Boston Common had been a space of productive labor, and would remain so into the early nineteenth century. New rules in the eighteenth century sought to maintain the Common as a working space. To prevent overgrazing, for instance, city leaders chose to limit the number of cows to one per family and levied a new tax on residents who chose to use the Common for grazing. The money from the tax went toward enforcing the new regulations.[11]

The growth of a new urban market economy also created a new social class in cities that increasingly saw their status reflected in their separation from productive animals. New and expanding wealthy classes (in Boston, New York, and other cities) asserted their political powers to create refined urban spaces out of parks and commons once considered places for working relationships with animals and the land. Within a generation, city parks, cemeteries, and pastures went from places where animals could graze and scavenge, to places that were increasingly defined by the absence of animals and the presence of cultivated trees, lawns, and gardens. These landscape ideals stood in opposition to each other; the sights, sounds, and smells of a refined urban park, by definition, excluded the more traditional, working relationships with those same places.[12]

By the 1820s and 1830s, the spaces available to graze animals in many cities were shrinking. Burial grounds—once a site for city grazing—were redesigned as nonproductive human spaces. Boston's City Council banned cows from all of the city's cemeteries in 1830 at the request of the city's wealthy residents, who wanted cows removed from the Granary Burying Grounds in particular.[13] Other cities also promoted the concept of refined gardens of leisure. Philadelphia (Franklin and Washington Squares) and New York (Union Square and Gramercy Park) sought to transform parks into relaxing oases of urban leisure, reconstructed in opposition to work. In so doing, they drove out cows and activities related to labor, often at the expense of the city's poorest residents who used open spaces to help provide for their daily needs.[14]

Many new regulations on common city spaces undermined the ability of urban residents to effectively maintain cows. It was perhaps no mere coincidence that a massive urban feedlot dairy industry emerged in New York in the wake of these new rules. In New York, the urban industrial dairies began as unusual private institutions that, in many ways, mimicked the functions of the declining public grazing systems. In many cases, residents paid a landlord to house and feed their animals, but still owned the animals and the milk and meat they produced. Along the fringes of major American cities emerged concentrated and specialized businesses devoted to the messy work of turning animal bodies and lives into commodities. The push to refine urban spaces in the 1820s and 1830s forced cows off of common spaces and concentrated their presence in other parts of the city.[15] But there were also strong forces that kept dairy cows in and near cities. Prior to effective transportation and refrigeration, consumer demands for fresh milk meant that animals needed to remain relatively close to where milk was purchased and consumed. Dairy cows became effectively suspended in a landscape that was neither too close to downtown residents, nor too far from them.

Another Mother's Milk

There is also some evidence to suggest that milk consumption was on the rise in nineteenth-century cities. Although there are no reliable statistics, ample evidence suggests that changes in dietary advice and wet-nursing practices in cities created new demands for milk among urban populations. From colonial times to the beginning of the nineteenth century, fresh milk was not a common beverage for most Americans.[16] But by the early and mid-nineteenth century that was beginning to change. Even Sylvester Graham—arguably the most influential health reformer of his generation—reversed his stance and ultimately endorsed milk consumption after seeing a "vast amount of evidence in favor of milk as an important article in the diet of mankind."[17]

Perhaps more important than adult consumption of milk, however, were shifts in the use of milk for infants. For the working poor, there were compelling reasons for women to "hand feed" their children using cow's milk instead of milk from their own bodies. In cities, women increasingly worked outside the home, or participated in the labor market in ways that undercut their capacity to nurse their own infants. These new demands on the labor of women likely cut down their productivity as nursing mothers. Because sustained and effective nursing requires frequent feedings, small shifts in the demands on women's time could cause major disruptions in their ability to consistently produce enough milk for their children.[18]

In addition to new demands on time and labor, urban mothers also faced weaker social bonds that once provided necessary support for nursing. One of the hallmarks of the early industrial economy was the increased flow of people in, out, and through burgeoning American cities. Amid this new social landscape, mothers left behind extended families and social networks that would have supported their abilities to nurse. Women often shared knowledge of the intricacies of how to nurse and often shared breast milk among family as well as members of a community. Those social networks were breaking down in early industrial cities, as nuclear families often became isolated from extended families and female social networks that were likely more conducive to breast-feeding.[19]

In many cases, women's entrance into the labor market meant selling the milk from their own bodies. Wet nursing was one way that many women entered the workforce. This was particularly true in cities, where wet nursing was increasingly a valuable form of paid labor available to women.[20] When women like Martha's mother sought income through the sale of their milk, they typically "put out" their own infants on cow's milk. The urban demand for wet nurses likely set off a chain reaction through the economy that created greater demands for cow's milk among poor families.

But urban lactation was a complicated matter. Many had concerns about the healthfulness of milk produced in cities—whether human or animal. Urban environments were dangerous because of both the physical and psychic problems they posed. According to many doctors, emotional distress brought on by the urban environment could create internal poisons in women's bodies that were then passed on to nursing children. Many believed that a woman who was emotionally distraught could harm or even kill her child if she nursed during or immediately after an emotional incident. Echoing the medical knowledge of the times, Robert Hartley noted that a woman might produce vastly different qualities of milk "under different circumstances." Irregularities in the quality of milk, he continued, "may generally be attributed, either to diet, the alternations of health or disease, or probably more frequently to the influence of the mental emotions." Emotions could directly alter the quality of milk and "seriously injure the health of the infant, and in some instances have proved fatal," he concluded.[21] The entirety of a woman's experience influenced the quality of her milk. And cities, in particular, contained physical and social conditions that could make toxic milk.

There were many plausible reasons for the rise in the use of cow's milk to feed infants. Hartley noted the trend in city mothers who no longer fed their children on breast milk. "Many mothers in our large towns," he wrote in 1842, "from constitutional feebleness, and others from infirm health, are incapable of nursing their offspring." Far more prevalent, though, were those mothers that Hartley identified as having "unnatural and justly reprehensible habits of life," which stifled their milk production and prevented women from doing "this important and endearing duty."[22] According to Hartley, women, themselves, were withdrawing from nursing—either by deliberate choice, through their inability to lactate, or because of their "reprehensible habits." By the early 1840s, according to Hartley, cow's milk constituted "the staple diet for infants and children" in New York, and was "indispensable ... in every family."[23] In New York, there were "few families, however humble their condition, who do not use at least one quart [of milk] daily." The more well-off drank "twice or thrice that quantity."[24] By many measures, the consumption of liquid cow's milk was increasing in New York. Many consumers believed they were consuming pure country milk—or at least hoped they were. The reality was more troubling.

Milking Profits

Although a growing number of urban consumers desired the milk of country cows, the early stages of the transportation revolution did little to alter the geography of fresh milk. Canals and roads effectively linked the city and the country in new ways in the 1820s and 1830s, but these technologies did relatively little at first to alter fresh milk production, which remained in and around urban centers. Because of milk's tendency to spoil, fresh milk producers found it necessary to remain physically close to consumers. Canals were radically remaking space for goods that could withstand dozens of hours or days in transit, but they did little to alter the landscape of dairies producing fresh milk. The same could not be said of butter and cheese production, which spread out from Manhattan into the countryside in the 1820s and 1830s. Butter and cheese could withstand the long and slow journey from country to city. But the production of liquid milk remained rooted in and near cities themselves. It was not until later advances in railroads—combined with new developments in ice production and refrigeration—that distances between city and country were sufficiently compressed to create new geographical possibilities for fresh milk production.[25]

Another important factor shaping the geography of urban dairy production was the dairy industry's strengthening relationship with a seemingly unrelated set of institutions: distilleries. As milk became harder for city families to produce on their own—and as demand for milk likely increased—specialized producers increasingly supplied urban milk markets. These dairies sought advantages in the competitive urban economy of the 1820s and turned to new dairying practices that would reduce costs and increase output. These new dairies were the outgrowth of a highly competitive market system of specialized production that was taking root in urban environments in the early nineteenth century.[26] In this profit-driven landscape, milk production was hidden from consumers through greater anonymity of production, a growing distance between consumers and producers, and the rise of adulteration of milk.

Without consumer oversight, and amid competitive production, dairies took to feeding cows distillery mash to reduce the costs of production. Mash, or "swill," was a by-product of alcohol production—what was left after beer or (more often) whiskey was distilled. As grain underwent fermentation, its sugar was stripped away. What remained was a hot, brownish, fibrous slush. Distilleries sought a way to dispose of this waste. Dairymen discovered that, in high volumes, it could be used as a cheap source of food for their cows. A city cow fed on "nothing but meal, grain, and hay," cost 20 to 26 cents per day to feed, and its milk could be sold for 8 cents a quart. By comparison, a cow fed on distillery mash cost, by one estimate, 9 cents per day to feed, and its milk could be sold for 3 to 4 cents per quart.[27] Distillery mash became an inexpensive food for urban dairy cows, and a rational outgrowth of a competitive market economy.

The practice of feeding refuse, or slop, to cows was not entirely new; colonial farmers were known to keep their cows in a "mean state" in winter, relying on a wide variety of foods to supplement animal diets when forage and pasturage were thin or unavailable. But feeding cows on swill year-round did seem to be an outgrowth of the new urban market economy that sought efficiency, low production costs, and high volume. Swill dairies solved two problems at once; animals would be supplied with inexpensive food, and distilleries would be relieved of their refuse. Keeping animals indoors and feeding them a consistent diet—even if that diet was swill—created greater predictability in the volume of production throughout the year.

Predictability and consistency in production were increasingly critical features of the new economy. Profits were made in the 1830s in knocking down or extending seasonal barriers. Ice, for example, was increasingly available in different seasons—and the growing uses of ice extended the life of other perishable foods from spoilage over time and across greater distances. Railroads allowed movement of goods and people between city and country in ways that were previously limited by seasonal hindrances such as mud and snow. Through human intervention, cows could also be manipulated to produce milk year-round. While colonial dairy farmers had long understood that a cow's diet was malleable, new urban dairymen realized that drastic and permanent alterations to a cow's diet could rationalize milk production. Even as winter set in—a period when farmers would traditionally rest their animals from lactation—cow's milk flowed in urban dairies and to urban consumers, often selling at higher prices. In a sense, the creation of the distillery cow—living indoors and fed, as it was, on a steady supply of swill—was an effort to elongate and rationalize the season of milk production. There were profits in extending seasonal limitations at the margins, and milk production was no exception. Extending seasonality and availability of fresh milk would also be important as milk became more commonly relied upon as a source of food for infants, whose hunger knew no seasonal bounds.[28]

These changes in dairy production turned animal bodies into living and breathing filters for city refuse. Although pigs have entered lore as the scavengers and filters of the nineteenth-century urban ecosystem, feedlot cows played perhaps an equal role, though in a far more structured way than free-roaming pigs.[29] Pigs turned street refuse into meat, and cows turned distillery waste into milk. Both processes reflected a human desire to produce food inexpensively using waste by-products, and to exploit undervalued resources in a competitive market system that valued cheap output of animals at the expense of their health. Distillery waste had been tried as food for swine, but pigs apparently did not respond well. They got sick and died at high rates, making it unprofitable. Cows were able to handle distillery mash with greater resilience.[30] Pigs had some degree of choice over what they scavenged on city streets, but cows were caged and coerced into consuming distillery mash.

For feedlot cows, distillery mash was an acquired taste. Hartley reported that cows avoided eating the mash for days or weeks, guided by a "mysterious instinct" that told them the slop was "deleterious" and improper nourishment. When cows refused to eat swill, dairymen found ways to coerce them. Feedlot cows were deprived of water and fed salty fodder to stimulate thirst. The cows eventually came around. By the second month, they slurped down hot slop with apparent relish. In time, wrote Hartley, the cows "learn to love the nauseous slush, as men acquire a relish for intoxicating drinks." Coerced and tempted, animals and men alike became addicted to aliments that were degrading to their bodies and violated what some reformers saw as divine order.[31]

As cows digested the steaming and acerbic mash in cramped pens, their bodies manifested what might have been the pain and displeasure they felt. According to Hartley, the animals became "flaccid" and flabby. Their teeth rotted and fell out. Their skin boiled with scabs and "cutaneous eruptions." The hair on their bodies fell off, creating bald spots that gave them the appearance they had been scalded. Without proper care or exercise, distillery cows faced a wide variety of skeletal and muscular injuries. Observers noted deformed hooves and feet, loss of joint articulation, lameness, and muscle atrophy.[32]

As luck would have it for swill-milk producers, feeding cows swill actually increased the output of "milk," as putrid and watery as it was. The increased output could have been the result of the large amount of liquid these cows consumed as part of the distillery slush, which might have been around thirty-two gallons per day. Hartley was convinced that distillery mash also created "an artificial thirst, which induces the cattle to swallow three times the quantity that is necessary of suitable food, for their proper nourishment." Milk producers "discovered that slop would produce more milk, and at a cheaper rate than any other food," wrote Hartley: "What was at first a matter of convenience or experiment soon became an object of choice."[33] To stay competitive in the urban milk market, however, producers might have felt that there was little choice at all.

But the liquid that came out of the cows' udders bore little resemblance to what people then and now would consider quality milk. The milk from distillery cows was bluish, thin, and watery. If marketed in its original form, there would be few, if any, consumers desperate enough to buy it.[34] But in the invisible and

FIGURE 1.1 "Sketch made in sixteenth street cow stables showing the manner in which the cows are crowded for room and lie in the reeking filth," from *Frank Leslie's Illustrated Newspaper,* May 15, 1858. This was one of a series of articles comprising a scathing exposé of the swill dairy industry in New York. Accessible Archives.

separate landscape of distillery stables—behind closed doors and high walls of "rectifying houses"—the rancid liquid was mixed with chalk, molasses, flour, starch, plaster of Paris, sugar, eggs, annatto, and a variety of other substances until it resembled something consumers were willing to purchase.[35] By some accounts, the mashed brains of calves and pigs were added to thicken up the liquid before it was loaded onto carts.[36] The large-scale mixing of milk from hundreds of cows also raised the possibility that harmful bacteria would be spread into a larger supply of milk—a scientific understanding that could not have been known at the time. After the milk's appearance was sufficiently altered, the white liquid was sent out for sale in city streets, often transported in milk carts that falsely proclaimed its virtues of purity and freshness.

By the 1830s, urban dairies were thriving alongside distilleries at the edges of urban settlements in New York. New contraptions allowed swill to be piped into the stables "reeking hot" from the still. Among the largest swill-milk producers in New York was Johnson's Dairy, located on Ninth Avenue at Fifteenth Street. At the time, the area was on the northwestern fringe of the highly settled parts of Manhattan. It was here that Johnson housed some two thousand dairy cows. Johnson was not alone; others in the vicinity kept hundreds of animals in large-scale operations similar to his. The new landscape combined elements of larger-scale production with older structures of the farm—a collection of "rude, unsightly wooden buildings, varying from fifty to two hundred feet in length, and about

Entered according to Act of Congress in the year 1857, by FRANK LESLIE, in the Clerk's Office of the District Court for the Southern District of New York.   (Copyrighted May 10, 1858.)

No. 128—VOL. V.] NEW YORK, SATURDAY, MAY 15, 1858. [PRICE 6 CENTS.

OUR EXPOSURE OF THE MILK TRADE OF NEW YORK AND BROOKLYN.

FROM a hundred sources we are receiving, day by day, thanks for our public spirit and fearless exposure of a nefarious and revolting trade, and good wishes and prayers for the ultimate and speedy success of our undertaking.

We feel sincerely gratified and deeply grateful for the outside encouragement we receive; it will move us to new exertions, for we feel that we have obtained the ear of the public; that its sympathies and hopes are with us, and armed with this assurance we feel our power equal to the emergency. That our blows have been dealt strongly and truly we have ample evidence. Our exposure has not only broken up all the milk

routes we have published, but one whose name we were fortunately enabled to give, is selling off his swill milk cows. His stable is broken up, his swill trade gone, and mark the consequence—he has contracted with the country dairies for the milk he requires for his customers. Is not the good work begun? May we not hope for the future?

EXPOSURE OF THE MILK TRADE.—MILKING THE DYING COW. WHEN THE ANIMAL, FROM DISEASE AND ULCERATION, CAN NO LONGER STAND, MECHANICAL MEANS ARE USED TO SUPPORT IT WHILE UNDER MILKING, AND THE PROCESS IS CONTINUED UNTIL THE COW DIES. THE MILK IS USED WITH THE REST. SEE PAGE 380.

thirty feet in breadth." These dairies were clustered on the western edge of the city, their long wooden stables stretching toward the Hudson River and separated by narrow avenues.[37]

Inside, cows were crammed into stalls that that were three feet wide (too small for them to turn around), organized in rows seven to ten across. In their confinement, the animals became lame and hobbled. Their muscles atrophied from lack of exercise. In some cases, too sick and run-down to stand, the animals collapsed into their own manure. Strapped and hoisted, raised from their feces, legs dangling, the milking went on.[38] In one case, when the supporting straps were removed, an observer was troubled to see that "she fell to the ground, where she lay till death put a period to her suffering."[39] Others noted the practice of posthumous milking.[40]

Reformers also showed concern for the poor ventilation of these distillery feedlots—the "foul air," and pestilential "vapors" that came from the concentration of animal bodies and waste. Reformers saw the low ceilings, cramped conditions, and lack of air flow as concentrating miasmas and degrading the health of the animals and the quality of milk.[41] The deprivation of good air was no small detail. In fact, the reformers' critique of poor ventilation for animals mirrored their parallel concern for the importance of fresh air for human health. Ventilation became a central concern of tenement house reform in the nineteenth century, as miasmas were understood as vectors of disease. For reformers of human and animal environments alike, fresh air was a priority for improved health. Though serious in the 1840s, concerns over miasmas and sanitation would grow in the 1850s and 1860s, and would lead to widespread urban environmental reform, including the reform of slaughterhouses and other animal spaces.[42]

For consumers, the adulteration of milk was rarely easy to detect. Historically, the characteristics of milk could vary greatly depending on where it was from, the time of year in which it was produced, the breed of cow that produced it, the food the animal had eaten that day, the distance and time the milk had traveled to market, and even the time of day when it was extracted. It was not unusual for milk to have inconsistent texture, consistency, fat content, flavor, and color. This range of possibilities created a more malleable expectation on the part of

---

FIGURE 1.2 "Exposure of the Milk Trade.—Milking the Dying Cow," from *Frank Leslie's Illustrated Newspaper,* May 15, 1858. The caption below the image reads: "When the animal, from disease and ulceration, can no longer stand, mechanical means are used to support it while under milking, and the process is continued until the cow dies. The milk is used with the rest." The man milking the cows is drawn using contemporary tropes that would have suggested to readers that he was Irish. Accessible Archives.

consumers and made it harder for buyers to judge whether milk was adulterated. If milk did not have a single taste or texture, then there was little basis for comparison with adulterated milk.[43] Dairymen worked hard to see that the bluish and watery substance that came from the swill-fed animals was superficially altered to fit a relatively wide range of quality that consumers found acceptable.[44]

The new economy of urban milk production and consumption marked the emergence of a highly specialized and commodified market for milk, and a new way of raising and treating dairy cows. Far from a twentieth-century development, densely confined animal feedlots were a pervasive feature of nineteenth-century American life, particularly in and around cities. Nineteenth-century urban dairies lacked modern antibiotics and corn subsidies, and yet they resembled something not wholly foreign to the crowded stables of modern industrial agriculture. The swill dairies did not need federal help or advanced industrial systems to function; they were an outgrowth of an economic system of large-scale urban production that accepted animals as an absolute form of property. Swill dairies were an outgrowth of actors in an economy that sought primarily to create profits by increasing output and reducing costs.[45]

In commodifying milk and the cows that produced it, Americans also came to commodify the lives of infants. How much was the health and safety of an infant worth? Four cents a day? In the new spatial, social and economic landscape of production, the goal for many dairymen was to produce the lowest priced milk whose true quality could not be readily discerned by consumers. Consumers were left peering into a bucket of opaque white liquid and wondering what the actual cost of that milk would be.

City Lots and Country Pastures

New concerns over urban dairy production reflected and reinforced pervasive cultural ideas of the city as a place of contamination, sickness, and death. The corollary—that the country was a place of health and vitality—had long been a fascination of Americans, and often for reasons that were understandable. As cities began looking, smelling, and sounding distinctly different from the countryside, those associations became further entrenched. Devastating outbreaks of smallpox, yellow fever, and cholera had ravaged urban areas at various points in the late eighteenth and early nineteenth centuries, destroying city populations in particular and sending residents fleeing for the safety of the countryside. Benjamin Rush, the most famous doctor of his generation, advocated sending children with cholera to the country to soak up the health of the natural environment.[46]

Increasingly, growing cities were understood as contaminated environments. Putrid urban dairies and growing rates of infant mortality served only to strengthen these associations of the city as an artificial and degraded space.[47]

Growing numbers of people believed that improving urban environments required improving the physical connections of urban residents to the health of the country. Food became a key intermediary between urban bodies and idealized rural environments. For the iconic food reformer, Sylvester Graham, human health suffered because connections between nature, food, and bodies were fundamentally broken in 1830s America—particularly in cities. Bodies in cities were sicker, he and others argued, because of impurities of the urban environment, along with the widespread adulteration of foods sold in urban market. This was far more than just a personal concern: sick and poisoned bodies committed crimes, spread sin, and disrupted the social order. Graham's dietary system held great promise for reforming society, and his drive for purity was not limited to flour alone; it was a larger dietary ideology that sought to link country environments with ravaged city bodies. He railed against improper tillage and adulteration, which in his mind were desecrations of God's designs for mankind and evidence of a breakdown in a sacred agricultural relationship. He feared that these broken relationships, particularly in cities, could cause "serious evil to the human family, through their effects on the flesh of animals which man devours, and on the milk and butter which he consumes."[48] Like Hartley, Graham saw broken relationships with nature and farming as forms of blasphemy.

Graham was among the earliest advocates for better milk for cities. The life and treatment of the cow mattered, he argued, because "every thing that affects the health of the cow correspondently affects the quality of her milk," he wrote. "Improper confinement, impure air, filthy stables, and every thing else that by absorption or otherwise affects her body unfavorably," he continued, "inevitably deteriorates the milk and renders it unwholesome." Cows kept in "dirty and ill-ventilated stables" produced milk that was "highly charged with the odor and taste of the filth." Even worse was the practice of feeding cows on "vile dregs of distilleries and other improper substances," which made the milk "any thing but wholesome, and can hardly fail to impair the health of those who use it freely as an article of diet."[49] Milk was only as good as the social and physical environments in which it was produced. "The best milk, therefore," Graham concluded, "can only be procured from perfectly healthy cows which, during the season of grazing, run at large in the open field and crop their food from pure soil, and during the winter are fed on good hay, and if housed at all, kept in clean and well-ventilated stables, and every day thoroughly curried and cleaned, and supplied with pure water for drink, and suffered to take regular exercise in the open air."[50] Human health depended on animal health. And animal health depended on proper environmental conditions that were defined by Graham and others in opposition to city environments.

There was a longer tradition of a romance with country milk production—and it was a tradition that did not exclude human milk production. Eighteenth- and nineteenth-century Americans saw milk as an odd and delicate substance that absorbed the flavors, characteristics, and qualities of the places in which it was produced. It was no coincidence that the advertisements for wet nurses in Boston emphasized the "country" health and geography of the wet nurses. One advertisement for a wet nurse in the eighteenth century touted that the woman for hire lived "in that part of Milton call'd the Blue Hills." Another woman from Marblehead, Massachusetts, mentioned that her town was "noted for children and noureches the most of any place for its bigness in North America, it's said the chief cause is attributed to their feeding on cods heads &c. which is their principall diett."[51] Arlington, a rural suburb of Boston with fresh air and numerous ponds, was the site of one of the main foundlings for that city, and other wet nursing institutions existed primarily in the city's hinterlands.[52] The geographic locations of these foundlings demonstrated a larger belief that environments had powerful influences on the quality of women's milk.

For Graham and others, the same environmental influences on women's milk also applied to cow's milk. Graham believed animal bodies, including humans, were unified as creations of God and therefore subject to the same set of natural rules. "If the cow or the female of any species of mammiferous animals, receive any poisonous or foreign substance into the vital domain by absorption, during the period of lactation, the milk is almost immediately affected by it," wrote Graham. But the mammary gland was seen as especially susceptible to environmental influences because it was understood by many as a primary means of expelling poison from the body. Graham cited experiments that showed lactating animals surviving doses of poisons, which were passed through milk and proved fatal to offspring. In these experiments, mothers survived but offspring died. He and others believed the same would be true of women and children.[53]

To many observers of nineteenth-century urban growth, the city, and its contaminated social and physical environments, was dangerous for lactation of any kind—human or bovine.[54] As reformers and residents came to see cities as increasingly contaminated environments, it became possible to imagine scenarios in which pure cow's milk from the country would be considered healthier for infants than the milk of mothers living in an impure city. In evaluating the health of milk, it was conceivable that the environment in which milk was produced could be more important to consumers than the species that produced it.

The complex set of factors influencing the quality of human and cow milk led to confusing and contradictory advice for women on the best ways to feed their infants. For Hartley, the solution to the infant mortality problem was not simply better practices in breast feeding and wet nursing, but, rather, greater access to the milk of country cows. The eighteenth century solution to improving the health of infants was to move a child from a city to a rural foundling, whereas new nineteenth-century transportation technologies offered another possibility for reformers by promising to deliver the health of the country to the doorsteps of consumers. Bottled, chilled, and shipped through a new rail system, many reformers believed that country animals could provide a safe and healthy food supply for children in ways that urban women could not. When regional railroads emerged in New York in the 1830s and 1840s—at the time of Hartley's first pure-milk campaigns—reformers imagined connections with the country as offering a way of reforming the health of the city. A purer, older, and more divine relationship between people and animals could emerge from the newest technologies of rail, and it promised to profoundly reform the city.

Purity and Nature: Robert Hartley and Milk Reform

Although Sylvester Graham was one of the prominent early critics of the emerging milk industry, Robert Hartley became known as the leading activist for milk reform in his generation. Hartley was no doubt influenced by Graham, along with a variety of other religious reformers that made up a "sisterhood" of antebellum reform movements.[55] Historically, Hartley would be most well-known for his longtime leadership of the New York Association for Improving the Condition of the Poor. But Hartley got his start trying to reform the massive and intractable swill-milk industry in New York City.

Hartley's personal history sheds light on a deeper cultural history that pervaded urban reform. His conception of his own life showed a certain historical thinking about urban and rural environments that would influence his reform efforts in the antebellum city. Hartley was born in 1796 in Cumberland County, in northwest England. His father, Isaac, had a childhood friendship with William Wordsworth and shared the poet's love of the Lake District and its scenic countryside.[56] Isaac arrived in New York in 1797, but did not plan to settle permanently. He was appalled by the state of urban life in America. But when he toured the rolling green countryside of upstate New York, Isaac changed his mind. He saw a landscape that reminded him, in part, of his homeland. Seeing possibilities for his family in this healthy and beautiful country, Isaac purchased land for a farm in Charlton, Saratoga County, near Schenectady. Isaac's family arrived two years later, in 1799, when his son, Robert, was three years old.

In his later years—after a long life lived as a reformer in New York City—Robert looked back fondly at his childhood in the New York countryside: the "deep blue hills," echoing with the sound of whip-poor-wills, forests of beech-nuts, and the "gorgeousness of the trees when dyed ten thousand hues by the autumnal frosts."[57] In some ways, the Hartleys were a personal connection in a cultural kinship between Wordsworth's romance with the Lake District and the emerging romantic view of the Hudson River Valley of Upstate New York.

Robert Hartley remembered his childhood as a romance with the country-side: "a pleasant country home, a pretty orchard and garden attached, sloping to the bank of a beautiful brook," the landscape "picturesquely diversified by forests, hills and dales, and in a rude and rather unsubdued state." Socially, the country held great advantages, too. The Hartley family lived close to a village church and schoolhouse, and the other townsfolk were a comfortable mix of "Scotch and New England" settlers. Robert remembered his country community and romanticized a time and place in which "there was little to corrupt the youthful mind, com-pared with the demoralizing influences of a dense city population."[58] Hartley had begun a lifelong romance with rural life in America.

Though Hartley minimized the challenges of rural living, his account suggests that country life was hard. Despite his love of Upstate New York, Isaac was over-whelmed with keeping a farm and was in over his head. He sought employment in the "mercantile business" in Schenectady, marking one of a series of moves the Hartley family would make between "country" and "city" over the course of Rob-ert's childhood. Isaac saw a number of advantages of city life in Schenectady, which at the time ranked in the top twenty largest cities in the United States in 1810 with a growing population of 5,900. When Isaac's wife became sick, "the only apparent hope for her recovery was a change to a more salubrious residence in the country." The family moved to a country home outside Schenectady. But the promises of country health failed to deliver. Robert's mother fell deeper into sick-ness and she died soon after the family's move.[59]

In their grief, the family moved again, this time twenty miles northwest of Schenectady, to Broadalbin, where Isaac bought a farm and supplied machinery for wool production, dividing his time between cultivation of the land and man-ufacturing for the early textile economy. When war broke out in 1812, young Robert left home to work in the nascent woolen mills that America now needed to support a domestic economy. Moving to a wool manufacturing center ten miles from home, Robert found himself "thrown amidst the thousand seductive and debasing temptations of city life."[60] In 1816, he moved back home to the country to help his father with the family business, only to leave the next year for employment "among strangers" in the town of Watervliet. Homesick, he returned to rural Broadalbin less than a year later, ebullient at "the sight of green fields, bubbling brooks, and rustling forests," which "awakened anew my feelings of thankfulness to the Author of all my mercies."[61] Looking back, Robert understood his life as a series of movements between these two distinct worlds of "country" and "city."

From a young age, Hartley was a deeply religious person. His diary entries were virtually silent on the happenings of everyday life, but were filled instead with profuse praise for God and requests for forgiveness, providence, and continued faith. In his teens, he organized a chapter of the Young People's Missionary Society, and later pursued a religious education at Fairfield Academy, where he was among the small minority of Presbyterian students. In 1822, Hartley fell ill, dropped out of college, and joined a "party of ladies" headed for New York, with the hope of regaining his health from the "tonic properties of sea air."[62] When the short sea trip was over Hartley stayed in New York City and took a job as a salesman in a dry goods house, but feared the "feverish atmosphere" and many dangers he saw lurking in city life. In his first summer in New York City, in 1822, Hartley saw a terrible outbreak of yellow fever, which tore through dense populations with great speed and ferocity. Hartley was also concerned with the "bilious, typhus and intermittent fevers which are very prevalent."[63] Soon, he pined for the "pure air and exercise" that were necessary for the body's continued "invigoration." The city would not be safe, he believed, "until the frosts have purified its miasmatic atmosphere."[64]

With a strong belief in God, sensitivity to the conditions of sickness and health, and rigid ideas of city and country, Hartley was poised to enter the emerging world of urban reform. He settled down in New York and married in 1824. Two years later, he became one of the founding members of the American Temperance Society, where he later served as an elected officer, corresponding secretary, and agent.[65] In 1836, he was invited to serve as secretary of the New York State Temperance Society. He refused the promotion. Hartley wanted to stay in New York City, where he believed there was serious reform work to be done.

By the 1830s, Hartley was a married man and a reformer. He was a deeply devout Presbyterian who reflected daily on his relationship with God and the eternal future of his own soul, and of the souls that surrounded him. He believed deeply in the health of the country and the perils of the city. Choosing to stay in New York City, rather than accept a position with the Temperance Society upstate, he made a decision to reform the urban environment and the poor souls who inhabited it, even if meant exposing himself to the city's many risks. But he did not give up his love of the countryside. In the years that followed, Hartley sought to improve the city by improving its connections to the country.

As Robert Hartley became more active in reform—particularly temperance reform—he discovered and exposed an underworld of milk production that was deeply interconnected with the production of inexpensive alcohol. Hartley estimated that there were some 18,000 cows in New York City and its surrounding areas that were, at any moment, fed on swill.[66] In the 1830s and 1840s, Hartley offered himself as an agent of God in the fight against this "vilest of evils," delivering a series of lectures and writing articles in the late 1830s, leading to the publication of a book-length exposé of the industry in 1842.[67]

The Sins of Swill Milk

Hartley's exposé, *An Historical, Scientific, and Practical Essay on Milk,* was a 358-page tract that presented a scathing critique of New York City's milk production. Swill milk was objectionable on many levels, but for reformers like Hartley, these reasons tended to stem from deep Christian ideals, which shaped sensibilities that clashed with the new capital-driven system of swill dairies. God had created the earth and all animals to function in an ideal way—a "natural" way—and the swill dairies represented a perversion of God's will on many levels.

Hartley's study included an extensive biological and anatomical description of cows, offering detailed descriptions of their body parts and functions. In studying the biological functions of animals, Hartley believed, humans could reveal and reconstruct God's intentions. In this respect, Hartley read the natural sciences as he read scripture: as a way of uncovering the designs of the Creator. In describing the digestive system of cows in intricate detail, Hartley was, in his view, outlining God's blueprints for these creatures. "From the teeth alone we are enabled to decide on the proper kind of aliment," wrote Hartley. He concluded that cows were designed to eat grass and live in open-air pastures. Anything else was a violation of God's intentions.[68] Thus, Hartley saw the New York swill dairymen as engaging in blasphemy against the "Author of nature."

For Hartley, the sin of improperly keeping cows went further. Not only were animals removed from their natural and God-given environment, but, as unknowing accomplices in the profitability of alcohol production, cows were unwittingly turned into agents in the spread of cheap alcohol. Living in confined pens, disobeying the "design of nature," and offering support to the business of alcohol production were all seen as affronts to the will of God and deeply disruptive of attempts to make the city a better and more virtuous place.[69]

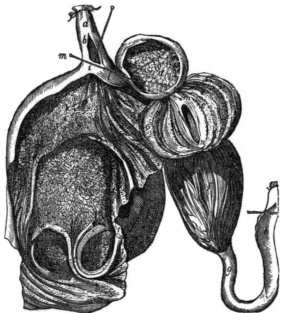

(*a*) The œsophagus. (*b*) The commencement of the œsophagean canal. (*cc*) The rumen. (*dd*) The reticulum. (*e*) The omasum. (*f*) The abomasum. (*g*) The duodenum.

The curious arrangement last referred to, is farther illustrated in the first plate. The arrow (*i*) points out that section of the œsophagean canal, through which the gullet communicates with the rumen.

FIGURE 1.3 "Internal View of the Cow's Stomach," from Robert Hartley's *An Historical, Scientific, and Practical Essay on Milk,* published in 1842. Hartley read the anatomy of cows as indicators of God's design. Library of Congress.

For Hartley and Graham, human and animal longevity were key indications of alignment with God's designs. When Graham argued that consuming cow's milk led to longer human lives, he was making a claim that milk was a food God had designed for human consumption. Similarly, the short life of the distillery cow also stood as evidence of blasphemy against God's "order of nature."[70] New urban dairies burned through their livestock at a remarkable rate, with many distillery cows dying within a year of their confinement. One doctor who joined the cause of milk reform noted that dairy stock became "so much diseased ... that they are always killed off in the fall and winter ... and a new set obtained every spring from the country."[71] This high turnover signaled to many a broken

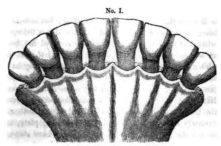

FIGURE 1.4 "Tooth of a Cow fed on natural diet." From Robert Hartley, *An Historical, Scientific, and Practical Essay on Milk,* published in 1842. Library of Congress.

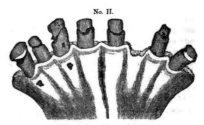

FIGURE 1.5 "Tooth of a Cow fed on artificial diet." From Robert Hartley, *An Historical, Scientific, and Practical Essay on Milk,* published in 1842. Library of Congress.

relationship of dominion. What was perhaps efficient in economic terms was wasteful and blasphemous in religious terms. The developing urban economy was creating animal lives that were disposable, and Hartley and others saw this as evidence of mankind's profligate waste and desecration of the divine creation.[72]

In the eyes of reformers, the new dairies were also tainted by the unsavory population of men they hired. Hartley argued that these men were willing to sacrifice God's natural order for the sake of money and profits. Other exposés of the 1840s and 1850s commonly noted the characteristics of men who worked at swill-milk dairies, highlighting their racial and ethnic differences. It was noteworthy that immigrant men (particularly Irish men) did most of the milking. When Frank Leslie published scathing stories on the New York swill dairies in the late 1850s, the writer ironically described the Irish workers as "milkmaids."[73] For Leslie and others, the Irish laborers—depicted as brute and animalistic—stood in sharp contrast to the idealized Anglo-American country mother milking a family cow. The new human faces in the human-animal relationship, noted Hartley, were the "drunken thieves and vagabonds, who, after prowling through the city for plunder during the day, resort to the lofts of the cow-stables at night to lodge." It was these "wretches" to whom the city entrusted the food of infants—a food so untrustworthy that the dairymen themselves "will not allow the use of this milk in their own families."[74] In the minds of reformers, the immigrant workers further degraded these urban dairies and the milk they produced.

The "Quadruple Alliance": Defining Morality in an Interdependent Economy

Although reformers like Hartley saw urban dairies as degraded and blasphemous spaces in their own right, what made them especially dangerous was that they were a linchpin in a larger interconnected social and economic network of vice and sin. For dairy reformers, swill milk was part of a larger system that was a cause and consequence of vice, greed, illness, and drunkenness. In particular, reformers understood the economic connections between swill milk and inexpensive alcohol. Alcohol created "human wickedness," and "spread vice, degradation and death, wherever its influence extends," wrote Hartley.[75]

Hartley's objection to the prevalence of swill-milk dairies was multifaceted, but at its core it was a critique of the new capitalist economy that incentivized the interdependence of profits among immoral and ungodly businesses. Hartley's original claim was true: swill dairies spread their influence by supporting a system that resulted in the production of inexpensive alcohol. Hartley realized that without dairies to purchase and remove the waste of alcohol producers, urban distilleries would become less profitable. "In order that expenses may not exceed the profits," wrote Hartley on the operations of distilleries, "the slop must be turned to good account; hence a milk dairy or a 'piggery' are indispensable adjuncts to every distillery."[76] In the cause of temperance, promoting teetotaling was not enough; to truly undermine the institutions of alcohol production and eradicate the temptation of alcohol, reformers needed to abolish swill dairies. At the center of the critique of this new economy was the way cows were treated in distillery dairies. The original sin of desecrating God's natural order spread sickness and vice like contagion through the new urban economy and society. The swill dairy, the sick cows, the dying children, the inexpensive alcohol, and the diseased milk were all symptoms of a depraved society that had embraced profits and greed and disregarded a larger set of Christian principles.

In confronting swill-milk dairies, Hartley was struggling to define his sense of Christian morality of the individual in an age of economic interdependence. Hartley identified this interconnected network of vice as a "quadruple alliance," which consisted "first, of distillers; second, of slop dairymen; third, the venders and consumers, of intoxicating liquors; and fourth, the consumers of the milk thus produced." "The distillers are supported by the slop-milkmen; and the milkmen by their customers," he concluded.[77] For an evangelical Christian like Hartley, acceptance and complicity at any one point in the system gave strength to the whole structure. By the same logic, severing a single bond of the structure would, he believed, break the forces holding the "quadruple alliance" in place. "Were it not for the use of still-slop milk," agreed Dr. Charles Lee, "our distilleries would most of them have to stop."[78]

In his effort to uproot the "quadruple alliance," Hartley honed an evangelical critique of relationships with animals in a capitalist economy. In the urban swill dairies, Hartley saw a broken relationship between people and livestock. Temperance might have attracted Hartley to study the city's swill milk industry, but he eventually came to see the urban feedlot cow as a problem in its own right. All city cows were, in a way, a degradation of a purer relationship between humans and nature. Hartley cited the latest science to suggest that even cows raised by families on small city lots produced milk that was inferior to country milk. Hartley wrote of one family cow, kept in a small city backyard, that ate a diet consisting largely of kitchen refuse, hay, leaves of vegetables, and Indian meal. Although the milk "was not deficient in nutrient properties," or offensive to taste, it was, according to tests, "invariably acid, even when fresh drawn." An "unfailing characteristic" of city milk, concluded Hartley, was that it was more acidic than alkaline country milk, and this caused long-term damage to human health.[79] Inferior quality milk suggested that something in the practice of keeping cows was misaligned with God's designs. Hartley's critique was not merely about the iniquity of swill dairies, but evolved into a broader opposition to keeping cows in cities. He was not alone in his growing conviction that cows belonged—by "nature" and by God—in the "country."[80]

The critique of urban feedlot dairies also contained a concept of animal welfare. Hartley expressed an ideal considering the way cows ought to be treated, an ideal that considered animal health and well-being. Reformers understood animals as something more than just machines in the city. To Christian reformers like Hartley, animals may not have had souls, but animals did have feelings and were, beyond question, creatures of God's creation and worthy of human respect.

For Hartley, God had given man dominion over animals, and the physical abuse of those animals represented a desecration of that sacred covenant.[81] Human sickness and mortality, reformers believed, were the physical indications of the sin of maltreatment of animals.

Although alcohol was likely the initial reason Hartley first explored the conditions of swill dairies, what he found when he got there was objectionable in its own ways. Amid the new urban market economy, the pursuit of profits had become the central force governing human relationships with cows. The "barbarous and unnatural treatment of this docile, inoffensive, and unfortunate animal," wrote Hartley, was a perversion of "one of the most valuable gifts of Providence to ungrateful men."[82] Mistreating cows was a mistreatment of the divine creation and order.

Ideas of health—inextricable as they were from religious beliefs—were also strong influences in constructing an informal concept of animal welfare in the antebellum city. "Nothing can be more certain," said a New England doctor, than the fact that "the quality of the milk is greatly influenced by the state of the health of the animal producing it."[83] The same was true of meat. Dairy reformers bemoaned the spread of diseased and rancid meat in the city, and blamed urban feedlot dairies.[84] For reformers, better quality milk and meat required green pastures, good forage, open space, fresh air, and clean water—all conditions that were understood as objectively better for cows than conditions in even the best city stables.

These conceptions of dominion and health buttressed an informal concept of animal welfare, even if it was not explicitly stated in such terms. In pursuing profits—and abandoning the principles of dominion—the dairyman showed "inhumanity" in "prematurely destroying the health and lives of his cattle." "The natural conditions of animal life . . . are grossly violated by the slop-milk system," said Hartley, "deranged health, and loathsome and fatal diseases are the necessary consequences." Although objectionable because of the "incalculable evils which it inflicts upon human beings," the swill dairies also showed a deep and disturbing "inhumanity to brutes."[85] Another journalist noticed the "leaden expression" in the eyes of urban distillery cows, who looked, to him, "miserable."[86] Reformers even objected to the treatment of animals after death. The "flayed carcases[sic]," which the swill dairymen casually had "thrown into the river" stood out to Hartley as evidence of a larger contempt for God's creation.[87] In relating to animals—in life and death—men were, in turn, relating to God.

The Swill-Milk Solution

When it came time to offer a remedy to the swill dairy, Hartley suggested several political solutions. There was, he believed, the possibility of a tax—not for the primary purpose of raising public funds, but as a way to discourage certain practices and to make distillery dairies unprofitable. If a tax were imposed, he argued, "Soon the whisky and the whisky-milk manufactories would die together."[88] A vice tax was one tool for reformers who wished to remake the marketplace to be more humane and moral.

But Hartley's greatest emphasis came in targeting the behaviors of consumers themselves. Changing consumer behaviors in the marketplace, he believed, would destabilize the dairies and distilleries. The "quadruple alliance" he spoke of included "the consumers of the milk thus produced." If customers were to "withdraw their patronage," he believed, then the whole system would unravel and come apart. Although he advocated for some level of collective regulation, his solution relied largely on an idea of consumer education and choice. Like many political reform movements, Hartley addressed consumers because he saw their buying power as a form of politics. In some ways, the politics of consumption were hardly new; they were exercised notably in boycotts on tea and stamps in the American Revolution, and again during the Free Produce Movement that sought to boycott products made by slaves. Although both of those movements offered different forms and dynamics of consumer politics, they all recognized the moral and political power of the consumer's dollar in a spatially vast and interconnected economy. Dollars could also speak where human and political voices held little or no power. With milk, as with other movements, buying and consuming took on new political meaning in an interconnected market economy.[89]

Political consumption also fit with Hartley's evangelical ideas of salvation and emphasis on individual choice. The evangelical reformer's obligations were primarily to the salvation of his own soul and spreading of the gospel to others. People could not be forced into believing in God, just as they could not be forced into temperance or milk reform; it was something that they had to decide and choose for themselves. In milk reform, the religious ideology that served as the foundation for opposition to urban dairies also forged the flawed political solutions that followed. Hartley could write books, give speeches, and try to convince the public that it was better to boycott the urban dairies than to turn a blind eye. While Hartley was not opposed to forcing dairies to adhere to rules or to heavy-handed governmental regulation, he seemed predisposed to a politics of consumer choice that mirrored evangelical methods and focused on the role of the individual in the marketplace.

Graham's evangelical politics also mirrored Hartley's in his desire to reform society one body and soul at a time. For Graham, the answer was consumption of wholesome bread and pure foods—an attempt to persuade individuals in cities to consume their way out of their social and physical problems by ingesting the health of the country. Regular and stable bodies would create a regular and stable society. But individuals had to choose the path to improvement on their own.

Hartley's interpretation of God's designs and absolute acceptance of human dominion over animals also limited the extent of his reforms. Animals were intended to be subordinates to humans, he said, asserting that man was given "superiority over the brute creation . . . by the Sovereign Creator, who in giving him dominion over every living thing that moveth upon the earth, appointed him lord of this lower world."[90] For Hartley and Graham, abstinence from milk was not an option. Milk itself was an "article of indispensable necessity, and universal use." Human consumption of milk was also divine, argued Hartley. "In nothing, perhaps, is the design of Providence more remarkable than in the adaptation of milk to the wants of the infant system," he wrote.[91] Graham agreed that God had made cows and milk for human consumption. He spoke of "some of the tribes of the Arabs of the desert," who subsisted solely on camels' milk and lived for two hundred to three hundred years. That sort of longevity was the stuff of the Old Testament, and proof that human consumption of animal milk was a way of living in accordance with the designs of God.[92] Dominion and human health not only justified human use of milk, but sanctified it. By this logic, the complete rejection of milk was as much an abandonment of God's designs as consuming swill milk.

Hartley's objections and proposed reforms were emblematic of a larger push by reformers to reshape the marketplace by encouraging consumers to choose country milk, even if it meant paying more. Like the proponents of the concurrent movement to bring pure country water into the city through the Croton Aqueduct, built between 1837 and 1842, milk reformers looked across greater distances in seeking new connections between the city and the health of the country. The Erie Canal, finished in 1828, and the Erie, Hudson, and Harlem Railroads (constructed in the 1830s and early 1840s) also promised new relationships between the impure city and the pure country. The movement for country milk was part of a broader set of reforms that sought to purify the city by connecting it more closely to the country.

Bobs and Kittens: The Failures of Reform

Hartley's lectures and published exposé drew some attention in the moment, but not enough to make a lasting impact or to inspire new regulations strong enough to uproot the swill dairies. By the time his lectures and articles were expanded and published in print in 1842, Hartley himself observed some subtle changes in the treatment of cows, which he described as "somewhat improved."[93] Others reported, naively, on the "speedy abandonment" of swill milk by an outraged public, and noted that many grocers made pure milk a "specialty" in their stores.[94] Perhaps most important, new associations of country dairy producers came together and established collectives to help ship country milk to the city. When Hartley's campaign began in the 1830s, not one dairy in the city sold country milk exclusively. According to one newspaper, "the whole population of this city was supplied from the over-crowded stables of the distilleries."[95] There was some evidence to suggest that the spatial dynamics of dairy production were beginning to change.

In the midst of Hartley's attacks on the urban dairies, more than sixty physicians lined up to condemn swill milk as "pernicious" and "detrimental to the health" of infants.[96] Following Hartley's exposé, grain distillers in the city went from eleven to four, and his work was said to inspire reforms in the milk supply of other American cities and even in Paris. In New York, Hartley's essay was republished in 1850 with a different title, *The Cow and the Dairy,* and in 1853, John Mullaly, a young journalist, published another exposé of the swill dairies, describing conditions nearly identical to what Hartley had lectured and written about a decade before.[97]

The attacks against city swill milk—along with the expansion of the railroads and collectives—did indeed cause an increase in the consumption of country milk. Orange County—located along the Hudson River, north of Manhattan—became a prominent site for milk production in the 1840s. Orange County became a sort of brand by the 1850s, filling the imaginations of urban consumers with rolling green pastures, fresh air, and roaming herds of hearty cows. Prior to the Erie Railroad's opening in 1841, "nearly all" of Orange County milk was "converted into butter." A year after the railroad opened, in 1842, train cars carried 388,505 quarts of fresh milk to the city in one year. That figure jumped to over 3,000,000 over the next year. By 1843, two milk trains ran from country to city—one in the morning and one in the evening.[98] By the railroad's third year, 5,095,763 quarts of fresh milk were shipped by rail to the city, and in each subsequent year the number seemed to grow. In 1851, it was at more than 12,000,000 quarts. By the late 1850s, milk arrived from the country dairies in the amount of 200,000 quarts per day (73,000,000 quarts annually). Newspapers reported favorably on the Orange

County dairy farms, which gave their animals regular bedding in winter, and supplied them with "daily rations of grain feed," which kept them in good health and often allowed them to "maintain their flow of milk throughout the season."[99] Urban residents eagerly sought to commune with the country through milk.

Taking a longer view, some observers argued that Hartley's attention to the swill dairies was the first shot in a longer war on the city's suppliers of impure milk. These observers and historians tuck Hartley's exposé neatly into a narrative of progress and improvement. "The earnest protest of Mr. Hartley against the use of swill milk, and the alarming disclosures which he made," said the *New-York Daily Tribune* in 1859, "did more than to excite a fleeting popular excitement, for it was the direct means ... of founding Pure Milk Associations, and opening this enormous traffic with the farmers of our adjacent counties."[100] But to lump Hartley into a progressive narrative of cleaning up the supply of city milk would be to dismiss the nuances of his ideology and to ignore the ways in which this ideology and proposed reforms were distinctive and specific to a certain time and place.

Although Hartley was among the first to object to the new system of swill-milk production, he did so using an ideology that contained the seeds of its own failure. There were blind spots and unintended consequences to his ideas and proposed solutions. For one, antebellum reformers reinforced and expanded the imagination of rural milk consumption, but they did so without substantively empowering consumers to discern the difference between pure country milk and impure city milk. The images, words, and popular dreams of the country spread throughout the works of reformers, but also through the false advertising and rhetoric of urban swill-milk producers. Both sides used the same discourse toward opposite ends. The exaltation of the country on all sides belied a deeper truth: people continued to drink swill milk and consumers were often powerless to do anything about it.

Although there were some improvements in the availability of country milk, the 200,000 quarts of milk that came each day by rail in 1859 still paled in comparison to the 500,000 quarts drawn daily from swill-milk dairies.[101] In response to Hartley, the urban swill-milk producers dug in and fought back. They argued that country milk was adulterated—and, increasingly they were right. The practices attributed to swill dairies were in fact spreading to the countryside in ways Hartley and others did not anticipate. By the 1850s, country dairy farms started looking more like city ones regarding the ways they were feeding and housing their animals. Urban swill dairymen pointed this out with delight and fought back to defend their products as normal and healthy.

Hartley's hopes of urban salvation through country milk were naively optimistic. If only consumers would choose to buy more country milk, he argued, so many problems of the city would be solved. Through transparency and consumer choice, the health of the city might be improved. Infant mortality rates would decline. The social and environmental landscape of the city could be remade to reflect God's designs. Although Hartley and other religious reformers were observant and critical of the new market economy, the political solutions they offered were simply incapable of keeping pace with the larger economic systems and behaviors they identified as central to the root causes of swill-milk dairies.

There was nothing inherently healthier about country milk, as Hartley and others believed. Hartley's idea of the country was built on the understanding that there was something permanent and stable about country relationships between people, land, and animals. In fact, as the hinterlands became connected to urban markets, country producers soon adopted many practices once associated with urban dairies. Country dairies even invented unsavory practices of their own. To stay in business, many milk producers had to abide by pressures to reduce production costs at the expense of the health of animals and the integrity of milk.

This promise of country milk failed to deliver for the cause of clean milk in New York City, and also failed to deliver for the well-being of animals themselves. As the market incentivized larger herds of country cows, farmers required more pasturage. But, increasingly, farmers understood that driving cows across larger pastures required the use of animal energy, which in turn cut into the amount of milk they were able to produce. More efficient production of country milk lay in European methods of bringing the pastures to the stables by keeping the animals in confined spaces and feeding them cut grass. This practice, known as "soiling," increasingly kept cows sedentary and indoors.[102] In confined spaces, animals saw less sunlight, breathed foul air, and got little exercise. The pressures of the market reached country dairies, which began resembling city dairies in ways reformers did not imagine.[103]

There were other unintended consequences of the increased demand for country milk that would have disappointed reformers who saw perfection in the country. For one, the boom in country milk prices created an economic landscape in which the calves of milk cows were turned into economic liabilities. In winter, when milk prices were highest, it was more profitable for Orange County dairymen to slaughter a newborn calf and sell its meat cheaply on the market than to allow the calf to consume its mother's valuable milk. A few days after birth, calves were sold to butchers at $1.50 to $3.00 apiece, then slaughtered and packed in baskets four-feet square. These newborn calves became known as "kittens" or "bobs," and their emergence marked a notable development in the marketplace. Traditional "veal" came from a calf that had been raised for several weeks, but "kittens" and "bobs" were animals that were only days old. Their meat was "red, flabby," and "disgusting," according to one newspaper, and was typically sold to the city's poor.[104]

The practice of slaughtering an animal so young struck many observers as objectionable. The practice violated what Hartley and others saw as a certain natural order and divine notion of livestock raising—an idealized relationship of dominion and a respect for the relationship of mother and calf. Surely, the emerging conditions on farms in the country were not what Hartley had imagined or idealized. The hope Hartley and others had that country milk production would follow traditional patterns was romantic and idealized fiction. Country milk—and the relationships with animals that produced it—was just as subject to market practices as the milk produced in city stables.

Amid spreading market practices, the lives of "country" cows appeared to be getting worse. By 1859, farmers reported an "epidemic" of bovine miscarriages on farms, causing losses in milk production. The popular concern was not so much the death of the calves as the fact that many cows were unable to produce milk when their calves "fell" early. The reason for the epidemic was unclear. Many speculated that environmental problems were causing it—something in the air or water. Others believed that a long wet season had caused a fungal growth in the pastures that was making the animals sick.[105] The notable spread of miscarriages proved again that the country was no panacea of public health and would not serve as a bulwark against disease.

Even if there were such a thing as pure country milk, the new distances milk traveled to city markets were fraught with dangers that Hartley and others were incapable of anticipating. The new distances between producers and consumers created greater opportunity for bacterial contamination of milk—a concept that Hartley and others were unable to understand at the time because of limitations in scientific knowledge.[106] Although perhaps better than many forms of adulterated milk, country milk was far from the perfect food Hartley promised. It did not drastically reduce or come close to eliminating infant mortality, which remained high in urban areas through the nineteenth century. A spate of reforms sought to regulate the composition of milk and prevent its adulteration, but it was not until the late nineteenth and early twentieth centuries that bacteria were identified as critical in milk sickness and infant mortality and targeted by regulatory reforms.[107]

Hartley's politics of consumption also failed to deliver meaningful reform. Because of the separation between consumers and producers—and the ruthless deception of swill dairymen in advertising their products as "pure"—consumers were in no position to discern the origins of their milk. To the extent that consumers could procure pure country milk, it was often at a price three to four times more

THE CITY MILK BUSINESS.

MARY, THE KITCHEN-MAID. "Why, John, what's the matter?"
MILKMAN. "Ah, Mary! If we don't have rain soon, I don't know what we'll do for Milk!"

FIGURE 1.6 "If we don't have rain soon, I don't know what we'll do for Milk!" From *Frank Leslie's Illustrated Newspaper,* July 16, 1859. Note the allegation of false advertisement for "Orange County Milk." Library of Congress Prints and Photographs Division.

than they would spend on standard milk, and far more than the city's poor could afford. This was true of Martha's family, and thousands of others who went on consuming impure milk for decades. Those who had enough money to purchase country milk at three to four times the price of regular milk could do so. Their babies probably died with less frequency. But they did not hold enough sway in the market to break the "quadruple alliance" and change industry practices, as Hartley hoped.

In advocating for the consumption of country milk without first accounting for false advertising or imposing rules on distillery dairy production, Hartley pushed consumers into the arms of urban swill dairymen. Without effective regulation, the urban dairies continued to peddle their swill to consumers under the guise of country milk. The milkmen repainted their carts with words that evoked the purity of the country: "Pure country milk from Bloomingdale," "Newtown,"

"Long Island," "New Jersey," "Washington Dairy," "Columbia Dairy," and "Pure Milk Dairy."[108] The fact that country milk had become glorified in the new and brighter world of railroads and canals created a basis of plausibility for these distended claims. The effects of the railroad were not simply progress and purity—they were not merely more country milk—but more urban swill milk, too. By increasing the plausibility of access to country milk, railroads expanded the imaginations of consumers and allowed space for urban dairymen to go on selling bad milk to the city's most vulnerable.

Reform was also limited by an ideology of dominion, which often granted some degree of respect and protection to animals but, moreover, affirmed their subordinate status as property. As a result, animals remained largely the responsibility of their owners. And owners could choose to feed them swill. In a sense, reformers accepted God's law of absolute dominion and the parallel laws of man that placed animals squarely under human control and ownership. Dominion blinded reformers and undercut their capacity to institute effective reform. It was not until another generation of reformers in the 1860s recast dominion and humane treatment as a public good, and the prerogative of the state, that stricter regulation of the treatment of animals emerged.

Conclusion

When Martha's story was documented in the city's medical report on swill milk in 1858, the problem of swill-milk dairies still plagued New York and other cities, and would continue to do so for decades. Nearly twenty years after Hartley's essay, the solution to impure milk remained unclear, and many continued to advocate a market-based politics of consumption that continued to fail the public interest. "The remedy is in our own hands," said the *New-York Daily Tribune* in 1859, echoing a common refrain that placed responsibility with consumers for the choices they made. "If city consumers were willing to pay an extra penny per quart for a pure, wholesome article, and eschewing the stuff that now pollutes their tea and coffee," said the *Tribune,* country dairies would grow and gain a greater foothold on the market.[109] It was the poor and uninformed residents of the city who continued to buy cheap milk and strengthen the swill dairies.

By 1860, the urban swill-fed cow was still a common resident in New York City. The swill dairies were well-connected and powerful institutions.[110] Journalistic exposés and reform movements were stymied by entrenched political interests. There was some truth in observations that industrial dairymen were among the roughest and most hardened men in the city. They worked in some of the foulest environments in all of New York, and in one of the least respected professions. Thick skin was a prerequisite. By one account Hartley was "assaulted" by swill-milk interests for his efforts to expose industry practices.[111] When a *New-York Daily Tribune* journalist tried to visit swill dairies in 1859, he was mocked and greeted with a shower of stones. Through bullying and political connections in Tammany Hall, swill-milk producers and urban dairies continued to dominate the urban milk market and stifle regulation for decades after Hartley's exposé.[112] In Brooklyn, in 1856, distilleries used their friends on the Common Council to gain a last-minute exemption from a new law limiting the number of cows on city lots.[113] Similar political corruption emerged in Manhattan, where Tammany alderman Michael Tuomey stifled regulation of urban dairies for years, until legislation reached the New York State government in the 1860s.[114]

But by the late 1850s and 1860s something was beginning to change in the way reformers spoke of the swill-milk crisis, and of urban animal reform more broadly. When Frank Leslie offered a scathing critique of the city's milk industry in 1858 he was increasingly appealing to consumers using a new discourse of health that was less laden with theology than was Hartley's exposé a generation earlier. Though the conditions of urban swill dairies remained largely unaffected, the public conversations around milk seemed to be changing. Leslie effectively broke milk reform away from temperance, and in so doing made it a secular public health question.[115] He also articulated a stronger case for animal welfare in the reform of urban swill dairies. Increasingly, by the 1860s, laws and bureaucracies were active in reshaping urban environments and urban animal populations in new ways. City and state health departments emerged with notable power and zeal and sought to regulate the lives of urban animals to promote a concept of common good and public health.

At the same time, the concept of dominion was also expanded and increasingly recast as a public good that escaped the narrow parameters of the private relationship between an owner and his animal. The emergence of Societies for the Prevention of Cruelty to Animals in the 1860s—especially in cities—demonstrated a growing sense of utmost public interest in the treatment of animals. The debate had changed by the 1860s, and the new focus on sanitation, animal welfare, and public regulation offered strength to the war on city cows, dairies, and other urban animals, increasingly recast in new terms and through new forms of political power. What remained unchanged was growing scales of capitalist production of animals, which would remain a lasting feature of the American landscape—both urban and rural. The features of these capitalistic relationships with animals would remain at the center of new challenges facing reformers and producers in the decades that followed.

CHAPTER TWO

"The War on Butchers"

San Francisco and the Remaking of Animal Space, 1850–1870

As NEW YORK CITY grappled with deeply entrenched conflicts over the proper role of animals in urban life, other American cities shared similar struggles. Perhaps nowhere did rapid urbanization meet head-on with urban animal issues than in the booming gold rush city of San Francisco. In 1850, a French journalist named Etienne Derbec arrived in San Francisco to report on what had become an international spectacle. In a series of letters, Derbec sketched scenes of everyday life in the thriving gold rush city that was growing before his eyes. After touring the California interior, he returned to San Francisco a few months later to find a city of more than 20,000 people expanding by such "extraordinary proportions" that it was "no longer recognizable."[1] Alongside the bustle of commerce and construction, Derbec noted the peculiar activities of other living creatures that shared densely settled spaces. Among the fortune-seekers were "domestic animals," including "horses, mules, sows, pigs, [and] chickens" who "live in freedom" in certain parts of the city. "You, sir, can imagine all the inconveniences such a population brings in its train," he continued, "one's sense of smell and of hearing are, as you can well believe, somewhat offended."[2]

San Francisco was hardly alone in the "inconveniences" of its animal populations—inconveniences that were deeply connected to the everyday lives of its citizens, and in many ways sources and symbols of the city's economic strength and stability. In the decades after the gold rush, however, city authorities, residents, and businesses struggled to regulate and remake animal populations in the growing city of San Francisco, as others did in additional American and European cities at the same time. As San Francisco's largely itinerant, single-male population of the early 1850s gave way to a growing, permanent urban culture of domesticity and family life in the 1860s, residents and elected officials focused new attention on reforming the city's animal populations to make the urban environment safe for the civilized family. The remaking of the geography and environmental characteristics of the city's collective relationships with animals promised social and economic stability, health, and a prosperous future and blazed a path for further regulation and animal exclusion in the years that followed.

Despite its unusual pattern of rapid urban development, San Francisco's story of urban animal reform was as much typical of nineteenth-century cities as it was distinctive. Where San Francisco differed most notably was in its explosive demographic and spatial growth as a city. In just over two decades, the population of the city went from approximately 850 residents in 1848 to more than 36,000 in 1852, to nearly 150,000 by 1870—inexact figures that denoted stunning urban growth and development.[3] With this rapid urban development, disputes over animals—and the nuisances they caused—flared up with notable intensity and frequency. In older American cities like New York and Boston, the creation of urban animal policies played out over decades. In the "instant city" of San Francisco, however, the nuisances of urban animal life came into frequent and intense conflict with an expanding population as city officials frantically groped their way toward a more stable system of animal regulation during a condensed period of urban growth.

In particular, residents, business owners, and city officials struggled with the widespread problem of urban slaughterhouses—the most acute of all nineteenth-century urban animal nuisances. The hoofed inhabitants that had grazed the hillsides of the San Francisco Peninsula and helped launch the development of the city of San Francisco soon came to threaten the city's very existence as a safe, healthy, prosperous, and civilized space for human habitation. From 1850 to 1870, human and animal geographies in San Francisco were increasingly at odds. So began a public battle that newspapers covered closely and called the "War on Butchers." When the dust settled in 1870, a new set of laws and enforcement mechanisms remade the city and led to a further separation of urban consumers from slaughterhouses and domesticated animals raised for food.

The development of strict regulations and physical separation of urban animal populations marked an important moment in human history. For millennia, most human beings lived alongside the animals that provided their meat, milk, and clothing.[4] Over time those connections and relationships changed, but by the 1870s, San Francisco officials had effectively created a city in which most animals that provided products for urban residents were almost completely divorced from human lives downtown. The reliance of human beings on the products of animals remained continuous, but the legally imposed separation of humans and certain domesticated animals was something new, and reflected clear desires on the part of the public to separate the "inconveniences" of urban animal life. These inconveniences were the animals themselves, but also included the qualitative relationships of certain human-animal interactions, along with underlying social status and relationships of people who worked with those animals.

The separation of animal nuisances like slaughterhouses had long been a goal of urban reformers throughout much of the nineteenth century. What changed from 1850 to 1870 was a notable shift in the character and force of laws. Efforts in San Francisco in the 1850s relied in large part on reactive policies of public complaints and lawsuits. This process was slow, clumsy, and riddled with corrupt exceptions for many businesses. In the 1860s, however, the city adopted a proactive and preemptive form of regulation using a growing police force and a new and powerful Board of Health—which were fueled by popular ideologies of urban reform that emphasized prevention (prevention of disease, prevention of cruelty, and prevention of various forms of "vice") in place of reaction. This emphasis on prevention led to the legal creation of a slaughterhouse and livestock district in the 1870s that was both more distant from downtown and more narrowly defined geographically. The creation of a "Butchers' Reservation" in 1870 realized the aspiration of removing slaughterhouses out of sight and smell from the city's downtown population of consumers, while effecting an idealized environmental relationship that promised to solve chronic urban pollution. The creation of "Butchertown," as it became known, was the result of years of struggle by public officials to find a solution to the problem of urban animal nuisances, and it marked a powerful new intervention of government in the lives of urban residents.

In excluding animals and creating Butchertown, politicians and residents legitimized and prioritized a certain form of residential life and took the controversial step of prejudging the work of raising and slaughtering animals as nuisances that necessitated confinement and geographic marginalization to ensure the proper development of the city. New ideologies of health, new advances in transportation, and new applications of law enabled this reorganization of space. Although technology played an important role in transforming slaughterhouse landscapes, the separation of slaughterhouses and animal nuisances was not merely the result of technological developments. Although laid out with railroads in mind, the new Butchertown would not have railroad lines to downtown San Francisco until decades after its creation. The stilted slaughterhouses built over the San Francisco Bay in Butchertown—another technological development—were ultimately inadequate and less effective than reformers had hoped. Like the possibilities of remaking New York City's supply of milk, the *imagination* of new technologies powerfully shaped the creation of Butchertown, but ultimately came up short.

The reform of slaughterhouses that played out in cities across the United States also represented a crucial moment in the history of law and governance. For many—including a vocal collection of butchers themselves—the tightening of regulations on slaughterhouses represented the overextension of governmental power into the labor and property rights of citizens. Many butchers—along with what was likely a small minority of San Franciscans—objected to the preventive and prejudicial tone of new animal-nuisance legislation. In San Francisco, a handful of butchers raised serious questions about individual rights and economic freedoms that reached the California Supreme Court in 1867. The San Francisco case of slaughterhouse regulation—and ensuing legal appeals—was one wave in a larger tidal shift in the late 1860s and early 1870s, as cities across the United States regulated slaughterhouses in new ways and courts grappled with the legal fallout. Questions about the legality of these new laws made their way through state and federal courts, culminating most famously in the Slaughterhouse Cases of 1873. Although infamous as test cases for the Fourteenth Amendment, the Slaughterhouse Cases also existed in the historical context of a key national moment in which cities were actively remaking urban space to improve the environmental conditions for residents. As the case of San Francisco suggests, the question of what to do with urban slaughterhouses was a major public policy question for city and state governments in the nineteenth century. Courts regularly sided with the city's or state's rights to legislate in new ways based on older legal precedent that upheld state police power.[5] San Francisco offered some unique ways of handling the slaughterhouse and livestock nuisance, but was also as typical of American cities as it was exceptional.

In creating Butchertown, along with a growing set of rules governing the geography and treatment of animals, San Francisco officials not only dealt a blow to the practice of urban animal husbandry but also fundamentally remade the geography and business practices of a large sector of the economy that raised, transported, killed, and processed animals for the market. Exclusion of these "noxious" elements of urban life was only one part of the new regulations. But the relocation of these businesses was also shaped by contemporary ideas of environment and public health. The slaughterhouses would be moved to the tidal marshes of the San Francisco Bay in the southern reaches of the city. In choosing this specific environment, city officials sought spatial separation from downtown, and also a way to harness the natural environment to mitigate nuisances. With slaughterhouses built on stilts over the tide, far from the city's population center, Butchertown contained elements of a modern concept of urban spatial organization without immediate changes in slaughtering technology. In the ideal, slaughterhouse waste would fall into the bay, and the tide would flush it away from human settlement. Prevailing winds from the west would dilute noxious fumes above the uninhabited expanse of the bay. While slaughterhouses built around the same time in Chicago were models of efficiency of labor and materials—famously known for selling "everything but the squeal"—San Francisco's slaughterhouses were something quite different. And yet, San Francisco wholesale butchers effectively maintained and defended their control of the regional meat economy and staved off Chicago and the omnipresent Meat Trust into the twentieth century. They did so, in most cases, using slaughterhouse methods that were hardly models of modern efficiency and sent an excess of blood and offal into the tides of the San Francisco Bay. San Francisco butchers, such as Henry Miller and Charles Lux, innovated meat production in other ways; they relied less on technological advances at the point of slaughtering and meatpacking, and focused instead on exploiting California land laws and environmental advantages to amass more than a million acres on which they could raise cattle efficiently. They integrated meat production vertically (from calf to steak), as well as horizontally (from Nevada to San Francisco).[6]

The final stop for many Miller & Lux cattle was the site of many battles in what urban residents called "the war on butchers." From 1850 to 1870, the city of San Francisco evolved from a reactive regulatory system of slaughterhouses to a proactive approach. They separated the smells and sounds of animals—and the working relationships with those animals that brought chronic violence, poor health, depleted property values, and social decay to the streets and neighborhoods of the growing city they imagined would become a beacon of civilization on the Pacific Coast. But, like any war, the final outcome was unclear to those living in the miasmatic fog of the moment; the creation of Butchertown had unintended social and environmental consequences.

Animal Settlement

The French journalist Etienne Derbec was not in San Francisco to report solely on the particular "inconveniences" of the city's animal populations. He was there, of course, to report on the gold rush. Although gold was essential to understanding the rise of San Francisco, domesticated animals played a lesser-known role in the city's emergence and development as a major Pacific port. The millions of cattle, sheep, horses, and mules that accompanied the comparatively smaller numbers of Spanish and Mexican settlers over the course of the late eighteenth and early nineteenth centuries helped establish and strengthen the missions and the small village of Yerba Buena, which became an important trading post on the Pacific Coast before becoming the booming gold rush city of San Francisco.[7]

In the early years of Spanish colonization, cattle and sheep were central to the work and operation of missions. By 1830, San Francisco's Mission Dolores alone had some 4,200 cattle and 2,000 sheep, along with hundreds of horses. In addition to supporting growing Spanish populations, cattle ranged beyond the small Spanish settlements and undermined Indian ecologies of subsistence across the peninsula. Animal grazing disrupted native food sources and disturbed lands that nearby tribes used to harvest a wide range of plants, including wild onions, wild oats, mustard, clover, dandelion, and many others. These ecological disruptions may have pushed native populations farther inland, and, more often, forced or attracted them onto mission settlements, where their crops nevertheless remained vulnerable to frequent invasions of domesticated animals of Spanish colonists.[8]

Mexican independence and shifting settlement patterns transformed human and animal activities on the peninsula beginning in the 1820s, turning the region into a place connected to global and regional markets in new ways. Cattle did the work of turning grass into meat, fat, and—most valuably—hides. Cattle hides became a chief export of Yerba Buena, built wealth in the region, and reinforced the economic importance of the Pacific port. By the 1830s, the small city was known for its booming hide and tallow trade, as materials from California cattle made their way to shops, factories, and homes across New England and the northeastern United States. Between 1826 and 1848, Yerba Buena exported the products of over 1 million cattle, including more than 62 million pounds of tallow.[9] Thousands of cattle grazed the valleys and hillsides of the ranchos that surrounded the small settlement on the northeastern edge of the peninsula. Rancho San Miguel, located near what is today downtown San Francisco, had a rotating population of some 2,000 cattle alone, and other nearby ranchos supported bovine populations that dwarfed the relatively small human settlement on the peninsula.[10]

With the gold rush and the settlement of Yerba Buena that followed, the peninsula morphed from a small port with a large cattle population to a sprawling city with a large commercial economy and a strong local provisioning economy of its own. The human population of San Francisco likely overtook its cattle population sometime around 1850.

Taming Livestock in the "Instant City"

As humans came to outnumber livestock in the region, individual animals became more valuable in San Francisco as regional demands for their products increased. In 1850, nearby farmers sold pigs, sheep, and chickens "very dearly" in urban markets. Milk and egg prices were notably high and dairy cows became so valuable that they were "difficult to obtain." Ranches farther from the city were often willing to sell cows at a premium, but they were, according to one observer, "difficult for a European to domesticate." Chickens sold for $5 each, sows for $100, and cows "worth only several dollars in the interior" fetched $80 in the city.[11] Pigs ranged freely in parts of New York and other cities for much of the nineteenth century, but the high price of animals in San Francisco meant that residents were likely to protect and enclose livestock. Although livestock no doubt inhabited all American cities, the ways in which animals existed in urban environments differed based on a variety of local conditions.[12]

From its beginnings as a boomtown, San Francisco faced public challenges related to the life, death, and decay of its significant animal populations. The city's 1850 charter gave the mayor and common council broad powers to tax and regulate widely—everything from "theatrical and other exhibitions" and "tipling houses," to the "weight, quality and price of bread to be sold within the city." Included in the charter were powers that would enable the municipal government to control its animal populations, "to make regulations to prevent the introduction of contagious and other diseases into the city," "to prevent and remove nuisances," and to "license, tax, and regulate" businesses.[13]

In its structures of government—and later, in its exercise of power—San Francisco was poised to advance a concept of public welfare typical of many nineteenth-century cities. As historian William Novak has convincingly shown, municipal governments actively embraced regulatory police powers to promote a concept of a "well regulated society."[14] Slaughterhouses and other urban animal industries and practices were among the most noisome and regulated in cities across the United States. San Francisco was no exception.

San Francisco's 1850 charter gave public officials immense power to control and regulate private and public spaces and to abate animal nuisances wherever they arose. The city had the authority to remove "all obstructions from the sidewalks, and to provide for the construction, repair and cleaning of the same and of the gutters." Article IV of the city's charter outlined the city government's capacity to create and regulate public space—to "take private property for the purpose of laying out or altering streets or alleys," so long as it compensated landholders.[15] The city had broad powers to regulate, shape, and create space—powers that typically surpassed personal economic freedom and property. Even though they were often unwilling to allow the same role for state and federal governments, residents in San Francisco and other American cities expected local governments to intervene to promote the concept of public good—particularly in matters related to nuisances that threatened public health, even if regulations came at the expense of the economic freedoms of its citizens.[16]

In the years that followed the 1850 charter of San Francisco, the city's lawmakers actively used their state-given powers to abate a wide range of nuisances, focusing notably on the city's animal populations and animal businesses. In his opening address in 1850, the city's first mayor, John Geary, noted the acute problems of animals and slaughter in San Francisco. "In some parts of the city an offensive effluvia is constantly arising from the offal thrown from slaughter houses, the carcasses of animals, and collections of various descriptions of decomposing substances." Geary saw these nuisances as "prejudicial to the comfort and health of the citizens," and encouraged common councilmen and political leaders to "take early steps for their removal, and for a proper supervision of the streets generally." The mayor included animal nuisances on a list of other problems he believed were urgent for the well-being of San Franciscans, including public market inspections and tight regulation of gunpowder.[17] These were matters of utmost public interest that were fundamental to the city's collective safety, security, and prosperity.

In their first years as leaders of San Francisco, the mayor and members of the common council placed nuisance mitigation front and center in legislation. The city's second ordinance, approved in May 1850, included "manure, waste water, or any animal or vegetable substance" on a list of materials that the mayor or city marshal could require to be "carried away . . . at the expense of the owner or occupant." Failure to clean up any of these substances within twenty-four hours of written notice from the mayor or city marshal would result in a hearing before the city recorder and a fine of "not less than twenty dollars, nor more than one hundred dollars." Similar rules applied to waste that was dumped in public streets, courts, squares, lanes, alleys, vacant lots, and ponds, with fines ranging between $5 and $50. By common standards at the time, the proper place for these materials was the San Francisco Bay. Although there were limitations in the city's ability to enforce laws—and corruption in enforcement—the actions and words of city officials placed the regulation of slaughterhouses and animal nuisances at the center of a concept of public welfare.[18]

The constant fine-tuning of slaughterhouse and animal regulations in the 1850s showed not only that regulating animals and slaughterhouses was an important legislative priority in San Francisco but also that the zones where slaughterhouses would be permitted were contested and constantly changing. In 1852, a new city law prohibited slaughterhouses north of Broadway, east of Larkin Street and north of Market Street, protecting and reinforcing real or imagined aesthetics of large sections of residential and commercial portions of the city (see figure 2.3). City officials appear to have enforced the new law, with one newspaper noting that the city recorder issued citations to "several butchers" in March and April of 1852 for violations of the ordinance. Butchers argued that they found the new laws "rather vague and indefinite," according to the *Daily Alta California*.[19]

In addition to regulating the geography of slaughterhouses, new municipal laws also dictated the physical structures and architecture of slaughterhouses. A city ordinance passed in May 1852 required all slaughterhouses to have a "tight plank floor, or be paved with brick or stone." Waste from slaughterhouses would need to be collected in sealed reservoirs and butchers were required to empty their containers "at the end of each day." The rules requiring butchers to contain their refuse and carry it to the waterfront reflected similar thinking about effluence more broadly. Regulations on "privy vaults" and outhouses in San Francisco and cities across the United States imposed policies of containment and removal in ways that would contrast to later efforts that sought to facilitate the flow of waste through sewer pipes with running water. Until the flow of effluence could be effectively controlled, cities often imposed rules that sought to control waste and prevent seepage of waste that caused foul odors and illness.[20]

San Francisco's 1852 ordinance also expanded enforcement powers for nuisance regulation. Under the new rules, the aldermen and assistant aldermen could order nuisances to be removed and could prosecute those responsible for animal-related nuisances, including the offensive "slaughter house, yard, pen, corral, or other enclosure used for slaughtering or keeping animals for sale." Any expenses incurred for compliance with the new law would be paid by the party responsible for the nuisance.[21]

City officials also used their power to issue licenses as a means of discouraging and controlling slaughterhouses. In 1854, the city charged slaughterhouses an exorbitant rate of $100 per quarter year—a staggering fee that was added to other existing butcher fees. The new slaughterhouse fee was among the highest in the city—rivaling fees assessed on other businesses deemed harmful, including drinking establishments and gambling houses. Although it is not clear whether the licensing law was intended to reduce the number of slaughterhouses, the expensive barrier to entry presumably had that effect and likely created a smaller number of slaughterhouses that operated at larger scales of production. In the same year, 1854, the municipal government expanded the space in which slaughterhouses were prohibited four blocks south, from Market Street to Harrison Street, while maintaining the Larkin Street boundary.[22]

Despite these laws and efforts to implement them, the city's means of enforcement remained slow and inefficient through the 1850s. City authorities often carved out exceptions for some businesses, and judges were often lenient with offenders, leading to allegations of corruption, unfairness, and favoritism. Although "numerous cases" were brought to the city's district attorney in the early and mid-1850s, many "exceptions have been taken by the counsel for the defendants," according to one newspaper. When complaints against slaughterhouses did make it before judges, they were often delayed and "lost sight of in the mazes of the law."[23] Residents and urban reformers became frustrated that nuisances continued unabated through special exemptions and lengthy waiting periods for adjudication and appeals. Many expressed their growing concern that laws, enforcement mechanisms, and courts were failing to quell nuisances and protect the public good.

By 1855, a cluster of slaughterhouses on the western edge of the city's advancing development was again causing stacks of unresolved nuisance complaints. In particular, a single block of Larkin Street, between Pacific and Broadway—the very edge of the established slaughterhouse boundary—had a cluster of five notorious slaughterhouses. "The sickening effluvia arising from these penetrates into every house in the vicinity," said one resident. These "effluvia" were not merely unpleasant, but popular miasmatic understandings of disease meant that foul odors from decaying organic matter were thought to be dangerous to permeable human bodies, public health, and the interconnected social order. In the mind of nineteenth-century urban residents, the foul smell of an urban slaughterhouse likely suggested the possibility of serious illness and death.[24]

But the possibility of sickness was only one concern of the residents who sought stronger slaughterhouse regulations. Their complaints bespoke a broader desire for safer, quieter, and more civilized urban space that increasingly stood in sharp contrast to the conditions associated with slaughterhouses. In particular, they feared the "herds of wild cattle" that "are daily driven through our streets," causing "danger of life and limb of every passer-by," according to one resident.[25] This was a common refrain across many American cities, as the driving of cattle through residential neighborhoods was seen as a threat to women and children in particular. As San Francisco became a city increasingly populated with women and children in the late 1850s, the remaking of the city for their safety was a refrain that echoed across urban policy for decades, and one that would become more pronounced as San Francisco became a place of domesticity and family life in the 1860s.

FIGURE 2.1 "Cattle Driving in the Streets—Who Cares for Old Women and Small Children?" A depiction of a street scene in New York in 1866, showing the dangers of urban cattle drives that plagued many cities. From *Frank Leslie's Illustrated Newspaper*, April 28, 1866. Library of Congress.

The urban environment itself compounded the dangers of livestock in the city. Even when slaughterhouses were regulated to the fringe of residential settlement, cattle and sheep still needed to traverse the center of the city—particularly if they were unloaded from boats at wharves downtown. The increasing density of San Francisco and other midcentury cities also made urban cattle drives increasingly dangerous. One concerned San Francisco resident noted that "of almost every drove one or two of the animals escape from their drivers," and are chased through the streets by men on horseback, as the whole neighborhood was thrown "in a turmoil."

Driving livestock through city streets often required a level of violence that many residents found abhorrent. This violence was objectionable on several levels—the cruelty it inflicted upon the animals themselves and the harm it did socially and psychologically to those who witnessed the atrocities. One concerned resident was horrified by the violence committed by cowboys in tracking down stray animals, describing how they lassoed, beat, and prodded them "mercilessly," sometimes driving sharp spikes "into their bodies" to get them to move. In one case, "hundreds of men, women, and children" observed a steer "beaten over the mouth with clubs, till blood ran in a stream, one of its hips thrown out of place, sharp pikes, six inches in length, thrust . . . in all parts of its body . . . till death put an end to the atrocious barbarity." The animal's limp body was dragged to the slaughterhouse in front of onlookers, "who were compelled to witness the disgusting sight," in "the great thoroughfares" of the city. Adding to the observer's outrage, the incident happened on the Sabbath.[26]

The sounds of urban cattle drives and slaughterhouses were also offensive to many. Intensive cattle drives and slaughterhouses transformed the city's soundscape, causing thunderous rumbling as heavy animals moved through city streets. Nearby slaughterhouses contained their own sounds of animal cries, to say nothing of the shouts of slaughterhouse workers as they maneuvered heavy animal bodies in dangerous work environments. One San Francisco resident commented on "the roar of cattle, the sound of the killing axe and the streams of running blood," that were "seen, and heard, and felt by those living in the vicinity, but [also] by every one passing the Pacific plank road."[27] Slaughterhouses—and the process of moving animals through crowded streets—represented a broad assault on the senses and refined aesthetics of urban residents, and therefore threatened social order.

Although San Francisco did not establish a Society for the Prevention of Cruelty to Animals until 1868, the concerns that residents raised against livestock brutality in the 1850s showed popular sensitivity to issues of animal abuse and the social problems supposedly wrought by animal cruelty. Foretelling the more formal humane movement that would emerge in later decades, many San Franciscans in the 1850s voiced concern that the brutality against animals in city streets was objectionable because of the suffering it caused the animals themselves. These concerns for animals were also inseparable from the social consequences many feared. A growing number of Americans believed that witnessing public animal abuse, particularly for children, could have grave social consequences.[28]

Despite the growing concerns of San Francisco residents and lawmakers in the 1850s, city officials seemed largely incompetent at addressing the public nuisances of livestock and slaughterhouses in the city. In 1855, a resident expressed deep frustration that "petitions, remonstrances, presentments, and even the order of Courts, have as yet failed to abate these nuisances."[29] Indeed, political ineffectiveness was ostensibly a cause for a broader revolt against the city's corrupt government in 1856, when the Committee of Vigilance staged a coup against the standing Democratic leadership of the city. The violent political upheaval of 1856 would remake city government, ushering in the People's Party on a platform of cleaner government, lower taxes, fiscal discipline, and social reform—part of a broad agenda that historians Robert Cherny and William Issel called the "desire on the part of the merchants—and especially their wives—to stamp the city political system with the seal of family-centered respectability."[30]

Despite its rhetoric of reform, the new People's Party seems to have done little to significantly change the city's animal nuisance regulations. In 1856, the leaders of the Committee of Vigilance sought a moderate candidate to run for mayor on the People's Reform ticket. After many attempts they persuaded the reluctant Ephraim Willard Burr—a Protestant merchant and banker from Rhode Island who had not been particularly active in the vigilance movement. Burr won election and led the city under the new terms of the Consolidation Act of 1856, which merged city and county governments of San Francisco and carefully defined city and county governmental powers so narrowly that "they were almost non-existent."[31] Burr's role as president of the newly formed Board of Supervisors remains a sketchy chapter in recent histories of San Francisco, perhaps because of the significant limitations imposed on city government. Burr enjoyed a relatively long, three-term tenure in office from 1856 to 1859, overseeing a contraction of city spending from $2.6 million in 1854–1855, to $856,120 in 1855–1856 to $1.1 million in 1859–1860, a period that also saw property taxes cut by half.[32]

But pressures of demographic growth persisted in San Francisco. In 1855, the Van Ness Ordinance opened lands west of Larkin Street for sale and development, extending the street grid on maps and setting off real-estate speculation and settlement in what became known as the Western Addition. In February 1857, the Board of Supervisors once again amended the nuisance ordinance to extend slightly the zone in which slaughterhouses were forbidden. The new ordinance also bolstered the power of residents to prosecute nuisances by creating a rule that "the complaint of any five persons, sustained by their oath," that a building was "used as a slaughter house, shall be sufficient to establish the fact of its being a nuisance." This part of the measure was an effort to streamline nuisance complaints and abatements, which in turn created a more adverse environment for butchers. The measure also toed the line between litigation and preemptive forms of regulation by turning over enforcement to the public, which came at almost no cost to the city. Violators, defined as any "butcher or workman," would be fined between $10 and $40, and butchers who continued to operate after a citation would be fined $10 per day.[33]

The question of what to do about the city's slaughterhouses emerged again in 1859, when residents and some city officials pushed for the passage of a bill in the California state legislature. The politics and motivations for the appeal to state-level government remain as unclear now as they did to many at the time. Faced with stacks of nuisance complaints and frustrated at their inability to carry on their trade, the city's butchers appeared eager to work with the Board of Supervisors in removing slaughterhouses to a part of the city where they could do their work without constantly battling aggravated residents. By 1859, the city had around seventy slaughterhouses, with those along Larkin Street continuing to cause most of the nuisance complaints. From 1854 to 1859 there had been some forty indictments against butchers on Larkin Street alone, and thirty-five remained unresolved.[34]

The politics behind the bill that came before Sacramento lawmakers were complicated and muddled. The bill would "provide for the location of corrals, cattle pens and slaughter houses in the city and county of San Francisco," something, many correctly noted, that had traditionally been the domain of city politics. Even more bizarre was that Ephraim Burr, the city's figurehead, was among the many voices supporting the bill. Burr offered written testimony to the state senate requesting their legislative intervention.

For Burr, the slaughterhouse problem may have been personal. In 1855, his eldest son died of an illness (cholera or typhoid) that Burr supposedly attributed to the open sewers and slaughterhouses near Larkin Street, not far from his home.[35] In written testimony to Sacramento lawmakers in 1859, Burr noted that there were "many citizens" now "living on the line of these slaughter-houses in sight of Larkin Street" who were inconvenienced by the filthy slaughterhouses. The city's laws and means of regulating slaughterhouses were simply not working. Other advocates for reform noted that the Court of Sessions was "continually annoyed by those indictments" related to slaughterhouses, "and the continued applications of those who had been indicted to be let off from paying those fines." Burr and others appealed to the state to intervene, believing that the special interests and failing legal and judicial infrastructure in the city itself could not effectively manage the slaughterhouse problem. In a rare moment of bipartisanship, a former Democratic judge and a former Democratic district attorney joined Burr in their support for state intervention.[36]

By some accounts, butchers also wanted stronger regulations. The complaint-activated abatement policies made life for the city's butchers unpredictable and itinerant, particularly as residential settlement expanded into areas once thought of as marginal and suitable for slaughterhouses. Some butchers grew frustrated at their inability to do business without being hassled and fined. In 1859, the butchers formed the Butchers' and Drovers' Association of San Francisco with the intention of finding a more permanent site for slaughtering animals. "It was the wish of the butchers, drovers" and other parties, Burr testified, "to purchase a tract of land for the purpose of placing the slaughter houses . . . believing it would be for the interests of the persons engaged in this business so to locate their business." The association of butchers lobbied the city and state to ask for help in purchasing the land. J. B. Forbes, an attorney for the butchers and other parties who carried on "offensive trades" in San Francisco, wrote to Sacramento to testify that his clients had been continually "harrassed [*sic*] by indictments for keeping nuisances" and that they sought the Board of Supervisors to "designate some piece of land on which they could carry on the said business." Ostensibly, many butchers disliked the subjective and unpredictable nuisance-based framework as much as residents.[37]

Prior to slaughterhouse regulation coming before Sacramento lawmakers in 1859, the San Francisco Board of Supervisors had supposedly sought a new place for the city's slaughterhouses, but had faced resistance by private-property owners whenever they came close to settling on a specific location. One large landowner nearly sold a large tract of land for the new slaughterhouse district, but backed out when he realized it would diminish the value on the rest of his adjoining lands. Slaughterhouses—and even the possibility of slaughterhouses—were enough to belittle property values. Despite a popular consensus to find a solution to the slaughterhouse nuisance in San Francisco, complex and conflicting local interests made slaughterhouse regulation a complicated political project in reality.[38]

It nevertheless remained unclear why, in 1859, the city was appealing to the state on a matter that had traditionally been handled locally. It seemed likely to blame a gridlock of local interests and backroom loyalties. Despite public support from butchers, many residents, and city leaders, inaction prevailed at the local level. By 1859, city leaders were asking the state to intervene. Many state legislators were puzzled by the demand and did not understand why the state would or should get involved. Senator Wheeler said he believed the power to regulate such nuisances was clearly given to the Board of Supervisors in San Francisco and outlined in the Consolidation Act of 1856. Intervening on a local matter such as this, he believed, would set a dangerous precedent. The state legislature, he said, should not "descend from the legitimate and proper functions of a legislative body" to concern itself with "the purlieus of a city to examine the streets and sewers." For Wheeler, the proposal to intervene was "an unheard of piece of legislation" and a radical expansion of state power on matters traditionally governed municipally. Senator Burton also believed that the senate had "no right" to regulate the slaughterhouses of the city, and said it was unclear why the state was being asked to make city policy. "Let us know the object of this bill," he demanded.[39]

Other legislators in Sacramento argued that state legislative power was precisely what was necessary because the "war on butchers" was corrupt and represented the worst form of special-interest politics that worked against the public good. Senator Anderson noted that the San Francisco delegation had continually sought city-level legislation over the past year, but that those efforts had failed. Williams believed there was "a disposition on the part of certain parties in San Francisco to force the butchers to remove from one portion of the city to another," and that "certain parties" in power "could make money out of it for themselves." The details of these corruption charges were not openly discussed, but it seems possible that butchers bribed city officials and judges to stall proceedings or to reduce or forgive penalties. Williams gave no specific names or details, but his explanation would certainly explain why a seemingly popular measure with outwardly supportive actors would remain politically stuck for so long.[40]

The debate in Sacramento exposed mounting pressures to *prevent* nuisances rather than to merely react to them. Senators Wheeler and Burton, and others who opposed the measure, maintained an older concept of regulation based on individual complaints and trials. Under this theory of liberalism—individuals pursuing personal freedoms could do so until they infringed on the rights of another—a slaughterhouse was only a nuisance if there was someone there to be offended by the smell. Wheeler believed there were "ample" remedies for the removal of nuisances, but that it "was a question that must be determined by the Courts."[41] Others saw the issue differently. Slaughterhouses, they implicitly argued, were inherently unpleasant and hazardous nuisances that required their removal from residential areas in totality.

The California Assembly passed the 1859 measure twice, but both times it was killed in the senate. Yet, two weeks later, the legislature enacted a law to extend the limits on "slaughter houses, corrals, and cattle pens" in San Francisco, extending the southern border to Mission Creek, and maintaining Larkin Street as the boundary on the western edge of the city.[42] The principled opposition against state intervention appeared to have failed—but so also did comprehensive and effective reform. By all appearances, the new rules—if they were enforced—did little to change the geography of nuisance and slaughter in San Francisco.

As city and state officials argued over new regulations in the 1850s, the city of San Francisco continued to expand rapidly, bringing new urban residents into greater contact with livestock and slaughterhouse nuisances. Charles Lux, a prominent San Francisco butcher, remembered that the residents moving to the western side of the city continued to raise complaints to the Board of Supervisors in the late 1850s and early 1860s. In the early 1860s, the slaughterhouses near Larkin Street eventually caved to public pressure and moved across town to join a cluster of noisome businesses on the southeastern edge of urban settlement, along Mission Creek at the corner of Ninth and Brannan Streets. That part of town was known at the time for its existing industrial nuisances, its heavily male and working-class population, its proximity to flowing water and prevailing winds that mitigated miasmas and pollution by pushing them "into the bay," where "they injured nobody."[43] Many butchers were willing to remove to a place they imagined might give them relief from the costly and sometimes unpredictable nuisance-abatement laws and litigation that imperfectly served the public good.

The relief that came from the relocation of slaughterhouses to Mission Creek was short-lived, however. Mission Creek slaughterhouses came under scrutiny again in 1861, when Senate Bill 80 proposed to outlaw slaughterhouses from the neighborhood in which they had just settled. By that time most of the slaughter-houses had relocated to the southern part of town, near Mission Creek. One resident estimated that "nine-tenths of the slaughter houses" in the city were located along Mission Creek.[44] At the urging of Senator Phelps of San Francisco, the state senate ultimately voted down the measure that would have uprooted slaughterhouses and corrals from Mission Creek.

Although comprehensive slaughterhouse regulation remained a chronic political issue into the 1860s, the city nevertheless continued to make other laws related to urban animal nuisances. In October 1859, city supervisor Gates passed an amendment to Order No. 88 that enhanced regulations on urban animals in San Francisco. The order made it unlawful to "drive any herds of animals not secured together" in residential parts of the city—ostensibly an effort to contain the nuisance of urban cattle drives and runaway steers. The city government had set aside new funds for a poundkeeper, who was instructed in 1859 to more aggressively "arrest and impound" all animals not secured within city limits. The law gave instructions to the poundkeeper and other officials to see that all animals driven through city streets were secured, but the statute also carved out exceptions for "sheep, hogs, and domestic milch cows," which were perhaps excluded because they were less threatening than loose cattle and horses. Those who did not secure their animals faced a steep fine of $5 per animal. One of San Francisco's leading newspapers, *Daily Alta California,* said the new law was "highly essential, as a protective measure against the furious herdes [*sic*] which have of late been driven through the streets."[45] But, a year later, in October 1860, the paper reported that the new law had failed to effectively reform urban cattle drives, saying that the laws were "never observed, as far as we can learn," like many city laws.[46] Newspapers continued to report on runaway cattle chasing people, charging crowds, and goring horses in city streets. "Accidents daily occur," reported the *Daily Alta California*, perhaps exaggerating the situation, "people are chased, knocked down, hooked, horned, and gored by the infuriate beasts, and it is merely a piece of miraculous good luck that some one is not killed."[47] In 1860, a ten-year-old girl was "severely injured" by a steer, raising public concern once more. The same newspaper warned that, under the current conditions, "there will be a funeral yet."[48]

Creatures of Progress

The demographic changes that began in the late 1850s continued to transform San Francisco into the 1860s. The numbers of women and children continued to grow as a percentage of the population, and the public protection of women and children remained a common refrain in city politics. These concerns for the safety of San Francisco's population of women and children in turn shaped a wide range of policies, including the regulation of the "wild cattle" and slaughterhouses in residential neighborhoods. Technological advancements in transportation further stimulated the impulse to reform, leading to new breakthroughs in municipal services and legal infrastructure necessary to effectively shape animal policy in the 1860s. In that decade, San Francisco laws profoundly remade the geography of slaughter and livestock in the city, marking a legal, political, environmental, and social transformation.

From 1850 to 1860, San Francisco was remade in almost every way: its buildings were built and rebuilt; its charter was twice rewritten; its economy was transformed from wild speculation to steady production and trade; and its itinerant population was replaced with permanent residents and families. The gold rush city of young single men and notorious rabble-rousers was giving way to a growing number of middle-class families, who settled away from the waterfront in neighborhoods, purchased property, and sought to create a form of permanence in the city. In 1849, San Francisco was roughly 98 percent male. By 1860, it was down to 61 percent. The most rapid demographic change came in the mid- and late 1850s, as women and children composed the entire net population gains in the city. From 1852 to 1860, the male population of San Francisco declined from 25,000 to 23,000, whereas the number of women and children increased from 12,000 to 34,000.[49] Despite the growing number of children, the average age of San Francisco residents also became older and wealthier, fitting with other demographic trends that ushered in a relatively stable group of permanent San Franciscans who inhabited high levels of governmental, civic, and economic leadership.[50]

With that expansion of permanence and civility came growing interests in property value and a broad desire among city leaders to make the city a clean, respectable, and healthy place. In the 1860s, mayors and city supervisors prioritized the creation and improvement of parks, new spatial zoning laws, and environmental management that promised to make San Francisco a healthy and prosperous city. Doing so required reforming the urban environment that extended into all facets of regulation—from the creation of parks, to greater restrictions on unpleasant and dangerous nuisances, and to tighter regulation of vice and crime. These impulses came together to remake the city's animal policies in the 1860s.

San Francisco was hardly New York in its population size and density, but city officials, boosters, and planners hoped that it would one day be a great city on par with older and larger cities on the East Coast. Eastern cities had long worked to establish and remake parks as a way to reform a variety of perceived urban problems. This was particularly true in the 1860s, as large urban parks became a means of combating urban vice. In the case of San Francisco, this ideology of park building took on a language and logic of its own, as the city's officials sought to protect and improve open spaces even before there was a perceived popular need. Population density and congestion—which helped inspire the creation of Central Park in New York—were not as significant in San Francisco as in eastern cities. Still, in the 1860s, San Francisco's leaders sought to improve public squares and solicited plans for an urban park to rival those in other cities, most notably New York's Central Park.[51] In the meantime, the city focused on improving smaller parks, and it fenced off squares downtown and in the Western Addition in 1863.[52] One important outcome of fencing was that it would help keep out unwanted animals. Although slaughterhouse regulation was not explicitly part of these plans, the new emphasis on park development fit a wider agenda in city hall to reorder urban space on a large scale.

In the 1860s, city supervisors and Mayor Henry Coon joined with private interests—including the landowner and financier William Ralston—to promote a new plan for urban parks and beautification. They hired the landscape architect Frederick Law Olmsted, of Central Park fame, to draw plans for a grand park for San Francisco that would declare the city's worldly aspirations. In 1866, Olmsted presented his plans for a series of connected parks, each with a distinct function, including a large promenade two blocks wide stretching more than two miles from Market Street north to the San Francisco Bay. Although the Board of Supervisors ultimately rejected the proposal, the plan set in motion a series of measures that would eventually lead to the establishment of Golden Gate Park in the early 1870s, which would transform the desolate Outside Lands into a public park larger than New York's Central Park. Before its transformation into a park—through intensive landscaping and irrigation—the Outside Lands was little more than a sprawling expanse of sandy dunes on the far western edge of the city.[53] On paper, Golden Gate Park was a symbol of the city's grand imagined future—"a feature of civic infrastructure that declared the city's world-class pretensions."[54] In reality, it was a sandy and desolate wasteland.

Designing a large park marked a new form and scale of spatial management in San Francisco. Olmsted's plan and the subsequent decision to build Golden Gate Park demonstrated a new type of urban planning. City spaces could be remade and manufactured to fit the supposed needs of the public, allowing for some features of city life to be distanced, and for other features to be brought close and cultivated. Nowhere was the conflict over space more notable, perhaps, than in the prominent two-mile promenade in Olmsted's original plan, which would have sliced through the part of the city known in the 1850s for its concentration of noxious slaughterhouses. By the 1860s, the slaughterhouses were largely gone from this neighborhood, but the proposed park showed how new forms of residential and refined space were increasingly in absolute conflict with certain noxious trades.

At about the same time that San Francisco sought to remake the geography and characteristics of slaughterhouses and parks, the city also began remaking spaces for the dead. Yerba Buena Cemetery was a thirteen-acre plot on Market Street, where City Hall now stands. In the 1860s, however, the cemetery was becoming a stubborn blight on the urban landscape and an impediment to development. In 1868, as the city imposed powerful new spatial regulations on slaughterhouses, it also began the work of exhuming bodies from the Yerba Buena Cemetery to make room for a new Civic Center. As they sought to do with animals, city leaders pushed out death and decay from the downtown landscape. Just as public health reformers feared slaughterhouses as places of disease, they increasingly worried that cemeteries posed similar threats.[55] An equally important reason for exhuming the bodies was an evolving centrality and significance of mourning in America, which matured during the Civil War. San Franciscans—and Americans generally—sought to establish new spaces for grieving. In the 1850s, many San Francisco residents pressured city authorities to create "ample and beautiful grounds for the resting places of the dead," that did not bring "fear to our mind," but allowed for calm and peaceful bereavement. Semirural cemeteries represented the convergence of art and nature, promising something "worthy of that great metropolis" many believed San Francisco would become.[56]

In 1868, city officials ordered bodies and headstones removed from Yerba Buena and relocated to the undeveloped Outside Lands, near Golden Gate Park in the windy and desolate landscape of sand dunes, described later as "sand and lupin and nothing else until the cliff's hanging over the ocean."[57] City leaders were on a mission to remake the residential city of San Francisco as a lively and healthy place; slaughterhouses and cemeteries had essential roles in urban life, but they would no longer be a visible part of life downtown.

======

The efforts of the Board of Supervisors to create a more pleasant and prosperous urban life were inextricably connected to emerging ideas of public health and the relationships between bodies and environments. The intervention of city leaders to drastically reorganize space was not merely an aesthetic choice, nor was it exclusively an effort to build and protect real estate values; built into these motivations were powerful ideas of environmental health that gained salience and influenced the creation of new forms of political power. In 1865, San Francisco established a permanent and powerful Board of Health and Health Department, which would profoundly shape slaughterhouse reform in the decades that followed. Combined with the city's growing police department and official agents of the Society for the Prevention of Cruelty to Animals, the 1860s marked the emergence of a set of laws and permanent police powers that shaped the treatment, killing, and processing of animals in San Francisco. Growing numbers of market inspectors, police officers, and Board of Health agents spread across the city with the intention of overseeing slaughterhouses and animals. Many carried newly minted badges backed by the power of the law.

The new emphasis on sanitation and environmental public health was a conversation that emerged with force in midcentury England and spread across European and American cities by medical doctors who believed that reforming urban environments would improve human health. The "sanitary idea" of Edwin Chadwick in London manifested in many ways in the growing institutionalized powers that shaped urban environments.[58] By the 1860s, Charles Rosenberg argues, sickness was seen increasingly as a "consequence of man's interaction with his environment" and "no longer an incident in a drama of moral choice and spiritual salvation."[59] The ideas of Chadwick and John Snow spread across cities in Europe and North America, and environmental sanitary reform became more central to city governance around the world. Improving environments, these reformers believed, would improve public health and create ordered and civilized social spaces. One Board of Health official in Cincinnati expressed the new spirit of health reform and its broader connection to progress and civilization: "Before erecting statues, building opera houses and art galleries, and buying expensive pictures, towns should be relieved of bad odours and fermenting pestilence. Good privies are far higher signs of civilization than grand palaces and fine art galleries."[60] Many American cities had created temporary committees to deal with specific urban health problems, but the creation of permanent and powerful health boards in American cities was something new in the 1860s and 1870s. San Francisco was a forerunner in this movement, establishing a city Board of Health in 1865—a year before New York City did so.[61]

In San Francisco, the city Board of Health was initially instructed to pursue a specific agenda. The Board of Supervisors tasked the Board of Health with administering charity hospitals, collecting license fees, and inspecting and quarantining ships entering the city's port. The influx of Chinese immigrants lay at the heart of some of these reforms. "The main cause for establishing a Board of Health and Quarantine System," said the city's health officer, was to tend to "the arrival of numerous vessels bringing Chinese passengers having malignant or infectious diseases."[62] The perceived threats of Chinese bodies to public health and social order were powerful ideological forces that remained politically salient well into the twentieth century.[63] Public officials and white San Franciscans commonly believed that the city's large and growing Chinese population posed a specific and urgent health threat to civilized white society and feared that Chinese bodies would not acclimate to San Francisco's particular environment. These fears contributed to San Franciscans' decision to establish a permanent city Board of Health, whose original purpose was to protect and improve the health of white residents amid a perceived onslaught of Chinese immigration.[64]

The scope of the city's Board of Health would expand to include widespread power to regulate many aspects of urban life, including control over environmental causes of sickness. Many white city officials and residents believed that Chinese bodies were dangerous to the progress of San Francisco, but also believed that animal bodies and industries were as much a threat. Sometimes health officials and San Francisco residents blurred the distinctions between Chinese bodies and animal bodies (as shown in Chapter 3). The city Health Department would eventually expand its role in regulating urban life by tracking statistics on illness and mortality, pushing for new infrastructure to manage human and animal waste, initiating campaigns to control smallpox and disease, and launching the city's food inspection system. The space devoted to the "Health Officer's Report" in the city's annual reports grew from less than twenty pages in the late 1860s to well over one hundred pages in the 1870s. Similarly, the city's Health Department budget expanded to support a growing team of agents and inspectors.[65]

The first head of San Francisco's Board of Health was Dr. James M. McNulty, whose understanding of health and science was a reflection of prevailing theories at the time. A graduate of Geneva Medical College in New York, McNulty served as a Civil War surgeon before returning to San Francisco in 1865 to head the city's new Board of Health.[66] Like many in his generation, the war was probably the pivotal event in his life—not only because of its unfathomable death and suffering but also because of its powerful role in developing sanitary ideas and practices and its central role in ushering in greater state intervention in public health.[67] Ideologically, McNulty was influenced by ideas of health that focused on the interaction of the body and the environment. In cities, that meant cleaning up environments that might produce unsanitary and miasmatic conditions. From the beginning, McNulty sought greater regulation of the city's animal population, in both life and death.

By the 1860s, the human and animal pressures on San Francisco's environment were extraordinary and still building. The city's population exploded by more than 90,000 residents in the 1860s, nearly tripling the total number of inhabitants to 149,000 by 1870. In his first report as health officer, McNulty noted the "rapid construction of buildings to contain this number of people, without any regard to drainage," which was creating a problem of "filth" that threatened to destabilize the city and stunt its development. In his first report, McNulty expressed concern for the unwieldy animal population and "the close proximity of the Slaughter Houses and Hog Ranches to the City," and the "great nuisance" they posed to public well-being. McNulty believed that efforts to regulate slaughterhouses in their existing geography would ultimately fall short. "So long as they remain in the present locality," he concluded, "I would strongly urge their removal."[68]

In particular, McNulty fixed his gaze on the Mission Creek slaughterhouses that had emerged amid reforms of the 1860s. The values of beauty and health downtown, coupled with the continued expansion of the residential city, meant that the cluster of slaughterhouses along Mission Creek reemerged as a problem for residents. Maps of the city over the 1850s and 1860s showed notable growth and development in the areas south of Market Street, just north of the slaughterhouses on Mission Creek.[69] Residential settlement and real estate speculation spread toward the slaughterhouses, fueled perhaps by the construction of the Brannan Street Bridge in 1857, which opened new areas south of Mission Creek for development. Parts of the mission were becoming known as working-class, residential neighborhoods. By the 1860s, the trend was clear: "The city has grown much within the last two years," declared the *Daily Alta California*, "especially in the neighborhood affected by the slaughter-houses," near Mission Creek.[70]

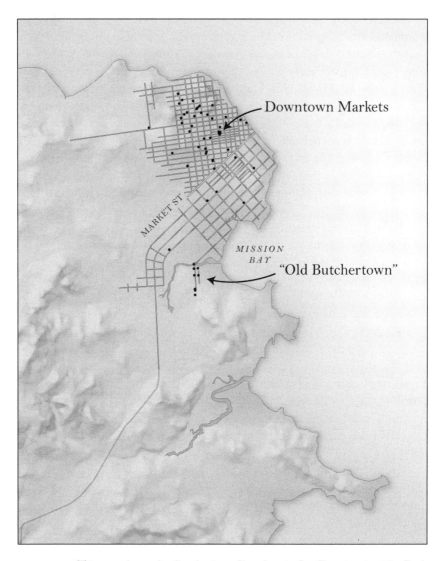

FIGURE 2.2 This map shows the distribution of butchers in San Francisco in 1860. Each dot represents an address listed in the city directory in the category "Butchers" (before directories distinguished between "wholesale" and "resale" butchers). Each dot does not necessarily represent a slaughterhouse, but the notable cluster of butchers near Mission Creek shows the growing slaughterhouse district that was emerging there by 1860, marked as "Old Butchertown." Cartography by Erik Steiner, Stanford Spatial History Project.

As new residential settlement came into greater contact with the slaughterhouses south of Market, new lines were being drawn in the war on butchers by the 1860s.

By the mid-1860s, Mission Creek was beginning to show the effects of intensive slaughterhouse pollution. The perpetual volume of blood and offal dumped in Mission Creek was overtaking the limited cleansing power the creek once offered. By December 1864, a letter to the editor of the *Daily Alta California* bemoaned the relentless stench of "fat-boiling, bone-burning, hide-curing, and slaughtering establishments in the vicinity of Brannan street Bridge." The letter was signed "One of the Many Sufferers." The writer proposed moving the slaughterhouses to "some more remote point, where they will not vitiate the very atmosphere breathed by a large and respectable portion of the people of San Francisco." The "sufferer" concluded with a point that may have revealed his true motivations: he was concerned for "the depreciation of property in that locality, on account of the above mentioned nuisances."[71] Property value, nuisance, environment, and health were deeply intertwined as motivations for reform, and nearly impossible to untangle.

Mission Creek continued to pose an acute and worsening nuisance in the years that followed. Hog ranches joined the slaughterhouses along Mission Creek, with yards of pigs "wallowing in blood to their hocks, and sucking up the warm stream [of blood]," according to one observer. Feeding slaughterhouse waste to pigs was a common practice in many American cities, but came under growing scrutiny in the last decades of the nineteenth century. By some estimates, somewhere between 500 and 1,500 hogs lived near Mission Creek, though their sounds and smells ranged far beyond their pens. A visitor to the Mission Creek hog ranches experienced the scene "through his nostrils," said one observer, and "his system will receive the greatest shock."[72] Others emphasized the auditory shock of the hog ranches—the "grunting and squealing of hundreds of the porcine race fills the air with discordant sounds." By 1867 the miasmas and stench of the hog ranches and slaughterhouses regularly saturated the air as far as Fifth Street, about a mile away—and under certain weather conditions, the decaying animal fumes reached all the way to Third Street to the north, and far south and west of Mission Creek, filling "the plain south of the Mission" that was hemmed in by hills. So constant and pervasive was the stench that one writer asked whether "the comfort of 10,000 people" was "to be sacrificed for the purpose of gratifying three or four men?"[73]

In the late 1860s, the public outcry no longer fell on deaf ears. The San Francisco Board of Health pushed for regulation in a way that marked a departure from prior policy, which had been based in nuisance complaints and litigation. The new laws and enforcement targeting the Mission Creek slaughterhouses offered a blueprint for a new form of regulation. Instead of a complaint-based system, new laws would prejudge slaughterhouses and hog ranches as nuisances and give the city's health and police departments power to wage a preemptive "war on butchers." In the Health Department's first four years in the late 1860s, agents actively monitored and sought to reform the city's slaughterhouse nuisance. Mc-Nulty persisted in his attempts to clean up the slaughterhouses on the "sluggish waters of Mission creek," which he said had become overrun with organic waste that required "two or three tides to carry the offal to the bay, where a great portion of it drifts in on our irregular water front, putrefying in the sun, and sending up its pestilential gases, poisoning the atmosphere of our city, and causing disease wherever it abounds."[74] Reformers had become increasingly concerned with improving the flow and movement of water and waste, which came to replace older models of environmental health reform that relied on trapping and containing waste. With the tides and streams around the southern part of San Francisco backed up with blood and offal, it was no longer enough to continue to react to the slaughterhouse nuisance; it had to be removed wholesale.

The need for a more permanent and preemptive solution to the complaint-based nuisance laws became clear again when slaughterhouses threatened to return to the neighborhoods where they were effectively removed a decade earlier. When some butchers sought to return in the late 1860s to the Western Addition—where residents had worked to eliminate their presence years before—concerned "citizens and taxpayers" wrote to the Board of Supervisors opposing the reestablishment of slaughterhouses in the area. The return of slaughterhouses, residents claimed, would be "prejudicial to health," "destructive to their property," and an assault on their rights to "personal comfort."[75]

Although it was immediately clear to Health Officer McNulty that the city's slaughterhouses needed to be removed, the specific place for their relocation remained uncertain. At one point McNulty proposed moving the butchers to the northern shore of the peninsula, near the Presidio, where the deeper waters of the bay and stronger tides and currents would more effectively flush refuse away from the shore and into the Pacific Ocean. But residents in the northern part of the city resisted. One resident said that the proposed site would pose a nuisance to "many of the older citizens" who had purchased property in that portion of the city "with a view of making for themselves homesteads." Already, "many improvements have been commenced—not only for our comfort but with a view of beautifying that portion of our city so long remaining untouched."[76] Homesteaders and property speculators no doubt made their preferences known to the Board of Supervisors, who, in turn, sought another location for the slaughterhouses.

Instead, the Board of Supervisors settled on separating the slaughterhouse nuisance to a more southern part of the city that had little or no political clout. Beginning in 1866, with the support of McNulty and the city Health Department, the city established new spatial parameters for animal keeping and slaughterhouses in Order 697—a far-reaching public-health measure that set stricter limitations on nuisances and sought new scales of separation of slaughterhouses, large populations of animals, and a variety of other "offensive trades." By 1870, the ordinance was revised to restrict animal nuisance industries to an even smaller area, confining slaughterhouses and animal nuisances in a way that sought to establish a particular environmental relationship that would facilitate the flow of waste into the San Francisco Bay.

The new reforms that emerged in the 1860s could not be divorced from the technological advances in transportation in that same period. The railroad established the possibility of new spatial relationships within cities and also between cities and their suburbs and hinterlands. For reformers, these new spatial relationships offered the possibility to improve urban health. In New York, railroads began delivering fresh milk from the country in the 1840s, ostensibly connecting the blighted city to the pure health of the country in ways that promised widespread renewal.[77] But railroads also had the capacity to separate waste from the residential city in new ways and on a new scale that promised serious improvements in urban health. The building of the San Francisco and San Jose Railroad in the early 1860s—and the continued expansion of railroad lines that connected California, the West, and North America in the decades that followed—not only remade the geography of markets on a scale of hundreds or thousands of miles but also offered cities like San Francisco opportunities to work at a scale of only a few miles to remake the geography of urban waste. With wire communication and railroads, the spatial possibilities of human-animal interactions changed; distant places on human scale (out of sight, scent, and sound) became relatively close on a new industrial scale (the flow of capital and the rapid movement of information and goods).

In theory, a trip from the city's outskirts to downtown markets by rail required a fraction of the time and cost it once did. Wire communication meant that a decision made in downtown San Francisco by someone in an office or on the stock market floor could be enacted immediately by someone miles away on the kill floor. The capacity to ship regularly, quickly, and inexpensively from hinterlands and urban outskirts to urban markets allowed for new spatial possibilities in slaughterhouse regulation. Railroads both connected and separated, creating an urban-periphery relationship that simultaneously pushed and pulled across the very same sets of tracks.[78]

In the remade landscape of a post-railroad world, San Francisco and cities around the world began separating their noxious trades on a new scale, chief among them slaughterhouses. One of the first things many cities did upon establishing a railroad was to more effectively export the messy businesses of killing and processing animals.[79] In Paris, slaughterhouse reform came amid widespread urban spatial reform, as Baron Haussmann remade the city for the enjoyment of flaneurs and the health and efficiency of those living downtown. Although Paris's makeover represented feats of engineering and modern organization—with public parks and wider streets and sidewalks—San Francisco's reforms were different mostly in scale. Animal life, death, and decay were not part of this new vision of Paris, just as they were not part of the way residents and leaders imagined the San Francisco of the future. The settlement that would become La Villette (Paris's large public abattoir) was made a part of Paris only two years before it became the new slaughterhouse district. The area that would become Butchertown in San Francisco was also something of a recent addition to the city, and was added to the municipality in the Consolidation Act of 1856.[80] In many cases in the mid- to late nineteenth century, cities annexed or extended their political reach into their immediate suburbs, making those places part of the city but also using those acquired spaces for separating and concentrating urban waste.

Like many new slaughterhouse spaces, the politics of siting slaughterhouses in Paris and San Francisco meant that the poorest and least powerful residents were often among those who sacrificed most for these downtown beautification and health projects. The abattoir at La Villette was built alongside one of the poorest areas of Paris, home to factories and warehouses and communities of people who worked low-wage jobs and would also seek employment in the abattoirs.[81] When Berlin created its slaughterhouse district in the early 1880s, city planners chose an uninhabited northeastern part of the city called Lichtenberg. The regulations that created the slaughterhouse districts of San Francisco and Chicago used marginal, ostensibly idle space: in Chicago an undeveloped swampland; in San Francisco a relatively uninhabited tidal marsh. All were designed with railroad connections in mind: to the city on one side, and to hinterlands on the other. All were built along moving water—rivers, tidal waters, canals—which planners imagined would provide natural flow and cleansing powers.[82] All were constructed to facilitate the movement of animal goods and waste in more predictable and efficient ways.

Although there were similarities in new slaughterhouse regulations in cities around the world, there were also key differences. European cities tended to favor public abattoirs, which were open for all butchers to use.[83] At first glance, American slaughterhouse regulations appear more favorable to private corporations.

Chicago, Boston, and New Orleans, among other cities, chartered monopolistic corporations that would centralize slaughterhouses outside downtowns. But chartering corporations was a key regulatory tool of cities and states in the nineteenth century, and the corporate charters of many of these slaughterhouse corporations required that they allow any butcher to use the facilities for a set fee. As was the case with many nineteenth-century regulations, American approaches to slaughterhouse reform are not easily defined in terms of "public" and "private."[84]

San Francisco's Butchertown was something of a hybrid of private and public space. The city did not create a corporation, but it chose instead to delineate a particular place for the butchers—what was to become known as the "Butchers' Reservation" or "Butchertown." By law, the new Butchers' Reservation was the only part of the city where animals could be killed and where large herds could be kept. It was a space ostensibly available to anyone to use, but whether it was truly open to all remains unclear. Butchers needed to have the financial resources to move their slaughterhouses to a distant part of town, and to purchase or rent space. San Francisco's Butchertown had no publicly owned structures for slaughter. The corporations that would be part of the remaking of slaughterhouse space in New Orleans and Boston, on the other hand, were public corporations that held land and built the slaughterhouses and were required to lease space to any butchers wishing to use the abattoirs at a set fee.[85]

Although innovative as a policy measure, San Francisco's new slaughterhouse district represented relatively modest technological gains. Its slaughterhouses were in some ways closer to the small-scale butcher stalls that inhabited the ostensibly modern La Villette (which centralized slaughter but still relied on master butchers who rented stalls and employed traditional butchering methods) than they were to the modern Chicago meatpacking operations that would emerge in the last decades of the nineteenth century. Nevertheless, the slaughterhouse regulations that emerged at this time all shared an interest in separating slaughterhouses and dense animal populations on a new spatial scale enabled by railroads. San Francisco and Paris were unlike Chicago in their organization and labor, even as San Francisco's Butchertown and Paris's La Villette had physical structures that were remarkably different. San Francisco and Paris slaughterhouses contained spatial elements of modern organization without notable advancements in production technology, labor, or scale.[86]

Although cities across the United States and around the world differed greatly in their approaches to advancing slaughterhouse reform and addressing animal nuisances, they all converged in creating spaces that would profoundly separate the keeping, killing, and processing of livestock. These new spaces took advantage of new spatial relationships, environmental features, and ideas of public health. Although they differed in their paths to reform and their embrace of technology, they shared a similar commitment to the construction of modern urban space through animal exclusion and slaughterhouse separation.

===

In San Francisco, the creation of a new slaughterhouse and nuisance district was a process of creation and revision. Butchertown was not created overnight. A major step came in early 1866, when the Board of Supervisors pushed slaughterhouses far beyond the residential downtown, to a swath of solid land and tidal marshes south of Islais Creek and east of San Bruno road, in the far southeastern reaches of the city (see figure 2.3). The new ordinance did more than limit slaughterhouses: it regulated a wide variety of animal nuisances, removing them to a remote stretch of land, which became the only place in the city where anyone could "maintain any slaughter house, keep herds of more than five swine; cure or keep hides, skins or peltry; slaughter cattle, sheep or any other kind of animal; pursue, maintain or carry on any other business or occupation offensive to the senses or prejudicial to the public health or comfort in any part of this city and county." While previous regulations sought to *protect* downtown from nuisances, the new measure showed a different form of spatial regulation. Rather than a "negative space" in which slaughterhouses and other noxious trades were prohibited, new laws assigned these nuisances to a geography with clear bounds, separated from residential areas. It was a legislative move that used space on a new scale to regulate the most toxic and dangerous businesses in the city. The new ordinance also implicitly created a space in which nuisances were acceptable and appropriate and would not be subject to traditional nuisance laws. It marked in unambiguous terms where the civilized city ended and where the city of nuisances would begin—creating environmental and social divisions that would deepen in the decades and century that followed.

City officials also showed how serious they were about enforcing the new laws through growing police and public health departments. If the late 1850s marked a temporary decline in the power of San Francisco's municipal authority, the 1860s saw a steady revival of city bureaucracy. The expenditures of the city in the year ending 1860 stood at $1.1 million; by 1870 the city's budget had steadily risen to $2.8 million. In addition to growth in the Health Department, the city's police force nearly doubled between 1864 and 1868 (from 54 officers to 104), with the number of total arrests rising from 5,422 in the year ending in 1863 to over 13,000 in the year ending in 1870.[87] The Health

Department saw a similar growth, marked by an increase in the number of officers and market inspectors.[88]

Slaughterhouse regulation had been largely reactive in the 1850s, but now city officers actively implemented the new rules on where slaughterhouses could operate in 1866. Within a year, the city police made several arrests and raided a large animal operation owned by wealthy wholesalers Miller & Lux. Numerous butchers lobbied the Board of Supervisors for more time to relocate, with one butcher, Shrader—himself a city supervisor—arguing before the board that a failure to extend the deadline for removal would cost the city "one hundred thousand dollars" and cause "three or four hundred persons" to be "thrown out of employment." It was unclear where he derived these figures, but his challenge to the new law seemed as much a threat as a warning to the Board of Supervisors. Consumers would suffer, too, Shrader argued, as "13,000 men, women and children of this city" would be "deprived of their 'beef steaks' in the morning." By a single vote, the Board of Supervisors denied Shrader's request for an extension for the butchers, but Shrader's protest of the law continued as a court case that reached the California Supreme Court in 1867.[89]

The Supreme Court heard the case of *Ex Parte Shrader* in 1867 and handed down its decision in November of the same year. Shrader, who was appealing his Police Court conviction under Order 697, argued that the city had violated his rights by effectively stripping him of property without due compensation required by the state constitution. Further, he argued, the slaughterhouse regulation represented legislative overreach into a realm previously handled through litigation and complaints. By prejudging slaughter and other noxious trades as nuisances, Shrader argued, the new laws were assuming guilt and stripping citizens of their rights to their own labor and use of property.

The court rejected Shrader's arguments on all grounds. The new law, they concluded, fit clearly within the powers of the 1863 state law authorizing San Francisco "to make all regulations which may be necessary or expedient for the preservation of the public health and the prevention of contagious diseases," which the court had upheld in a previous case related to a law protecting the Sabbath.[90] As part of the same act, in 1863, the state legislature authorized the city of San Francisco to specifically "prohibit and suppress, or to exclude from certain limits, or to regulate all occupations, houses, places, pastimes, exhibitions, amusements, exhibitions and practices which are against good morals and contrary to public order and decency, or dangerous to the public safety."[91] The capacious law reflected the broad regulatory powers vested in San Francisco's municipal government—not unlike those in cities across the country—to mitigate and preclude nuisances, even at the expense of individual claims of property and labor rights.[92]

But the California Supreme Court went even further in rejecting Shrader's claim that the city infringed on his right to property and labor. The court emphasized that the new ordinance did not violate rules of eminent domain or constitute the stripping of personal property. "Voluntary obedience to the order," the court held, would have involved "neither a surrender of the right nor a disuse or suspension of the capacity, and a disobedience to it on the part of the prisoner has been visited with no description of civil disability," the justices concluded. Telling butchers where they could practice their trade was not a violation of civil liberties. The California Supreme Court further defended the ordinance by arguing that its intent was consistent with "all the forms of the common law," and that the individual rights of property did "not deprive the Legislature of the power of prescribing the mode of acquisition or of regulating the conduct and relations of the members of society in respect to property rights." For the court, there was little doubt that cities and states could regulate intensively to "suppress particular branches of business deemed by it immoral and prejudicial to the general good."[93] Few businesses threatened that "general good" more than slaughterhouses.

As for the butchers' argument that courts were the proper place for nuisance mitigation—and not preemptive legislation—the California Supreme Court also disagreed. "We are not aware that the limits of that power are to be determined in any case by the mere rigor of common law definitions or categories," said the court. "Common law definitions or schedules, so far from being limitations upon legislative power here, are the most familiar subjects of legislative action." Judicial and legislative forms of regulation were not separate and competing, but were mutually reinforcing and aligned in a common law tradition of regulation for public welfare. On whether the new law treated slaughterhouses with prejudice, the court agreed that it did, but for valid reasons: slaughterhouses were a particular variety of nuisance that, "with reasonable probability," posed a threat to public health by spreading contagious disease. "The power conferred has been exercised intelligently and in good faith," the majority opinion concluded.[94] The law forcing the relocation of slaughterhouses would stand.

In its unanimous opinion in *Ex Parte Shrader*, the California Supreme Court offered unambiguous legitimacy to the city's power to preemptively regulate nuisances in San Francisco. In addition to its citation of *Ex Parte Andrews*, which in 1863 confirmed municipal powers to regulate activities on the Sabbath, the court also cited *Cooper v. Metropolitan Board of Health*, a New York case that upheld a law limiting cattle drives and cattle ownership and required license fees for butchers. The verdict in *Shrader* fit within a larger legal network of cases that largely upheld municipal intervention for the social good, despite loss of—and severe limits to—personal property. When the United States Supreme Court took up the Slaughterhouse Cases six years later, there was already an extensive case law to support the extensive use of policy power by city and state authorities to mitigate public health nuisances. The arguments in the Slaughterhouse Cases in many ways rehashed arguments similar to those in *Shrader* on a federal level, and in the immediate wake of the passage of the Fourteenth Amendment. The key issues remained questions of free labor, the free uses of property, and the appropriate role and powers of city and state governments.[95] Although the Slaughterhouse Cases are typically considered as a federal test case of the Fourteenth Amendment, they also existed in the immediate context of a wave of city and state regulations on slaughterhouses. In most cases—federal and state—courts upheld the legitimacy of powerful municipal slaughterhouse regulations.[96] Had the Supreme Court found the use of such police powers to run contrary to the newly passed Fourteenth Amendment, they would have effectively stripped cities of an important set of regulatory tools used to minimize the worst environmental nuisances of the nineteenth century.

Perhaps bolstered by the verdict in *Shrader*, San Francisco officials actively enforced and tightened slaughterhouse laws in the years that followed. In 1867, the Board of Supervisors revised the initial boundaries to push slaughterhouses farther from the city center and increased the penalty for violators, with fines of $20 to $500 per incident, or ten days to six months in prison. The higher limit of $500 for fines perhaps marked the recognition of a new corporate scale of wholesale and slaughtering operations taking root in San Francisco. In December 1867, city officials also showed notable enthusiasm for enforcing the new slaughterhouse laws. The city's deputy health officer arrested Michael McCarthy, a pig rancher, at the corner of Broadway and Van Ness, and charged him with a misdemeanor.[97] When butchers near Mission Creek failed to relocate by the June 1, 1868, deadline, the *Daily Alta California* declared, "The Butchertown War Resumed." On June 4, Officer Becker and his men marched down to Mission Creek and arrested nine owners of slaughterhouses still operating there.[98]

Despite the focused efforts of public officials and the full-throated assent of the state Supreme Court, the war on butchers continued at a halting pace. Writing in 1868, one observer called the slaughterhouses, brickyards, and pig ranches as "firmly fixed and immovable in its place as Mount Diablo or Tamalpais," whose towering peaks could be seen from many parts of San Francisco. Despite a growing police department, city orders were still "laughed at and defied," according to this observer, and the force of public opinion and city laws were "as powerless as the idle wind."[99] Another editorial decried the "dead letters" of the nuisance laws: "There is not one prosecution for a thousand violations of the law, and there would

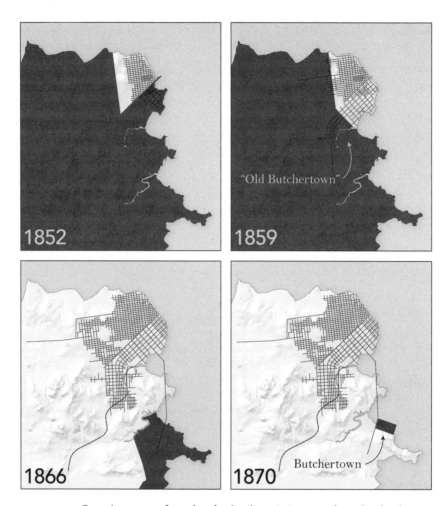

FIGURE 2.3 Over the course of two decades, legal restrictions on where slaughterhouses could operate changed drastically in San Francisco. These four images show the transformation of areas where slaughterhouses were permitted to operate. Most of the laws also limited the number of livestock that residents could keep. Research by Liz Fenje and cartography by Erik Steiner, Stanford Spatial History Project.

not be one punishment if there were a thousand prosecutions."[100] For many, city regulations remained far too feeble.

Amid these criticisms, the city's Board of Health and Police Department soldiered on in enforcing the new laws. In 1870, the Board of Health instructed the city's health officer to "make incessant war on the butchers till they leave the

Potrero."[101] Soon after, the city's market inspector—a member of the Health Department—testified in Police Court against numerous butchers accused of violating the slaughterhouse law. Weeks later, the Board of Health ordered the arrest of thirty more butchers. This time the cases were dismissed in court based on an unintentional glitch in the language of the law. Within days, the Board of Supervisors immediately cobbled together a new law that left little room for misinterpretation.[102] Two weeks later, the Board of Supervisors pressed the Board of Health to pursue the butchers with "stubborn determination," and to "prosecute them vigorously" until they removed to their new location. Relentless prosecutions took their toll on the butchers. By October 1870—four months later— newspaper reports suggested that the butchers were finally relenting and making arrangements to "break camp and depart."[103] By 1871, reports of butchers near Mission Creek and the Potrero vanished from city records, directories, and newspaper reports, suggesting that their removal to Butchertown was complete.

The twenty-year "war on butchers" was not easily won; it took the collective work of city supervisors, state legislators, city judges, Supreme Court justices, police officers, health officers, and active citizens to uproot the slaughterhouses, corrals, and hog ranches. By 1871, with the butchers and animal businesses largely removed to the shores of the new Butchertown, out of sight and smell of downtown residents, city officials and residents finally seemed to be free of the animal nuisances they had long seen as intractable threats to the health, safety, and progress of the city. Few, if any, anticipated the consequences of the new urban world they were about to create.

For the butchers themselves the twenty years from 1850 to 1870 were times of extraordinary change and uncertainty. Some likely benefited more than others in the revised slaughterhouse landscape of 1871, including Henry Miller. Miller was "one of the prominent butchers in the great emporium" of San Francisco, who arrived in 1850 and lived out the rest of his life in California. Like a large share of the city's butchers, Miller was born in Germany, the son of a "master butcher," and trained in a traditional craft of butchering—a craft that required a seven-year apprenticeship and extensive expertise. In Germany, Miller learned all parts of the business: from purchasing and raising animals, to running a shop, to making a large variety of products from sausages to fiddle strings. He left in 1847 and worked for two years in New York as a semiskilled butcher for a slaughterhouse operation that paid him largely in guts, hearts, livers, and offal that the company's owner allowed workers like Miller to collect and sell as part of their compensation. Born Heinrich Kreiser, he changed his name in 1849 to Henry Miller, to match the name printed on a one-way ticket to San Francisco.[104]

In San Francisco, Miller's business bounced from one part of the city to another in the 1850s. This was perhaps a result of the loose slaughterhouse laws and the unpredictable urban growth that characterized the decade. At one of his first jobs in the 1850s, Miller remembered taking a cart from his boss's shop to the slaughterhouse, located at the far northern edge of the city. Before the 1852 ordinance, Miller may have owned a slaughterhouse in what would become known as Chinatown, but soon abandoned it for a more permanent shop and slaughterhouse on the corner of Fifth and Howard Streets.[105] Miller's various locations across the city in the 1850s and early 1860s marked an itinerancy and impermanence perhaps typical of many butchers trying to make a living in a city that was changing so quickly that it kept butchers in constant fear of fines or costly displacement.

Miller's success as a butcher came through several good investments he made on small stock purchases, leading him to work with Charles Lux, another German butcher who had established similar success in the trade. In 1857, Miller joined Lux in a wholesale venture, purchasing a herd of 1,600 underfed Texas cattle, fattening them on Lux's 1,700-acre Buri Buri ranch (in what is now South San Francisco), and killing them at a handsome profit. In 1858, Miller and Lux formed a permanent partnership that would become one of the largest corporations in California and transform the region's cattle trade and larger patterns of land ownership, land use, and settlement in the San Joaquin Valley. By 1866, one California newspaper said Miller was "known throughout California wherever stock is raised."[106] By the twentieth century, Miller & Lux had amassed some 1.25 million acres of land along with valuable water rights, primarily in California, but also in Oregon and Nevada. Miller & Lux moved animals and feed through a complex network of landholdings, driving cattle north from Gilroy, pasturing them at Buri Buri, and driving them north to Butchertown. The two men began constructing this network in the 1860s with seed money they made as butchers in the gold rush city. By the late 1860s, Miller & Lux controlled a large share of the cattle and butchering industry in California.[107]

The parallel rise of Miller & Lux and the new slaughterhouse regulations in San Francisco may be no coincidence. Although there is no evidence to suggest that Miller & Lux had a direct hand in creating Butchertown, it seems likely they benefited immensely from its creation and specific location. Butchertown was perfectly situated between their Buri Buri ranch, just south of the city, and retail markets just to the north downtown. While historians have often imagined the "imperial" influence of the city of San Francisco on the California hinterlands, the emergence of Butchertown suggests a complicated dialogue of city and hinterland.[108] San Francisco businessmen were not only transforming land use and ownership in the California interior but also, in turn, shaping the built urban environment to fit their needs of rural production. If Henry Miller and Charles Lux could have written the slaughterhouse rules themselves it seems likely that those rules would have looked similar to what emerged in 1870. If Miller & Lux's exploitations of political and insider connections in other parts of their business were at all indicative, it would be surprising if the two men recused themselves from slaughterhouse debates of the late 1860s.[109]

For the city's butchers who operated on a smaller scale than Miller & Lux, there were good reasons for resisting the move to the distant shores of Islais Creek. In most cases, the move to the new Butchertown represented an investment of thousands of dollars. Although the removal of slaughterhouses marked progress for urban residents, it was an inexpensive solution for taxpayers that came with enormous costs for butchers themselves. One Board of Health estimate—perhaps inflated—put the cost of moving at $20,000 to $30,000 for some individual butchers.[110] Purchasing land at auction and building new pens and slaughterhouses represented enormous immediate costs that likely drove many slaughterhouse operations out of business. Adding to the initial costs of relocating, wholesale butchers would now face new and ongoing transportation costs across greater distances. These costs likely favored businesses operating at higher volume and scales of production. Spatial shifts affecting *where* butchers could exist utterly remade the structures and costs of production, sales, and distribution, and remade a connected network of animal by-product industries. Without state or city help in compensating the costs of relocation, butchers and other businesses were forced to pay for the move themselves. Faced with mounting costs and annoyances, many businesses, it seems, perished.

———

By 1870, the Board of Health and city supervisors had transformed nuisance law in San Francisco. The late 1860s marked a fundamental shift in slaughterhouse regulations across the United States, and San Francisco was on the cutting edge of these new laws. What was radical about the laws was not so much the expansive role of police power in municipal legislation. Rather, it was the intensity of police power to preemptively assume slaughterhouses were themselves a nuisance. Spatially, the new slaughterhouse districts—such as Butchertown, San Francisco— also operated on a new scale enabled by the advent of railroads. Connecting the city's wastes to the bay and separating them from downtown residents had long been the goal of many city regulations. In pushing slaughterhouses into the tidelands far south of residents downtown, San Francisco lawmakers imposed a new level of intervention toward those ends. They were also fundamentally remaking urban ecology, culture, and social relationships in ways they could not have imagined.

By 1871, with the butchers completely relocated, San Francisco authorities had effectively remade the downtown urban environment for its human and animal populations. The twenty-year "war on butchers" finally seemed to be nearing a temporary period of peace and tranquility. What emerged was a healthier, more pleasant downtown for a city that increasingly imagined itself as the "Paris of the West." But the story that would unfold in and around Butchertown in the subsequent decades was one quite different from the pursuit of refined progress downtown. The concentration of slaughterhouses, offensive trades, and large populations of livestock transformed these new spaces into a sort of "animal suburb," and a nuisance suburb—at once connected and disconnected from life downtown. In creating Butchertown, San Francisco officials were writing in clear geographic terms where progress and civilization would begin and end in the city.

One immediate outcome of the creation of Butchertown was that it marked a fundamental shift in how people and animals moved through San Francisco. Animals moved from pastures and stables to slaughterhouses in new ways, increasingly bypassing crowded downtown streets. The new geography imposed on slaughterhouses, tanneries, and other businesses no doubt shaped the geography of where workers lived and the distances they commuted to work. A growing number of "jobbers"—who transported animal products from slaughterhouses to shops downtown—moved through the city along new and different streets, connecting wholesalers, retailers, and consumers. Unhealthy miasmas and offal moved in new ways, too, flushed out into the strong, salty currents of San Francisco Bay and out into the Pacific Ocean. Prevailing winds forced foul odors into the open space above the bay, where they dissipated and bothered few. This, at least, was the hope. Regulating the geography of one element in the city's collective relationship with animals shifted the physical and social networks of the city, with profound implications for urban life, both human and animal.

Eliminating livestock from the city—in both life and death—offered reformers a pathway toward a healthier and safer city for the majority of San Franciscans. The creation of Butchertown presented the possibility of a permanent environmental relationship that would solve the nineteenth-century urban crisis of animal nuisances. The human city would thrive without the physical presence of living cattle, pigs, and other livestock—and without the businesses and workers that did the messy and unpleasant (though essential) work of turning the animals' bodies into products. Butchertown, by all appearances, would be a panacea. In reality, it turned out quite differently.

Conclusion: The View from Nob Hill

In 1878, only a few years before building his forty-two room mansion atop Nob Hill in downtown San Francisco, James Flood—a pioneer forty-niner turned millionaire silver king in the Comstock Lode—commissioned George Henry Burgess to paint the city of San Francisco as it would have appeared in 1850. The world Burgess created on canvas probably bore only some resemblance to the actual gold rush city. Like all aging memories, this conjuring of the past was perhaps smudged and altered in the hands of time. In the three decades since the gold rush, the city had become a major American metropolis of more than 200,000 residents. The civilized city that wealthy men like Flood claimed as their own creation was beyond even the outsized dreams of many residents in the early 1850s. As numerous San Franciscans came to understand their historical trajectory as one of progress and change, what stood out in their memory of the gold rush city were elements of urban life that had disappeared in the three intervening decades.

Almost an allegory, the painting, *A View of San Francisco in 1850*, shows the development of the city in stark terms. Read from foreground to background, it tells a story of progress and change: from the shadows to the light; from the tent settlements of Spanish and Mexican inhabitants to the illuminated bay with its iconic ship masts that signified prosperity in the years after the gold rush. Occupying a middle ground—between a tent city on the edge of civilization and the commercial downtown—were livestock. On the left side of the canvas, a man on horseback is herding cattle toward the city center, probably to slaughterhouses near downtown. Farther in the background two men on horseback pursue what might be a runaway steer or hog. The painted city is one in transition—a city in movement, in flux, with a multiplicity of cultures and stages of progress—but one that was, inevitably, giving way to the Gilded Age city Flood and Burgess knew and inhabited. Flood and Burgess knew how the story in the painting would end.

By 1878, the cattle herds through downtown were something of the past, but their memories were important for those who told stories of the city's history and progress. Cattle were a feature of urban life that essentially distinguished the city in 1850 from the one Flood and others believed they had built of gold, silver, wood, ore, and steam. But the streets in the painting have been scrubbed clean with the painter's brush. They are devoid of the gritty environmental and social reality of the gold rush city. The soft glow of the painting suggests that memories of the bygone animal city may also have contained feelings of loss and nostalgia for those looking backward in time from 1878. The cattle are not menacing, but calm.

FIGURE 2.4 George Henry Burgess, *A View of San Francisco in 1850*," 1878, oil on canvas. The Picture Art Collection/Alamy Stock Photos.

The early city, full of cattle and livestock, was perhaps a necessary stopping point in the linear progression that many understood as the ascendance of city, state, and nation in the late nineteenth century.[111] By 1878, no longer just a port city on the edge of the Pacific, San Francisco was a city that faced east, toward the continental United States—like the eastward view in Burgess's painting. When Burgess sat down to a blank canvas, it was the very absence of cattle downtown in the late 1870s that caused him to so prominently paint them into an assemblage of memories and a narrative of progress and development. The removal of animals and slaughterhouses from downtown between 1850 and 1870 was an important piece of a larger set of transformations in San Francisco that marked the decline of the gold rush city and the rise of the Gilded Age metropolis.[112]

The new Butchertown was two miles south of the slaughterhouses on Mission Creek, and farther still from the growing majority of downtown residences and settlements that spread west toward the Pacific. A few years after the establishment of the slaughterhouse reservation, the city's former mayor, Ephraim Burr—by then one of the wealthiest men in San Francisco—would begin construction on his lavish Italianate mansion at 1772 Vallejo Street. The house was just a few blocks from the cluster of slaughterhouses he fought to remove only years before—the slaughterhouses he blamed for the death of his eldest son. Looking out from the circular windows on the building's third story, Burr might have been able to see the distant shores of Islais Creek to the southeast, and the plumes of white steam rising from the new bone-boiling and tallow-rendering establishments. But he would have been unable to smell the mass of animal bodies or the stench of decaying offal. He would not have heard the "roar of cattle" or the "sound of the killing axe," or have seen the thick streams of blood that ran into the bay.[113] For Burr and other San Franciscans living downtown, those experiences were from a city that existed in the past.

CHAPTER THREE

Blood in the Water

*The Butchers' Reservation
and the Reshaping of
San Francisco*

PEERING DOWN FROM the Golden Gate Bridge—above the one-mile channel that connects the San Francisco, Suisun, and San Pablo Bays to the Pacific Ocean—the forces of nature are staggering. Tides and currents churn and swirl with a force more powerful than any river in the world. It is here—in this narrow stretch—that the vast network of bays and inlets of hundreds of square miles engages in a constant push-and-pull of tides and swift currents. In a single day, around 400 billion gallons of water rush in and out of the channel—a number too abstract to effectively capture the forces one encounters when standing on or beneath the Golden Gate Bridge watching the roiling waters below.[1]

It was the cleansing power of these waters that city officials sought to harness in 1870 to solve some of the greatest pollution problems in the city. City planners did not merely wish to separate slaughterhouses from downtown on a new industrial scale; rather, they sought to establish a permanent and sustainable relationship between the city's "noxious trades" and seemingly unrelenting cleansing powers of the San Francisco Bay. Most of the slaughterhouses would be built on stilts over those inexorable tides, and the blood and offal would fall into the bay, where they would be washed away twice daily by the ebb and flow of salt water.

Although seen by some of its architects and supporters as a permanent solution to the city's slaughterhouse and pollution crisis, the creation of Butchertown had pervasive unintended consequences. The creation of Butchertown fundamentally transformed the social and ecological landscape of San Francisco. By the mid-1870s, it was apparent to public health officials that Butchertown was far from the panacea some had hoped it would be. Slaughterhouse regulation seemed to be one endless game of whack-a-mole: the solution for one generation sowed the seeds for the health crisis of the next. Butchertown created a deep disruption in the ecology of the San Francisco Peninsula that sent ripple effects throughout the city. The transformation of the extensive tidelands and marshes around Butchertown sent waves of disruption into a variety of other environmental relationships: from waterfowl hunting, to shrimp farming, to small-scale milk production. But the decision to create Butchertown endured long past the late nineteenth century. The development of San Francisco into the late twentieth century and to the present shows the ways in which decisions about slaughterhouses continue to shape our cities.

Islais Creek

The location lawmakers chose for Butchertown in 1870 lay at the mouth of Islais Creek, one of the few tidal inlets on the eastern edge of the San Francisco Peninsula. What San Franciscans called "Islais Creek" was in fact a large tidal area made of a network of marshes and creeks. The largest of these creeks started more than three miles inland, in the steep hills that rose from the center of the peninsula. As a watershed, Islais Creek drained a large swath of the southern reaches of the city—including the Mission District, which was growing rapidly in the last decades of the nineteenth century. As the creek wound its way down the hills, it joined smaller streams and fanned out into a large tidal plane that stretched almost two miles wide by the time it reached the San Francisco Bay. At high tide, this delta often contained several feet of water—deeper in some parts than others—that covered the low tidelands for more than a square mile, much of it covered with thick mud and tall grass. Although the waters of the Pacific were powerful as they washed in and out of the Golden Gate, by the time they reached the inland marshes of Islais Creek, they had become slow and gentle.

The name "Islais" had mythical origins as a Spanish word, adapted from the Salinan Indian word "slay"—a wild holly-leaf cherry bush that may once have flourished along the banks of the creek.[2] The word "Islay" appeared on a Spanish map in 1834, and, as early as 1868, a newspaper article printed a story of the wild cherry trees as the creek's namesake.[3] This legend continued into the late nineteenth century, and even up to the present. Whether or not there were once wild cherry trees, the Edenic myth of a pristine creek lined with fruit trees said perhaps

FIGURE 3.1 Detail of Islais Creek, before the construction of Butchertown, from U.S. Coast Survey of San Francisco in 1869. Islais Creek and the extensive tidal marshes are shown near the center of the frame in dark gray. Courtesy of David Rumsey Map Collection.

as much about the massive environmental changes that would follow as it did about the original character of the creek itself.

After the wild cherry trees came the cattle. The area that would become Butchertown was part of José Cornelia Bernal's 4,500-acre Mexican land grant in 1839, descriptively named "Rincon de las Salinas y Potrero de Viejo"—"the corner of the salt marsh and the old grazing land."[4] The name change reflected the shifting laws, interests, and environmental relationships of the new settlers—concerned as they were with marking property and the grasses that would feed their cattle trade. With the establishment of Butchertown thirty years later, cattle returned to the Potrero de Viejo in larger numbers than ever before. The new name—Butchertown—again reflected the ways in which people saw and interacted with the changing landscape in new ways. But, by the late nineteenth century, the cattle themselves looked increasingly different from those only decades before; they were bulkier breeds designed to produce meat, not merely hides.

In the years after the gold rush, as Mexican land grants were eaten away by expanding white settlements and homesteaders, the fate of the southeastern parts of the city remained in question. Some residents and speculators believed and hoped that areas around Islais Creek would share in the rising tide of prosperity after the gold rush. Some even expected that the tidelands near Islais Creek would be filled to make solid land for homesteads.[5] New roads and bridges shortened the trip from southeast San Francisco to downtown by the 1860s. In 1858, the distance from City Hall to Hunters Point was eight miles by road—a circuitous path around the sprawling Islais Creek tidelands. In the 1860s, the construction of several bridges and roads cut the trip from downtown to Hunters Point to 4.5 miles. In many areas near Islais Creek, land values more than doubled.[6] A horse-drawn railroad across the Long Bridge connecting Hunters Point to downtown created a smoother surface for transportation, and further eased overland movement. Even before the arrival of steam-powered locomotives, public and private construction of roads, bridges, and rails radically altered the spatial connections of the areas south of Islais Creek, opening it to prospectors and settlers—and fueling the ideas of city planners and speculators in ways previously unimaginable.[7] By the mid-1860s, speculators and large landholders had laid out numerous homestead lots for sale near Islais Creek.[8]

The lands just south of the area that would become Butchertown showed promise as an industrial suburb even prior to the creation of the slaughterhouse reservation in 1870. In the 1860s, the construction of Dry Docks at Hunters Point and the Pacific Consolidated Woolen Mills, in nearby Bayview, promised to employ thousands of San Franciscans and return large profits to investors downtown. Some saw a "southward drift of the city" as industry and some residential settlements took root in the southeast—even inspiring a proposal to move City Hall south to the Potrero to account for the increasingly north–south orientation of urban development. Boosters noted the "beautiful and fertile valleys" of Bayview and Visitacion Valley, both south of Islais Creek, along with the numerous homesteads ready for purchase with "the best soil and most pleasing sites for homes within the limits of the county."[9] One booster noted that the future prosperity and settlement of San Francisco lay in the "streets in the southeastern part of the city," which were "advancing more rapidly than any other" with the construction of roads and other improvements.[10]

For these numerous San Franciscans who owned land in the southeastern part of the city, the addition of slaughterhouses, tanneries, hog ranches, and large populations of livestock posed a threat to their land values and investments. The environmental and social characteristics of a zone devoted to heavy nuisances stood in sharp contrast to the world of imagined homesteads and families.

Roads Not Taken

With the creation of Butchertown, many city officials believed they were creating a lasting and permanent solution to the slaughterhouse crisis of the 1860s. It was not obvious to planners that the new Butchertown would soon create a new health crisis in the 1870s. The designs for Butchertown bespoke new intentions for the slaughterhouse district that would be something more than a scaled-up spatial solution to an old nuisance problem. The slaughterhouses themselves were built to effect a new relationship with the natural world—not one of intentional domination or subversion, but a place where the built and natural environment (human work and ecological work) would coexist in perpetuity. The stilted structures, where waste would fall into the tides and wash away, exemplified hopes that the city might find a permanent solution for the worst forms of pollution and that permanent growth and prosperity would prevail in San Francisco. The new location was "unexceptionable" as a place of development, according to one city newspaper, and planners agreed that it would "hardly be possible for the [slaughterhouse] business to again become a nuisance to the neighboring community."[11]

Some saw through the sanguine rhetoric and criticized the plans for Butchertown, arguing that it would not solve the problem of slaughterhouse nuisances. One critic, writing anonymously as "A Nose from South San Francisco," argued that the removal of slaughterhouses would simply relocate the problem and not provide a long-term solution. The old slaughterhouse district near Mission Creek—that "Garden of Eden," in "full bloom and fragrance,"—could hardly be corrected simply by transplanting the animal businesses to the southeastern tidelands, he argued. The root cause of the nuisance—the scale of dumping and the wasteful practices of wholesale butchers—would remain uncorrected by the new law. He warned that the southern lands would become overrun with waste from the "abattoirs and the herding of Moses' pets," which would accumulate and "spread all over the flats of Islais Creek, knee deep."[12] "The nuisance will be merely changed and not abated," said another critic of the plan.[13]

Other alternatives were proposed at the time—paths not taken in the development of the city. The same critic of the relocation plan proposed another method for disposing of slaughterhouse waste. Rather than facilitate the dumping of blood and offal into the tidelands, he argued, the city supervisors would better serve the public by passing laws to promote the recycling of waste as fertilizer. In particular, the construction of a *poudrette*—to convert waste into fertilizer through heat—was seen by some as a solution that had helped European cities manage organic waste. Through laws or construction of public facilities, the city could promote the conversion of slaughterhouse wastes into "valuable composts for our gardeners and farmers." If cities forced slaughterhouses to reuse their wastes, slaughterhouses and animal industries could exist anywhere, he argued, "in any Plaza of the city," and could operate "without annoyance to the public."[14] Reusing organic materials, some believed, would stitch the city and hinterlands once more into a sustainable, productive, and healthy organic network.

Indeed, by some measures, the reuse of organic matter was in sharp decline over the course of the nineteenth century. The "organic city" of antebellum America— in which organic waste was intensively reused by various means—created something resembling a "closed ecological loop."[15] The profligate dumping of slaughterhouse waste in San Francisco—a solution apparently embraced by policymakers—stood in sharp contrast to this older model of waste management. The large-scale pollution that would emerge in Butchertown also stood in contrast to contemporary slaughterhouse waste management that was emerging in places such as Chicago, which was known for using "everything but the squeal."[16]

The fact that butchers discarded such high volumes of organic materials is something of a puzzle. This is especially true when one considers the apparent crisis in available fertilizer that was emerging in the 1850s. So broken was the "ecological loop" that the growing demand for fertilizer in the United States had become a matter of national and international importance. Demand for guano fertilizer was causing international conflicts in the Pacific in the 1850s and 1860s, and the US market was spurred by the passage of the Guano Islands Act in 1856. Despite the market demand for fertilizer, local businesses were apparently unable or unwilling to profitably process organic waste into fertilizer. Critics of the Butchertown plan noted this apparent paradox. "A navy is employed by the Atlantic States and England to transport concentrated manures to their shores," said one critic, while the capacities to produce fertilizer at home were going largely untapped.[17] Harvesting Butchertown's waste for fertilizer was not something businesses were doing on their own; it was, it seems, less expensive to allow blood and offal to fall into the tides than it was to process that waste into fertilizer or other by-products.

The bracing rhetoric of progress and civilization pervaded both sides of the debate over how to manage the city's slaughterhouses. The organic foundations upon which the civilized city would be constructed mattered greatly to its long-term success or failure. If San Francisco were to become a world-class city—that "we all believe is to be the richest and most populous [city] on earth"—it would need to follow and learn from the "experience of the most civilized nations and the counsels and warnings of science" to abate the "most abominable" nuisance using the best possible methods. Some saw perfection in the tidal cleansing of stilted slaughterhouses, while others saw perfection in transforming slaughterhouse

FIGURE 3.2 The "Butchers' Reservation" (commonly known as "Butchertown") is shown on this 1911 map. Imposed on the image is an outline of the area where it was legal to operate a slaughterhouse in San Francisco. Note the slaughterhouses clustered in the northern corner of Butchertown, built on piers over the tides. Tanneries and ramps for unloading animals from train cars are also depicted on the map. Map detail from August Chevalier, "The 'Chevalier' Commercial, Pictorial and Tourist Map of San Francisco From Latest U.S. Gov. and Official Surveys" (1911), courtesy of David Rumsey Map Collection. Cartography by Erik Steiner, Stanford Spatial History Project.

waste into the building blocks for of a regional farm economy. Both sides believed their plans would promote and preserve the "health and comfort of the citizens" downtown and advance the overall progress of the city.[18]

The proposal to remake laws and customs in San Francisco to encourage slaughterhouse waste conversion into fertilizer was a path not taken in nineteenth-century San Francisco. Such a solution would have required a far greater intervention on the part of the city supervisors into the intricacies of waste management of slaughterhouses, and not merely laws of greater spatial separation. It might also have required funds for a public *poudrette* or other investments that would have incentivized the reuse of slaughterhouse waste for fertilizer. Forcing butchers to collect their blood and offal might have hampered businesses and added to their operating costs. The cheaper and easier form of regulation—selling off tidelands and improving the flow of slaughterhouse waste into the bay—triumphed.

By the early 1870s, a new city ordinance forced all slaughterhouses, hog ranches, and corrals into a thirty-five-block "Butchers' Reservation" that quickly became known as Butchertown. The biggest slaughterhouses opened shop along a single pier at the northernmost edge of Butchertown—the point nearest to their downtown consumers. Hog ranches, cattle pens, and additional slaughterhouses filled the more southern lands and tidal marshes to the south. A constellation of tanneries, tallow works, and bone boilers filled in the marshes just west of Butchertown, along the interior tidelands of Islais Creek.

Bloody Nuisance

But the designs of the new Butchertown soon showed serious flaws. Blood and offal inundated the shallow waters around Butchertown and sent out waves of ecological disruption that transformed other environmental and urban animal relationships in unanticipated ways. The city grew from 149,000 in 1870 to 343,000 in 1900, and the wholesale butcher industry expanded to feed downtown residents. The increased waste of feeding that booming population was now concentrated into what was, in effect, only a few acres.[19]

The animals that would become the blood and offal that fell into the San Francisco Bay had their origins dozens or hundreds of miles away—increasingly in the large pastures of the San Joaquin Valley. Seeds, sun, nutrients, and water combined to create grassy pastures, which fed and fattened livestock destined for San Francisco markets. Animal bodies turned grass into muscle, fat, blood, skin, and bones. From these distant pastures, cows were driven up the peninsula—typically by Spanish-speaking vaqueros, who maintained a niche role in the industry through the nineteenth century. As the animals walked to Butchertown, they metabolized some of that stored energy along the way. The increasing use of railroads in transporting animals to slaughter in the late nineteenth century might have reduced some of this weight loss, though animals also lost significant weight in transit. But even as rail became important in moving livestock nationally, large numbers still arrived in San Francisco on hoof. Many cattle were shepherded through a network of landholdings of a handful of powerful cattle giants, namely, Miller & Lux, who were also wholesale butchers in San Francisco.[20]

From pastures hundreds of miles away, animals made the last leg of their trip to Butchertown, where men turned their living bodies into consumable parts. In the process, animal blood and offal were dumped into the tides. Cattle were funneled into Butchertown from all parts of California and large swaths of the American West. On the other side of Butchertown, consumable animal body parts were sent out across a vast consumer network in the city and beyond—in some cases animal parts were shipped as far as New England and East Asia. Consumers living in San Francisco digested this animal food, converting it into energy for work and life, and made waste of their own. The construction of new city sewer systems caused much of this human waste also to flow through Islais Creek, past Butchertown, and out into the bay.[21] Seen through flows of energy and waste, Butchertown was essentially a two-block bottleneck in a vast network of animal production and consumption that fanned out in all directions. It quickly became what was likely one of the most concentrated zones of pollution in the United States.

Butchertown's new environmental pollution problems became perceptible in the 1870s, soon after it was established. The few voices that warned of flaws in the proposed slaughterhouse laws and designs were prophetic. In 1874, a *New York Times* article warned visitors riding to San Francisco—"Prepare to hold your noses"—when approaching Butchertown, then "Hold hard!" when passing through. The writer for the *Times* acknowledged the discomfort with this new hidden landscape of condensed slaughterhouses, adding: "If people will eat they must take the consequences." Although almost all major cities had their own noisome slaughterhouse districts by the 1870s, the *Times* reporter noted that San Francisco's slaughterhouse district was especially revolting, observing "the spicy gales of this Araby" that were "particularly odiferous."[22]

Part of the problem may have been that the depths of the San Francisco Bay were themselves changing, which in turn limited the cleansing capacities of the tides. When the *Baltimore Sun* published an article about San Francisco's Butchertown in 1876, it noted that water had once washed out the slaughterhouse wastes at high tide, but that the tides were no longer deep enough to keep pace with a growing scale of pollution. "There never was a wider discrepancy between theory and practice," wrote the correspondent about the intentions and realities of Butchertown. The result was a "suffocating stench" that poisoned the atmosphere. "The offal drops into the bay," said the observer, "and the tides come and go," but "do little to remedy the situation."[23]

The causes of these changes in tidal depth around Butchertown are hard to pin down precisely. The perpetual dumping of animal matter into the tidelands no doubt contributed to the shallower waters beneath the slaughterhouses. But there were other likely contributing factors as well. The San Francisco Bay was undergoing larger-scale changes in water depth at the same time that Butchertown began facing new pollution problems. Hydraulic mining in the Sierra Nevada mountain range, beginning in the 1860s, was causing massive sediment flows that reached the network of bays around San Francisco. Geologist Grove Karl Gilbert estimated that between 1856 and 1897, 1.5 billion cubic yards of sand and mud—more than eight times the amount excavated in the creation of the Panama Canal—flowed from mining sites upstream, filling some 30 square miles of Suisun Bay with an average of 3.3 feet of sediment. The effects farther south, near San Francisco, were less severe but still significant: 272 square miles of San Francisco Bay lost an average of about 8 inches in water depth, wreaking havoc on the bay's fisheries and oyster farms.[24] The sedimentation of the San Francisco Bay from distant mining likely contributed to the shrinking depths of water that were essential to the original designs of Butchertown.

Just four years after creating the new slaughterhouse district, the Health Department expressed grave concerns over what they had wrought. As early as 1874, the head of the Health Department said that the new slaughterhouse district was becoming as "great a nuisance as the former," and would soon require "action of some kind." The promises of cleanliness only a few years before had given way to a new reality: "A vast amount of blood and offal is thrown directly into the bay, rendering its waters, the mud beneath, and the marshes adjoining, inky black with filth, and odoriferous with the putrefying animal materials." On warm days when the tide was low "the stench is intolerable."[25] The situation would show few signs of improvement into the 1870s and 1880s, as the scale of industry and volume of slaughterhouse waste grew.[26]

Ripple Effects

The pollution that emanated from Butchertown and the industries along Islais Creek sent out ripples across the urban landscape and transformed a wide range of other environmental and human-animal relationships across the city and peninsula. From Butchertown, pollution washed up into the vast tidal flats of Islais Creek, mixing with waste from adjacent tanneries and hog ranches, along with sewage from the growing residential neighborhoods in the Mission District. This pollution affected a wide range of animal life in San Francisco—from changing populations of waterfowl to the spread of rats. Butchertown's pollution also took a heavy toll on small-scale urban producers, including immigrant dairy farmers and Chinese shrimp farmers. These less powerful groups ended up sacrificing the most as large wholesale butchers were given priority to freely dump their waste into the tides in the last decades of the nineteenth century.

In spatial terms, the creation of Butchertown also contributed to the rise of horse populations in San Francisco. Horse populations rose sharply in late nineteenth-century American cities—enabling and reflecting urban geographic expansion. But, as the creation of Butchertown suggests, these changes were also ushered in by new laws that facilitated the geographic spread of development. Distance from downtown was a key feature of Butchertown. Horses enabled this expansion, but also were the living beings that stitched the spreading city back together into a somewhat coherent whole.[27] Although exact numbers of horses are hard to determine, the number of businesses devoted to the horse economy in San Francisco expanded greatly over the last decades of the nineteenth century. The number of shops listed as "Harness and Saddlery" in San Francisco grew by more than 35 percent, from 45 to 63 between 1869 and 1900. "Hay and Grain" re-tailers increased at a faster rate, from 40 in 1869 to 100 in 1900. Most telling, perhaps, was the number of "stables," which rose from 41 in 1860 to 121 in 1910. By 1900 the city also had at least 107 "horse shoers." These figures offer some mea-surement of the rise in the number of urban horses in San Francisco—a trend common in most American cities at the time.[28]

One important promise of removing slaughterhouses from downtowns was that it would reduce the number of large, dangerous animals in city streets. But as meat and other products traveled greater distances across spreading cities, horse traffic came to present its own set of nuisances and dangers. In the 1850s, the labor of bringing meat to consumer markets was often done by livestock themselves; cattle and sheep walked to slaughterhouses near downtown. In a sense, the living muscle of horses replaced the living muscle of livestock that previously moved meat through city streets. Because horses could be more easily trained and con-trolled than cattle, sheep, and pigs, the use of equine muscle power brought a new level of homogeneity and order to city streets, even as traffic became a growing urban concern. The legal solution to one animal problem—separating the slaughterhouse nuisance and urban cattle drives—in turn exacerbated another animal problem: the traffic and waste that resulted from booming urban horse populations.

In terms of pollution, among the first ecologies to see the effects of Butchertown were bird wildlife populations. Long before the establishment of slaughterhouses and tanneries near its shores, Islais Creek served as a seasonal habitat for migratory birds. At certain times of the year, San Franciscans traveled to the Islais marshes to hunt waterfowl in one of the few estuarine habitats near the city. "The flats on the other side of Islais Bay afford magnificent duck shooting," noted an article in the *Sacramento Daily Union* in 1869—a year before the creation of Butchertown. A "good sportsman" could stand on the newly built long bridge and shoot flocks that flew overhead toward the creek and "fill his bag." One particularly notable prize was "an immense pelican," shot near the bridge that same year—a species that had become rare since its decline in the region over the previous two decades.[29] This recreation was particularly popular among boys who traveled out to Islais Creek to practice their shooting skills and to bring home trophies or food.[30] By the 1890s, newspaper reports suggest that many populations of waterfowl that once inhabited Islais Creek and Butchertown were in decline. "There is nothing in the district that they can shoot, every feathered wild thing seeming to have left for good," said one paper of the areas around Hunters Point and Islais Creek.[31] Although 1892 saw a return of "ducks of all kinds," the newspapers spoke generally of avian decline from unknown causes.[32]

The pollution of Islais Creek also affected those who hunted and consumed wildfowl. Some hunters no longer wanted to eat the birds they shot, believing that they were "poisoned with the filth of the sewers and the slime from Butchertown slaughter-houses and tanneries."[33] That same pollution may have caused the birds' disappearance. By 1895, others decrying the contamination of the creek noted that "even the ducks avoid the poisoned waters and fly past them to better feeding ground."[34] The pollution could sometimes prove deadly to humans as well. A duck hunter who accidentally shot himself near Islais Creek made the mistake of smearing mud on the wound to try to stop the bleeding. One of the city's newspapers blamed the polluted mud for causing an infection that killed the man.[35] Decades of pollution sacrificed a distinctive habitat for certain bird species—and a distinctive sport and subsistence activity for people.[36]

In other ways, slaughterhouse waste supported new bird populations. Butchertown became a habitat for massive flocks of seagulls that typically appeared in published observations of the slaughterhouse district. According to one report in 1892, the waters off Butchertown were "whitened by thousands of gulls" that congregated to feed on the floating offal and to mate before returning to their nesting grounds on the Farallon Islands.[37] A reporter visiting in 1881 also noted the "clamorous seagulls" that fed on "floating offal."[38] Another described the feeding frenzy when offal fell into the tides from the stilted slaughterhouses, saying that "the gulls fight and scream over it."[39] Apparently gulls were not much of a hunting prize, and it seems that bird hunters had little interest.

Domesticated birds also flourished in the new Butchertown, particularly on "duck ranches." As duck became popular on menus and dinner tables in downtown San Francisco, raising ducks offered opportunities for small-scale farmers. The *Pacific Rural Press* gave sage advice to those wanting to start their own duck ranch: to obtain "cheap feed . . . go to Butchertown," where "boiled beef heads" and other scraps can be procured at little cost.[40] Another observer in 1877 noted the common practice of feeding offal to ducks, which "makes very fattening food for hogs and for those 'wild' ducks of which we are so fond at our restaurant dinners."[41] The areas in and around Butchertown were ideal for raising ducks in San Francisco because of their proximity to inexpensive land and feed.

Given its low overhead and quick return on investment, duck ranching appealed to small-scale farmers—most notably Chinese farmers.[42] As with many forms of discrimination against Chinese Americans, new laws increasingly targeted Chinese practices as a way of targeting people.[43] This was true of duck farming, as Chinese San Franciscans came under growing public scrutiny, leading to the passage of a law in 1889 that prohibited feeding offal to ducks. The Health Department struggled to assert its powers, however, and city officials were still battling Chinese duck ranches near Butchertown as late as 1908.[44]

The concentration of discarded offal also supported the "ever-present dog" in Butchertown, which became a staple of descriptions of the neighborhood. Whether dogs were actually more numerous in Butchertown than in other parts of the city is unclear. But descriptions of Butchertown dogs echoed emerging social divisions of downtown and Butchertown. Butchertown was home to "dogs of every kind," said one observer in 1881—especially "mongrels and curs of low degree." The writer noted the "dozen dogs" that hung around one group of slaughterhouses, "reared in an atmosphere of blood," and lying "promiscuously" around some of the shops.[45] Another observer described, in detail, the dogs that inhabited the old slaughterhouse district in 1870 as "an ugly, ill-favored species" with "bullet heads, small upright ears, little stubs of tails, and short porcupine-like hair stuck in bunches all over their carcass." The dogs had a "disagreeable way of leering upon strangers with a pair of savage eyes," and snarled and growled at passersby. The same writer concluded that these Old Butchertown "curs" would "answer to any name but 'Beauty.'"[46]

To outside observers, these dogs embodied the physically and socially degraded environment of Butchertown itself. Descriptions of dogs in Butchertown reflected wider social divisions that were emerging between downtown and Butchertown in the late nineteenth century. At times, it was hard to know whether observers were describing Butchertown dogs or the ostensibly brutish men who worked in the slaughterhouses and lived on the outskirts of town. The men living and working near the slaughterhouses were, by one description, "broad-chested fellows," "apparently indifferent to the pain they inflict, or to the disgusting sights and smells around them." The men acquired "a taste for blood," and "drink it like milk, warm from the veins of their victim."[47] According to some, the brutal world of Butchertown created a substandard and savage human world—an inferior colony of the civilized city.[48]

Slaughterhouse workers likely understood the presence of those "curs" in a different way. Dogs provided companionship to workers, who disproportionately worked and lived in overwhelmingly male environments and performed the physically grueling, emotionally taxing, and socially alienating work of killing and butchering animals in the city. "In order to insure a quiet and contented mind to the butcher, he must have a dog," said a writer for the San Francisco Chronicle, recognizing in some way the emotional labor of slaughterhouse workers.[49] For some butcher shop owners, dogs were valuable in keeping down rat populations and protecting property from theft. But to outsiders, these "mongrels" and "curs" were merely symbols of savagery and distinct from the pets they had in their downtown homes.

Butchertown's slaughterhouses also became a key habitat for the city's growing population of rats. Rats had long been a concern in San Francisco, according to the Daily Alta California in 1884, "since the pioneers of the rodent army of occupation came out here in the ships which brought the Argonauts." But San Franciscans soon came to think of Butchertown rats as a different sort of creature altogether. "The Butchertown brand of rat is different from the ordinary hotel rat," said one writer, "he is larger and stronger, and has a wonderful appetite for raw meat."[50] Once again, descriptions of animals in Butchertown served as a proxy for widening social divisions within the city. Butchertown was a place apart from downtown—a place of savagery and brutality. These meanings became ascribed onto rats themselves.

Although Butchertown rats were rarely seen downtown, they made brief and celebrated appearances as animal embodiments of savagery. Rat baiting as a sport had a strong following in San Francisco well into the late nineteenth century. The sport typically involved releasing well-bred and well-trained dogs on a pit of rats to see how many they could kill in an allotted time. Advertisements for the rat-baiting events in San Francisco often touted that the rats used in a particular contest would be taken from Butchertown.[51] The Butchertown rat was something of a brand by the 1880s: seen by those who followed rat baiting as the most savage and vicious rats in the city—and, therefore, better sport.

One of the most famous rat catchers in America earned a living catching Butchertown rats. Richard Toner—known affectionately as "Dick the Rat"—was

FIGURE 3.3 Richard Toner, known widely as "Dick the Rat," is among the subjects depicted here in the *National Police Gazette,* February 14, 1891.

well-known in New York City by the 1880s. In 1884, Toner went to San Francisco to begin "a crusade against his namesake." His method of collection was itself a form of skilled labor that was in high demand among butchers, hotel owners, granaries, and other businesses that were vulnerable to infestation. He was, by one description, a "rat-charmer," and a sort of Pied Piper. But Toner's work catching rats demonstrated a sophisticated understanding of the animals' behaviors. He attracted rats using lamps and a special blend of oils of cloves and rhodium— along with his ability to "squeak like one"—then used special tongs to gather them up without injury by the hundreds. Toner thought of himself as a respectable person. Even when catching rats he wore a "nice dark suit," with "immaculate" linens and could "pass anywhere for a well-to-do business man."[52] In San Francisco, about half of Toner's rats came from Butchertown. The other half— presumably to make up for a shortage—were taken from the basements of hotels downtown. "Hotel rats" were usable, but reputedly more docile and less fierce than their Butchertown rivals. When confined together, some noted that Butchertown rats often killed and cannibalized hotel rats.[53] Toner not only collected money from businesses fighting infestation but also sold living rats to rat-baiting contests.

The social and political meanings ascribed to Butchertown rats and rat-baiting contests were thinly veiled. Like Butchertown dogs, Butchertown rats were seen as savage and ferocious. For those watching or competing in rat-baiting contests, Butchertown rats were the "fine and strapping gladiators" of the rat world—a trope that likely revealed as much about perceptions and imaginations of social, environmental, and spatial distinctions as it did about animals themselves. In pursuing the toughest, most savage creatures as sport for their dogs, San Francisco's sporting men were experimenting with what they understood as a controlled, man-made experiment of "survival of the fittest," as one observer called it.[54]

The underlying social implications were also quite clear: in ascribing savagery and ferocity to Butchertown rats, San Franciscans were also defining people and spaces. Rat fights were the entertainment of many of the city's elites, "senators, county officials, doctors and merchants," according to one city paper, "who enjoyed the novel sport of witnessing the mode of generalship used by the dogs when chased around the pit by several savage rodents who fought savagely."[55] In setting their well-bred dogs on the Butchertown rats, the city's downtown elites in some way played out underlying social conflict. It was a controlled and symbolic form of violence. The sport was justified, in part, because of its dubious claims of advancing public good by reducing the number of dangerous rats. As Toner himself put it: "Rats is no good."[56]

In the 1890s, rat baiting came under the scrutiny of Societies for the Prevention of Cruelty to Animals (SPCAs), both in San Francisco and in other cities across the United States. In San Francisco, agents of the SFSPCA forced rat baiting underground and into suburban retreats that were outside the jurisdictional authority of the San Francisco society. One rat-baiting match that was broken up had attracted some "thirty odd people," many of whom were among the city's professional elite. In 1894, San Francisco police intervened to stop a rat-baiting contest that resulted in the prosecution of twenty-eight men who were charged with cruelty to animals. When brought before the court, the judge agreed that the men had violated the law, but believed that killing rats was not such a terrible crime. He reduced their bail from $40 to $10 each, and in numerous cases released men with little more than a slap on the wrist.[57]

The rats that thrived in Butchertown gained further notoriety in the wake of the 1906 earthquake. As the city crumbled and burned in the 1906 earthquake, one estimate suggested that some five hundred animal carcasses, mostly horses, littered the city streets. With resources diverted and no running water or working incinerators, organic waste, animal carcasses, and abandoned buildings created ideal conditions for rats.[58] When the plague broke out in San Francisco in 1907, rats became the central target, with Butchertown as ground zero of a new public health war on rats. The outbreak caused the death of 89 San Franciscans and came just two years after the discovery that rats—specifically the fleas that lived on their bodies—spread the disease. Officials quickly identified Butchertown as the center of the largest rat populations in San Francisco, and public efforts targeted the slaughterhouse district.[59] San Francisco responded through a massive public-private partnership that raised hundreds of thousands of dollars and distributed thousands of leaflets to citizens and businesses. In six weeks in 1908 alone there were 162 meetings in San Francisco to educate the public on rat eradication. The city set bounties on rats at 5 cents apiece, which was later increased to maintain pressure on declining rat populations. At its peak, the effort to kill rats employed more than 900 people and was responsible for the deaths of over 200,000 rats, including some 13,000 rats in a single week. Thousands more rats likely died of poison, their bodies never found or collected.[60]

In Butchertown, the slatted floors that many slaughterhouses still maintained became the bane of the anti-rat crusaders. Spaces beneath the floor—designed in the 1870s to mitigate the nuisance of waste—were now recast as the root cause of the city's greatest public health crisis because they provided habitats for the city's rats. The solution to a previous generation's health crisis of controlling slaughterhouse waste and nuisance had sowed the seeds of a new generation's health emergency. In response to these and other concerns, city officials rewrote rules to make Butchertown a landscape of impermeable cement—regulations that changed buildings in Butchertown and also downtown. Rat-proofing the city meant pouring concrete, sealing off and rationalizing the flows of waste into the San Francisco Bay, and exerting a new level of control over organic material that could become food for rats—especially slaughterhouse waste. Concerns over urban animal life once again remade the built environment, this time ushering in a landscape of concrete and undoing a previous architectural and environmental logic of slatted floors and flows of waste.

Understory

As Butchertown developed in the last decades of the nineteenth century, it also transformed the geography and characteristics of another important animal industry in San Francisco: hog ranches. Hog ranches had long been a feature of urban slaughterhouse landscapes in many American cities—including in San Francisco's old slaughterhouse district in the 1860s. Like distillery dairies, hog ranches used animal bodies as machines to transform organic waste into animal products. Arguably, these hogs were as important as creeks and waterways in disposing of waste, but they added, in turn, their own share of public health nuisances: unpleasant smells, cacophonous squeals, sporadic threats of disease, and potentially unwholesome meat. Public health reformers saw the hog ranches of Old Butchertown as a key piece of the nuisance problem they sought to address in creating the new slaughterhouse district.

The laws creating Butchertown were also designed to limit the urban geography of large concentrations of pigs and other livestock. The new law in 1870 restricting the geography of slaughterhouses also explicitly prohibited residents from keeping more than five swine outside certain limits that overlapped significantly with Butchertown, but extended several blocks to the south. With respect to keeping pigs, the law appears to have been loosely enforced or revised over the years, as hog ranches emerged along Islais Creek in areas outside the limits stated in the original ordinance. In the new Butchertown, wholesale slaughterhouses, like Miller & Lux, increasingly incorporated hog ranching into their large-scale production methods, feeding pigs on the copious supply of offal.[61] Nevertheless, one important outcome of the Butchertown ordinances was that it shifted the geography of the city's hog ranches to the southeast. Like duck ranches, hog ranches depended on the proximity of slaughterhouses for supplies of inexpensive feed. As slaughterhouses populated the shores of Islais Creek and the areas in and around new Butchertown in the 1870s, the practice of keeping hogs near—and even beneath—slaughterhouses continued unabated. "The worthless portion" of animal bodies, said one observer in 1881, "if not dumped into the bay, are fed to hogs, which, in turn, yield to the same knife."[62] Ironically, the public health laws creating Butchertown may have reinforced the connections of hog ranches and slaughterhouses by locking them in close proximity.

In 1888, a new mayor and Board of Health became increasingly concerned over the practice of keeping pigs near or below slaughterhouses. The city's veterinary surgeon condemned the practice, but for surprising reasons. He was not primarily concerned for the welfare of the hogs—many of whom lived in filthy, dark understories of slaughterhouses. Nor was his primary concern for the poor health of the pigs and the quality of the pork they produced under such filthy conditions. Rather, his chief concern was that hog pens produced "foul air from below" that drifted up into the slaughterhouses and was "absorbed by freshly killed meat."[63] The "mass of filth" of hog ranches acted "as a means of contamination to the carcasses which hang up above them to cool." Only as a secondary concern did he believed that the hog ranches should be regulated because the meat from offal-fed hogs was "unhealthy and unfit for human food."[64] The primary concern was for consumers downtown.

In November 1888, city supervisors passed a new ordinance that explicitly banned the practice of keeping hogs beneath slaughterhouses. The city's health officer notified firms in Butchertown that the Health Department would no longer tolerate the practice of having hog pens that were in any way physically connected to slaughterhouses.[65] The Health Department maintained pressure on businesses by creating a special committee to oversee the slaughterhouse district, with a particular concern for the places where living hogs and hanging meat shared the same air. Similar to later city efforts to reduce rat populations in 1907, the commission recommended architectural reforms and advocated for the abandonment of permeable structures in favor of impermeable floors and receptacles for collecting slaughterhouse waste. The Board of Health encouraged wholesalers to collect waste, load it on barges, and dump it into the deeper waters of the bay. If firms were to feed offal to hogs, new rules required that it be boiled before it was fed to pigs.[66]

Despite new laws and recommendations in the late 1880s, enforcement appears to have been lax. Many butchers and businesses in and around Butchertown apparently ignored the new rules. Hog ranches continued to operate in forbidden parts of the city, including the Potrero, long after they were banned by law. By August 1889, Miller & Lux was supposedly the only company following the new rules on boiling offal before feeding it to hogs, and many companies remained in violation of orders banning hog ranches beneath slaughterhouses. The nonchalance with which wholesalers and hog ranchers disobeyed Health Department rules led, in part, to proposals to expand the number of city inspectors. The city's mayor in 1889, Edward Pond, opposed additional enforcement, arguing that there were already enough health officials, who were "tumbling over each other" in Butchertown. Other city supervisors, however, supported an expansion of the Health Department to monitor slaughterhouses and hog ranches.[67]

The 1890s would see further growth in the Health Department's inspection powers and the number of agents who patrolled the city. In 1890, the health inspector, A. B. Kinne, issued a report in which he named those responsible for the sanitary disaster that continued to unfold in Butchertown. Hogs were still feeding on offal in pens connected to kill floors, and it was in these cellars that "the worst conditions" were found. Of the twelve slaughterhouses in the report, ten kept hogs next to or beneath the slaughterhouse floors, including all of the biggest wholesale companies. Rather than new laws, however, Kinne encouraged inspectors to enforce existing laws.[68] The problems of enforcing health laws on hog ranches in Butchertown showed the strengths and weaknesses of municipal regulation. The effectiveness of slaughterhouse removal marked the strengths of municipal power, but the struggles to prohibit untoward hog ranching showed the limitations of city government. Regulating practices was, perhaps, a greater challenge than regulating geography. Regulating *where* certain animal industries could operate was somehow easier for public officials than regulating *how* they operated.

Nevertheless, the city was in some ways successful in reforming hog ranches in the 1890s. Ironically, this too might have sowed the seeds for the rat crisis of 1907. In some ways, hogs and rats occupied similar ecological niches in Butchertown, feeding on the same deluge of slaughterhouse waste. In reducing or eliminating the practice of feeding offal to hogs in the 1890s, the city might have created a greater food supply for rats. The thriving population of Butchertown rats by 1907 may have been the result of well-meaning animal reforms from the 1890s.

Wading into the Waters: Gleaners and Shrimpers

Pollution from Butchertown and other animal industries along the Islais Creek marshes also influenced the productive environmental relationships of market gardeners and small-scale food producers. The San Bruno road was the main road connecting downtown San Francisco to the productive hinterlands to the south. Market farmers driving north to the city would have approached San Francisco along the San Bruno road, which skirted the western edge of the Islais Creek marshes for more than one mile.[69] For many farmers, the wetlands provided one last stop along the way to downtown markets, where they gathered wild watercress that grew at the edges of the marsh. Islais Creek supplied "a large part of the city's supply of watercress," which grew "so thick and rank and is of such easy access to the San Bruno road that it is a matter of only a few minutes to lay in a supply for the day," said one observer.[70] By the 1890s, however, health officials grew concerned that pollution of the creek was making watercress harmful for downtown consumers. The fight against the market gardeners who gathered watercress—a group that city newspapers typically identified as Chinese and Italian—unfolded at the same time that the marshes around Islais Creek were brought under greater public scrutiny and amid renewed efforts to stop grazing that had long existed there.

Pollution also wreaked havoc on productive environmental relationships on the other side of Butchertown, along the San Francisco Bay near Hunters Point. It was here that numerous Chinese shrimpers lived and worked in one of the more fertile shrimping beds in the San Francisco Bay. Chinese San Franciscans had dominated the shrimping industry in the region going back to the 1870s. By 1895, the 5.4 million pounds of shrimp harvested in the Bay Area—almost entirely by Chinese fishermen—was among the most valuable fisheries, second only to the Bay Area oyster industry in market value and tonnage.[71]

The Chinese "shrimp camps" that appeared in the 1870s were more than just work environments. Shrimp farmers often lived alongside the shores where they worked—sometimes in the very same structures. In some ways, the spatial isolation of these camps probably offered refuge for Chinese men, away from a discriminatory landscape downtown. To outsiders, however, the lives and work environments of Chinese shrimpers were improper. Not only did Chinese men live in the same places they worked in substandard conditions, but—even more shocking to white observers—Chinese men used their bare feet and wooden shoes to separate meat from the shells. Adding to white hostility, most of the shrimp were exported to China, where their meat was sold as inexpensive food and their pulverized shells as fertilizer. This export economy angered many whites, who saw the natural bounty of the bay sold away to China for the profit of Chinese immigrants and merchants.[72] To white observers, the whole operation was backward.

As Butchertown waste washed up along the shores of nearby shrimp farms, public health officials found fault not with the wholesale butchers, but with the Chinese shrimp farmers. It seems unlikely that the Chinese encampment near Butchertown preceded the slaughterhouses there. What is clear, however, is that the interests of Chinese shrimpers were quickly deemed secondary to those of the large-scale slaughterhouses that grew along those shores in the years that followed.

It was once again the protection of downtown consumers that ostensibly justified the targeting of Chinese residents, though the social discrimination was thinly veiled. Public health officials engaged in aggressive public attacks on Chinese shrimp camps in the 1890s, focusing in particular on encampments near Butchertown.

The attack on Butchertown shrimp farmers came in the broader context of other attacks on Chinese fishermen in the last decades of the nineteenth century. Chinese fishing practices angered and frustrated nativist white fishermen who saw Chinese netting practices as destructive of young fish and fish populations.[73] Widespread anti-Chinese sentiment became cloaked in a new language of fisheries conservation. "If the mode adopted by the Chinese is allowed to be continued in a few years they will have the Bay of San Francisco entirely drained of all kinds of food fish," said one critic in 1885.[74] Anglers and sportsmen joined state conservation officials in the fight against Chinese fisheries in the 1880s, with the director of the California State Sportsmen's Association of San Francisco offering his support to the fish commissioners in seeking a ban on shrimp exports. With mounting pressure, the California legislature passed a ban on "Chinese shrimp or bag nets" in 1887.[75] California's State Board of Fish Commissioners set numerous rules that sought to handcuff Chinese shrimpers, though historians have since concluded that Chinese practices were not to blame for declining fisheries.[76] It was in this larger social, political, and environmental context that concern for the shrimp farms near Butchertown surfaced in the 1890s—this time cloaked in the language and laws of public health.

The city's new focus on microscopic threats to public health in the 1890s led to allegations that Butchertown shrimp (harvested by Chinese shrimpers) were contaminated with ptomaine—a protein produced by bacteria when they consumed organic waste coming from the slaughterhouses. The Board of Health did "extensive analysis" and declared a prohibition on the catching and selling of all shrimp caught in and around Butchertown. But Chinese workers living there refused to obey the orders, according to the city's papers. In 1899, the city's health officer enlisted the help of the city's chemist and police officers, along with an army of fourteen Health Department inspectors. They marched down to the Chinese encampment near Butchertown, and condemned and set fire to 15,000 pounds of shrimp. Months later, the city's Board of Health concluded that the shrimp from Butchertown were not "germ-ridden," as previously thought. Their mea culpa ran on page 7 of the *San Francisco Call*, but their uncompensated damage had been done.[77]

Quagmire: The Islais Creek Cows

Perhaps the most significant consequences of the pollution of the Islais marshes came in the transformation of the tidal pastures used for raising dairy cows. The grassy tidelands—one of the wettest and greenest parts of the peninsula near San Francisco—had long been used for grazing livestock. This was true even before new ordinances began pushing dairy cows farther from the city center beginning in 1880. These ordinances would become known as the "Two-Cow Limit" because they banned San Franciscans from keeping more than two cows in large and growing sections of the residential city. Islais Creek and its extensive marshes were just outside the initial Two-Cow Limit, making it an ideal location for cows producing milk for urban consumers. The Islais marshes also seemed to function as a sort of unclaimed commons, making the grasslands around Islais Creek a distinctive environment for small-scale dairy farmers seeking close proximity to downtown markets.

By the 1890s, however, the pollution of the "swamps" of Islais Creek was becoming a growing concern for city health officials, who increasingly saw the tidal marshes as dangerous places for food production for downtown consumers. These new concerns were the result of physical changes to the marshes and also in changes in scientific knowledge. Although miasma had long been central to the ideology of health reform, new concerns over germs and bacteria increasingly drove municipal health policy in the 1890s. The city health department pursued these new microscopic threats by expanding the number of Health Department inspectors and scientists as part of an aggressive system of food and milk reform.

The 1890s also saw a wider national and international reconsideration of pure milk and public health, along with new forms of governmental regulations. Increasingly, scientists and health officers of the city and state understood milk as a key vector for germs.[78] But the new scientific paradigm that accounted for microscopic actors did not merely replace older miasmatic theories of disease, but often integrated these knowledge systems in ways that were complimentary. Public concerns over the health of city milk combined elements of both modes of thinking—miasmatic and microscopic. Environmental understandings of health did not simply disappear with the advent of germ theory. Rather, environment remained an important part of the way that the public and health professionals understood disease. Public health officials continued to focus on environmental conditions of cows because they believed those conditions could make cows more susceptible to bovine tuberculosis and other diseases. In the case of cows and milk, microscopic and miasmatic health paradigms did not necessarily clash, and often merged.

In the 1890s, popular and governmental fears over typhoid and tuberculosis in milk spread across the San Francisco Bay Area. These fears led to the creation of tighter food inspection laws and expansions in the number of Health Department inspectors to enforce old and new laws. When typhoid broke out in the early 1890s, city officials mapped the disease and found that it appeared throughout the city in a pattern suggesting that its spread was not purely miasmatic, environmental, or transmitted from human-to-human contact. Officials concluded that the city's milk supply was to blame. Throughout the 1890s, city officials looked to reform dairy practices as a means of addressing public health. "Milk is largely if not altogether responsible for this extraordinary condition of the City health," said one report. Dr. Williamson, who sat on the city's Board of Health, declared that "there is hardly anything that produces more disease than impure milk."[79]

Despite new microscopic understandings of disease, public health efforts in the 1890s continued to target environments for reform. Public health officials identified a combination of factors that affected animal health and the quality of milk they produced. They believed that cows feeding in fetid swamps were particularly susceptible to becoming diseased. It was a hybrid understanding of bodily health that wove together bodies of animals, germs, people, and environments. In the early 1890s, public officials traced bovine tuberculosis to polluted marshes in Oakland, where dairy cows produced milk for the San Francisco market. San Francisco authorities came away from that epidemic believing that swamps—particularly polluted swamps—were breeding grounds for bovine diseases that poisoned the city's milk supply.

As San Francisco officials sought a solution to the milk crisis of the 1890s, they looked to cities across the United States to construct the laws and administrative infrastructures they saw as necessary to improving the public supply of milk. In 1895, San Francisco's health officer, Dr. Morse, produced a "stack of health reports from various cities" to help the Board of Health build appropriate municipal structures. For San Francisco officials, Cincinnati emerged as a notable model. In 1893, Cincinnati had created a milk inspection system that employed six "business men" as inspectors, who collected samples of milk they suspected as impure. In a time of public-private models of regulation, it was not entirely surprising that inspectors were drawn from "expert" businessmen, who were experienced in assessing milk quality.[80] Milk suspected of contamination or adulteration was sent to a city-employed bacteriologist, who understood milk differently from the businessmen—through a rapidly evolving science. Using a microscope and other instruments, the city bacteriologist "would decide the matter [of contamination] beyond a doubt."[81] In theory, business and scientific knowledge would combine to deliver a healthier supply of milk for urban consumers.

But governmental action in San Francisco remained mired in city politics. When city supervisors dragged their feet on developing a new system of milk inspection, the Board of Health circumvented the Board of Supervisors and the mayor. In 1895, the Board of Health appointed two new officials to monitor the city's supply of milk. James Dockery would serve as milk inspector, and Dr. John Spencer—a medical doctor and professor of pathology and histology—would serve as city bacteriologist.[82]

The Board of Health's decision to appoint two new salaried officers without the approval of the Board of Supervisors and the mayor was something of coup of nonelected experts. Elected city officials, including Mayor Adolph Sutro, questioned the legality of the appointment, noting that the city had "no money" for the new inspectors. When the Board of Health bucked Sutro's warnings and voted to set Spencer and Dockery's salaries at $150 a month, Sutro "laughed heartily." But the city's auditor upheld the legitimacy of the appointments as being within the expansive powers of the Board of Health. The Board of Supervisors and the mayor eventually came around to supporting what became a popular measure. Within a short time the city's new milk inspection team went to work.[83] It was yet another example of the extensive political power of the city's nonelected Health Department.

The head of the new milk inspection regime would be James Dockery. Dockery was neither a medical doctor nor a scientist; he was a prominent restaurateur and hotelier. Ostensibly he knew milk because he purchased large volumes of it for his establishments, and for that reason was thought to be a discriminating consumer with some claim to a capacity to discern good milk from bad. Dockery also imagined himself a man of culture and civilization. For years he was a leader in the Native Sons of the Golden West—a nativist organization that celebrated the first generation of white settlers in California, and what they saw as the progress of the civilized city. Dockery was also a "Grand Protector" of the Knights and Ladies of Honor in San Francisco, a prominent charitable organization.[84] Ensuring pure and healthy milk was part of Dockery's larger project of civilizing San Francisco—with ideas of race and gender mixed in to milk reform. For Dockery and others, city milk contained shades of whiteness.

In the 1890s Dockery pursued milk inspection with notable zeal, animated by a rigid ideology that public and private efforts could guide the city on a path of progress. The four years Dockery spent at the helm of the city's nascent milk inspection system, from 1895 to 1899, would mark the most notable years of his public life, and a period of intense public intervention into the city's milk markets and sites of production. As head of the dairy inspection system—and later the expanded food inspection system created by the Board of Health and Board of Supervisors—Dockery aggressively pursued the popular agenda of pure food reform in ways that gained him fame among the city's consumers. When he died in 1913, Dockery's obituary stated that "if the women of San Francisco had had a vote the mothers of young babies would have elected Dockery to any office he might have wished for."[85] But for others, Dockery's willingness—even eagerness—to brandish and fire a pistol at those who evaded or refused inspection gave him mixed popularity and reputation. Some dairymen came to see Dockery's work as mere public theater, and his confiscations as unfair destruction of private property. The courts never seemed to doubt his legal authority to seize and destroy large quantities of milk without trial or compensation. In basic terms, Dockery was a nonelected armed official who canvased the city, conducted searches at will, used threats of violence, employed questionable methods to test milk on the spot, and seized and destroyed private property when he deemed milk unsuitable.

In his first two months on the job, at the end of 1895, Dockery was primarily concerned with the practice of adulteration. Dockery and his team employed the "Babcock test," a method developed at the University of Wisconsin in 1890, which allowed inspectors to quickly measure the fat content of milk using a small hand-crank machine that separated milk using centrifugal force. The Babcock method could not determine the microscopic contamination of milk, but it was an imperfect way of testing whether milk was adulterated. Milk that failed this inspection was often poured out onto the street. Dockery could also send milk samples to Spencer's lab, where test results could be used in later prosecutions of dairymen. The discovery of germs and bacteria were key in leading to greater inspection of milk, but Dockery's technologies in conducting roadside tests were limited to measuring the "solid particle" and fat content of milk, and revealed nothing about the microscopic qualities of milk. New scientific ideas and knowledge may have necessitated greater milk inspection, but the inspections themselves were still quite rudimentary.

Dockery's inspection system showed immediate results. He targeted city markets, but also spent much of his time at roadside checkpoints, stopping milk wagons on their early morning trips into the city. On the busiest roads connecting city and suburbs—such as San Bruno road—Dockery's checkpoints often caused traffic jams with dozens of milkmen lined up for inspection. In his first twenty-three days on the job Dockery destroyed more than two thousand gallons of milk and initiated prosecutions against more than forty milkmen. The city courts were quickly full of cases, the outcomes of which overwhelmingly supported Dockery and his cause. Milkmen who transported or sold adulterated milk faced harsh fines.[86]

As Dockery's tenure entered its second month, the wet season arrived in San Francisco. The marshes around Islais Creek began filling with water and the grasses turned green and lush. But the rains that year intensified, spreading pollution across the flats surrounding Islais Creek. In November 1895, Dockery fixed his gaze on the Islais marshes—the pools of fetid water and sludge—and the cows that grazed there and made milk for consumers downtown. By November 1895, Dockery had found an important new battleground in his crusade for pure milk: the Islais Creek "swamps."

For Dockery and the San Francisco Health Department, the Islais Creek "swamps" were a looming public health menace—and were in worse environmental condition than the Oakland marshes where bovine tuberculosis had broken out only two years earlier. Health Department officials decided that "from now on a determined war will be waged against all dairymen who allow their milch cows to feed on swamp lands," according to the *San Francisco Call* in December 1895.[87] The wide swath of marshes connected to Islais Creek was chief among these "swamp lands" in San Francisco. It was here that dairymen allowed their cows free range "to wade into the swamp and eat of the rank grass which grows in the infected water."[88] The "concentrated filth" from various sources, said the *San Francisco Chronicle,* "penetrates the grass and soil of the swamp, and renders the former utterly unfit for nourishment for a beast." Echoing older miasmatic ideas, many warned that at night, "the vapor and fog rise like a poisonous breath from the marshes and spread over the adjacent places." Even in a time of emerging germ theory, "vapors and fog" from marshes and sewers presented acute health risks.[89]

But the regulation of the Islais swamps and the city's supply of milk was no small task. Dockery needed to coordinate enforcement across numerous branches of city and state government. By the 1890s, the powers to regulate animals in San Francisco were spread across several distinct municipal departments, each with separate badges, rules, duties, budgets, agents, and tools of enforcement. The poundmaster was responsible for rounding up stray animals of all kinds (mostly dogs, but also livestock) within designated areas of the city known as the "pound limits." The city pound also killed dozens of unclaimed animals each day. The city's Health Department regulated all facets of animals used for food, focusing on markets, but also attending to live animals themselves. The growing number of market inspectors—a branch of the Health Department—enforced regulations on animals in both life and death. The city's police department independently enforced a growing set of ordinances related to how and where residents could keep animals. Sometimes police arrests were triggered by complaints from the SFSPCA, which was established in 1868, and which also had its own professional and volunteer agents who patrolled the city with police power.[90] The city's Park Commission, which ran the expansive Golden Gate Park, also enforced animal policies and had its own pound, and focused on preventing livestock from illegally entering the park and grazing on the grasses, gardens, and trees dedicated to human leisure. Collectively, these agencies reveal the pervasiveness of animal life in San Francisco in the nineteenth century, along with the growing and expansive government power dedicated to regulating animals and shaping urban life.[91] Seen in this larger regulatory context, Dockery was merely one piece of a larger public intervention in the city's collective relationships with animals.

To reform the city's milk supply in the 1890s, Dockery would have to coordinate these various departments and city officials. The city's new veterinary surgeon, Dr. Creeley, played an especially important role in growing efforts to police the city's cows and dairy farms. Creeley also set his sights on Islais Creek, arguing that cows there fed on "grasses grown in water which is thick with the seepage from slaughter-houses, soap factories and tanneries," and produced milk that was dangerously unhealthy. The grasses in the Islais swamps were "laden with the germs of typhoid fever and consumption," Creeley continued. For Creeley, milk reform was an issue of "greatest importance" for the "community." Some of the worst milk in the city, he concluded, came from cows pastured in and around Islais Creek.[92]

Dockery and Creeley soon began inspecting and surveilling the Islais Creek cows. On November 27, 1895, Dockery and Creeley accompanied the city's pound-master and his five assistants to the Islais Creek marshes. When the team arrived they discovered the marshes full of cows—as many as two hundred standing in the swamps, with many more on the nearby slopes, their legs wet or caked with mud. Creeley believed that some of the animals showed external signs of tuberculosis.[93] In the coming days and years, these sorts of visits to Islais Creek marshes would become a common practice.

As with all cases of animal regulation, there were underlying social conflicts that played out in creating and enforcing new policies. The human beings connected to the animals that grazed in the swamps were an important element in the Islais Creek story. The *San Francisco Chronicle* called the Islais marshes a "swamp land which the Italian ranchers use as a pasture."[94] When Dockery and his men approached the dairies and shanties along the shores of Islais Creek, they saw not only sick cows and polluted swamps but also what they believed were degraded and backward human lives. To Dockery and others, the Italian dairy farmers likely presented their own threat to white San Francisco.[95] Americans had long judged one another by how they raised their animals, and San Francisco in 1890 was no exception. The Italian farmers' failure to graze animals properly was an affront to social order and the greater health and progress of the white, civilized city.

The vilification of the Italian dairy farmers along Islais Creek occurred in a larger economic and technological context. The small and squalid operations around Islais Creek stood in sharp contrast to a growing market presence of larger, scientifically managed dairy producers. These producers advertised their production methods as modern and sanitary—and an efficient and effective management of nature. By the 1890s, the wealthiest and most successful of the dairies that supplied San Francisco were far from the city center and far from the marginal urban pastures like Islais Creek. Increasingly, San Francisco's milk came from large dairies to the south, in San Mateo County, and also from large-scale dairies across the bay—in Oakland, Alameda, Marin, and even Sonoma.

The Jersey Dairy Farm was one of these large-scale operations. Founded in 1875 by Richard George Sneath, a wealthy San Francisco businessman and politician, the dairy operated on some 2,700 acres of land fourteen miles south of the city in what is today Daly City. Sneath had made his fortune as a grocer in the gold rush, and went on to become a prominent banker and city leader, serving as president of the San Francisco Chamber of Commerce and also as a city supervisor from 1856 to 1860. Sneath's efforts to produce pure milk for San Francisco and his active civic engagement were deeply intertwined. He saw pure foods as foundational for urban advancement and progress, and sought to contribute to the improvement of the city by raising cows and producing milk.[96] Sneath's brochures described the dairy farm as a contribution to public welfare—a "great philanthropic work—for there can be no question of the fact that thousands of lives, particularly of children, have been lost in this city through the use of bad milk." To produce "absolutely perfect milk," he argued, "must be considered in the light of a great public benefaction."[97]

Publicly, Sneath presented a romanticized idea of nature as a source of healing and health for the city of San Francisco, and actively contrasted his milk production methods to those in the city. Company brochures and observers described the Jersey Dairy Farm in glowing naturalistic language. "Springs of pure water in every field" supplied a network of troughs, reservoirs, and canals to provide drinkable water for animals, irrigation for fields, and "motive power to grind the grain, cut the hay, wash the cans, and sluice the barns, besides raising all the fish needed as food for the tables." Sneath's workers planted fruit trees, grew vegetables and flowers for the city's markets, and raised chickens and fish for city consumers. In describing the purity and cleanliness of his dairy, Sneath was speaking directly to urban retailers and consumers and offering an alternative to the dingy urban dairies that operated in San Francisco. "Cows are much more likely to become diseased in the city yards, on such defective food as is generally given them, than in the country," said a Jersey Dairy Farm brochure. Without "good air, water and exercise," cows were soon left "effeminate, and an easy prey to the many disorders they are liable to."[98] By his own measure, Sneath was trying to save the city through the production of pure country milk.

Although Sneath romanticized nature in his farm publications, he also embraced modern technology, environmental management, and large-scale production. The Jersey Dairy Farm was a massive operation that dwarfed the smaller dairies along the city's fringe—like those along Islais Creek. His 2,700 acres started at Mission Road (El Camino Real) and continued more than two miles to the Pacific Ocean. The company boasted of its herd of more than 1,000 cows, with plans to double the herd in the late 1880s. Sneath proudly professed his use of the "finest Jersey breeds" and the best methods of producing clean, natural milk. Sneath's operation involved cooling and processing technologies to create enormous batches of milk that were sent north to San Francisco in 7,000-pound loads that required six mules and three hours to reach city markets.[99] Sneath told consumers that inferior milk was removed from distribution and fed to hogs, which the farm raised at a rate of 100 per year. Animal waste from barns was channeled through ducts, stored in pits, and then spread over pastures to improve their fertility. Milk cans and vessels were scrubbed using revolving, waterpowered "Russia bristle brushes," which "cleansed much better and cheaper than by hand." Sneath had his own in-house blacksmith, wagon shop, and mill—a self-contained world of mechanical and ecological efficiency. All told, the Jersey Dairy Farm employed some 100 men and nearly as many horses and mules. By Sneath's own account, he sought to make the farm a modern, large-scale—almost utopian—system of production. Those who managed the farm did not seek to overcome natural impediments, but rather to improve and manage nature on a new scale using modern ideas and systems for greater natural productivity.[100]

It was in this broader context of changing dairy production in and around San Francisco that Dockery pursued stricter regulation and exclusion of small-scale Italian dairies around Islais Creek. Although Dockery showed an eagerness to target small-scale production of urban immigrants, he also inspected wagons of large-scale dairy farmers, including the Jersey Dairy Farm. The fact that Sneath's dairy failed basic adulteration tests in June 1896 showed that Sneath's advertisements were likely as much fantasy as they were reality.[101]

Despite some semblance of impartiality, Dockery's regulatory measures likely favored large milk producers and hindered small ones. Because fines were not adjusted based on the size of a business, the Jersey Dairy farm paid the same fine as a small-scale producer or distributor of milk. With their deeper pockets and greater production capacities, larger dairies could easily pay what would be a steep fine to a small dairy. Large-scale dairies were also apparently more willing to monitor and cull their herds of sick animals. For large-scale dairies, individual animals represented a smaller percentage of overall financial investments, making a preemptive culling less costly. Large dairies also had greater resources and technologies to manipulate milk to pass the Babcock test, which analyzed milk for unacceptable levels of adulteration but not for microbes. With a larger number of animals, a greater volume of milk, and the organizational and technological capacity to test and alter milk in large batches, large-scale dairies were more capable of smoothing natural inconsistencies of milk production and creating milk that would meet particulate standards. Scale of production, in effect, became a form of insurance in a new regulatory environment.

In the 1890s, Dockery continued his crusade to remove the immigrant dairymen on Islais Creek, but not without resistance. By December 1895, Dockery's warnings to Italian dairymen were going unheeded, and the San Francisco newspapers wrote that he was again "on the Warpath," summoning the city police, poundmaster, and veterinary surgeon to initiate a "raid on Italian ranchers" in the Islais swamps. This time Dockery and Creeley were not about to let the milkmen off with just a warning. Dockery began ordering the impoundment of cows grazing in the marshes, but was quickly met with resistance from the farmers. One dairyman rushed in on horseback to gather up his animals and drive them away from Dockery in "border style." Dockery fired three shots, supposedly to alert the patrol wagon that was parked along a distant road. But the immigrant ranchers apparently interpreted the gunshots as targeted aggression; the women living in the shanties around Islais Creek—unable to speak English—believed they were under attack and fled in a panic. Dockery ordered the arrest of three Italian dairymen and seized and impounded their cows.[102]

In the years that followed, Dockery would continue to marshal his teams of city authorities to impose law and order on farmers who grazed their cows in the marshes of Islais Creek.[103] Instead of actively pursuing the source of pollution—large wholesale meat corporations like Miller & Lux, large-scale tanneries and hog ranches, and the city's own sewer pipes—city officials targeted the Islais Creek dairymen. Although "Italian dairymen" featured prominently in descriptions of the first wave of reform, by 1897 the names of those arrested—Chambers, Barry, McDonough, Marty, and Baumann—suggested a broader targeting of fringe urban dairy farmers. Many were likely immigrants, but they were no longer described exclusively as Italian.

As Dockery made his raids on small dairies in and around the city, large-scale dairies like Sneath's thrived in the rural suburbs. The milk of those large-scale dairies entered Dockery's jurisdiction only when it crossed into San Francisco County. But the living animals and the environments that produced milk for San Francisco were beyond his direct control. In fact, the Milkmen's Association—a regional organization of the largest dairy operations in and around San Francisco—endorsed Dockery and his inspection system from the outset, perhaps realizing they would benefit from the new regulations that disproportionately affected dairies located in San Francisco. "Upright milkmen" with large volumes of production claimed they wanted to compete honestly under stricter regulation if it meant they would exist in a marketplace without smaller competition that often refused to set common prices. Large-scale dairymen like Sneath believed they had little to hide and much to gain from regulation. "Dockery is becoming a sort of dairy Moses, leading upright milkmen to a promised land they have hitherto hardly dared to dream of," said the *Pacific Rural Press* in 1895.[104]

But the Islais dairymen did not go quietly. Two years after Dockery began his campaign, dozens of cows still fed on the Islais marshes. Dockery staged another raid in October 1897, which again ended in "warning shots" that buzzed past the heads of resisting dairymen. When one of the dairymen fled the scene, he was intercepted by a police officer and beaten with a club before being taken to the city hospital for "several lacerations to the scalp." After firing more warning shots at another dairy farmer, Dockery finished his work of driving the offending cows to the pound, except for one cow that looked consumptive. Dockery pulled out his gun and shot her between the eyes. No compensation was paid to the owners, and Dockery boasted that when the dairymen arrived to retrieve their impounded cows that their permits to sell milk would be revoked, as would "all the permits of all other milkmen who allow their cows to feed in Islais creek swamp." The patrolling of Islais Creek continued through the late 1890s, with Dockery impounding cows and revoking licenses whenever he could, and often in quite public displays of power.[105]

The urban dairy crisis and the removal of cows from Islais Creek in the 1890s was part of a larger set of environmental and social transformations that resulted, in part, from the 1870 ordinance that relocated slaughterhouses and animal nuisances to Butchertown. Whether intentionally or not, city policies had the effect of enabling pollution around Butchertown and across the Islais Creek flats. The winners tended to be the large meat and milk producers and the companies that were given free rein to dump in the muddy flats around Islais Creek. Although

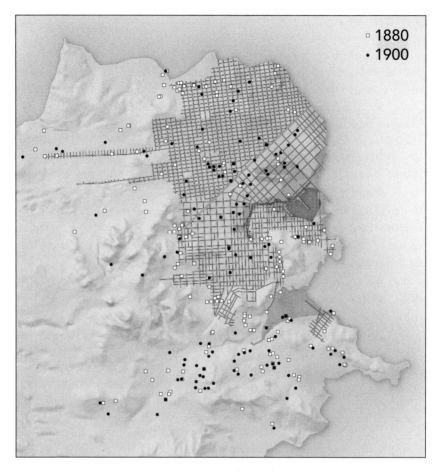

FIGURE 3.4 Each dot on this map is an address listed under "Milk Dealers" in the San Francisco City Directory for 1880 and 1900 (see key). Not all milk dealers had cows, but many did, offering a rough landscape for where cows lived in the city. Note the extensive movement of milk production away from Islais Creek and the Potrero, which coincides with the passage and enforcement of new laws restricting cows in those areas. Research by Liz Fenje and cartography by Erik Steiner, Stanford Spatial History Project.

some reformers sought to address the source of the pollution, the rapid degradation of the tidelands continued largely unabated. With Islais Creek quickly turned into a dumping ground for many powerful and entrenched groups, officials turned instead to the low-hanging fruit: market gardeners, Italian and immigrant dairymen, and Chinese shrimp farmers. None of these groups had created the environmental problem, but they paid dearly for the public health menace that ostensibly threatened urban residents and consumers. The city's regulatory capacities and political will were laid bare: authorities seemed far more effective at removing small-scale farmers along Islais Creek than they were at regulating the pollution of the city's noxious trades around Butchertown. One result was that productive relationships with animals were increasingly legislated into the "country," in part to protect the health of urban consumers.

The new regulations that emerged in the 1890s caused an important transformation into the early twentieth century. From 1880 to 1910, the distribution of "Milk Dealers" in San Francisco underwent a notable transformation as a result of new regulations. Addresses of "Milk Dealers" listed in city directories—an imperfect measurement of where cows were living in the city—suggest that these new laws and enforcement regimes changed the geography and distribution of the city's dairy producers. From 1890 to 1900, city directories showed a reduction in the number of "Milk Dealers" in San Francisco by almost one-third, from 179 to 138—perhaps marking a migration of dairy farms to areas outside of San Francisco. Further, the mapping of those addresses suggests a notable movement away from Islais Creek, to areas farther south. San Francisco was becoming a place where milk was consumed in greater volume, but where one was less likely to see a dairy cow or a dairy farmer.[106]

But the regulation of the dairy industry in San Francisco was not continuous or everlasting. As soon as 1899, newly elected governor Henry Gage went about scaling back many regulations affecting San Francisco by weakening the state food-inspection laws and seeing that the Board of Health was reappointed with railroad-employed physicians. Dockery was removed and replaced with a saloon-keeper crony of the San Francisco political machine.[107] The *San Francisco Call* decried the gutting of the Board of Health, which became part of the "machine to do politics of the lowest kind for the lowest purposes and for the lowest persons."[108]

Despite these changes to the Board of Health, the limits on where cows and dairies could exist within the city remained. The city's Two-Cow Limit was extended gradually as new neighborhoods applied successfully for inclusion. As they did, small dairy farms continued their retreat from urban spaces. The emerging distinctions between city and country were in part the result of laws that reinforced the separation between productive animal relationships and residential, consumer culture downtown.

By the last decades of the nineteenth century, Islais Creek was becoming the nuisance many San Franciscans wished would disappear. The opportunity to make that happen emerged in 1906, in the wake of the devastating earthquake and fire that left downtown San Francisco a heap of ash and rubble. What would the city do with the massive amounts of debris downtown? Yet again, city officials looked to the tidelands. In one final act of sacrifice, officials authorized the filling of Islais Creek one cartload at a time, burying the putrid marshes and wetlands with the ashes of the former city. The Southern Pacific Railroad continued to fill the creek in the years that followed, turning tidal lands that they owned into salable property.[109]

===

Born in the late 1860s, before the creation of Butchertown, Dockery may have been among the boys who went to Islais Creek to pass time hunting waterfowl. The city had changed by the early twentieth century—not least in the complete transformation of its animal populations that had once been a greater part of everyday life, but which now existed largely outside the residential city. Dockery lived just long enough to witness the first automobiles in San Francisco, which signaled the rapid decline of the city's largest remaining animal population: horses. The number of commercial stables listed in the city directory went from 121 in 1910 to only 22 in 1920. The organic animal city of the 1860s had come a long way in Dockery's lifetime, with the emerging world of concrete and automobiles enabling further shifts in the city's collective relationships with animals. But the decline of the organic animal city was hardly inevitable or purely the result of market change; it was forged in the political actions and decisions of people like Dockery himself.

Dockery made another passing appearance in the historical record when he briefly returned as chief milk inspector in 1910, traveling as far as Sonoma County in 1911 to track down impure milk sold in San Francisco markets.[110] In 1912, he joined the effort to extend the "two-cow limit" to the entire city and county of San Francisco. The ordinance passed and effectively spelled the end of commercial dairy production within city limits.[111] With city dairies gone or soon departing, one of the most notable causes of Dockery's life was complete. He died the next year, in 1913.[112]

Legacy of Neglect

Butchertown's legacy of environmental change lasted long into the twentieth century. The decision to site slaughterhouses and animal industries along the southeastern shores of the city set those neighborhoods on a distinctive long-term path of development. The Butchertown slaughterhouses would eventually disappear gradually over the twentieth century, beginning in the 1890s with the arrival of Chicago packers who built their modern slaughterhouses just outside the city limits, in Baden (in today's South San Francisco)—an area not subject to the same municipal regulations as San Francisco. The national meatpacking companies touted modern sanitation, factory-style labor, large-scale production, and new systems of refrigeration. In the face of this onslaught, San Francisco wholesalers in Butchertown were surprisingly effective at maintaining their place in the city's wholesale meat market. San Francisco was one of the few places in the United States where local companies held off the Chicago-based meat trust into the twentieth century.[113]

One important reason that so many San Francisco wholesalers survived national competition was that many were themselves large corporations. Cattle and land giants like Miller & Lux had long been operating on extraordinary scales of production. They matched Chicago in the market by vertically and horizontally integrating meat production across a geographically vast system of production, with Butchertown serving as a key part of that integrated network. Western laws and urban regulations had, for decades, fostered corporate growth in meat production. When Chicago dealers and packers arrived, they temporarily met their match.

Local retail and wholesale butchers also mobilized anti-Chinese sentiment in battling the Chicago companies in Baden. They accused the Baden meatpackers of employing low-wage Chinese labor, and the issue became a unifying rallying cry in boycotts of Baden meat. The efforts to cripple these outside corporations and their Chinese workforce were, by all appearances, effective. Anti-Chinese sentiment was a key feature of the coordinated campaign against Chicago packers in San Francisco, and was effectively weaponized to maintain the relevance of chiefly white butchers in Butchertown well into the twentieth century.

But the dam holding back the Chicago meatpackers in San Francisco would effectively break with the 1906 earthquake, which tumbled the stilted structures of Butchertown into the bay. The facilities in Baden were relatively unaffected by the earthquake. When federal and state emergency aid poured into the region to feed the hungry and homeless residents of San Francisco, government contracts went to those companies that could fulfill the large and urgent orders. With Baden largely unscathed and Butchertown in shambles, the large-scale producers south of the city received most of those contracts. The temporary monopoly caused a key shift in the city's meat production, and the national meatpackers won a lasting advantage in provisioning the city into the twentieth century.

FIGURE 3.5 Butchertown in ruins, 1906. The stilted structures of Butchertown—designed to allow blood and offal to fall into the tides—fared poorly in the 1906 earthquake. California History Room, California State Library, Sacramento, California.

Some of the Butchertown slaughterhouses were rebuilt, but they were relics of a bygone era. They were cramped by modern standards, and the 1907 "war on rats" forced them to turn their slatted floors into impermeable concrete, thereby eliminating any environmental distinctiveness or advantage that Butchertown once offered. There was a slow and steady decline in meatpacking in Butchertown in the twentieth century, with the final slaughterhouse closing its doors in 1971.

Pollution in and around Butchertown cast a long shadow into the twentieth century. The spaces first dedicated to slaughterhouse pollution and other nuisances attracted new institutional nuisances in the twentieth century. City and state laws reinforced the space's characteristics as a zone dedicated to pollution. Nearly every unpleasant, polluting, and noxious industry in San Francisco found its home in or around Butchertown in the twentieth century. It was here that the city sited the largest coal- and oil-fired power plants in 1929, which helped electrify downtown San Francisco until 2006.[114] It was here, where the tanneries once stood—across the old railroad tracks from Butchertown—that the city constructed its largest wastewater treatment plant in 1952, which has continued to grow in the intervening decades. It is here where 80 percent of the city's sewage ends up today, with the poor air quality to prove it. From 1948 to 1969, the Naval Radiological Defense Laboratory operated on the southeast border of Butchertown. It was here that scientists studied the effects of radiological exposure, and ships underwent radiological decontamination. The result was widespread radiological contamination of the soil that remains to this day. In 1989, the Environmental Protection Agency declared the area a Superfund National Priorities List site, making it the only Superfund site in San Francisco.[115]

But pollution was, in some cases, the by-product of production and jobs. The Naval base had been a major employer in the area during World War II. In the 1940s, African Americans settled in the areas around Butchertown, filling low-wage jobs in the shipbuilding industry, while escaping oppression of the American South. When the shipyards closed after World War II, employment in the area dropped, and the barracks were converted to public housing. In the 1960s, a powerful new Redevelopment Agency effectively uprooted large parts of the city's African American population downtown and relocated black San Franciscans to public housing and low-rent homes around Butchertown—most notably in Hunters Point, just south of Butchertown.

In some ways, the creation of the African American ghetto near Butchertown in the postwar years echoed earlier battles over race, environment, and space in San Francisco. In 1888—in an effort to uproot the Chinese population in Chinatown over fears of disease—city supervisors passed an ordinance limiting where Chinese residents could live in San Francisco. The area they chose was the thirty-six-block Butchers' Reservation. Although the courts struck down the measure as a violation of civil rights, the intentions of lawmakers were clear. In the mid- to late twentieth century, city ordinances had essentially created a new ghetto for the city's African American population, though the legal and social construction of that place was only slightly more subtle than the 1888 ordinance. The lands around Butchertown would remain the place where powerful public and private interests sought to remove, separate, and conceal unwanted urban problems—human and animal alike.[116]

=====

When James Baldwin visited San Francisco in 1963, he described the neighborhood adjacent to Butchertown as "the San Francisco America pretends does not exist."[117] By then it was the city's urban ghetto, made up overwhelmingly of poor

African Americans who faced widespread discrimination and difficulty finding housing and employment. But Baldwin's words would have rung as true—for different reasons—a century earlier, when the city sought to hide its animal nuisances and killing practices beyond the perception of downtown residents. Butchertown's history has been one of willful invisibility, neglect, and denial—or worse, outright desecration. In many ways it was a sacrificial landscape that continues to shape the area today.

Things may be changing. The flood of capital into the city resulting from tech booms of the late 1990s and today is remaking Butchertown and its environs once more. Since the 1980s, the city has invested in rehabilitating the area around Butchertown in numerous ways, but the benefits seem to be accruing to major development companies. A new light rail line connects Butchertown and Bayview with downtown, and real estate prices are rising. Although social and environmental factors have long limited the development of the neighborhood, the tech boom appears to be elevating rents and housing prices, with gentrification pushing in at the edges of Butchertown and Bayview, which for years had been a slow-moving backwater of the city's real estate market. One of the last African American communities in San Francisco—estimated at around 65 percent black in the mid-twentieth century—has dwindled to 30 percent and falling. As wealthier white residents move in, the invisibility and neglect of Butchertown seems likely to fade.

Although neglect is no longer the central characteristic of the city's public efforts around Butchertown, many residents wonder who will actually benefit from the changes that are causing massive transformations and pricing out longtime residents. "They're fixing things up, but it isn't for us," said a longtime resident in 2008, who has seen the exodus of black families over time: "This is all for the new residents."[118] Butchertown may be on its way to being remade in the name of progress and wealth—resembling the battles over urban development in the 1860s. The forces transforming Butchertown today—the shiny promises of technology, growth, and progress—are perhaps no less quixotic than the plans to permanently solve urban industrial pollution 150 years ago. There are, of course, many contingencies that went into creating Butchertown, Bayview, and Hunters Point today. But a critically important one—and arguably the first of great significance that set the region on its developmental path—was the creation of the "Butchers Reservation" in 1870. In a sense, these neighborhoods are unknowingly haunted by animal ghosts, reminding us that livestock not only shaped nineteenth-century cities and politics in important ways, but that decisions about animal exclusion 150 years ago continue to have profound significance today.

Big changes happened in and around the emergent animal suburbs of the late nineteenth century. But animal life was changing downtown as well. As slaughterhouses and livestock disappeared from downtown life, other species flourished in the Gilded Age city. Horses and pets occupied a growing space in urban environments. These animals did not step into the same social and ecological spaces once inhabited by urban livestock, but their ascendance in the Gilded Age city marked an important shift in the social and cultural composition of urban life.

CHAPTER FOUR

How to Kill a Horse

SPCAs, Urban Order, and
State Power, 1866–1910

O N AN APRIL MORNING in 1878, as the sun came up over the hills east of the San Francisco Bay, Captain Henry Burns left his home on Seventeenth Street and walked out into the cool San Francisco dawn. Burns was entering a city charged with the sounds and smells of animals: the braying of horses in city stables, the rhythmic clopping of hooves on streets, the distant barking and howling of stray dogs, the anxious bleating of sheep as they jostled their way off boats and railroad cars, and the occasional mooing of cows from a neighbor's backyard. There were subtler experiences, too—those encountered only in the close presence of animals: the heavy breaths and snorts of workhorses as they struggled to pull wagons up steep hills; the sideways and downward glances of stray dogs as they crossed streets at odd angles; and the twitches on a horse's skin that momentarily revealed the sinewy muscles that powered the urban economy. The dry and earthy smell of hay—stashed in all corners of the city—and the sharp and familiar whiff of animal urine and manure, were so prevalent they must have felt, at times, like the smell of air itself.

Despite industrialization and livestock exclusion policies, the city Captain Burns entered was still crawling with animal life. The thousands of horses that graded streets, worked on construction crews, and carried all types of goods across the city, sustained a large secondary economy of horseshoers, bitters, clippers, feed stores, saddle makers, stables, veterinarians, and numerous other businesses that filled page after page of the city's directories. Despite the growing use of railroads, streetcars, and steamships, life in nineteenth-century American cities still depended heavily on animal power—fueled by grasses and grains, contained by whips and harnesses and bits, and powered by animal muscles, blood, and bones. Despite the millions of pounds of waste and ubiquitous nuisance, horses were indispensable to urban life; their presence must have seemed as permanent and immovable to San Francisco as the summer fog, the tides that flowed through the Golden Gate, and the silhouetted peak of Mount Tamalpais.[1]

Captain Burns had a special relationship to this world of animal life in the late nineteenth century. Toward the end of the 1870s, he began serving as the sole full-time salaried officer of the city's nascent San Francisco Society for the Prevention of Cruelty to Animals (SFSPCA)—an organization established in 1868, which sought to improve the lives of animals and human morality in turn. Because of the sheer scale of the animal economy, Captain Burns's duties bordered on Sisyphean: he was responsible for the well-being of the tens of thousands of horses, cows, dogs, cats, and chickens that lived and worked within city limits—to say nothing of the countless undomesticated animals that only occasionally appeared in SFSPCA records. Along with these more permanent urban animal residents, Burns also diligently monitored the hundreds of thousands of cattle, pigs, and sheep that annually passed through the city to their final destination in Butchertown. All told, it was an animal population far too numerous, dynamic, and spatially vast for any one man to effectively oversee. But its vastness and variation were themselves constructed in time and space; new zoning laws—especially those passed in the 1860s, pushing slaughterhouses and livestock far from the city center—made Burns's job all the more difficult. New animal geographies limited and shaped emerging forms of animal law enforcement. The new humane laws and agencies formed in the 1860s and 1870s had real geographic limits.

===

Captain Burns was no stranger to great civilizing projects in the American West. A veteran of the Apache Wars, he was stationed in the early 1870s at Camp Mc-Dowell, in Arizona Territory, where he led numerous attacks on the stubborn and ostensibly savage Apaches. Fresh from those battles to make white civilization safe from savagery and barbarism, Burns returned to San Francisco in 1873 to continue the fight. He became the leader of the Sumner Light Guard, a "gallant" private militia company that had been formed in 1861, which practiced military games and performed public shows of marksmanship. The Light Guard took seriously its objective of protecting the public good and maintaining social order. But its interpretation of the public good was often contentious. When miners struck in Amador County for higher wages and better working conditions in 1871, the Sumner Light Guard was called on to restore order—a job the Pinkertons might have been hired to do years later.[2]

Through his experiences in the Sumner Light Guard, Captain Burns understood private police and military power as central to protecting the public good. This sort of public-private alliance structured numerous aspects of law and order in late nineteenth-century American life, including the organization that would hire Burns in 1876, the San Francisco Society for the Prevention of Cruelty to Animals. Burns seemed an especially good candidate to become the first agent of the SFSPCA—not least because of the apparent enjoyment he took in discharging a gun. One of the most important duties of the Society's agent would be to shoot injured and suffering horses. Despite accidentally shooting and killing a man hired to tend targets for the Sumner Light Guard, Burns maintained a reputation as an upright citizen and one of the best shots in San Francisco.[3] In some ways it seemed a waste of his skills as a marksman for him to be employed by the SFSPCA, shooting injured horses between the eyes at point-blank range.

When Burns left his house that spring morning in 1878, the sun might have caught the glint of his officer's badge and the buckle of his belt, which held a holster and pistol. The gun and badge were the heavy metal objects that signified and conducted power. The weapon was ostensibly a tool to kill injured horses, sheep, pigs, and cattle, but Burns's gun and badge no doubt gave him great authority in dealing with members of his own species.

=

From their inception in American cities in the late 1860s, regional SPCAs were, in many ways emblematic of public-private government power—a form of power that scholars have increasingly understood as a hallmark of governance in late nineteenth–century America. The widespread presence and legal authority of these SPCAs offer evidence in understanding the nuance and meaning of the nineteenth-century regulatory state. In looking at animal regulations, we see a strong role of state intervention, bolstering William Novak's claim of a "myth of the weak state" in nineteenth-century America.[4] Although the size and budgets of governmental bureaucracies were small by twentieth-century standards, cities and states found ways of governing and policing that were nevertheless influential. Often, they did so by chartering corporations and handing over state powers to private companies in exchange for law enforcement and private financing that circumnavigated public taxation. It was governance "off the books." Once chartered, regional SPCAs employed agents and enlisted vast voluntary and social networks to enforce a growing set of laws designed to promote a specific public good. The laws these corporations enforced were often laws they helped write. The SPCA operated in what seems like an odd space that mixed public and private, law making and law enforcement, and held both police and special prosecutorial powers. In fact, the corporate structures of SPCAs destabilize the very concepts of "public" and "private" sectors in nineteenth-century American life.[5]

Formal public-private partnerships in the name of public good had deeper roots going back to the early nineteenth century. Governments chartered corporations for bridges, banks, waste removal, and water delivery, and their charters typically outlined explicitly the public obligations of the corporation or monopoly.[6] These private corporations, including SPCAs, allowed cities and states to provide public goods and services without taxation. But the private management and implementation of public law caused uneven enforcement across space, social class, and—in the case of the SPCAs—across species. By the late nineteenth century, the flaws and shortcomings of government-by-incorporation were becoming all too apparent.

In examining the characteristics and nuances of these private forms of state power, scholars have often neglected geography as central to understanding the dimensions of that power. The strength or weakness of governmental power was constructed in real space, and these spatial inequalities were widely understood by people living at the time. The geographies of urban law enforcement and the location of animal industries and livestock populations were moving pieces in this legal landscape of the last decades of the nineteenth century. As livestock and various animal industries were pushed across the urban landscape through new zoning laws, their interactions with emerging forms of law enforcement also changed. SFSPCA power looked starkly different depending on where in San Francisco one stood. For the cows and pigs that lived on an advancing fringe of urban development, miles from downtown, the power of the SPCA was virtually nonexistent. For horses and pets living downtown, however, the proximity to SPCA power offered greater access to legal protection. With different animals inhabiting different and increasingly distinct urban spaces, some animals became "more equal than others," to appropriate George Orwell's memorable words.[7] Of course, SFSPCA enforcement records suggest that some humans were also "more equal" than others.

——

As early as 1867—just a year after Henry Bergh established the American Society for the Prevention of Cruelty to Animals (ASPCA) in New York City— newspapers in San Francisco anticipated that the West Coast city might soon see its own SPCA dedicated to the improvement of conditions for animals and, in turn, the morality of humans. Many San Francisco residents had aspirations of building a first-class city, but also saw an urban environment with "all the cruelties" of a metropolis with a large animal population, according to an editorial in the *Daily Alta California*.[8] The overdriving and beating of horses, the tying of calves and sheep in transit, and the fighting of dogs and birds were widely seen as unnecessary forms of animal suffering that plagued the city. These activities not only caused suffering of animals, but reformers argued that their very existence degraded morality and social order, threatened the public good, and insulted the city's civility.[9] Hearing these calls—and seeing the spread of the SPCA in other prominent cities across the United States and around the world—the California legislature took up the issue early in 1868 on the urging of some of San Francisco's most prominent residents.

By February 1868, An Act for the More Effectual Prevention of Cruelty to Animals was making its way through legislative committees in Sacramento. The bill started in the Committee on Public Morals, but was referred to the Committee on Corporations, where it made the docket alongside laws relating to the charter of railroads, turnpikes, cities, and towns.[10] The bill passed the Committee on Corporations in March 1868, and came to the floor of the State Assembly that same month, where it was debated with few objections.

The little debate there was over the bill did, however, reveal the social dimensions and aspirations of animal protection and the uses of state power. One representative proposed an amendment that would have added "Chinamen and Indians" to those protected under the law, but withdrew the amendment for unknown reasons after meeting with the Speaker of the Assembly. By all appearances, the amendment to add Chinese and Native Americans to the law was earnest. Months later, one supporter regretted that the legislature had not extended prohibitions on cruelty to "cases of cruelty to human beings—Chinamen and others—as the children of San Francisco are likely to become thoroughly demoralized by witnessing the murderous outrages and wantonly brutal attacks made upon that race by the vilest dregs of our own, every day, in our public streets."[11] For some, the protection of animals fit within a larger concern for the protection of other vulnerable groups—racial and ethnic minorities, children, and other "defenseless" populations across species. The Act for the More Effectual Prevention of Cruelty to Animals passed overwhelmingly, with fifty-two votes in favor and only ten opposed. It sailed through the state senate and was signed by Governor Henry Haight in March 1868.[12]

Although the legislation marked a major step in the movement to protect animals, the California Act for the More Effectual Prevention of Cruelty to

Animals—and others like it that were making their way through legislatures across the country—was not the first legal protection granted to animals. Laws against animal cruelty already existed in San Francisco and other American cities before the 1860s, many of which fit with a longer tradition of common law that prohibited animal abuse.[13] But the new law in California was part of a wave of city, state, and federal legislation across the United States that clarified and codified animal cruelty in new ways. More important, perhaps, the spate of animal protection laws in the 1860s and 1870s offered new means of enforcement by laying the foundations for the creation of SPCAs. These anticruelty corporations would become the new legal and law enforcement structures that would give animal protection laws their teeth.

The new California law did much to delineate cruelty in clear terms. The law listed three definitions of animal cruelty explicitly prohibited by law—definitions that would be expanded in subsequent amendments in the 1870s. The first explicitly forbade torturing, tormenting, starving, "unmercifully or cruelly" beating, mutilating, or killing "any living creature." A second section of the law—in some ways redundant—added prohibitions on neglect, malicious killing, maiming, wounding, injuring, torturing, and cruelly beating "any animal belonging to himself or another." A third section of the law addressed a rather specific form of cruelty, "carrying or transporting any living creature" in a way that caused "unnecessary pain and suffering," torture, injury, or torment. This appeared to be directly targeting the transportation of livestock. Taken together, the law outlined a clear and far-reaching statement of animal protection in many forms—and one that protected "any living creature." Although human intent and human-centric social reform were important parts of the movement to prevent animal cruelty, the new laws also protected animal suffering in its own right. Animal suffering was a punishable crime whether or not it resulted from intentional or malevolent human actions. The suffering of animals mattered intrinsically.[14]

Despite its far reach, the law also offered a statement on what did *not* count as cruelty. The new rules would not interfere with existing game laws and bird protection laws, or the right of people to "destroy venomous reptiles or animals dangerous to life, limb or property." Although the law explicitly forbade cruel transportation of livestock, it also stopped short of calling animal slaughter cruel. The law would not interfere with "the killing of animals used for food, and with scientific experiments." Lawmakers were willing to protect animals to a point, but did not interfere in cases where certain human interests deemed essential would be compromised. By explicitly exempting it, the law effectively reinforced the right to kill animals for food and personal defense, and to use animals to promote medical knowledge and practice. Even if they were cruel, these forms of animal treatment were deemed too essential for regulatory prohibition. The laws bespoke a belief that these human practices could be reformed but not eliminated.[15]

Perhaps the most important feature of the new law was the foundation it laid for the establishment of Societies for the Prevention of Cruelty to Animals in California. The act's initial referral to the Committee on Corporations was no coincidence; a significant portion of the act detailed the terms of incorporation for SPCAs in California, and the special legal powers Societies could access through incorporation. The first section of the act made it possible for any three or more citizens of the state to incorporate an SPCA, so long as their "corporate body" was the first in their county. Section 2 of the act reaffirmed the private corporate characteristics of the SPCA, giving the Society autonomy to make and adopt its own bylaws, determine who could be a member, and select who would be on the board of directors. The legislature handed over special police powers to an organization that would effectively manage and wield them without intense governmental intervention or oversight. The Society needed only to provide annual reports to the legislature, with a "full account of their acts," and could not violate laws of the State of California or of the United States, or any provisions of the act itself.[16]

Central to the Society's powers was its capacity to deputize officers of the law. Section 5 of the act permitted the Society's Board of Trustees to appoint officers, who would have the same power as police officers, but were limited to enforcing laws specific to animal protection. The Board of Trustees merely had to submit nominees to a county judge for approval. When confirmed, the officers would be "sworn in the same manner as are Constables and peace officers," and could make arrests for violations of the law so long as they wore a "suitable badge." Like other police officers, SPCA officers did not need a warrant to make arrests for any violations they witnessed firsthand. Only cases reported to officers required a warrant from a judge to make an arrest. When the Act for the More Effectual Prevention of Cruelty to Animals was amended in 1874, new instructions were given to judges to "issue and deliver immediately" such warrants, effectively expanding the enforcement powers of the SPCA. The amended act of 1874 also allowed SPCA officers to carry "the same weapons" as other police officers, and explicitly sanctioned officers to "enter any place, building, or tenement," without a warrant to stop or prevent the "exhibition of the fighting of birds or animals." The new laws designed a private police force with expansive powers.[17]

Finally, the act enlarged powers of California SPCAs by granting them special access to courts. Section 8 of the 1868 act allowed SPCA officers to prosecute any case of animal cruelty "whether or not he be an attorney and counselor at law."

The officer would do so in the name of "the people of the State of California."[18] In lowering the bar for public prosecutions, the new law granted the SPCA special access to courts—a primary channel of governance across the United States. Special access to courts was powerful public-private governance in yet another form.[19]

Among the most remarkable features of the 1868 act were the structures it erected for funding the SPCA. Not wanting to raise taxes to fund law enforcement—but still wishing to promote a new public service—the state sought an independent funding stream for Societies. Under the act, any convictions for animal cruelty were deemed misdemeanors and subject to a court-ordered fine. When the Society secured a conviction, the "Judge or Court" was legally bound to "direct the whole of the fine" to the president, secretary, or treasurer of the SPCA.[20] The transfer of funds would need to be publicly recorded, but the Society could spend the money in whatever way it pleased. Although the reduction of visible forms of animal cruelty was often framed as a public good, the financing of that public good would be paid by a minority of the population convicted of violating animal protection laws. The system of fines also bespoke a certain understanding of fairness: as opposed to blanket taxation, those who paid ostensibly deserved to pay because they had committed wrongdoing. But the system of financing also meant, potentially, that the SPCA in California might unintentionally become dependent on the very behaviors SPCAs were designed to prevent. All told, the act created a perverse set of incentives and structures: a system in which a private corporation could deputize officers of the law to enforce laws they helped write. The SPCA could effectively write the law, deputize the officer, make the arrest, prosecute the case, and collect the fine. In many ways, the SPCA in California was a private fiefdom of state governance.

In passing the Act for the More Effectual Prevention of Cruelty to Animals, California lawmakers put in motion the creation of a corporation capable of governing on its own terms, with the capacity for its own financial autonomy. It was a massive transfer of public forms of power—police, courts, and fines—into the hands of a few private citizens who sat on the Society's Board of Trustees. Although the humane movement was a social and cultural movement with important intellectual roots and networks, the legal and financial structures of SPCAs bespoke their particular autonomy. Although the San Francisco SPCA shared the name and broadly defined agenda of its eastern counterparts, it was not merely a "chapter" of the ASPCA in New York City. Rather, it was its own corporate entity with its own certificate of incorporation, charter, and bylaws in the state of California. It had its own members, officers, and trustees. In its printed publications and lobbying efforts, the SFSPCA may have operated across city, county, state, and even national boundaries. But its legal and police powers—some of its primary expressions of power—stopped at the San Francisco County line. Within those political and geographic boundaries it possessed immense legal and financial power. But in a spatially expanding economy of animal production, those geographic boundaries seemed increasingly constricting.

Although the state legislature drew up the blueprints for the structures of SPCAs in California, the San Francisco SPCA did not immediately assume the ideal form. In fact, in their first years, SFSPCA leaders seemed uncomfortable with their organization's powerful police and prosecutorial powers. In their first decade, SFSPCA leaders aspired, instead, to sustain the Society through donations and annual membership dues, not fines. Other SPCAs across the United States struggled with the appropriate tone and expression of their police powers (as outlined in Chapter 5). Eventually the SFSPCA would fall back on the organizational and financial structures that were imbedded in its certificate of incorporation. The SFSPCA ultimately became a chimerical entity that embraced its police powers while also asserting widespread social and cultural influence.

Within weeks of the passage of the 1868 act, some of San Francisco's most prominent citizens signed and filed a certificate of incorporation for the San Francisco Society for the Prevention of Cruelty to Animals. Its charter declared the objectives of the Society as enforcing the state's new anticruelty laws and working in "the education of a public sentiment of humanity and gentleness towards domestic and other animals." They issued 5,000 shares of capital stock at $1 per share, which they hoped would lay a solid financial foundation for the Society's work. Despite its corporate characteristics, its charter explicitly said that no dividends would be paid to stockholders and that profit was not the aim of the Society.[21]

The original Board of Trustees was a veritable cross-section of the civic, business, and social elite in San Francisco. The initial set of leaders—appointed on a temporary basis until elections could be held—included some of the city's most prominent political, religious, and business leaders. Mayor Frank McCoppin and District Attorney H. H. Byrne topped the list, and were joined by public health officials Henry Gibbons and Isaac Rowell. Other founding members were successful businessmen, top bankers, insurance company managers, lawyers, and politicians. It was a group made up overwhelmingly of Republicans and reformers, eager to extend political and social activism in the name of progress in the years after the Civil War. For many of the SFSPCA's leaders, the Society was only one of several organizations in which they were involved. They sat on boards of medical colleges and universities, the Old Ladies Home, the California Prison Commission, the Chamber of Commerce, the Mechanics' Institute, the Mercantile Library Association, the San Francisco Benevolent Society, and countless other libraries, museums, hospitals, asylums, orphanages, and philanthropic organizations. Quakers and Unitarians may have been overrepresented in the SFSPCA, but the Society also enjoyed the support of the city's most prominent Jewish leader and philanthropist, August Helbing, who headed numerous Jewish organizations in the city.[22]

Robert Swain, one of these prominent businessmen, was a founding member of the SFSPCA. Swain was a merchant and an active Unitarian who sat on numerous boards of private relief organizations in his lifetime. For Swain, involvement in private reform organizations was one of the spoils and obligations of success, and the highest form of civic engagement. "I regard honorable distinction as a merchant as infinitely more valuable than I do the highest glory that can come from any office in the gift of people or President," he said of his role as benefactor. According to Swain, the successful businessman had earned his status and had a special ability as a leader of men, "not because he has become possessed of huge wealth but because his mind has been disciplined while accumulating that wealth to a correct knowledge of the uses to which it should be applied which so few understand."[23] For Swain, wealth revealed something about his character, which in turn justified—and indeed necessitated—his involvement in improving society. For Swain and others who pursued private forms of politics, organizations like the SFSPCA also offered a cleaner and purer form of political action that required little compromise. Governance through private organizations offered a form of public control among men who had ostensibly proved themselves worthy through the fortunes they made. Some even suggested, unsuccessfully, that municipalities should be run like private corporations, with those contributing the most in taxes making the most important decisions in cities.[24]

Organizations like the SFSPCA offered a parallel and independent form of governance for wealthy board members, without any need to show deference to voters or others' definitions of public good. In the years after its establishment, other wealthy residents topped the list of SFSPCA trustees, including Leland Stanford, head of the Southern and Central Pacific Railroads, and Andrew Smith Hallidie, who ran a large manufacturing and construction company, and developed the city's famous cable car system. For Hallidie, highlighting and regulating the suffering of horses also happened to benefit his business of transporting San Franciscans without horsepower. The cost of becoming a member and a leader in the SFSPCA demonstrated a deeper truth: the humane treatment of animals—and leadership in the Society itself—was, in many ways, a luxury good.[25]

Prominent doctors and public health officials also joined some of the city's wealthiest businessmen in the establishment of the SFSPCA and in its leadership in the years that followed. Dr. Isaac Rowell and Dr. Henry Gibbons were founding members and leaders of the SFSPCA. Both Rowell and Gibbons served as public health leaders in California and San Francisco, and each served terms as the city's health officer, the highest-ranking member of the Health Department, in the late 1860s and early 1870s. Gibbons would go on to serve as president of the SFSPCA from 1868 until 1875.

The involvement of Gibbons and Rowell in both the humane and public health movements suggests the ways in which these movements were interconnected. In some ways it was unsurprising that Gibbons and Rowell would become involved in these formal efforts to protect animals—a project that offered many of the same promises of improvement and civilization as urban sanitation and health reform. But these two agendas—public health and humane treatment of animals—had a more complicated relationship than reformers might have imagined in their own time. Both movements were at the heart of popular conversations about progress and civilization, but both movements also imagined new urban spatial arrangements that were unintentionally counterproductive. Effective public health efforts to remove animal populations and slaughterhouses from certain urban areas had the eventual result of limiting the effectiveness of SPCA law enforcement. As health officers, Rowell and Gibbons presided over an environmental and spatial transformation in urban animal life by helping create and enforce new zoning laws that established Butchertown and other limitations to the geography of livestock and noxious trades. But reformers' interests in creating invisible landscapes of animal suffering and death undercut their parallel interest in protecting animal welfare, at least in the short term. New zoning laws made large populations of animals mainly invisible to a public that, ironically, was increasingly concerned about the well-being of animals. Although animal welfare and public health overlapped, new health laws controlling where animals could live also presented challenges to the SFSPCA that was emerging at the same moment. Livestock, in particular, were increasingly separated from the laws, organizations, and agents that were established to protect their well-being.

=====

In the eyes of many San Franciscans, the establishment of the SFSPCA advanced the city farther along a path toward civilization and progress. The *Daily Alta*

California hailed the formation of the SFSCPA as a "step in a right direction," adding that "every friend of humanity will join us in the wish that [the Society] may be able to stop some of the brutalizing practices and exhibitions that now torture the lives of dumb animals, and harrow the feelings of men who have any feelings to harrow."[26] In the SPCA, reformers saw another panacea of urban progress and politics. As an added bonus, the world would be remade at no discernible financial cost to the taxpayer.

But the grand hopes and ambitions did not materialize in the ways that Society boosters had first hoped. Membership roles were thinner than initial estimates, and only a fraction of the shares of capital stock sold. Founders had hoped to have 5,000 members—made up of both men and women, who would play distinct roles within the organization. But a year after the SFSPCA was established, there were only 100 members.[27] The following year the SFSPCA reported having only 50 "active members."[28] Part of the problem may have been the high cost of joining. Annual membership was $5—a significant sum considering the annual per capita income in San Francisco was around $165 in 1870.[29] But the relatively high price of membership also ensured that the Society would maintain a certain social composition and status, which may have attracted many members in the first place.

Despite its expansive legal and police powers, the SFSCPA appeared hesitant at first to embrace its state-sponsored role as police and special prosecutor. Their arrests, prosecutions, and fines were meager in their first several years, and often intentionally so. In 1868, Society leaders stated their goals and objectives: "It is desired that the public understand that it is not at all the desire of the Society to arrest and prosecute, or to make displays in Court. It rather desires to work by the *morale* of its presence in this community."[30] The use of hard force was, in the early years, a last resort. For many Society leaders—in San Francisco and in other cities—arrests and prosecutions were indications that softer forms of influence were failing. "Prevention" still remained a principal tenet of the SFPSCA, and leaders believed that police power could be used toward that end without necessarily making arrests and initiating prosecutions.[31]

Through the 1870s, the SFSPCA's leadership celebrated the Society's low and declining numbers of arrests, prosecutions, and convictions, taking these statistics as evidence of its effective work. The Society made only thirty-three arrests in 1869, with declining numbers of arrests and prosecutions through the early 1870s. In 1872, the Society made only seven arrests and prosecutions, though all seven ended in conviction. One favorable newspaper article in 1870 declared that "the best proof of [the SFSPCA's] usefulness is to [be] found in the fact that few arrests have been made, in comparison with those of preceding years."[32] Declining arrests were, ostensibly, a reflection of declining incidents of abuse in the first years of the Society.

By the late 1870s, however, there was a notable shift in how the Society understood its law enforcement powers, and how it sought to use those powers to raise funds. The first sign of these changing times was the retirement of Dr. Henry Gibbons as president of the Society in 1876, and his replacement with Joseph Winans. Unlike Gibbons, Winans was not a public health reformer. Rather, he was the son of a wealthy New York businessman, and a Whig turned Republican reformer. Born in New York, he attended Columbia College and studied law before coming to California in 1849, where he established a successful law practice in Sacramento before moving to San Francisco in the 1860s. Though he shied away from formal political and elective office, Winans served as a member and president of the San Francisco Board of Education, a regent for the University of California, and a leader in the creation and direction of numerous public and private libraries and educational institutions across California. In some ways, this interest in education fit well with the Society's overall goals, which also emphasized the formation of humane sympathies in childhood.

But Winans was best known as one of the most prominent lawyers in California, and "the first scholar of the bar" in the state, according to Oscar Tully Shuck who wrote a short biography of Winans as one of the "representative and leading men of the Pacific." Winans was a founder of the San Francisco Bar Association and served as a trustee until 1879. It was, in some part, Winans's legal orientation that pushed the Society to fully utilize and embrace its legal powers in the 1870s and 1880s.[33]

The shift toward law enforcement and prosecution in the late 1870s also marked a significant shift in how the Society raised funds. Through the early 1870s, the SFSPCA was financed largely through membership dues and donations. In 1870, 89 percent of revenue came from annual memberships. Only $30 of the Society's revenue came from fines. In 1871, revenues from membership continued to supply 76 percent of the Society's annual revenue, and membership grew to 87 people. By 1876, when Winans took over as president, the SFSPCA's membership had nearly doubled in just five years, to 170 annual members. This growing base of supporters would provide the small operating budget of the Society. By the SFSPCA's own accounting, membership dues seemed to be financing the organization adequately, leaving little apparent incentive to tap its dormant police, prosecution, and fine-collection powers under the law. By 1876, the Society was running heavily in the black, expending less than a third of the money it brought in. That fall, under the new leadership of Winans, the Society used some of that surplus revenue to hire Captain Burns as the Society's first special agent.[34] It was a decision that would pay dividends in the years that followed.

The Society experienced a notable financial shift soon after hiring a full-time agent. The SFSPCA had prosecuted only seven cases in 1876, but in the first year with Burns as special agent, prosecutions soared to ninety-eight. The Society secured convictions in all but five of those cases, resulting in fines amounting to more than $2,100 that went directly into the Society's coffers.[35] A majority of these ninety-eight cases and fines were related to the raid of a single cockfight, which brought more than sixty-five people to court and resulted in the collection of more than $1,300 in fines. Routine infractions made up the remainder, about $825, mostly from convictions in cases involving beating and overdriving horses, but also in the inhumane transportation of calves and the abuse of dogs. The shift in revenue collection was stark: for the first time in its short history, fines collected in the fiscal year ending in 1877 amounted to more than 60 percent of the Society's total revenue. This new reliance on prosecutions as a main source of revenue would continue into the 1890s, and in many years it vastly exceeded revenues from donations and membership dues. The Society's shift in 1877 toward law enforcement marked the beginning of a new era for the organization. In the decade that followed, the Society's special agent and officers routinely arrested and prosecuted hundreds of cases each year.[36]

As prosecutions rose, membership in the SFSPCA dropped. The rise in revenue from prosecutions may have reduced pressure on the Society to recruit new members, and annual membership fell by more than 25 percent, hovering at around 150 members through the 1880s. Although increased prosecutions were something of a failure by its own president's appraisal, there was no question that they were profitable. Prosecutions allowed the Society to cover the costs of a salaried agent and lawyers, while also raising funds for other social and cultural types of reform. By the end of the 1870s, Winans reported that the SFSPCA was "now upheld, in the main, by the pecuniary penalties which *the law* inflicts upon those who are convicted of cruelty to animals."[37] The Society was now making most of its money from incidents of animal suffering.

It is worth noting that this shift in the Society's finances happened amid the greatest economic disruption of a generation. The Panic of 1873 and the ensuing national and international economic downturn of the 1870s took a few years to hit San Francisco, but it hit hard in 1877, with high unemployment, the rise of the Workingmen's Party, and anti-Chinese labor strikes in 1877.[38] Paradoxically, the economic depression did not cause the decline of SFSPCA membership. Throughout the 1870s, SFSPCA membership, annual dues, and donations, grew steadily, but modestly. Annual membership grew from 50 in 1869, to 126 in 1872, to 155 in 1875, to 170 in 1876, to 200 in 1877, and to 216 in 1879.[39] Hard economic times did little to stop the membership growth of the Society, suggesting perhaps that those wealthy enough to afford membership were not hit hard enough by the panic to influence their decision to donate. Despite rising membership rates, the SPCA president spoke in dire terms in his annual address for the fiscal year ending in 1879, noting that the "business depression which everywhere exists" had caused the SPCA to suspend operations and threatened its extinction.[40] But when it came time to make difficult decisions in how the Society would save money, it seemed odd that its leadership would choose to cut Agent Burns's position—a job that had provided a main source of revenue for the Society.

Part of the decision to cut the agent's salary may have been that Special Agent Burns was not making as many arrests by mid-1878. The decline in arrests translated into a decline in prosecutions, and in turn a decline in revenue for the Society. Even though arrests and fines were down, Burns was pursuing cases of animal cruelty with zeal. But by 1878, Burns seemed to have become more interested in using his police powers in ways that were influential, but not necessarily financially rewarding to the society. In particular, Burns was becoming fixated on the tens of thousands of livestock landed each month in San Francisco. Cruelty to livestock was pervasive and troubling to the SFSPCA, but it was also hard to enforce through existing laws and a system of arrests and fines. Livestock injuries were often unintentional and systematic, making them not conducive to arrests and convictions, which still favored human intentionality. Cases involving apparent intent to injure animals were often those that received the highest fines and punishments in the late nineteenth century. The responsibility for livestock injuries was increasingly difficult to pin on a single party—especially in a spatially vast and segmented system of animal production and shipping that had emerged in California and across the United States.[41]

In San Francisco, this vast and dynamic system of livestock production funneled livestock through two places: the Second Street Wharf and Butchertown. Although Butchertown was designed along a proposed railroad line of the Southern Pacific Railroad, the transcontinental line would not be built through the adjoining neighborhood until 1907.[42] Further, the stilted structures in Butchertown were built on shallow tidelands, and presumably not deep enough to serve as a port. As a result, hopes of fully relocating livestock to the urban fringe were not immediately realized. The Second Street Wharf downtown remained a central gateway for bringing livestock into the city well into the 1870s and 1880s. It was here that animals were unloaded off railroad cars and steamships and driven on foot to Butchertown through a network of streets carefully delineated by law—

an urban cow path that zigzagged through an industrial and working-class part of town.[43] In one month alone, some 30,000 cattle, sheep, and hogs might be unloaded at the Second Street Wharf before making their way to Butchertown.[44]

By the spring of 1878, Burns had become fixated on the Second Street Wharf as a site of animal suffering. Animals were often injured, starved, dehydrated or weary after journeys that lasted hundreds of miles and days on end. By the spring of 1878, Burns was visiting the Second Street Wharf almost every day to monitor the unloading of boats and railroad cars, and the driving of animals to Butchertown.[45] In May 1878, Burns mentioned visiting the Second Street Wharf in twenty-three out of twenty-six diary entries. On two of the three days Burns did not mention the Second Street Wharf, he was in Butchertown—far from downtown—where he was "cautioning" the butchers about the treatment of their stock. In all, Burns made at least four trips to Butchertown in May 1878—more visits in one month than later agents in the 1880s and 1890s would make in an entire year.[46] Burns's preoccupation with the welfare of livestock continued into the summer of 1878, when he visited the Second Street Wharf nearly every day in June and July.[47]

But Burns's concerns with livestock did not result in the collection of fines for the SFSPCA. He made numerous interventions in the landing and driving of livestock, but few, if any, arrests. In May 1878, he made only four arrests, and got convictions in two of those cases, both for dogfighting. Although he was not getting convictions and collecting fines, Burns was nevertheless using police power to actively intervene in cases of animal suffering. He ordered suffering livestock killed immediately, or taken by horse cart to Butchertown. In one typical entry Burns described arriving at the Second Street Wharf: "Found one yelling calf not able to travel with the drove (has been down in the cars and trampled on) ordered it taken out to Butcher Town in a[n] express wagon."[48] Burns made hundreds of interventions like this, but rarely, if ever, made arrests for these forms of routine cruelty that were part of an emerging—and seemingly unstoppable and vast—system of raising and shipping animals for food. Toward the end of his term, Burns was using his police power to improve the lives of hundreds of animals each month. But the small number of fines he collected could not even cover the cost of his salary. By the summer of 1878, the Society was hemorrhaging cash. In August it spent more than $200 and brought in only $40. In that month Burns investigated fifty-five cases but made only four arrests and got convictions in only two, one for "fast driving" of horses. "As the Society is very short of funds it was deemed unavoidable to dispense with the services of Captain Burns," reported the *San Francisco Call* that August. The decision came with "expressions of regret," according to the Society, as Burns had "served the Society faithfully for several years, and gained the esteem of all the Directors."[49]

As Burns's experience would suggest, the laws governing anticruelty and the structures of animal policing were showing serious flaws. Laws and penalties were designed to punish human intention, guilt, and wrongdoing. But animal cruelty often existed beyond this limited context. In monitoring the Second Street Wharf, Burns was observing what he knew to be a form of animal suffering that was real and vast, but also was difficult to prosecute and convict under the law. The challenges were many. For one thing, human guilt and innocence in large-scale shipping of livestock were harder to determine than in cases involving simple ownership and deliberate abuse. When Burns visited the Second Street Wharf, he almost always observed animals that had been injured in transit—typically through negligence and economic frugality, but rarely through outright human malevolence. Although not essential to prosecute, human intent was nevertheless an important factor in the Society's decisions to bring cases to court and a factor in the likelihood of conviction. Malice, or "wanton cruelty," made a case more favorable for prosecution, conviction, and large fines. In many cases, wanton cruelty led to fines that were dozens of times greater than those for standard or routine infractions, such as cases involving lame or overdriven horses.[50]

This sort of intentionality and malevolence was often absent in livestock shipping. Shippers might decide to overcrowd a railroad car or a steamboat, but that decision was seen as one of financial calculation, and not malicious intent. Arguably, it was cool and rational, but animals nevertheless suffered. On longer trips, livestock might suffer from lack of food or water on railroad cars. When trains experienced unexpected delays and inclement weather, animals faced starvation and dehydration. This form of suffering was in many cases seen as beyond immediate human control, and certainly beyond human intention. They were rational decisions based on shipping rates and times—of calculated rates of average weight loss and mortality in transit. Such cruelties were merely part of a new railroad geography and economy of animal production far too colossal for the SPCA and the humane movement to overturn.[51]

This large-scale system of animal production also created a fragmented set of relationships between people and livestock that defined the new economy and presented challenges for enforcement of animal welfare laws. In a geographically vast system of production, animals interacted with numerous handlers. When injured livestock arrived in San Francisco, who was responsible? Ranchers? Sellers? Shippers? Drovers? Buyers? Butchers? The process of raising, shipping, and killing animals was, in fact, a human-animal relationship increasingly segmented into many short-term temporary relationships across greater distances, making guilt and responsibility for injuries elusive. Within this vast chain of animal handlers, the point of culpability was hard to pin down—certainly more so than in cases where abuse was witnessed firsthand, or where ownership and responsibility were unmistakable. It was easier to arrest a man overdriving a lame horse on a city street than it was to prosecute the suffering of livestock moving through a segmented system of production and transportation. There were ideological reasons for wanting to protect horses in certain ways, but there were practical reasons as well. Laws designed to protect animals were still based in an older human-centric legal framework of individual human responsibility, and designed to punish relationships that were failing an older patriarchal model of accountability. New corporate relationships that segmented human-animal relationships into shorter interactions did not mesh well with these older models of the law.[52]

Another seemingly antiquated aspect of laws and enforcement came in the jurisdictional limitations and challenges of enforcing laws on livestock shipping. New forms of livestock production and shipping contained spatial characteristics that were not tailored to traditional geographies of police and legal powers, including those of the SFSPCA. The SFPSCA's authority was limited to the county—and SPCAs across the United States had geographic limitations that hindered their capacity to police a geographically vast system of animal production and shipping. In one typical case, SFSPCA officer Hooper complained of the overcrowding of cattle in railroad cars: "23 cattle is to[o] many to put in a car," he said, but added that "the man that shipped the cattle did not come with them soe I did not get to see him."[53] On another occasion, Agent Burns expressed frustration at trying to track down a man named Morton who "brought two hundred hogs from Los Angeles in two cars when sixty is considered a large number for one car." Twelve of the hogs were dead on arrival in San Francisco, "and very many others nearly so." Burns took a ferry to Oakland to get a warrant for Morton's arrest, but when he arrived he learned that his suspect had returned to Los Angeles the night before.[54] Suffering livestock may have been within Burns's jurisdiction, but the people responsible for that suffering were increasingly outside county lines.

Burns was experiencing the frustrations of systems of laws that had not yet caught up with the new spatial relationships and realities of a railroaded West.[55] As the livestock production network spread far beyond county lines in an era of private western land empires and railroad lines, SFSPCA agents were increasingly powerless to pursue shippers who overpacked cattle, pigs, and sheep on railroad cars and boats, or who failed to adequately water and feed animals in transit. While regional SPCAs pursued these abuses through new federal alliances and legislation, such infractions remained evasive in the everyday police actions of Society agents. New federal laws—passed in response to the emergence of the American Humane Association, a collection of regional Humane Societies—

limited the number of hours livestock could be confined on railroad cars without food or water. But enforcement was spotty at best, and it did not establish appropriate financial incentives for regional SPCA enforcement.[56]

When SFSPCA officers did intervene on matters related to the shipment of livestock, they often did so in ways that did not address the underlying causes of suffering. When SFSPCA agents found livestock suffering, the typical remedy was to order that the animal be shot on the spot, or else transported by horse-drawn cart to the slaughterhouse. Neither of these remedies fundamentally disrupted the operations or profits of livestock handlers and dealers, as the value of the animal's flesh was still preserved for resale. SPCA agents also shot horses, and this was a far more severe punishment because it deprived owners of the animal's labor, thereby sending a strong message to horse owners to take care of their animals or else face severe financial loss. Shooting livestock, on the other hand, did little to affect the bottom line of butchers and drovers. A suffering calf ordered slaughtered by the SPCA agent still sold the next day at market. Shooting livestock to alleviate their suffering may have solved the immediate problem, but it was a solution that did little to alter the root causes of livestock suffering in shipping.[57]

Despite the many challenges of prosecuting cases against livestock handlers and owners, Special Agent Burns nevertheless attempted to use his police powers to alleviate livestock suffering in the late 1870s. Burns remained vigilant in his efforts to see that the hundreds of thousands of cattle, sheep, and pigs that arrived in the city each year were treated well in transit. It must have felt, at times, as though he were swimming against an endless and powerful current. But almost every morning he visited the Second Street Wharf, where animals arrived in the city with injuries including broken legs or bloody gashes, or were thirsty or hungry to the point of exhaustion. This interminable work at the ports of entry did not bring in money for the SFSPCA, but it did offer some reprieve for animals themselves. Because it did not pay, Burns's vigilance in alleviating the suffering of livestock may have ultimately cost him his job.

There was another important change in the Society that might explain Burns's departure: the Board of Directors of the SFSPCA was increasingly made up of railroad and shipping interests, though they were not a majority. Although there is no smoking gun to show that the directors of the SFSPCA remade the Society's police powers to fit their private economic interests, the timing of Burns's dismissal raises some suspicions. Leland Stanford was a trustee of the SFSPCA in 1876, and by 1877 he was joined by Charles Crocker and Henry Newhall (president of the San Francisco and San Jose Railroad, before it was sold to the Southern Pacific). Crocker and Newhall were "Life Members"—a designation given to those who made extremely large donations—and they shared that membership status with numerous friends in banking, business, and shipping. Many life members, like Newhall, were also large landholders in California who, no doubt, understood that the true value of their land often depended on the livestock that grazed those remote spaces, and who turned soil, water, and grass into meat and hides.[58] These railroad executives likely shared a pecuniary interest in easing restrictions on shipping livestock.

Although the corruption of San Francisco animal policy by corporate interests is difficult to prove, it would have fit with a broader current of corruption in humane activism by railroad and shipping interests happening across the country. The American Humane Association (AHA)—founded in 1877 for the cooperation of regional animal welfare organizations—had its origins in addressing the cruelties of interstate cattle transportation. But the AHA chose to work with railroad companies rather than against them.[59] In Chicago, corporate interests also captured the work of the Illinois Humane Society (IHS) and appeared to shape the law enforcement in Chicago's stockyards and slaughterhouses on the city's South Side. By the mid-1880s, a former IHS agent complained that the new agent assigned to the slaughterhouses was neglecting his obligations, and was "ignorant" and "incompetent." Writing to the IHS vice president in 1885, the former agent claimed that he had a damning letter "written by one of the leading members of the society, begging of me, not to make public, the society's record at the Stock Yards, for the last five years."[60] The new IHS agent—a man named Mitchell—had undone many of the gains of the 1880s, according to the retired IHS agent.

By the 1890s, IHS agent Mitchell appeared to be firmly in the pocket of the major Chicago meatpackers, some of whom also sat on the IHS Board of Directors. An employee of the Union Stock Yards wrote to the IHS president in 1890 saying that Mitchell was a "good man" and "had no enemies in the Stock Yard. . . . [He] attends to his own business and lets other people's alone. For that reason, he makes plenty of friends here." Mitchell stood loyal to the meatpackers, even lobbying the IHS president on their behalf when he argued that their modern systems allowed for animals to be slaughtered in "as Humane a manner as possible." Philip Armour, who sat on the Board of Directors of the IHS, joined Gustavus Swift and IHS president William Shortall in requesting that the governor of Illinois reappoint Mitchell in 1893.[61] While modern slaughtering methods were, in many cases, faster and more efficient in killing animals, the convergence of IHS and corporate livestock and meatpacking interests nevertheless raised concerns that officers of the law—and humane societies themselves—could be captured by monied interests.

Back in San Francisco, the relationship of the SFSPCA to other powerful corporations was also complicated. At times, Agents Burns and Hooper appeared adversarial in their relationship with the city's butchers and drovers. At other times, in dealing with the city's horse population, they appeared to be friendly with the numerous "stable bosses" who ran the large railroad, streetcar, and stable companies in the city. Despite the influence of wealthy businessmen within the SFSPCA, there is little evidence to prove that they fundamentally altered the organization's operations to fit the interests of large animal companies. More likely, the mechanisms of law enforcement and the ideological and practical structures of laws favored prosecutions of individual animal owners within the city itself. The dismissal of Agent Burns marked an important shift in the SFSPCA's turn away from livestock and toward other domesticated animals that inhabited downtown San Francisco.

====

Just a month after Captain Burns was let go by the SFSPCA—ostensibly because of financial shortfalls—a city police officer named William Hooper was assigned to be the Society's chief law enforcement officer. In his first few months on the job, Hooper seemed to have picked up where Burns left off. The sorts of cases in which he intervened—and the city spaces that he monitored—were not notably different from those in the last few months of Burns's tenure. But over the next few years, and over his two-decade tenure as an SFSPCA officer, Hooper shifted his influence and showed greater interest in enforcing laws in downtown San Francisco—particularly cases involving cruelty to horses. With Hooper as the Society's agent, the SFSPCA fully embraced its police powers and its authority to take legal action and collect fines by initiating hundreds of prosecutions each year. The fines collected on convictions would become the primary source of funding for the Society in the last decades of the nineteenth century.

Although SFSPCA police power expanded under Hooper, it also became more geographically concentrated. Indeed, it was partly the growing numbers of prosecutions themselves that placed unanticipated limitations on Hooper's geographic range. With each arrest, Hooper needed to appear in court as a witness. The time he spent in court was time he could not spend enforcing laws on the streets. Even more, his need to be downtown for court appearances limited the geographic extent of his enforcement. A visit to Butchertown required at least several hours or a full day. On days when Hooper needed to appear in court, trips to Butchertown were nearly impossible. Not only was Butchertown distant, but the abuses to livestock there rarely translated into convictions and fines. As

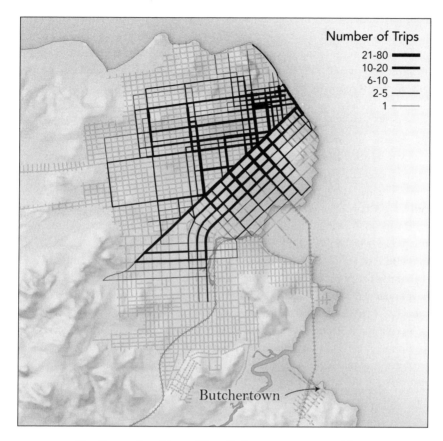

FIGURE 4.1 The Geography of Animal Law Enforcement, 1878–1883. This visualization shows the extent of Officer Hooper's daily routes in San Francisco. The map was created using a sample of routes from cases that led to prosecutions between 1878 and 1883. Thicker lines indicate areas of greater enforcement. Note the concentration of enforcement downtown, and the complete absence in Butchertown. Research by Mark Sanchez and cartography by Erik Steiner, Stanford Spatial History Project.

a result, policing Butchertown became less relevant than policing downtown. By the 1880s and 1890s, Hooper was making hundreds of arrests and prosecutions each year—most of which resulted in fines that supported the SFSPCA. What emerged was a cyclical pattern of arrests and prosecutions downtown, often in close proximity to courthouses and the main office of the SFSPCA. It was a system that filled the Society's coffers with record numbers of fines and revenue, but limited its agent from accessing more remote parts of the county that contained large populations of livestock and some of the worst animal abuses in the city and state.

An additional geographic constraint on the Society's enforcement of laws for livestock was that SFSPCA policing leaned heavily on ordinary citizens and Society members to report animal abuses. Residents were, in many cases, the eyes and ears of the Society—especially those who were active and contributing members of the SFSPCA. Residents often called the Society to report abuses they had seen in the streets—almost all of which involved horses, dogs, cats, and small animals sold in city markets.[62] Under this system of neighborhood policing, Butchertown once again was beyond popular surveillance and law enforcement. Butchertown was designed as a place apart from downtown—a place for work in the most noxious trades, and largely devoid of residents. Those who spent time in Butchertown or lived nearby were more likely to have been employees of livestock and slaughterhouse companies, who had numerous incentives to keep their heads down and voices silent in the face of animal abuse. Even if employees were attuned to the sufferings of the animals they drove and slaughtered, reporting a case to the SFSPCA might have endangered their jobs. As a result, abuses were rarely reported in Butchertown, though they no doubt existed. Residential law enforcement had geographic limitations, creating a resounding silence in Butchertown in SFSPCA enforcement.

Indeed, the citizen surveillance and law enforcement of animal abuses was also part of the system lawmakers and SFSPCA leaders envisioned and designed. The 1868 Act for the More Effectual Prevention of Cruelty to Animals in California authorized the Society to deputize as many agents as it wished, and that same year SFSPCA leaders proposed having an "unlimited number of these officers."[63] But it was also a form of policing that SFSPCA hoped would be both diffuse and organized. Each city ward would have a district officer, who would oversee a number of deputized "monitors," creating a web of citizen officers would monitor the city for animal abuses. The goal was not primarily arrests, but it was a show of force: it was these officers' mere "power and presence in our midst," SFSPCA leaders believed, that would act as a deterrent to animal abuse.[64] That ideal of a diffuse, citizen-based police power remained a part of the SFSCPA into the late nineteenth century. In his annual address as president in 1877, Joseph Winans expressed his interest in developing "a corpus of ministerial agents." He wished to see "every citizen whose philanthropic instincts impel him" be able to participate as an officer in the "noble work" of the Society. In his own words, Winans was "creating . . . a secret police formidable for its efficiency and omnipresence."[65] The dispersed police power was an idealized form of state power and governance that would exist without obvious bureaucratic structures or taxation, and without the legal traces of arrests, prosecutions, and fines.[66]

The number of officers deputized by the SFSPCA bespoke this ongoing vision of a self-regulating society with strong and scattered police power. In the very first year of its existence, the SFSPCA deputized 12 officers to head each district, and was working to get badges for 20 more members. The number of officers in the Society rose from 36 in 1869, to 45 in 1872, to 100 in 1877, to 275 in 1902, and to 321 in 1907.[67] Whereas these officers rarely made arrests on their own, they no doubt provided surveillance for the Society's agents and leaders, and for the city's Police Department.

A similar fascination with surveillance and police work emerged in a kindred organization of SPCAs: the Bands of Mercy—a national children's organization with thousands of local chapters across the United States. Invented by the founder and president of the Massachusetts SPCA, George Angell, the Bands of Mercy were meant to bring children into the humane movement and to encourage them to practice kindness toward animals. Bands distributed readings, lessons, and songbooks free of charge, and, by the 1890s, had over 11,000 chapters across the United States, with more than 500,000 children as members.[68] "Every school child," said one pamphlet, "as soon as he is old enough to write his name, is made a member of an army for the prevention of all the old evils." Members pledged "kindness and justice to all living creatures," and as part of their membership, children signed a card with the words: "I will try to be kind to all harmless living creatures, and try to protect them from cruel usage." Children were instructed that they could "cross out the word *harmless* from [their] pledge" if they wished.[69] An essential element of membership in a Band of Mercy was a pledge to intervene on behalf of animals unable to defend themselves.

Despite its veneer of soft power, more formal elements of police power were folded into the work and symbols of the Bands of Mercy. With the signatures of thirty adults or children, local chapters could receive a packet containing copies of the SPCA publication *Our Dumb Animals,* a book of songs, a pamphlet called *Twelve Lessons on Kindness to Animals,* and eight humane leaflets. In that package was also an "imitation gold badge" for the president of the chapter, which resembled those worn by SPCA officers of the law. Any child member could purchase a gold or silver badge for 8 cents. At each Band of Mercy meeting, time was set aside for children to share "what they have done to make human and dumb creatures happier and better," which often involved stories of intervening to stop abuse they had witnessed.[70] One young female member of the San Francisco chapter of the Band of Mercy saw a tired horse beaten on the side of a hill. She told a blacksmith, who notified the police.[71] Bands of Mercy taught and supported children in observing, reporting, and intervening in cases of animal cruelty.

In wearing badges and interceding to stop animal cruelty, child members of the Bands of Mercy were mimicking and reproducing a form of disperse police power idealized at the highest levels of SPCA leadership. SPCA leaders no doubt understood children as part of a broader surveillance system. One San Francisco newspaper called the members of the Band of Mercy "detectives."[72] "No blue-frocked, brass-buttoned guardian of the peace could have done a tithe of the good that those children have accomplished," said one pamphlet promoting the Bands of Mercy.[73]

While the protection of animals was central to the work of the Bands of Mercy, the organization also advanced the notion that kindness toward animals would ultimately cause broader social improvement and reform society from the bottom up. As Chapter 5 shows in greater detail, humane reformers saw humane treatment of animals as the foundation for improving society more broadly—including improving relationships between groups of people. The Bands of Mercy often celebrated this expanded view of social reform. In one instance, a boy in San Francisco who was a member of a Band of Mercy shared his story of seeing another boy throwing stones at a "Chinaman with a bag o' rags on his back." When the Chinese man began to run away, the boy "kept a–chasing of him and firing at him, until I runs up and sticks out my foot and trips the boy head over heels."[74] The SFSPCA was not primarily concerned with discrimination against Chinese Americans, though there was no doubt a segment of the organization that cared about improving fraught social relations. Bands of Mercy and SPCAs often recognized children as central to both the operation of an expansive law enforcement element of the humane movement, and also as primary agents in a broader agenda of social reform that crossed species.

=====

As children became more important in the humane movement—and as livestock disappeared from urban life downtown—the legal and cultural work of SPCA's shifted geographically and qualitatively. In San Francisco, the SPCA was fast becoming a police force for fewer and fewer species of animals living downtown—overwhelmingly horses, but also pets. Whereas Burns had been preoccupied with the city's livestock in the late 1870s, the SFSPCA appeared fully committed to other downtown species by the 1890s. Of 268 cases prosecuted in 1895, 262 cases—98 percent—were for abuse of horses or mules (250 cases for horses, 12 cases for mules). The remaining 6 cases involved dogs (3), chickens (1), a turkey (1), and a cat (1).[75] In that year, not a single case involving a pig, cow, or sheep was prosecuted, though agents may have intervened in nonprosecutorial ways to help those species.[76] This role as a police force for the protection of animals down-town kept the SFSPCA in the black for decades. But it also failed to protect large livestock populations within city limits.

Even downtown, however, the SFSPCA encountered numerous challenges re-lated to the enforcement of animal protection laws. New corporate structures of ownership continued to distort the enforcement of laws built on older concepts of legal responsibility and guilt. As with the shipping of livestock, large companies were also pervasive in downtown transportation. Companies with large numbers of employees and horses proved more difficult to arrest and prosecute than indi-vidual owners. The Society was either unwilling or unable to take on city transit companies and railroad lines. Agents Hooper and Burns were also sympathetic to company drivers, who they understood were simply working horses their bosses had provided them. Agent diaries show that company drivers would typically get off with a warning. "Saw a horse in car no 11 of the Folsom St. Line," wrote Officer Hooper on October 9, 1879. The horse was "very lame," but it was not the obvious responsibility of the man driving it. Hooper "told the driver to tell the Stable Boss to take him out." Later that day, another man driving a coal cart was instructed to "tell his Boss that he must not work him [the horse] till well."[77] These sorts of warnings were typical in cases where drivers were not owners of the horses they drove. The fragmentation of human-animal relationships in an industrial corpo-rate economy caused problems for law enforcement reliant on older concepts of re-sponsibility, intention, and guilt. For the SFSPCA, it was unfair to hold a driver responsible for the condition of a horse owned by his employer.

In contrast to these company drivers were thousands of horses owned by in-dividuals and small-scale producers that also inhabited the city. Special Agents Hooper and Burns actively monitored these horses—particularly when they gath-ered at city markets, where horses brought goods from suburban farms into San Francisco. These horses were often owned by the men who held their reins, making the line of responsibility and accountability unambiguous. The Italian "vegetable peddlers" were among the most frequently mentioned subset of this class, but others also relied on old horses and mules to do their work. Within a decade of their founding the SFSPCA had already made great strides in clearing the streets of old and lame horses—often at the expense of poor San Franciscans. "The old bottles and rag men," whose horses were notoriously decrepit, "have been over-hauled," declared the *San Francisco Bulletin* in 1878, in discussing the effective-ness of the SFSPCA's work over the previous decade. Men with poor horses, they continued, had "come to the conclusion that it is cheaper for them to make use of younger and sounder horses."[78] But "making use" of younger horses was also a costly decision for small-scale producers. Efforts to improve the lives of animals may have been earnest, but the city's poor and working class often paid the greatest price for this form of progress.

Consistent with their other forms of corporate kinship, the SFSPCA established strong relationships with stable bosses—the men who managed stables for large companies. Society agents and leaders seemed satisfied by the reassurances they received from company managers. Like the large-scale dairy farmers facing new regulations, big companies with horses were buffered financially by their scale of operation. Companies with tens or hundreds of horses could more easily conform to new regulations that forbade driving injured or weary horses. A large portion of SFSPCA cases were those that involved overworked or lame horses—injuries that occurred simply because of frequent use. Large companies adjusted to regulations by keeping animals in reserve and rotating and resting their stock. They could easily swap out horses in ways that may have offered them a comparative advantage; by having reserves, companies did not lose a day of work on a horse that was slow, sick, or injured. As with dairies, scales of production once again acted as a form of insurance in the face of new regulations. Agent Burns described his relationships with stable bosses and "Superintendents of the different railroads" as cooperative. They were, he said, "willing and anxious to do all in their power to alleviate the sufferings of stock carried over their roads." In the thousands of cases prosecuted from 1878 to 1919, none—or an elusive few—were cases brought against corporations.[79]

The case of regulating horses once again showed the ways in which the laws and mechanisms of enforcement seemed unable—and legal and political powers seemed unwilling—to adjust to new realities of animal ownership and relationships. The segmentation of human-horse relationships—like the segmentation of cattle production—made legal responsibility a tricky concept. "Junk wagons," "vegetable peddlers," "milk wagons," and "butcher wagons," were overrepresented in SFSPCA prosecutions. These wagons and carts were pulled by horses of workers who not only stood out as needing reform, but whose relationships to and accountability for their workhorses was unmediated by corporate structures. Many probably only owned one horse and did not have the means to rest or replace old or lame animals. The enforcement of animal welfare laws fell disproportionately on them.

====

The SFSPCA remained locked in this spatial, legal, and financial logic of enforcement for decades. Horses and pets—and downtown surveillance, arrests, and fines—became the central focus of the SFSPCA, as Butchertown and livestock disappeared from agent diaries. In the 1880s and 1890s, Butchertown was mentioned only a handful of times, and visits there never ended in prosecutions for the abuse of livestock.[80]

By the 1890s, the SFSPCA stumbled onto another source of revenue when they took over what had been a corrupt city pound. For the next decade, the city pound would become a new cash cow for the SFSPCA through redemption fees and the sale of strays (mostly dogs). The San Francisco SPCA was not alone in moving toward this financial model of operating city pounds.[81] But the new focus on downtown pets reinforced a spatial and intellectual pattern of caring primarily about animals that were in plain sight and physically present in downtown city streets. The transition to focusing on pet keeping in the 1890s was fortuitous timing for the SFSPCA. With the decline in horse populations in cities in the beginning of the twentieth century, the SFSPCA lost what had been its largest source of income. As horse populations rapidly declined in cities in the first two decades of the twentieth century, prosecutions (and fine collections) plummeted from 177 cases in 1899, to 91 in 1914, to a mere 28 in 1920. From 1922 until 1936, the SFSCPA prosecuted less than 20 cases each year—including one year, 1927, in which they prosecuted only 2.[82] With the decline of the horse, the age of the SFSPCA as a police and prosecutorial force also declined, remade once more with an emphasis on revenue from membership dues and pound fees—both of which depended on pets.

SFSPCA records from the late nineteenth century also suggested a stark reality: the SFSPCA was in the business of animal slaughter. In the 1870s, 1880s, and 1890s, agents ordered dozens of animals killed each month, with agents themselves often pulling the trigger. For decades, beginning in the 1880s, SPCAs across the United States distributed pamphlets with instructions on how to kill animals humanely, complete with illustrations.[83] San Francisco annual reports included detailed instructions to officers to "place the muzzle of the pistol within a few inches of the skull, aiming at a point in the middle of a line drawn across the forehead from the centers of the pits above the eyes."[84] As directors of the city pound in the 1890s, the SFSPCA euthanized thousands of unwanted dogs and cats each year, and leaders prided themselves on developing new humane ways of gassing animals that caused less suffering than older methods. Death was not some horrible manifestation of cruel treatment of animals; rather, it was a humane and merciful solution to animal suffering. "Kill, if necessary, but torture not," said ASPCA president Henry Bergh.[85]

━━

As the SFSPCA sharpened its police and legal powers in the late 1870s, there was a glimmering but brief moment that humane reform might reach all species

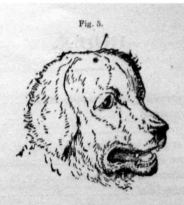

Fig. 5.

DOG.

Place the muzzle of the pistol within an inch of the head at the side, just over and in front of the ear, shooting downward toward the neck.

killed by blows with a heavy axe or hammer directed to the same place indicated for shooting. Animals to be killed by blows should first be blindfolded.

43

FIGURE 4.2 "How to Kill Animals Humanely." SPSPCAs and Humane Societies often printed instructions like these in various publications. From *An Act for the More Effectual Prevention of Cruelty to Animals* (San Francisco: San Francisco Society for the Prevention of Cruelty to Animals, 1907), 42–45. San Francisco Society for the Prevention of Cruelty to Animals.

in all parts of the city. Agents Burns and Hooper both expressed interest in protecting the transitory populations of livestock that walked off boats and trains
and made their way to slaughterhouses. But concern for those animals did not
yield prosecutions and income, and largely vanished from SFSPCA enforcement
records in the 1880s and 1890s. A significant challenge to the agenda of protecting
livestock from cruelty was the new urban geography of livestock that emerged in
the last decades of the nineteenth century. A greater chasm was opening up, with
the Society's officers and members downtown, on one side, and the lives of livestock and workers in Butchertown on the other.

"Saw 30 cattle killed," Hooper scrawled in his agent diary on October 21, 1878,
after visiting Butchertown—a trip he would make rarely in the decades that followed. The butchers behaved well while Hooper was present, driving and killing
the animals in ways that met his approval. But Hooper was frustrated by having
to return downtown, knowing that the butchers would go back to harming animals when law enforcement disappeared. "I was told by a man," Burns wrote,
"that if there was no officer around that they punch them [the cattle] with a
stick that has a sharp spike on the end of it."[86] A week later, Hooper visited the
slaughterhouses again, and again the butchers "took good care not to abuse them
while I was there," he wrote. But all around him were the grim signs of silent
animal suffering and abuse: many of the cattle, he said, had "their eyes punched
out."[87]

On many levels, seeing was power. The distance to Butchertown—the distance
that health officials and property owners so ardently pushed to create in the prior
decade—made seeing Butchertown difficult for SFSPCA officers and San Francisco residents alike. Out of sight, the abuse of livestock faded from public con-
sciousness and lost the urgency of other animal abuses that happened in more
central and visible parts of town. "Cases occurring in the streets are checked by
public opinion," said the leader of the Illinois Humane Society, "but, as a rule,
there is no disinterested person to see how animals shipped from one point to
another are treated."[88] It was a sad irony for livestock that efforts to improve their
lives emerged with force at the same moment that they were increasingly invisible
to most urban residents. Civilization and progress demanded both their improvement and their absence, but the realities of those demands were increasingly at
odds. It was not for complete lack of will that places like Butchertown became
places of neglect. The new distances that were essential in separating the health
nuisances of animal industries unintentionally blinded and limited the SFSPCA,
too. The SFSPCA had immense legal powers, but also immense challenges,
limitations, and blind spots in asserting those powers across the city of San
Francisco.

The invisibility of slaughter and livestock from urban life was comfortable and familiar by 1906, when Upton Sinclair wrote *The Jungle*. The "slaughtering machine ran on, visitors or no visitors," he wrote, "like some horrible crime committed in a dungeon, all unseen and unheeded, buried out of sight and of memory."[89] The lives of laborers who interacted with livestock had also become invisible in many ways, which led to a variety of workplace abuses that were as shocking to many as the horrors of meat production. Burns and Hooper would have understood quite well the blind spots of a new geography of human-animal interaction.

On the afternoon of October 21, 1878, Hooper left the livestock in Butchertown and returned to the streets of downtown San Francisco. Although Butchertown proved a frustrating site of reform, Hooper's efforts to enforce animal cruelty laws were duly rewarded downtown. He stopped the driver of a milk wagon for driving a horse with a sore shoulder and ordered the man to rest the animal. He visited a neighborhood under development to check on the city's "grading horses"—the bulky breeds that smoothed the steepest San Francisco slopes and moved hills, one cartload at a time, to fill the bay. Late in the day, he responded to a call from Mrs. Wheeler, a dues-paying member of the SFSPCA, about a horse in "poor condition" in her well-off neighborhood on Russian Hill.[90] The visible world downtown told a different story of SFSPCA power and the lives of animals in San Francisco. In the visible and civilizing world downtown, all indications were that the treatment of animals was getting better.

CHAPTER FIVE

That Doggy in the Window

The SPCA and the Making of Pets in America

O N T H E A F T E R N O O N of May 13, 1874, Henry Bergh left his office on the corner of Fourth Avenue and Twenty-Second Street in Manhattan and traveled more than twenty blocks south to the corner of Broadway and Houston. Bergh was the founder and president of the American Society for the Prevention of Cruelty to Animals (ASPCA) in New York City. Although a man of means who could have held a comfortable desk job as president of the ASPCA—or no job at all—Bergh preferred to spend his days walking the streets of New York City, flagging down drivers of lame horses, issuing warnings, and making arrests. On that May day, Bergh was out to investigate a specific complaint that the owners of the Walker cider shop were committing cruelty to an animal. When Bergh arrived he saw what the fuss was about; there, in the shop's front window, was a dog on a treadmill, powering a small cider press.

According to later court testimony, Bergh had known about the dog-powered cider press for some time, but had done nothing until May 13. It took numerous letters from concerned citizens and members of his Society for Bergh to become involved—including a complaint that day from James Goodrich, a lawyer who often passed by the store. Goodrich had seen enough and decided that day to take action.[1]

In the coming days, the Society backed Goodrich's efforts to arrest and arraign Charles Walker, the proprietor of the shop, on charges that his use of a dog on a treadmill amounted to cruelty. When the case was finally brought before the Court of Special Sessions months later, Walker was accused of cruelty under the 1867 New York State law on the "More Effectual Prevention of Cruelty to Animals." The court convicted him and fined him the steep sum of $25, roughly equivalent to at least two or three weeks of work, and a fine hefty enough for Walker to pursue a legal appeal that went all the way to the state's Supreme Court.[2]

What was on trial in these cases was the increasingly contested relationship between people and dogs in New York. That relationship was undergoing notable changes across the United States at precisely the same moment that Walker's case was making its way through courts. As dogs became central to a new ideology of humane education—and key figures in an important branch of social reform—many sought to eliminate numerous forms of relationships with dogs they deemed objectionable, including working relationships.

Although the dog churn at Walker's cider shop was something of a public attraction in New York City of 1874, dog machines were somewhat common at the time. Throughout much of the nineteenth century, dogs powered a variety of machines, while also serving as a source of locomotive power in cities. But as dogs became increasingly defined as pets—whose lives were dedicated to leisure and not labor—their presence as beasts of burden came under greater attack from overlapping groups of urban elites, pet owners and breeders, and members of regional SPCAs. Dogs played a key role in a new humane ideology that placed the kindness of pet ownership at the center of its reform agenda. The laboring dog—and the inevitable strain and suffering of canine work—had no place within this new ideology and within the civilized city where the ideology thrived. Culturally and legally, human relationships with dogs—particularly in cities like New York—were becoming contested and regulated. By the end of the nineteenth century, the wide range of relationships with dogs known to many Americans at midcentury had been narrowed to an acceptable few in cities like New York. Powerful reformers were gradually remaking dogs exclusively as animals of leisure.

Working Like a Dog

The creation of dogs as creatures of leisure in the late nineteenth century city was hardly inevitable or obvious to those living in the moment. Indeed, dogs provided a niche form of power that was unfulfilled by water, coal, steam, and horses. Dogs offered the possibility for new, smaller machines that promised real labor-saving improvements for Americans on farms, in homes, and in cramped city spaces alike.

Dogs also served as locomotive power for New York City's poorest residents—the ragpickers who owned dogs to pull carts as they scavenged city streets. For many who relied on dog labor, remaking canines exclusively as creatures of leisure was far from an improvement.

Dog labor was nothing new to human history. For thousands of years, dogs evolved alongside humans in a relationship that provided humans with numerous benefits and services. In the nineteenth century, dogs protected property, worked at firehouses, thwarted predators like wolves, and guarded and herded livestock. In snowy regions, they pulled sleds. In the South, they tracked and terrorized runaway slaves.[3] Quite often, these forms of labor relied on the specific traits and abilities of dogs: their keen sense of smell, their distinct forms of intelligence, their loyalty and obedience to owners, and their capacity to communicate and interact with people.

But, increasingly, dogs also worked in a variety of relatively toilsome jobs. As Americans avidly took to machine power in the nineteenth century, they also employed dogs as compact and pliable sources of power. Dogs offered a unique capacity to power small machines. As early as the 1820s, American newspapers—particularly agricultural journals—touted the possibilities and benefits of dog labor for machine power. Mentions of these machines were most prevalent from 1840 to 1870. The dog that turned Walker's cider press was, in some ways, more typical than it was unusual, part of a longer technological story that had developed over decades in America.[4]

Some of the first discussions about dog power emerged in 1828, when several newspapers published an article celebrating a "very ingenious mechanic" in Troy, New York, who had designed a mill for sawing small, delicate pieces of wood for sashes and window blinds. This new machine was "driven not by steam power, nor water, nor cattle power, but by *dog power*."[5] News of the Troy invention reached England through the *Kaleidescope*, which published an article on the inventive machine in 1829. "Fire and water, and their joint offspring, steam, have long been obliged to work for their living in our land of steady habits of industry," said the newspaper. "The wind has been compelled to contribute something of moving power. The horse and ox have trudged diligently along the road or over the farm." But now the "lazy and gentlemanlike dog" could be put to work in "giving motion to machinery." With a little instruction, dogs could become "sagacious and docile labourers, regarding the exercise as sport rather than toil."[6]

For other European visitors in search of American character and essence, the use of dog power suggested something fundamental about American zeitgeist in the nineteenth century. Alexis de Tocqueville noted the American obsession with efficiency and machines: "To minds thus predisposed, every new method that leads by a shorter road to wealth, every machine that spares labor, every instrument that diminishes the cost of production, every discovery that facilitates pleasure or augments them, seems to be the grandest effort of the human intellect."[7] Although Tocqueville never mentioned dog power by name, the innovative dog machines fit his observation of a broader American obsession with machines that "spared labor." An Englishman touring the American countryside in the 1860s mentioned dog labor specifically in discussing Americans' obsession with "what they call 'labor-saving machines.'" Where there was a "scarcity of hands" and high wages, he wrote, Americans had made the most efficient use of labor, including the development of the "dog churning apparatus."[8] Dog machines fit within this larger popular impulse to develop machines that maximized efficiency and minimized human labor.

Dog power was not merely a novelty or a symbol of this cultural obsession with efficiency, but in many cases offered real savings and value to those who used it. Dogs themselves were relatively inexpensive to purchase and feed. One article noted the economy of dog power, claiming that keeping four dogs cost "only 6d per day."[9] For the needs of a small producer, dogs could often do the work of horses and other beasts of burden at a much smaller price. In many cases, using a large animal to power a small machine or perform a light-duty task was excessive— and the cost of maintaining a larger animal and machine amounted to unnecessary expenses. While many Americans owned horses, they were hardly ideal as machine animals. Their "eyes bulge out," wrote Reverend Frederic Shelton in 1853, describing the ways in which horses developed health problems when put to work as machine animals. In some cases, he argued, the horse "soon becomes blind and dies." "The dog," on the other hand, he continued, "was the very animal to accomplish this kind of work."[10] The distinctive physical and mental makeup of dogs made their labor contribution unique.

Shelton observed the prevalence of dog labor on dairy farms in particular, where dogs labored to turn milk into butter. "Those who have large dairies" Shelton observed, "candidly confess that they could not do without them [dogs]." As dairies became larger and specialized producers for growing urban and regional markets, the work of processing milk and churning it into butter became something of a part-time job. What had once been only a small part of a person's workday was increasingly a full-time occupation, and dairy farmers struggled to deal with this new labor demand. Hiram Olmstead, a dairy farmer in Upstate New York, expressed the challenges of specialized, large-scale butter production in 1859: "The tax of time and patience to do up the churning at all times," he said, "is sufficient to prevent many from entering into the business." Dog labor for

FIGURE 5.1 "The Dog Churn." From *Harper's Weekly*, December 11, 1869. Here a sheep is powering the "dog churn." Note the old machine in storage above the doorway, which may have been human-powered.

churning enabled much of the rise of large-scale butter production in Upstate New York.[11]

Dog-powered churns also promised to save labor for a particular group of Americans: women. Traditionally, churning was women's work. But as specialized butter production spread, women suddenly faced a daunting and impossible workload of churning. The butter churn also arrived at a time when the absence of women's work was often understood as a mark of status and gentility. "Reasonable men will not require the women to do the churning," said Olmstead, which could take up hours of the day and was physically exhausting. "No one milking three cows," he concluded, "can afford to churn by hand."[12] In 1834, a Vermont man advertised the benefits of his patented "dog churn," which did more than just churn butter, and could also be used for "turning grindstones and washing clothes."[13] "Women may now introduce 'dog power' into their kitchens and dining rooms," claimed the Vermont inventor, "and seat themselves in the parlor."[14] For a small cost, dog power offered dreams of middle-class leisure and refinement.[15]

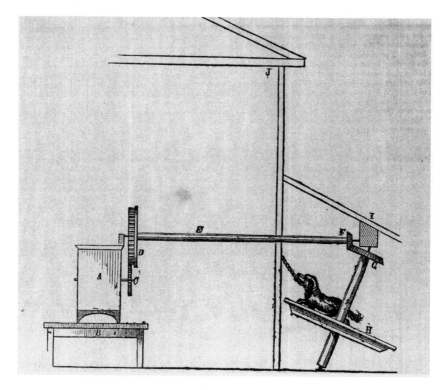

Churning butter was only one form of dog labor in rural production. On dairy farms, dogs often labored in various ways—from protecting animals and property, to herding livestock, to providing human companionship. Most farms already had dogs, so putting them to work in a machine was added labor with little additional cost to farmers. Where grass was plentiful, sheep also provided machine power with little additional cost for food, and could use the same small machines designed for dogs. But dogs and sheep had different dietary needs. In crowded pastures, dogs offered savings in the type of food they consumed. As dairy farmers measured their productivity and wealth in their number of cows, volume of milk, and available pasturage, dogs offered a distinct advantage in their diet of table scraps, offal, and leftovers that were inedible or undesirable for human consumption. Dogs did not compete for pasturage, which was where many dairy farmers counted their profits. For many Americans the care and protection dogs received from their owners also justified the use of their labor. "As long as dogs are kept," said the *Cultivator* in 1865, "they should partially pay their keeping."[16] For these owners, it was only fair that dogs contribute to their privileged way of life, and dog machines offered just such an opportunity.

Dog machines themselves were inexpensive and easy for farmers to build. The simple machines required less raw material to construct than larger machines for heavier force. In most cases, dog machines could be made by handy farmers themselves. "The whole machinery is very simple," according to the *Southern Cultivator*, which printed basic blueprints for building a dog machine in 1852: "Anyone who has the slightest knowledge of using tools can build one."[17]

Dog power offered the possibility of liberation from spatial and geographic restrictions of other forms of machine power. On the smallest spatial scale, dog machines could fit in spaces where larger machinery could not. Promoters noted that dog power could remake spaces and labor in homes, but also on larger spatial scales. In particular, dog power offered the possibility of machine power without dependence on the geography of wind and water. Olmsted noted that "water power answers a very good purpose for those situated so as to employ it," but that it was "expensive to establish and keep in repair, owing to the liability to decay."[18] While running water could potentially run small churns, it remained usable in only certain locations—"for those situated so as to employ it."[19] A dairy farmer whose land was distant from running water was out of luck and disconnected from an important market advantage. But dog power could be used anywhere and was highly portable, making it even more attractive to the mythologized independent producers settling new lands. Equal in importance to its actual use, dog power tapped into the dreams of small producers by promising an affordable machine for everyday life that would save time and labor, and provide power that was free of traditional geographic limitations. Dogs promised to power rural America and to bring relief to the long and laborious days of farm families, and to deliver greater profits for farmers.

=====

The naturalist and writer John Burroughs remembered the dog churn on his family farm, in the Catskill Mountains of Upstate New York. Burroughs was later famous for his scathing attack on "nature fakers" and those who, he claimed, distorted and anthropomorphized the lives of animals.[20] As a boy, in the 1840s and 1850s, Burroughs worked on the family farm and remembered the summers, when they used a dog churn to keep up with the greater volume of milk. When it was churning time, the dog, Old Cuff, perhaps knew to make himself scarce—to find "important business with the woodchucks in a distant field." In Old Cuff's absence, the family employed an old ram to run the churn—and when animals would not cooperate, Burroughs and his brother Eden would take turns in the machine. "I've been the dog," Burroughs said. John and his brother rigged a hackle to prod the ram back to work when he grew tired and lay down. One day Burroughs returned to find that the ram had jumped or fell from the machine, hanging himself with the rope that had been fastened around his neck.[21]

Dog Labor in the City

Dog labor also offered new possibilities for urban labor and production. One of the greatest advantages of dog power was that it occupied "much less room" than other technologies—making it suitable for cramped urban spaces.[22] There was no shortage of by-products and leftovers of the urban economy to feed to dogs, making them relatively inexpensive to maintain. Novelty and the curiosity of dog labor was also a large part of its urban appeal. For many in nineteenth-century America, seeing dogs working machines was sensational—and also an implicit celebration of technical achievement and inventiveness. Reverend Shelton was "much amused" in observing dog machines, and he was excited to learn that dogs "work extremely well" in producing machine labor. Though unable to move a "gigantic engine," dogs nevertheless were quite useful in providing energy, and demonstrating "power and ingenuity combined."[23]

Indeed, the spectacle of dog labor likely played a key role in the modest spread of dog power in urban environments. In Boston, dogs powered six "knitting machines" at Marlboro Chapel in the 1840s, where women produced stockings, gloves, and other textiles. Visitors came to the chapel daily "for the purpose of seeing the operation."[24] The Walker cider shop in New York City also used dogs for pressing apples and also as a prominent display in the shop's front windows, where onlookers gathered to see dogs turning the wheels of machines. Dog labor not only served as productive labor, in many cases, but also as a form of entertainment that could be converted into advertising. The curiosity of dog labor emerged in part because it contested the very definition of what a dog was and ought to be. For some, dogs were not supposed to work in repetitive labor, as power for machines—and yet they did the task quite well. The dog in the machine also stood in increasingly sharp contrast to the dog in the home. As dogs were becoming pets and creatures of leisure, their place in powering machines

FIGURE 5.3 "The Rag Picker," *Harper's Weekly*, May 7, 1870. This image was printed soon after the initial crackdown on dog carts in the late 1860s. The artist's inclusion of a passive police officer in the background suggests the criticism that new laws were not aggressively enforced in the spring of 1870. Library of Congress.

was becoming more objectionable. Dogs as unthinking machine power stood in sharp contrast to their other developing roles in society.

Machine power accounted for only one form of urban dog labor. More significant and widespread was another form of canine work that also emerged in cities in the nineteenth century. In New York, in particular, the city's poorest residents used dogs to pull their carts. Although the practice was not entirely new, by most accounts it was spreading in urban environments, particularly among a specific subset of New York immigrants commonly known as "ragpickers." "Dog power is coming into use in New York to a large extent," noted the *New England Farmer* in 1862, especially among the "German ash-mongers and rag-pickers" who used the "economizing power" of harnessing "stout dogs" to pull carts.[25] Dogs were not only capable of powering machines, but could also be harnessed and made into beasts of burden.

The ragpickers who harnessed dog power were a growing population in New York, and among the city's poorest residents. Ragpickers were professional scavengers who wandered the city in search of scraps of material they could resell. This included rags as well as a wide variety of other materials like bones, "bits of old iron, pieces of wire, old boots, shoes, scraps of leather, half-burned coal from the ash-barrel, broken glass, and every other sort of rubbish thrown out into the streets and alleys." These materials were resold to shops and small factories at minuscule profits. In some cases, ragpickers consumed the scraps of food they found.[26]

Although the racial and immigrant composition of ragpickers varied and changed over time, by most accounts German immigrants made up a majority of ragpickers for much of the nineteenth century. The German background of these workers was not lost on reformers, who saw ragpickers and their ways of life as foreign and odd. Ragpickers clustered in a variety of neighborhoods, from "Rag-Picker's Paradise" near the Five Points, to certain parts of the Lower East Side, to "Shantytown" uptown, and in the southern outskirts of Brooklyn. By the 1850s, according to one estimate, they numbered in the thousands in New York City alone.[27]

The ragpicker's workday typically started before dawn, between four and six in the morning, before professional street sweepers and garbage collectors made their rounds. On a good day a ragpicker could earn 25–50 cents per day in the 1850s, and might expect to pay between $3.50 and $5 per month for rent.[28] Those rag-pickers who were slightly "better off" could afford a cart and a couple of dogs to improve their efficiency and to ease the physical burdens of the job.[29]

Ragpickers came under growing scrutiny from reformers beginning in the mid-nineteenth century. City, state, and private groups formed commissions, wrote reports, and carefully observed the lives of ragpickers in the second half of the nineteenth century. Many reports and observations of ragpickers focused on their overcrowded and filthy living conditions in tenements and shanties. The first thing observers noted about ragpicker tenements was the sheer number of rags hanging out to dry. An article in *Harper's Weekly* described one residence known as "Rag-Picker's Court," near Mulberry and Bayard streets. Staring up from the courtyard, "one beholds a sight that can not be imagined. Rags to the right of him, rags to the left of him, on all sides, rags, rags, nothing but rags. Lines in the yard strung with them, balconies festooned with them, fire-escapes draped with them, windows hung with them; in short, every available object dressed in rags—and such rags!"[30] The rags were not merely unsightly, but were also "reeking with pestiferous smells," which purportedly posed grave threats to public health.[31]

When observers described ragpicker settlements in the 1850s and 1860s, they nearly always mentioned the dogs that shared the crowded tenements and sprawling shantytowns. When the Legislative Committee to investigate the condition of tenant houses in New York went on an observational visit in 1856, they noted the prevalence of dogs in the crowded apartments and courtyards. The tenements on Sheriff Street, known as "Rag-Pickers' Paradise," were packed with human and animal bodies: "Every inch of space is appropriated with beds, dog kennels and rags," and the dogs "set up occasional howls, adding to the delight of the visit."[32] Observers noted the "scores of dogs" and the "bones of dead animals and noisome collection of every kind."[33] The *New-York Tribune* observed one tenement where "at least fifty or sixty dogs are kenneled within the yards and houses," and many had been "harnessed to the rag carts in the transportation of the sickening nuisances" across the city. In visiting the ragpickers' tenements, the *New-York Tribune* concluded, "You may regard yourself fortunate if you escape a bite."[34]

The lives and homes of ragpickers were quickly becoming key sites of urban reform in the 1850s and 1860s, and dogs became a key battleground in that larger conflict. It was not merely the number and concentration of dogs in ragpicker tenements that was striking and objectionable to observers and reformers, but also the qualitative lives of dogs, immigrants, and the relationships between people and their animals. At the heart of the complaint was a disgust with the immigrants themselves. One reformer, speaking of the situation on Sheriff Street, called the German ragpickers "of the lowest order, having no national or personal pride; they are exceedingly filthy in person . . . their food is of the poorest quality. . . . They have a peculiar taste for the association of dogs and cats, there being about 50 of the former and 30 of the latter," in a building containing thirty-two apartments, twenty-eight families, and sixty adults.[35] For reformers, the relationships between ragpickers and their dogs marked a degraded social state and posed an affront to the social order of the city.

From the perspective of ragpickers—whose voices are largely missing from the historical record—dogs were likely valued workers and companions. The dogs that howled by night did important work for ragpickers by day. Dogs helped ragpickers pull heavy carts across miles of city streets, with ragpickers often pulling alongside their canine companions. When ragpickers ventured away from their carts, "up alleys or in basements carrying out buckets of loading for his cart," the dogs remained with the cargo and guarded it "from all invasion." Rag buyers and garbage collectors also used dog power, suggesting that dogs provided a more expansive form of locomotion for low-value goods in the garbage and recycling economies within the city. It was an "unnatural vocation" for dogs, said one observer, but one that they performed quite well.[36]

Although outside observers largely saw ragpickers and their dogs as performing a kind of unskilled labor, the ragpickers used dogs in ways that relied on training and the specific forms of canine intelligence. The dogs who pulled carts were "docile" and "teachable," noted one curious observer.[37] Many dogs could pull and stop carts on command, allowing scavengers to range farther from their carts, onto sidewalks and down alleyways, and allowing the team to more efficiently advance down a street without the ragpicker constantly returning to the cart. "The intelligence of these dogs is remarkable," said another writer in 1857, "they seem to know almost as much about the management of the cart as their human associate, and obey every word and look, and even anticipate approaching necessities."[38] At the end of a long workday, dogs likely offered immigrant ragpickers companionship. But to many outside observers—who knew dogs in a different social and labor context—the sight of immigrant ragpickers and their harnessed dogs was a real and powerful symbol of both human and canine degradation.

Making Pets in the Gilded Age

The social tensions between ragpickers and reformers were tangible by the 1870s. Even a compliment about the intelligence of dogs contained a backhanded jab at the "human associates" who scavenged city streets. Animals composed a key feature of a larger set of social tensions and conflicts. Dog labor came under growing public scrutiny and greater regulation in the late 1860s and early 1870s. The New York–based ASPCA led a mix of reformers seeking to prohibit the use of working dogs in the city. Bergh's New York Society—based on the decades-old English Society of a similar name—was the first of the independent American chapters that quickly sprouted up across the United States in the late nineteenth century—especially in cities. But the regional Societies took pride in the humane movement's national expansion, publishing lists of city, county, and state organizations in their annual reports in ways that suggested an evangelical impulse and an imagined geography of progress and civilization that was advancing across the United States and around the world.

These regional American SPCAs were loosely affiliated. Each was committed to animal welfare and an underlying agenda of social reform, but the humane organizations pursued their independent agendas in different ways. Each SPCA and Humane Society had separate leadership and administration, separate boards of directors, separate priorities and agendas on animal welfare, and separate legal jurisdictions typically limited to the city, county, or state in which they were chartered. The American Humane Association, founded in 1877, sought greater coordination across regional SPCAs and Humane Societies in the late 1870s, but there was still a large degree of regional autonomy.[39]

By 1874—when the Walker cider shop case went to court in New York City—there were over fifty branches of the SPCA in over twenty-five states, a number

FIGURE 5.4 Henry Bergh, founder and president of the American Society for the Prevention of Cruelty to Animals in New York. Library of Congress.

that would grow to nearly three hundred animal protection organizations across American states and territories by 1900.[40] These Societies pushed through state and city laws—often leaning on political friendships—and most chapters gained some form of police power to enforce a variety of new laws. As in the case of San Francisco (discussed in Chapter 4), many Societies employed agents or officers to police cities on their own terms. Cities and states readily handed over police power to SPCAs, which, in turn, offered to enforce and prosecute the new laws at no additional expense to taxpayers. In 1873, New York State alone had over fifty officers of the SPCA, with some capacity to enforce the growing set of animal cruelty laws.[41]

By the early 1870s, Henry Bergh had become one of the most famous New Yorkers, and had even begun to develop national notoriety. The New York press covered Bergh endlessly—sometimes praising and sometimes mocking the eccentric president of the ASPCA. "Since Horace Greeley's death, no figure more familiar to the public has walked the streets of the metropolis," wrote one observer of Bergh in 1879.[42] Part of Bergh's fame came from his notable physical appearance. At six feet in height, he towered above his fellow New Yorkers, and walked the streets with a "slow, slightly swinging pace peculiar to himself." He was a thin man—a "spare yet sinewy figure"—with a "long, solemn" face, downward-sweeping hair, a thin nose, sleepy eyes, and a "drooping moustache" that, in pictures, created the illusion of a permanent frown. Bergh was, in some ways, the embodiment of Victorian privilege and its fixation on suffering. Armed with a police badge, a top hat, and the financial security of his father's massive shipbuilding fortune, Bergh spent most of his days standing on street corners, flashing his badge, and stopping drivers and informing them of their ignorant cruelties to horses. He demanded that drivers lighten their loads, rest and water their animals, and attend to their wounds—and he did so with the threat of a fine and arrest—powers he was unafraid to use.[43]

In its first few years, Bergh's ASPCA paid surprisingly little attention to the many dogs that inhabited New York City. The ASPCA's earliest efforts focused deliberately on the treatment of animals used for transportation and food. Bergh and the ASPCA sought to end the practice of transporting sheep and calves by tying their legs and stacking them alive in carts. The ASPCA also used its legislative and police powers to end the common practice of plucking fowl alive. In its first years, Bergh's Society brought public attention to the cruel manner of transporting hundreds of thousands of live turtles each year, which were imported as food for New Yorkers. Their "fins pierced and tied," turtles were thrown into stifling ship holds, "lying for weeks on their backs without nourishment" as they made the trip from the "Tropics" to northern markets.[44] This focus on improving conditions for animals used for food was common not only in early ASPCA efforts in New York, but also in similar organizations across the United States, including San Francisco.[45]

Like most American SPCAs in the 1860s and 1870s, the ASPCA also focused its early efforts on improving the lives of tens of thousands of horses in New York City. Bergh's Society constantly battled the overloading of horse-drawn carts, omnibuses, and railroad cars that moved a growing volume of people and goods throughout the expanding city. Beyond the immediate suffering of overloaded and lame horses, the ASPCA also sought to improve the quality of roads and pavements that caused a slow and steady degradation and suffering of horses. They also worked to improve the purity of horse feed, which—like human food—was often adulterated with additives like plaster of paris, which reformers said caused intestinal problems and sometimes death. The population of urban horses grew dramatically over the course of the nineteenth century, as horses moved all sorts of goods across expanding cities. The growth of urban horse populations likely made animal suffering more visible to a growing number of Americans. Like the San Francisco SPCA, the New York ASPCA spent most of its energy and resources in the last decades of the nineteenth century trying to lessen the suffering of the urban horse.[46]

===

Amid this early push to improve the lives of animals, relatively little was said about dogs. Although dogfights were targeted as examples of "wanton cruelty" that caused the suffering of animals for the degrading pleasure of humans, the ASPCA's early spotlight rarely shone on the plight of canines. Prosecution records bear this out: in the ASPCA's first year, ending in 1867, only 4 of 110 cases prosecuted (3.6 percent) involved dogs. In the next year, only 19 of 266 cases (7.1 percent) involved dogs—with many of those 19 cases related to charges of dogfighting. In the year ending on March 31, 1870, only 8 of 369 cases (2.2 percent) involved canines. Dogs were noticeably absent from the early annual reports of the ASPCA.[47]

The absence of dogs in the ASPCA's first years seems to have been a deliberate choice. "There are certain creatures," said Bergh, that "the public have long regarded as unworthy of consideration. Among such are the turtle and many other animals, not large enough, or handsome enough, or sufficiently domesticated to be entitled to sympathy." Culturally and socially, dogs already enjoyed some degree of esteem among most New Yorkers—respect that typically resulted in favorable treatment and better status than that received by other creatures. It was the less charismatic creatures, argued Bergh, that most needed the protection of the Society.[48]

In many ways, it seems Bergh was less motivated by a deep affection for animals than by a keen sensitivity to animal suffering. By one account, Bergh recoiled at the affections of a small dog before telling its owner, "I don't like dogs."[49] By another account, Bergh was a man of "rueful countenance" who merely tolerated his wife's pet terrier. Typical of a man of his wealth, Bergh owned a Dalmatian to run alongside his carriage horses—a common practice to ward of stray dogs and to keep the horses calm. With Bergh as president, the ASPCA would seek to diminish animal suffering for a variety of species, and would not prioritize the suffering of dogs above that of the turtles or the nameless cattle that suffered on boats and trains on their way to urban markets.[50]

Although the ASPCA in New York was the first American organization of its kind, other SPCAs soon emerged in the United States. In 1867, regional SPCAs sprouted up in Brooklyn and Buffalo. In 1868, Philadelphia, Massachusetts, and San Francisco formed their own independent Societies. The origin stories of these

Societies read like narratives of enlightenment or conversion. In Boston, George Thorndike Angell was inspired to start the Massachusetts SPCA (MSPCA) after learning of a forty-mile horse race from Boston to Worcester in February 1868, which left both horses driven to exhaustion and dead in the road. Angell, a lawyer, was astonished and outraged to learn that the drivers had broken no law.[51] He formed the MSPCA that same year. In San Francisco, James Hutchinson, a banker, witnessed a cowboy—a vaquero—tie a stubborn pig to a horse cart and drag the animal by its legs over the cobblestone streets. He intervened to stop the cruelty and, soon after, established the San Francisco SPCA.[52] Few, if any, of these compelling origin stories were concerned with pets. Rather, they sought protection for the vast number of working animals and livestock that inhabited and passed through cities, and whose bodies and lives were sacrificed for the convenience and sustenance of people.

The emergence of SPCAs also coincided with the growth of pet ownership and pet culture in ways that marked their interconnectivity. While Bergh noted that dogs enjoyed some degree of status in society, American pet culture was largely in the process of development in the mid- to late nineteenth century. It was not until the 1860s that dog shows appeared regularly in the United States, and not until 1884 that the American Kennel Club would be established.[53] The end of the nineteenth century was the period in which breeds became rigidly categorized and regulated.[54] At the time that the first SPCAs were established, popular pet culture was not as widespread as it would become by the turn of the twentieth century.[55]

As new Societies were organized, differences emerged over animal welfare ideologies and approaches to reform—and over the status of centrality of dogs within the movement. Whereas the ASPCA in New York seemed to give dogs no special attention in the organization's first years, dogs were more central to other Societies' approaches to animal welfare. In particular, George Angell's Massachusetts SPCA began forging a larger culture and ideology of animal welfare that promoted animal kindness and pet ownership. Angell's MSPCA quickly became the intellectual and cultural center of the movement, producing millions of copies of a monthly publication called *Our Dumb Animals*, which the MSPCA shipped to emerging societies across the country. Within its first year, the MSPCA printed 260,000 copies of its publication, with many thousands circulating across New England and beyond. Of that initial distribution, 1,000 copies were sent to New York, 1,000 to Philadelphia, and a "considerable number" to cities in the American West and around the world.[56]

Angell's approach to effecting social change and improving animal welfare was fundamentally different from Bergh's. Whereas Bergh spent his days standing on street corners and using the Society's police and prosecutorial powers, Angell spent his days at a desk and on the lecture circuit. By the 1870s, Bergh's Society was prosecuting hundreds of cases per year—statistics that featured prominently in the ASPCA's Annual Reports as evidence of the movement's work and success. Angell's Society, on the other hand, rarely published data showing its prosecutions, even though such records existed. For the MSPCA the numbers of prosecutions and convictions were not indicators of success; rather, they were a necessary evil—a temporary solution until educational and cultural reform could effectively remake society from the bottom up. To reformers like Angell, arrests and prosecutions attested to the organization's own failures to prevent cruelty from happening in the first place. "Law is important, and prosecutions a necessary part of its machinery," declared Angell's *Our Dumb Animals* in its fourth issue, "but when we can enlist the writers, the poets and the orators, the men and women who make the ballads and sing the songs of the nation, then will come such a revolution as humanity has never witnessed." Under Angell's leadership, the MSPCA was attempting to remake society through the production of a culture of kindness—a culture that relied, fundamentally, on human relationships with pets, particularly dogs.[57]

The differences between the MSPCA and ASPCA models of reform were visible to contemporary observers. In 1870, the *New York Times* noted that, while Bergh's ASPCA was working primarily through Police Courts, its Boston counterpart was pursuing a more "advanced" type of reform that supposedly engaged philanthropists, philosophers, and poets in creating a "programme of work" that "the Bostonians regard as a triumph of social science, destined not only to save our dumb animals from abuse, but to strike at the foundations of society."[58] The Boston approach did not completely disavow punishment or prosecution, but it relied primarily on a concept of "humane education" to reform society in a gradual and permanent way by educating a future generation to become kind and empathetic adults. "We shall strive to prevent rather than punish," was the Massachusetts SPCA's motto, and their pursuit of that goal was threefold: "to protect dumb animals," to "convert human brutes into merciful men," and to "educate the children" in humane ways. "We must educate the children," emphasized the MSPCA: "We must create a great public opinion. We must wake up the Pulpit and Press, and scatter the literature of humanity until it shall be read in the homes, taught in the schools, hung upon the walls, and all the children of the State shall feel that these animals have been mercifully given us to use, but not to abuse."[59] In its large, poetic claims for the centrality and urgency of improving relationships with animals, MSPCA literature offered a vision of a different form of political change distinct from Bergh's ASPCA.

For Angell and his followers in Boston, the MSPCA was striving to do something quite radical: to completely remake society through education and new forms of culture. Angell saw animal protection as a centerpiece of a much larger social agenda. Spreading "humane literature and education into all the schools of the country" he wrote, would "not only insure the protection of animals, but also the prevention of crime, unnecessary wars, and forms of violence."[60] It was a movement that had the potential to "unite all religious and political parties on one platform" and might lead to "the abolition of war and the brotherhood of man."[61] Angell carried this message to an international audience, arguing in Zurich in 1869 that when the "leading minds of all nations" come together to support humane education "wars between nations will end."[62] Angell went to the grave believing that humane education—and its linchpin of childhood relationships of kindness toward animals—would save humanity. He died in 1909, humanely spared the horrors of World War I.

To effect their ambitious program, Angell and the MSPCA focused their efforts on cultivating kindness in society through the production of culture—particularly through the publication of *Our Dumb Animals*. The *New York Times* called *Our Dumb Animals* the "first publication of the kind in the world for general circulation," and a "journalistic enterprise" that sought to spread "humane education," through "stories, paragraphs, poetry and pictures, illustrating the beauty of kindness to animals addressed in general of the young."[63] In contrast to the ASPCA's Annual Reports, *Our Dumb Animals* consistently devoted large parts of the publication to stories about pets, and dogs in particular.

At first, the ASPCA in New York resisted the MSPCA's soft, intellectual approach to a problem they saw as one of law and order. Angell and Bergh had little to do with each other. They rarely collaborated or corresponded, despite being the two most prominent figures in the animal welfare movement in North America. The *New York Times* argued that a high-minded method of reform might work in the intellectual Hub of Boston, but that the "vicious classes of this great world-maelstrom" of New York City would hardly respond to such an approach. New York "is not to be controlled so easily" as Massachusetts, said the *Times*. In New York, "Pamphlet propagandism would not go far among swill-milk merchants," said the *Times*, "and it is to be feared that neither dog pit frequenters nor railroad corporations are to be reached through the Sunday schools."[64] For the writer in the *Times*, the soft social and cultural reforms developed in Boston—that intellectual "Hub" of the universe—hardly stood a chance with the hardscrabble, greedy, and corrupt individuals who saw profits in animal cruelty in New York.

In Boston, Angell continued to develop these distinct methods of social reform, which brought women and children into politics in important ways. Whereas New York relied on a heavy-handed, masculine, male-dominated politics of arrests, trials, fines, and imprisonment, Boston sought to promote a different sort of politics that played to the distinctive roles of women as mothers, educators of young children, and guardians of the domestic sphere who were uniquely situated to teach empathy and kindness to a new generation. Massachusetts was not alone in emphasizing the important place of women within the movement. In Philadelphia, Caroline Earle White stepped forward as a local and national leader of the humane movement, and in cities across the United States women played essential roles in the emergence of SPCAs and humane education. "It is safe to say that were the support of the women of America suddenly withdrawn, the large majority of societies for the prevention of cruelty to children and animals would cease to exist," wrote an early historian of the humane movement in 1924.[65] The active role of women seemed to mark American Societies in important ways. George Angell believed it was the participation of women in such high numbers that distinguished the American humane movement from the English and European models. Although Americans had imported many of the ideas and structures of the English and European anticruelty Societies, by the late 1860s, they were exporting a new form of politics of their own. Angell proudly touted his role in assisting the women of London to organize the Ladies' Humane Educational Committee when he traveled there in 1869.[66]

At the core of the differences between the approaches of the Boston and New York Societies was a fundamental debate about human nature itself: Was the most effective way to reform society through punishment and fear, or was it through positive reinforcement and cultivation of certain ideas, sentiments, and social customs? For Bergh, society needed to be coerced and compelled into humane behaviors through laws and enforcement. For Angell, change was gradual and behavioral. Dogs mattered little for Bergh's method of social reform, but they were foundational to the cultivation of kindness that was so central to Angell's agenda. Nowhere was Angell's positive concept of animal relationships more pertinent than in the promotion of the dog as a domestic pet, to be cared for and loved within the home. Beginning in the late 1860s, the humane education branch of the animal welfare movement began a long process of converting the dog into a central figure of social reform. But cultivating dogs as agents of friendship and kindness also presented an ideological challenge to the use of dogs that did not fit these values. Dogs in machines and dogs that were harnessed to carts did not fit the emerging ideals of dogs as companions, friends, and pets.

=====

Although not central to the first years of the ASPCA, dogs were nevertheless part of an urban animal population that fell under humane laws and enforcement in New York in the late 1860s and early 1870s. Bergh's ASPCA received an expansive charter in 1866 that gave it special use of police forces across the state, to "aid the Society, its members or agents" in enforcing all laws "for the protection of dumb animals."[67] Two weeks after granting the Society's charter, on April 19, 1866, the New York state legislature passed An Act Better to Prevent Cruelty to Animals, a short but expansive statement prohibiting animal cruelty. The words of the act stated clearly that those who "neglect, maliciously kill, maim, wound, injure, torture, or cruelly beat any horse, mule, ox, cattle, sheep, or other animal belonging to himself or another, shall, upon conviction, be adjudged guilty of a misdemeanor." Though some animals were listed specifically by name, dogs were not. Canines fell into the broad category of "other animal." When Walker went to trial years later, he was charged with violating this law and its broad application.[68]

In April 1867, the ASPCA expanded its lobby in Albany and gained a more extensive law composed of ten sections. This time dogs were mentioned specifically, but only in one part of the law, section 6, which required licenses for dogs used "for the purpose of drawing or helping to draw any cart, carriage, truck, barrow, or other vehicle." Licensing was left to the discretion of a city's mayor, or village "president." Dog cart owners operating without a license would pay $1 for the first offense, and $10 for each subsequent offense—a sum that must have seemed unimaginable to ragpickers, who may typically have paid less than $5 per month in rent.[69] A month after the passage of the new law, in June 1867, New York City police rounded up more than fifty ragpickers and brought them to City Hall Park. *Harper's Weekly* derisively called the event a "convention of chiffoniers." The ragpickers had no licenses for their dog carts and were in violation of the new law.[70]

Although the enforcement record is unclear, it appears that new laws regulating the harnessing of dogs were effective. Later observations of the ragpicker settlements near downtown suggest a decline in the use of dogs among the city's poor, particularly those living in tenements. By the late 1870s, the depictions of the ragpickers' apartments rarely, if ever, included descriptions of the dogs that were once a staple of these same observational accounts in the 1850s, suggesting that the practice of keeping dogs for pulling carts was in decline among those living in downtown tenements.[71] When *Harper's* ran a story on ragpickers and their tenement dwellings in 1879, they meticulously mentioned all manners of

FIGURE 5.5 "Arrested Rag-Pickers in City Hall Park, New York." From *Harper's Weekly,* July 6, 1867. Library of Congress.

"filth" and "wretchedness" that characterized the tenements. Missing from the description and artistic sketches—where one would expect to find them—were working dogs of any kind.[72] An article on the city's Italian population in 1884 noted that they had supplanted Germans as the primary scavengers of the city refuse, having "driven out the old-time German men and women, who were such a feature and familiar sight some fifteen years ago." The Italian women were known for their peculiar style of carrying large loads of items "balanced upon the head, having been taught to be bearers of burdens from their youth." The German ragpickers and their dog carts had been "driven to the wall," "like many another ancient institutions."[73] The ragpicker's dog cart was a fading part of life in downtown New York by 1880.

═══

Where working dogs and dog carts did seem to remain in the lives of poor New Yorkers was in the sprawling shantytowns on the distant fringes of the city near

Central Park. Dogs joined a variety of other species in parts of the city that were distant from law enforcement, urban reformers, and wealthy residents. "The dog is the goat's only rival as the typical animal of the colony," said *Scribner's* about a part of the city called Shantytown in 1880. The animals themselves once again stood in for the strained social relationships within the city: "The dog in Shantytown," *Scribner's* continued, was "everything that is vile, degraded and low in canine nature. In him survives the native savagery of the wolf, blent with an abnormal cunning learnt from association with men." The dogs on the outskirts of New York City also continued to pull the carts of ragpickers, but did so largely out of sight of ASPCA agents and police officers downtown.[74] Like many unwanted or unpleasant forms of animal labor and suffering, dog carts were not utterly eliminated from New York City, but they were no longer as much a part of downtown urban life.

The apparent decline of dog power in the late nineteenth century coincided with notable efforts of the ASPCA and public officials to eliminate the practice through laws and policing—though the decline may also have been related to shifting cultural practices as Italians replaced German immigrants as the predominant group of ragpickers. By the 1890s, "dog carts" were no longer associated with the city's poorest residents, but were lightweight carriages attached to horses and used as sports cars of the city's wealthy residents. In 1880, *Scribner's* celebrated the decline of some of the squatter colonies in the uptown area, which was becoming "graded, curbed, and paved," with its "whitewashed cabins" giving way to "six-story mansions." The old dog carts were also giving way to the new: "The aristocratic anglo-maniac's dog cart has replaced the rag-picker's," they noted.[75] Although called "dog carts," the lightweight carriages were not usually pulled by dogs, and were attached instead to horses to give wealthy residents a fast and thrilling ride.[76] City streets had been largely cleansed of the ragpicker's dog cart and made safe for the "aristocrat's."

"Dog Days"

Although Bergh's ASPCA showed little interest in dogs in the late 1860s, the organization was rapidly changing and shaped by the broader urban animal landscape and the national and international humane movement. One indication of this new interest in dogs was the ASPCA's growing involvement in the ongoing problems of stray dogs and rabies. A particularly bad rabies scare in the early 1870s sent New York into a frenzy. For years the city had imposed "dog laws" during the summer months, known casually as the "dog days," when dogs were believed to be most susceptible to rabies—a misconception based on the fact that dogs salivate and pant more in the summer, suggesting symptoms of rabies. In 1854, a fairly typical year, the city ordered more than two thousand dogs killed between June 26 and August 15 alone, in what was often a messy and brutal process. Much of this work was done by men and boys with clubs.[77]

Roundups were not evenly enforced among breeds. The city paid only 25 cents for smaller dogs. Valuable purebred dogs were treated differently once impounded. "Whenever a really valuable dog is found he is put aside and kept for sale," whereas the "curs" were tossed into the cistern at 5:30 each day, two hundred at a time, and sprayed with a hose. "To those on top the cooling bath must have been a temporary relief, and they seemed rather to enjoy it," but as the "water rose higher, the yelps became fainter and fainter, and in a short time all was still."[78] More valuable dogs were often spared this fate, as poundkeepers set them aside for wealthy owners who redeemed their animals at a premium.

Reformers saw these scenes of brutality—of public clubbings and drownings—as cruel to the animals and also degrading to the public good and social order. As dogs became pets and the foundation of humane education and kindness, these visible scenes of suffering dogs would not be tolerated. The New York ASPCA became involved in the reform of the dog laws in the 1870s, first banning payments to children for the collection of strays in 1873, then, in 1875, successfully lobbying for the repeal of the dog bounty law altogether. A key feature of early reforms of the ASPCA and other urban SPCAs was to remove children from the economy of killing dogs, and to spare them "the frightful scenes of bloodshed and cruelty" that were part of urban dog catching and killing, particularly during rabies scares.[79]

In Boston, fears over dogs even reached a point where the city considered an outright ban on canines. As new laws imposed greater restrictions on other urban animal species, it was not clear that dogs would survive as a significant population in the city. In 1878, the Massachusetts legislature sought to impose an expensive tax of $10 dollars on every male dog and $20 on every female dog. George Angell and others came to the defense of dogs, testifying on Beacon Hill that the "dog haters"—not least of whom were agriculturalists who wanted to protect their sheep—were taking advantage of the rabies scare of the previous summer to try to eliminate dogs from the city. Angell testified before a packed committee room of over two hundred people and argued that dogs deserved a place in the city because of their special relationship with people. In one notable portion of his testimony, he read a story of three small children trapped in a snowdrift who were saved by a dog. For Angell and others, the possibility that dogs might be eliminated from everyday life was not only troubling, but posed a mortal threat to the very ideology and reforms that promised to save civilization. The Massachusetts dog tax failed to pass, and other attacks on Boston's dog population, particularly in the 1870s, generally failed amid Angell's staunch opposition.[80] Angell's humane ideology required that dogs be part of everyday urban life as agents to cultivate human kindness and affection.

Bergh was somewhat slow to adopt Angell's embrace of dogs. Bergh himself did not so much love dogs as he despised suffering. In fact, in the case involving the Walker cider shop, Bergh had passed the shop numerous times, and had even stepped inside. But Bergh saw no problem. It was not until he began receiving letters from constituents that he began to confront Walker more seriously. By the 1870s, despite Bergh's own inclinations, the New York Society was caring more about the plight of urban dogs. As thousands of copies of the MSPCA's *Our Dumb Animals* flooded into New York, Bergh's Society no doubt felt the influence of the powerful ideology of humane education. Dogs became an increasingly important part of the ASPCA's everyday operations.

The People vs. Charles W. Walker

Amid these many debates and tensions over the appropriate role of dogs in American cities, Charles Walker appeared before the New York City Court of Special Sessions in October 1874. Walker's case had been delayed since his arrest in May, on account of his poor health. When the court heard the case in October, the courtroom became something of a local spectacle, "crowded with interested parties," including aldermen and notable city residents, and complete with a roster of celebrity witnesses on both sides, including prominent lawyers, Henry Bergh himself, the powerful city recorder John Hackett, and former mayors A. Oakey Hall and Daniel F. Tiemann. Important and prominent New Yorkers took time to engage in a hearty debate over the very meaning of dogs.

The case brought together some of the city's most powerful figures, but the incident at trial involved a little-known lawyer who made a complaint against a little-known cider maker. The lawyer, James Goodrich, was walking past the Walker cider shop on May 13, 1874, when, according to his testimony, he saw a bulldog working a treadmill, "tied up by his collar to the front of the mill he was treading." The dog, which Goodrich had seen before, seemed "very much exhausted, and his mouth was running." Whenever the animal tried to stop, said Goodrich, "the collar drew so hard on his neck that he had to start again." The underside of the dog's neck "was discolored with blood where the collar had chafed it."[81]

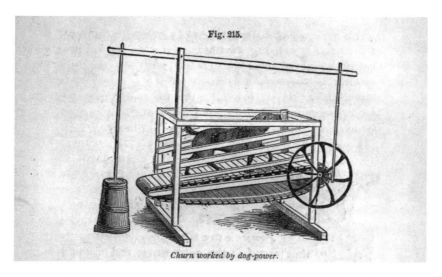

Fig. 215.

Churn worked by dog-power.

FIGURE 5.6 A dog treadmill operating on the "endless chain" principle, similar to the machine used at Walker's shop. 1854. John Jacob Thomas, *Farm Implements, and the Principles of Their Construction and Use* (New York: Harper, 1854), 165.

Goodrich took his complaint to Judge Wandell on May 18, and the next day Walker was arrested and arraigned.

Goodrich was not listed as a member of the ASPCA, nor did he leave much of a historical paper trail. The same was true of Walker, who was a shopkeeper and cider maker apparently of ordinary means. But as Charles Walker entered the courtroom that October, his case had become something larger than life; the witnesses for Bergh's ASPCA attested to his Society's powerful connections to the social and political elite of New York City. Bergh had friends in high places, and they turned out in force to testify in a seemingly ordinary case.

The prosecution sought to prove not only that Walker's dogs were treated cruelly in that particular case but also that dog machine labor in general was a form of animal cruelty. Goodrich was the first to testify as an eyewitness to the case at hand—and told the court that the dog suffered from exhaustion and injury. Goodrich's testimony was corroborated by two others, including the Society's salaried veterinary doctor, William Ennever. Former mayor A. Oakey Hall and city recorder John Hackett testified that they had passed the cider shop together that May and had also seen a Newfoundland dog on the treadmill, who looked "very much distressed."[82] The prosecution's witnesses all testified that they saw all the outward, bodily signs of cruelty: apparent fatigue, excessive salivation, abrasions, and blood—and the appearance of "distress" and sickness. Although, as "dumb animals," dogs could not testify, their bodies took on greater significance as testimony of suffering. A city judge named Butler Bixby also joined the others in testifying that the Walker cider press had long used dog power, and that the dogs they used often looked "overworked" and seemed to be "suffering considerably."[83]

Among the most notable witnesses for the prosecution was recorder John Hackett. As recorder—a position rooted in New York's royal government and eliminated in 1907—Hackett stood at the center of New York City politics: he was on the Board of Supervisors (second only to the mayor); he sat as a judge in General Court; and he served as a member of the Police Board. He also participated as a voting member of other financial, executive, and legal institutions of the city and state. Hackett was a large man with a "well-knit and sturdy frame," and the separation of city powers was, quite often, no greater than the width of his broad shoulders.[84]

The prosecution called Hackett as a dog expert. And in certain ways he was. Hackett was among the "grand lot of sportsmen" who "trained their dogs, till there was hardly a more beautiful sight," said the editor of *Forest and Stream*.[85] He was considered one of New York's "keen sportsmen and excellent shots," and was a founding member of the elite South Side Sportsmen's Club of Long Island, where he served as president from 1868 to 1879.[86] The editor of *Forest and Stream* called Hackett "the most perfect shot whether with gun or pistol, who lived in my time."[87] Hackett was known for his "extraordinary exhibitions of marksmanship" that were mythologized by the New York press. He "knocked off chippy birds' heads and shot holes through coins thrown into the air or held by some trustful friends," including his own wife. But his favorite trick was to shoot the ashes off a gentleman's cigar as he "sat placidly puffing away in an armchair" at the Sportsmen's Club.[88] In short, Hackett was a gentleman.

As an eyewitness to the Walker dog machine, and an expert in breeding and training hunting dogs, Hackett testified on behalf of the ASPCA to claim that Walker's dogs were treated cruelly. Despite his support for the prosecution, Hackett was not a member of the ASPCA—in fact, he later butted heads with Bergh's organization over its intervention in pigeon shooting, fox hunting, and other animal cruelties related to sporting activities. Nevertheless, Hackett was willing to testify that Walker's use of a dog in a machine was cruel, "by his breathing, and his appearance in a thousand ways, to a man accustomed to dogs." The dog he saw in the cider press, he concluded, was "in great distress."[89]

Although Hackett never argued that there was inherent cruelty in using a dog to turn a machine, his testimony spoke to a cultural division and an objection to using dogs to power machines as beasts of burden. Hackett was not categorically opposed to putting dogs to work, but dog labor of this kind—repetitive and laborious—stood in sharp contrast to his own idealized understanding of dog labor. For sportsmen like Hackett, machine work was a perversion of a dog's higher skills and abilities. In court, Hackett spoke of his own relationships with dogs, "exercising them generally; playing with them; shooting with them; hunting with them, etc." Hunting and sport were activities constructed in opposition to menial human labor and urban life, but used skilled work in nature as a form of leisure.[90] Hackett and other sportsmen relied on dog labor to simulate a purer, higher form of work that was not commercially driven and that constituted an idealized working relationship with dogs. Hackett's relationships with dogs occurred outside the commercial marketplace and in the fields and streams of the Long Island countryside—far from the cities that contained degraded human populations and their downtrodden curs.

The idealized forms of dog labor Hackett appreciated contained its own forms of cruelty that he and others often overlooked. In idealizing his own relationship with dogs, Hackett and other breeders believed they were doing important work in producing higher orders of animals. Hackett testified that he had owned three- or four hundred dogs in his lifetime. To get the numbers and characteristics they desired, breeders like Hackett participated in experiments with dogs perhaps as novel as the dog machines themselves. Dogs were a sort of technology, too. Breeding for recessive traits required accelerating the generational passage of time, such that an owner like Hackett could own three- or four hundred dogs. Breeders sought to refine traits and characteristics through generations of canine bodies.

This process of creating and reinforcing breeds could at time be grisly. Breeders killed off a large percentage of puppies that were failed experiments—animals that did not carry the desired traits, were deformed from inbreeding, or simply part of a litter that was too large. Breeding was a constant grind against forces of biological diversity, and likely caused another sort of cruelty rarely, if ever, challenged by the nascent SPCA. George Washington, a famous breeder of his generation, was known to drown many of his experimental breeds.[91] One breeding book from 1891 instructed breeders to "examine the puppies; harden your heart, and decide which are to be given to the bucket and which to the world."[92] As a result of intensive breeding, many breeds became saddled with various chronic ailments and diminished quality of life. Hackett himself was, perhaps, blinded to these cruelties out of a belief that he was giving to himself and the world a higher order of animal and a more perfect form of nature.[93]

Hackett joined a growing number of sportsmen of his generation who celebrated skilled forms of dog labor. It seems likely that Hackett would have been familiar with the canine legends that circulated in sporting circles, and which celebrated the breeding culture among elite hunters. In 1876, *Forest and Stream* ran a story about a setter named Old Grouse. By then, Old Grouse was widely known in sporting circles as one of the finest and most prolific setters in the world. The story of Old Grouse—as it was told in 1876—began back in 1838, when a group of hunters came across a cabinetmaker named Taylor in Lambertville, New Jersey. The man had been using a team of dogs to run a small machine that powered his lathe. Two of the dogs were "of mongrel breed." But what really concerned the hunters was that Taylor was also using a purebred setter to power his machine. *Forest and Stream* described the dog in obsessive detail: a "full-sized, heavy moulded liver and white *double*-nosed setter, the liver color in some places shading to something of a tan; legs, indistinctly ticked; head, rather short; eyes, rather light, but exceedingly bright; ears, well set; tail, straight; back, short; and legs and feet good, and altogether presenting the appearance of a well-bred, serviceable setter." It was the archetype of its breed. But its use on a treadmill was a desecration of the animal, the breed, and the owner himself.[94] The mythology of Old Grouse ended in a story of redemption for the noble dog, with the sportsman cast in the role of hero. One of the hunters paid Taylor to liberate Old Grouse from the machine, where his work was once again elevated to its highest ideal in the hunting world. His vast progeny would go on to work alongside sporting men for decades to come. "It would be hard to convince us that any dog ever produced better dogs than were the descendants of Old Grouse," said *Forest and Stream*.[95]

Whether or not the story of Old Grouse was true, it spoke to social and cultural tensions that played out through relationships with dogs. Sportsmen celebrated the Old Grouse tale as an American liberation and redemption story: plucked from the countryside and saved from mindless monotony and hard mechanical labor, Old Grouse saw a rebirth into a life that allowed him to live out his true calling, and to fully use his senses and intelligence for higher purposes. No longer forced to toil for the profits of his owner, Old Grouse went about another sort of work that was true to his intellectual and physical strengths. The sportsmen who celebrated skilled dog work would "never forget the old fellow."[96] They saw in Old Grouse what they wished for themselves and their society.

But not all dogs could move up the canine hierarchy in the same way that Old Grouse did. There was something deeply predetermined about Old Grouse's story that resided in his own physical, genetic makeup. For those who idealized Old Grouse's story, it mattered little that the other dogs at Taylor's farm were left to toil in the sawmill because their nature limited their status and purpose. For many sportsmen and dog breeders, only certain animals had a higher calling. "Mongrel" dogs had no higher purpose. At Walker's trial, it was no triviality that many of the witnesses who complained about the treatment of Walker's machine dogs mentioned their breeds: a Newfoundland, a Mastiff, and a Bulldog—valuable breeds designed by people for purposes other than turning a wheel. The curs that worked mills rarely got the same attention or provoked the same outrage as their purebred brethren.

Hackett's testimony and perspective as a sportsman reflected one idealized form of human relationships with dogs in New York—and one that was likely common among sporting men who held elite and powerful positions within the city, even as they spent large amounts of their time in the forests and rivers of the countryside. Henry Bergh was not a sporting man—far from it—and he would later butt heads with elite sportsmen over the course of his tenure as president of the ASPCA. The network of SPCAs and humane education, in fact, came to idealize the care of curs as part of their ethic of kindness. Many SPCA publications expressed pity and sympathy for mixed-breed curs and street dogs—including *Beautiful Joe,* a story narrated by a cur that escaped abuse because of the kindness of a child. The book was second only to *Black Beauty* as a staple of childhood literature and humane education. It was dedicated to George Angell and sold hundreds of thousands of copies.[97] To evoke pity and inspire the most profound expressions of kindness, curs joined other breeds as valued symbols of the humane movement.

Although Bergh believed in focusing the ASPCA's attention on a variety of species—even prioritizing other species over canines—he did hold a rather rigid concept of dogs and dog labor. Horses, he said in testimony, "are beasts of burden in contradistinction to the dog, which is not a beast of burden." It was breeding and human intervention that made dogs what they were and were not. To put a dog in a job that he was not designed to do amounted inherently to a form of cruelty, argued Bergh in the Walker case. In court, the defense pressed Bergh to defend his position, "Would it be any more cruelty for the dog to work than for the horse?" Bergh replied, "Yes sir, certainly," stating in clear terms that the dog was not designed to do menial work.[98] Disrupting the order of animal labor itself amounted to a form of cruelty and signaled underlying social and cultural disorder.

Despite his willingness to testify in the case, Bergh showed signs of his own ambivalence and that he was serving less his own interests than the broader interests of other SPCA members in prosecuting the Walker case. When pressed by the defense, Bergh admitted that he had visited the Walker press before and had been aware that dogs worked in the machine—even admitting that he believed it was not "so cruel as persons thought."[99] At trial, the defense attorney suggested that Bergh had initially asked Walker to simply conceal the dog labor, to "put the dog to the same work, but put him out of sight."[100] Bergh denied that he had made any such request, but his ambivalence and uncertainty about the dog machine was clear from his testimony and the larger context of his work at the ASPCA. If Bergh did suggest concealing rather than eliminating what many believed was a cause of animal suffering, it would fit with a larger set of solutions that SPCAs often adopted out of convenience. If animal abuse harmed society in large part because of its visibility to people, as many humane leaders believed, then conducting the abuse out of sight was a practical compromise.

In contrast to Bergh's argument that dogs were not designed for heavy labor, the defense in the Walker trial sought to show that dog labor was commonplace and good. When used properly, the defense argued, dog labor benefited both people and animals. The defense did its best to depict Walker as a responsible and reasonable dog owner and manager. The prosecution had called some of the city's most highly regarded doctors, lawyers, and politicians to make its case. The defense countered with two star witnesses of its own, enlisting former mayor Daniel Tiemann and the prominent lawyer Cephas Brainerd. The workers at Walker's shop also testified about their experiences working alongside the dogs. With growing testimony on both sides, the question was, increasingly: Who could speak for the experience of the dogs themselves?

The defense sought to establish two facts: that dog labor in general was not inherently abusive, and that Walker's dogs, specifically, were well treated. The fact that the defense felt the need to explain the uses of dog power in court suggests that such uses were not universally known. The fact that the defense called prominent and respectable New Yorkers to show the benefits and uses of dog labor may also have been a way of confronting the stereotype that dog labor was associated with lower-class and working-class New Yorkers.

To prove that dog machine labor was respectable, the defense called former mayor Tiemann, who spoke to the "dog power question." Tiemann had a large industrial company on Twenty-Third Street and Fourth Avenue, and had long used dogs for "manufacturing paints and colors and pumping water." He testified that dog machines were "very easily worked," and did not pose serious burdens on animals. It was, he said, "no more labor for a dog to go up the incline of a hill than to go up that machine." Not only was dog labor harmless, he argued, but in many cases the exercise benefited the animals. In his own experience, dogs improved under the conditions of regular work; their limbs grew stronger and they became "heavier," "sleek," and "healthy."[101] When the dogs were tired, he said, they learned they could rest by lying down in a way that stopped the machines.

Given the broader historical context that emphasized a legal and moral concept of "consent," it perhaps comes as little surprise that a central question in the case was whether the dogs on Walker's treadmill were capable of giving consent

for the use of their labor. In many ways, the debate was reflective of those surrounding human labor. The "free labor ideology," constructed as it was in opposition to slavery, relied on a concept of consent, which, by the late nineteenth century,
was transformed into a discourse of "contract."[102] Dogs could not enter formal
contracts, but there was some question about whether they could express consent. Determining whether—and how—dogs could give their consent became a
key point at the Walker trial.

The prosecution argued that the dog had no choice in the use of his labor. He
was tied to the machine in a way that prevented him from stopping the treadmill
or escaping, forcing him to continue walking or else choke. The defense implicitly agreed that forcing an animal to work against its will would have been objectionable. But they also sought to show that Walker and his men never tied the
dogs to the machines in ways that forced the animals to labor against their will.
The dogs, the defense argued, were able to lie down to stop the machine whenever they wished, and, according to witnesses, they often did. Both sides agreed
that animals deserved some modicum of agency in the use of their labor.

But the defense went further and argued that dog machines were actually good
for the animals and often made for enjoyable work. Among the prominent witnesses for the defense was Cephas Brainerd, a New York lawyer involved in a variety of conservative reform efforts, who would go on to lead the expansion of
the YMCA in the late nineteenth century. Brainerd testified that the dogs in question were "sleek," "fat and comfortable," and showed no signs of abuse or over-
work. John McGinn, a police officer stationed in Walker's neighborhood, who
often watched the dogs work, testified that he "never thought they were in a suffering condition." If he had, he said, he "would have examined them."[103] Walker's
father and brothers spoke of the health of the animals, and even their apparent
enjoyment of the work. They testified that they had to put brakes on the machine
and wedge sticks in the mill to prevent the dogs from turning the treadmill at
night when the shop was closed.[104] The dogs, the defense claimed, enjoyed the
work and exercise of turning the press; they were free laborers in the cider shop.
Walker defended his practices even further by arguing that he employed dogs
that had been rescued from destitution. Acquiring them as "thin" and in "poor
health," Walker fed them well and restored them to "strong," "fat," and "sleek"
creatures.[105] In this ideal, Walker's paternalism mixed with the animals' own
agency in the creation of good and productive labor.

Others disagreed that the dogs were well treated or that they had agency in
their labor. The debates in court revealed a contradictory set of testimonies that
suggested coerced motivations of the people involved. Many witnesses were employees of Walker's, and likely had a financial interest in testifying on behalf of

their boss. The first witness, John Bolger had been arrested before on charges that he had pinched a dog "in the nuts," but the case had been discharged. Another witness for the defense, an African American man named Washington Williams, worked for Walker and appeared to have provided contradictory testimony—first testifying that the dogs were tied to the mill in such a way that they were forced to walk, but later saying that they could stop if they wished.[106] It was unclear what was actually happening at the Walker cider press. But the courtroom testimony revealed the stories that the Walkers and their workers told themselves about dog labor, and human labor in turn.[107]

The trial also blurred the distinction between dogs as laborers and dogs as pets. Charles Walker's father, William Walker, testified that he grew up on Sheriff Street—known as "rag-picker's row"—and he no doubt knew about the hundreds of dogs that pulled carts for scavengers. In his testimony, William Walker expressed an enthusiasm about dog labor and also about his dogs. He argued that dog power was not used merely in the "country," where it was most known, but also across the city. "We have used the dog power for ten or twelve years," he testified, and he had used dogs to grind apples and do other work "as long ago as I can remember."[108] William Walker also professed his love for the dogs that worked for him. He wistfully recounted one dog in particular, whom he remembered by having "a picture or profile of him in my house." William Walker said that dog could "grind nine barrels of apples in a day, himself alone," and that the dog loved the work so much that he "had to chain the mill to keep him out of it." William Walker claimed to speak for his dogs, whom he believed were well treated and content. Of course, the dogs never took the stand. But to William Walker and many who had working relationships with dogs, these relationships combined characteristics that the SPCA was seeking to split apart and control. William Walker imagined his relationship with dogs as paternalistic: he cared for them and they gave him productive labor in return. But he also valued their loyalty and affections, making the relationship a complex amalgamation of leisure and labor that clashed with the ASPCA's ideal relationship with dogs as pets.

Charles Walker's own testimony also showed his paternalistic belief that he both loved his dogs and valued their work. He testified that he had used dogs to turn the treadmill since 1869—the year when ragpickers were arrested for using dogs in their carts. Walker knew his dogs by name. The dog working the treadmill on that day in May 1874 was named Bounce, and was one of seven dogs that worked the mill, never longer than one hour at a time, according to Walker. Walker spoke of his adoption of Bounce as an act of benevolence. According to his testimony, Walker acquired Bounce in "terribly poor" condition, and had nursed him back to health and strength before putting him to work in the machine. Since the dog had stopped working in May—by order of the ASPCA—Bounce had gone from healthy and "sleek" to sickly. Walker said he took pride as a caretaker, even allowing his dogs to sleep in his bedroom. When his dogs got sick, he would give them good "meat from the Quaker Dairy" to help them recover. He admitted that his dogs were "worn with the collar," as the ASPCA alleged, but that there was "no mark or abrasion at all."[109]

But another important twist in the Walker case came out at trial. The dog machine was not all that it appeared to be. When Bergh visited Walker's shop in May 1874, he saw the dog in the window, working in the machine, turning an arm that extended beneath the floorboards into the basement below. Bergh entered the shop and asked to have a look around. As he descended the stairs to inspect the basement, he expected to see and hear the commotion of men making cider, and to smell crushed apples. What he found, instead, was surprising—"no apples, nothing but this endless ladder which turned the wheel down in the basement, and there was not an apple on the premises, nor was the machine doing any work at all."[110] The dogs toiled in futility. Walker testified that he did use dogs to press apples, but that when there was no work to be done, he put dogs in the machine, in the window, as a form of "advertisement."[111]

Perhaps this was the detail that changed Bergh's mind about prosecuting the case. He accepted some level of animal suffering when it was used toward productive ends or the sustenance of human life. In 1870s New York, some degree of animal suffering was an unavoidable part of everyday life. But animal suffering for entertainment, or advertising, was something entirely different; it was unnecessary, extravagant, and "wanton." There was a sort of pragmatism in this understanding of animal cruelty that existed in the midst of an animal-dependent economy—the belief that practical context mattered above the objective conditions of animals themselves. Although the new spate of laws in the 1860s increasingly sought to recognize objective conditions of animals as the basis of protection laws, there was still a great deal of social context and human intention that influenced Bergh and other SPCAs as to whether a case was worthy of prosecution.[112] For Bergh, a dog turning a treadmill was actionable cruelty only in the context of the human relationships and intentions that surrounded it. Animal suffering for entertainment and advertising was an unacceptable and unproductive form of animal suffering.

—

After a "few moments' deliberation," the three judges on the Court of Special Sessions found Walker guilty of animal cruelty and sentenced him to pay a steep fine of $25. When the State Supreme Court upheld the conviction later that year, they noted that dogs enjoyed no special status under the animal cruelty laws—a point belied by the unusually steep fine assessed by the lower court. "A dog, although not a beast of burden," said the Supreme Court "may lawfully be used upon a treadmill or in any other service employment; but if he is cruelly used, it becomes a crime."[113] It was a mixed opinion for the ASPCA: Walker's conviction was upheld, but the court also rejected the notion that a dog working in a machine was inherently cruel.

The conflict between Walker and the ASPCA did not end there, however. A month after the court of Special Sessions verdict, on November 21, 1874, the ASPCA's Veterinarian, Dr. Ennever, again intervened on behalf of the Society, directing the Society's deputy sheriff Timothy Kelly to arrest Joseph Bailey, an African American employee at Walker's shop. Ennever claimed that Bailey was "torturing" a Siberian Bloodhound by forcing him to turn the mill. Judge Kasmire, who was one of the three judges in the Walker case, ordered Bailey released after he spent a night in prison, saying that the charge of cruelty had not been proved.[114]

In the wake of the arrest, the Walker brothers were incensed at what they saw as continued harassment by the ASPCA. The Walkers supported Bailey in pursuing a lawsuit against the arresting officer, Timothy Kelly, for "felonious assault" with a deadly weapon and without legal authority. Kelly, they said, had made an unjust arrest without a warrant and used excessively "rough and violent" force against Bailey. The case was testing the limits of the ASPCA's police power, according to the *New York Herald,* and of great importance, "affecting as it does the entire community, a great portion of whom are frequently brought into unpleasant relations with Mr. Bergh's society."[115]

When the case came to Police Court in January 1875, many of the courtroom actors were the same as those who had convened for the Walker case only months before, but now in reverse roles; now sitting at the defense table was the ASPCA's attorney, Elbridge Gerry, who represented Officer Kelly, the defendant; the Walker family testified on behalf of Bailey; Henry Bergh attended the proceedings, at one point shouting from the gallery asking to be left out of the discussion; and Judge Kasmire presided. Key testimony came from James Deester, a boy who worked for Walker, and others who said that Kelly barged into the shop and demanded Bailey's arrest. When Bailey asked to see a warrant, Kelly pointed a pistol at him, purportedly saying, "This is my warrant," and threatening to shoot if he did not comply with the arrest.[116]

In his decision, Judge Kasmire ruled that the charge of pointing a pistol at Bailey had not been sufficiently proved, but that Kelly had exceeded his authority in making the arrest without a warrant in a case that showed "no probable cause for the arrest." Kasmire's ruling—the third of its kind—effectively limited the police power of the ASPCA. It went further by saying that Kelly, although deputized, was not specifically authorized as an agent to make arrests under the law of 1867 to prevent cruelty to animals, and was therefore trespassing. Kelly was held on a simple assault and battery charge, and the charge of felonious assault dismissed.[117] In this case, the court restrained the police powers of the ASPCA.

The ASPCA again quarreled with Charles Walker in October 1875, with the *New York Herald* running the headline "Bergh Again on the Rampage." This time Bergh brought the complaint himself, arguing before the Police Court that Walker had attached a dog to the treadmill with a rope around the animal's neck, preventing it from stopping the mill. Walker again denied the charges in court and accused Bergh of singling him out and using his Society to settle old scores. "I would like to ask," said Walker, "why Mr. Bergh does not pay any attention to several notifications he has received of dogs being worked in the same manner in an establishment in Mangin Street, where they are cruelly treated and literally starved." Judge Wandell saw no reason why dogs could not be used to work in machines, as long as they were treated well. Berg responded again that dogs deserved a special status: "The dog, Your Honor, is not a beast of burden . . . he is the friend of mankind—a watchman and a sentinel to look after the wellbeing of the human family, and therefore should be nourished and protected." Judge Wandell sided with Walker, saying that there was no evidence of cruelty and that dogs had no special status under the anticruelty laws. The case was dismissed, dealing another check to the police powers of Bergh's ASPCA.[118]

Despite a spate of losses in court over Walker's use of dog power, Bergh and his private police force nevertheless formed a powerful agency of change. They could wield immense surveillance, police, and prosecutorial powers, the full force of which would not be fully measured by the number of arrests, trials, and convictions, but also happened in the daily patrolling of city streets. Walker fought back, but countless others without means likely complied with ASPCA orders, fearing fines and prosecution. With active salaried agents, vigilant members, and shrewd lawyers at their disposal, the ASPCA could make life difficult for Walker and others, even when their work did not end in conviction.

=====

As new laws remade American life with respect to the treatment of animals, apparent contradictions also emerged over the uneven expansion of rights across species. As Charles Walker awaited trial between May and October 1874, he put his dogs to rest, perhaps fearing additional charges. But the treadmill did not remain idle. In the summer of 1874, crowds gathered in front of the cider press to witness another spectacle: running the machine, in place of the dogs, was an African American boy, not more than "about eight years of age," with "sweat drops cours[ing] down his sable cheeks, blinding his eyes," according to the *New York Herald.* The newspaper called it "an outrage upon youth, and perhaps, upon poverty, that the boy should be allowed to wear his little body out in acting the part of a dog."[119] New Yorkers wondered how it was possible that a dog was protected from certain harsh labor conditions, but that a human child was not? For some it was a signal that the humane movement had gone too far; for others it was a call to action to expand protection to children.

Bergh and his Society were equally outraged at the treatment of the African American boy. They raised the issue in court in an attempt to vilify Walker, but lacked legal authority to prosecute child abuse cases. The advancement of animal protection would notably advance child protection laws in the years that followed. With the more prominent case of child abuse committed against Mary Ellen Wilson, also in 1874, Bergh and ASPCA lawyer Elbridge Gerry argued for the protection of children by appealing to their status as animals.[120] For a brief window of time, animals enjoyed legal protections above those afforded to children. Seeing Walker's dog replaced by a black child, one letter to the editor of the *New York Herald* said, "I am forced to arrive at the conclusion that the quadruped is more valuable than human life, and that it would be better for that child to be a dog than . . . an American citizen." In 1875, SPCA members, led by Elbridge Gerry, established the Society for the Prevention of Cruelty to Children.[121]

Through the advancement of protections for animals, reformers made another crack in the protective shell of legal patriarchy that had shielded state intervention. In establishing basic standards for the treatment of "dumb," defenseless, and powerless animals, new laws set off a series of dominoes in moral and legal logic that returned back to humans. Placing the capacity to suffer—rather than the capacity to reason—at the center of rights and protections, early safeguards for "dependents" in many cases protected those members of the patriarchal order least able to voice dissent or consent: animals. When it became clear that the humane treatment standards afforded to animals did not explicitly apply to children, state power again expanded into the home in areas previously considered private and protected from the state. There were limits and rules on family and social relationships that belonged to the public—not only because they affected the well-being of sentient creatures, but also, as the humane reformers argued, because they affected the greater social order and public good. "The child is an animal," argued

Gerry, and deserved "at least [to] have the rights of the cur in the street. It shall not be abused."[122]

Conclusion

Whether in dog machines or in ragpickers' carts, the apparent decline of dog labor was likely the result of emerging efforts of SPCAs across the United States. Although dog power continued in urban environments into the late nineteenth century, the number of working dogs and the variety of their work seemingly dwindled. After the ASPCA's interventions, ragpickers no longer seemed to rely as heavily on the labor of dogs. Those that did lived in the northern shantytowns of New York, or on the outskirts of town—away from the police powers that enforced animal cruelty laws. By the late nineteenth century, dog machines were mentioned with far less frequency and enthusiasm in American newspapers. Electricity may have driven dog machines into obsolescence, but it was also the cultural and legal pressures of the late nineteenth century—spearheaded by humane activists—that effectively transformed dogs into creatures of leisure. Decades after the Walker case, Jack London had to travel to the Yukon to find dogs that "did all manner of work that horses did in Santa Clara Valley," though there were still a small handful of examples of dog labor that San Francisco newspapers occasionally mentioned as oddities.[123] Dogs pulling sleds had a certain romantic and rugged connotation that many saw as the antidote to modern urban life, but there was nothing romantic or noble about a dog turning a machine in the city, or carting the dirty rags of the city's poor.[124]

The humane ideal of pet ownership was firmly entrenched by the turn of the twentieth century. It was part of what gave London's story such salience. What was gained was a strong and powerful ethic of kindness and care for dogs as pets. What was lost was some of the diversity and variety of human relationships with dogs, which sharply narrowed compared to just decades before. Ambrose Bierce, writing in the last decade of the nineteenth century, was among a shrinking number of voices who grumbled about the new pet culture in America. He excoriated the "loafing" pet dog and those that loved them, calling canines America's "only true 'leisure class.'"[125] Was this new life of leisure an improvement for dogs? Or, as Walker and others suggested, did they want for vigorous exercise and labor? Dogs, no doubt, suffered less visibly under the new rules and culture, but their lives may have also reflected the boredom, ease, and leisure that many urbanites saw as the downfall of their own modern human culture.

Though their words and perspectives are largely missing from historical records, ragpickers must have understood viscerally the loss of dog labor; carrying heavy sacks and pulling their own carts, they no doubt felt the absence of working dogs in their sore muscles, throbbing knees, and aching backs. They were free laborers in a market economy, and there were no laws or agents to prevent that sort of suffering.

CHAPTER SIX

Captivating Spectacles

Public Battles over Animal Entertainment

O N T H E M O R N I N G of September 8, 1827, thousands of spectators crowded along the cliffs overlooking Niagara Falls. The event they were there to see had been advertised and promoted across the expanding geography of newsprint—from Maine to Georgia, New York to Ohio, and countless cities and towns in between. As the crowds grew thick that September, it became clear that the small upstate towns would be unable to accommodate the thousands of visitors. Bars and restaurants were running short of food for guests, and hotels as far as Lewiston—more than seven miles from Niagara Falls—were overrun with "distant visitors." Some travelers pitched tents outdoors, and two took to the comforts of sleeping above and below a billiard table.[1]

For a country whose population was still spread thin across agrarian towns and villages, the size of the crowds that September morning was itself noteworthy. One writer described the mob that was "brought together from motives the most opposite," from peddlers to refined ladies, "and composed of persons of every age and from every walk of life."[2] The crowd was a "force" to be feared, which "may be supposed to produce an evil effect."[3] Another observer said that "such a mass of heterogeneous humanity, we never before witnessed."[4]

The crowds that filled the upstate towns that weekend and gathered along Niagara Falls were, by some estimates, equal to or greater than those that came to see Andrew Jackson's inauguration only sixteen months later, in 1829.[5] At its largest, the crowd at Niagara likely exceeded even the largest numbers that had gathered for the Great Revival at Cane Ridge only decades before, in 1801.[6] The election of Andrew Jackson and the iconic revival that launched the Second Great Awakening loom large in our imagination as popular and essential moments in American history.

But those who made the long trek to Niagara Falls that September day did not come to participate in a religious revival or to find God—though they may have sought a similar experience. They did not come to bark like dogs or to speak in tongues—though they no doubt came to engage with something beyond the confines of their humanity. They did not come to hear the fiery rhetoric of a preacher or politician, or to seek political offices and drink wildly on the White House lawn. They came to watch a boat full of living animals go over Niagara Falls.

Crude as it was, the Animal Boat was, in many ways, an innovative and elaborate form of popular animal entertainment. It celebrated the growing tourism of Niagara Falls, the growing mythology of American nature and the frontier, and growing curiosity about the new technologies of the time—canals and steamboats. But the animal entertainment on display that September was of a type that would come under greater scrutiny over the course of the nineteenth century—particularly in cities. It was entertainment that in some ways required and celebrated animal suffering and death. But the Animal Boat was not merely a brutal and sadistic sacrifice of living creatures; beneath its facade was a complicated set of popular desires and interests, and perhaps even the seeds of empathy that would fuel the humane movement in the decades that followed. Over the course of the century, popular exhibitions of animals would reveal much about intricacies and changes in American culture and society. Such exhibitions would be made and remade by entertainers, showmen, and reformers alike to match evolving moral and emotional qualities and ideals. Through animals, nineteenth century audiences sought answers to essential questions about what constituted humanity and nature. Through animal entertainments, Americans expressed their evolving popular wishes and aspirations, often leading to disagreement and conflict. By the late nineteenth century, animal entertainments looked much different from the way they had looked decades before. Shows like the Animal Boat would be largely regulated into invisibility, cleansed of visible suffering and death that had pervaded earlier forms of animal shows.[7]

The Falls of Niagara

That spectacle of November 8, 1827, revealed an extensive world of animal entertainment in America, as entertainers far and wide followed the crowds that assembled around Niagara Falls. Although the "descent was the only topic of conversation among all classes," there were countless numbers of other smaller attractions, including "men with wild beasts, gingerbread people, cake and beer stalls, [and] wheel of fortune men."[8] A famous dog, Apollo, made the trip from New York City, and entertained the crowds by "playing cards" and offering "lectures" on astronomy. Apollo joined other "grosser amusements, for vulgar tastes," according to one observer, including a "learned pig."[9] The air was thick with sounds: "bands of music," "the roar of the African lion in the menagerie, and the din of the passing multitude," which mixed with the perpetual rumble of the falls.[10] So overwhelming was the cacophony of sounds that one observer called it "almost too much for the human organs."[11]

Indeed, the powerful emotions visitors felt when they were in large crowds in some ways mirrored the experiences they sought in the "sublime" and terrifying Niagara Falls. The animals onboard were part of that sublime, too—embodiments of the powerful and terrifying wilderness they imagined spreading mythically to the west from Niagara.[12] Advertisements for the event promised animals "of the most ferocious kind."[13] The American West, wild animals, and the sublime were interconnected popular curiosities that were hard to parse out. When organizers eventually settled on the animals that would constitute the floating menagerie, the geographic origins of those species were carefully listed in newspapers as important information: a buffalo from the Rocky Mountains, two bears from Green Bay and Grand River, a North American fox, which joined a raccoon, an eagle, a "vicious" dog, a cat, and four geese. Numerous reports suggested that the bears were actually quite tame, one of which was later sold to Sam Patch, the famous jumper of waterfalls.[14]

The Animal Boat was not merely a sacrifice. Many believed that the boat might survive the 185-foot drop if the hull were properly sealed. The animals were chosen for durability—"muscular strength" and solid bones, and some believed that greatest part of the spectacle would be "the closing scene, in seeing them [the animals] successfully arise among the billows in the basin below . . . and shape their course to the shore."[15] For these spectators, it was not certain death and destruction that they came to see, but a "contest between the products of human art and the powers of nature" and the test of animal strength against the powerful falls.[16] The exhibition at Niagara Falls highlighted the central importance of animals in the popular creation of the sublime. People feared and admired the awesome and terrifying power of the bison and bear as they did the power of the falls. Sending the ship over the falls with a cargo of animals offered viewers a version of the most wild and terrifying elements of North America, thrown together and stirred in the foaming cauldron of Niagara Falls. Though utterly a human creation of the hotelkeepers and restaurant owners of Niagara to increase revenue in the off-season, it was ostensibly a contest of nature.

And yet human empathy for animals was in fact central to the show. Days before the event, paying visitors could step aboard the floating menagerie to see the ill-fated animal passengers up close. They could board the ship and look into the eyes of the animals, and perhaps, with their own knowledge of what would ensue, imagine the fate that would befall the creatures the next day. A small number of visitors willing to pay an additional fee of 50 cents could ride with the floating menagerie from where it was docked on Navy Island to the boat's final stop, just above the falls.[17] The animals were a living presence on the boat—a presence that people understood as something similar to their own, and a presence that enabled their vicarious experience of the fall.

Many visitors that day were familiar with animals through the work of their daily lives. Being able to think like animals was an important skill that most Americans understood in some way, through raising livestock and thwarting predators and pests on farms. The animals aboard the *Michigan*, like the animals that inhabited various parts of everyday life, were not Cartesian others, but creatures that people understood as sharing elements with themselves.[18] In a sense, sending living animals over the falls was an expression of human empathy, perverse as it was. Spectators would experience the falls through the eyes of animals.

<hr/>

The day of the Animal Boat spectacle the crowds pushed their way toward the falls. "Buffalo itself seemed to be moving en masse towards the grand point of attraction," said one observer, and crowds clustered on the edges of cliffs surrounding the cataract.[19] A famous captain from the Great Lakes, and his crew, towed the boat a quarter mile from the precipice, launched the boat toward the falls, then rowed frantically for the shore. The clamor of the crowds ceased at the cry "She's coming!"[20]

But before the boat reached the falls, as a final human act, the animals were freed from their confinements—except the eagle, which was chained to the boat. What did the animals think and feel as they stood on the deck of a boat careening down rough waters toward the abyss? Onlookers described what they believed was a sense of fear among the animals onboard. Perhaps some of the animals did sense the peril they were in. But the descriptions of the animals onboard said as much about the fears and excitement of the spectators themselves. Some noted the fox running up and down the deck in an apparent frenzy. Others described one of the bears climbing the mast before both bears jumped into the river and swam to the safety of the Canadian shore, where they were ultimately captured. By one account, the bison jumped ship and was swimming in the river, but was seen thrashing in the water before going over the falls alive. Its body was never found.[21] Whatever the animals may have thought or felt, the descriptions bespoke the panic and fears that many visitors wished to experience vicariously.

With the other living animals presumably still onboard, the *Michigan* slid off the glassy edge of the waterfall, fell through midair, and disappeared into the thick white foam. In the moments that followed, the river beneath the falls "exhibited a singular appearance from the thousands of floating fragments, there being scarcely to be seen any two boards nailed together."[22] Transforming a boat into unrecognizable fragments and splinters proved that the waterfall had won the contest between "human art and the powers of nature." In the contest between elements of nature itself, the sublime falls seemingly swallowed the animals whole. They disappeared into the turbulent waters below. But it was not a resounding victory: By jumping ship and swimming to shore, some of the animals made the outcome of the contest uncertain. The animals themselves revealed a certain degree of agency that sabotaged the man-made spectacle. The only clear winners were the hotel and restaurant owners who financed and arranged the exhibit for an off-season bonus, and who filled their coffers.

———

Two larger debates over the proper role and character of animal entertainment in America intersected at Niagara Falls that September of 1827. The first was a popular concern over the proper treatment of animals. Many visitors objected to the way in which animals were treated onboard the schooner *Michigan,* with one journalist describing the event as a "vain curiosity" and a "childish amusement" that unnecessarily harmed the animals involved. The same journalist said he would have been just as excited to watch "a mass of uprooted trees or a field of ice" descend the falls, which would have spared the animals.[23] Others spoke of the "unjustifiable cruelty to the animals."[24] "The exposure of a number of unoffending animals to such a terrible death," one journalist wrote, "I must pronounce wanton cruelty, and inhuman."[25] Nearly forty years before the formation of the ASPCA, many in attendance openly objected to what they saw as animal cruelty.

Within these objections, however, lay a complicated set of beliefs about animals and nature. The writer who spoke of the "unjustifiable cruelty to the animals" was not necessarily concerned for the individual lives of animals onboard, but for human relationships with larger natural or supernatural forces that may have been more than just metaphor. "Why should the elements hush their commotion for the safety of man," he asked, "if man is deaf to the cries of things under his subjection?" Many saw injustice in the wanton cruelty to animals, for which nature might exact revenge for the sins of mankind in this perversion of Noah's Ark.[26] A decade later, a tourism guidebook reflected on the Animal Boat incident: "The putting of animals on board, for certain destruction, for mere amusement, was not generally approved," they wrote, but excused the cruelty by adding that "none had been taken but the useless and vicious, and such as would have been destroyed, if they had not been selected for this purpose."[27]

The second thread that passed through the Niagara Falls spectacle concerned the social effects of the animal exhibition. Through animals, people sought to experience what they believed were the most intense forms of human emotion: fear, awe, and visceral excitement. In the coming decades, Americans debated whether such emotional states were beneficial or appropriate to cultivate, and what the larger social effects would be. They also debated the role of animals in accessing certain emotional states. While some sought to use animals to allow people to access fear, pity, and excitement, others increasingly questioned both the use of animals in these ways and the very act of promoting such emotions. Many reformers believed that certain animal exhibits cultivated detrimental thoughts and emotions, and in turn degraded people and society. Animal entertainments that inspired pity, fear, or excessive stimulation were increasingly regulated and policed, and replaced with forms of animal interaction that emphasized bonds of passivity and kindness between people and animals.

Tensions over animal entertainments were particularly acute in cities, where a profound reordering of human-animal relationships was unfolding over the course of the nineteenth century. As livestock populations and slaughterhouses declined in downtowns, other species experienced greater presence and visibility as pets, in animal shows, and in zoos. Wild animals that had in some cases been hunted and driven out of human settlements returned to cities as captive entertainments, joining more exotic species from around the world. Ostensibly wild animals experienced a rebirth in the urban environment just as certain domesticated species were zoned out of the visible world of downtown city life.[28]

The development of animal exhibits and the exclusion of livestock shared a common social impulse. Removing animal death and suffering and enlarging the visibility of animals as creatures deserving of human affection, attention, enjoyment, and popular entertainment offered a way of improving human life in various ways. Zoo animals were commodified and made safe for popular enjoyment, as urban residents sought naturalistic retreats as antidotes to the enervating conditions of urban life. Rural and suburban Americans also flocked to urban zoos and animal displays, though circuses increasingly brought animal entertainments to wider populations by the late nineteenth century. As zoos developed in the 1800s, they often sought to connect people to some form of a more authentic, wild nature. But urban zoos offered visitors a refined and limited view of that world that contained invisible contradictions. Zookeepers and animal exhibitors in the late nineteenth century increasingly created exhibits that would not upset the public's sense of order and decency—masking, in the process, a set of animal behaviors and relationships that were cleansed and made safe for civilized life. Animal life remained narrowly constructed to meet and reflect certain social values.

The rise, decline, and transformation of animal spectacles in nineteenth-century America presents a layered, contradictory, and contentious set of social and cultural changes. This was true even looking at the isolated case of the Animal Boat at Niagara Falls, where observers disagreed about the meaning and consequences of the exhibition. When Niagara's tourism boosters planned the next shipwreck spectacle in 1829, the boat slated to travel down the falls did not have living animals onboard. Perhaps this was a reaction to the apparent backlash organizers experienced in 1827 over the plight of the animals. The 1829 exhibition still drew large crowds, but ultimately disappointed. The boat struck a rock above the falls and remained stuck until spectators cleared out and returned to their lodgings after waiting expectantly for hours. In the middle of night the boat broke free, then crashed, unseen, into the dark void.[29]

Dead Animals and the Life of the Republic:
The American Museum

Animal exhibitions of the nineteenth century had historical antecedents in colonial America and the Early Republic. Although the emergence and growth of concentrated human populations and surplus wealth in nineteenth-century America created favorable markets for animal exhibits, traveling menageries nevertheless existed in limited numbers in the American colonies of the eighteenth century. Newspapers heralded the arrival of the first lion to visit the continent in a menagerie in 1720, the first camel in 1721, a polar bear in 1733, and a leopard in 1768.[30] Although colonial Americans were curious about wild and exotic animals, the rise of large-scale, permanent institutions and companies specializing in animal exhibitions only flourished in the nineteenth century.

Charles Willson Peale's American Museum in Philadelphia was perhaps the largest and most notable animal exhibit of its day. In many ways, the spectacle at Niagara Falls and the popular animal entertainments that would emerge in antebellum America were responses to the sort of passive and refined forms of animal exhibits that comprised Peale's museum of republican virtue. Established in 1784—as the newly independent collection of American states struggled to find a stable system of governance—Peale's museum was a bold physical embodiment of the highest ideals of the new republic. Like the American Philosophical Society, which Benjamin Franklin helped establish in 1743, Peale's museum emphasized rational thought and scientific knowledge over popular entertainment and emotional excitement. Peale aspired to engage and shape the public, but he sought to do so through higher intellectual faculties and by improving accessibility to science, art, and natural history. Natural science and philosophy had, after all, served as the basis of republican rights and values. Franklin and Peale both believed that society benefited when leisure was cultivated and trained. Fostering an understanding of the natural world was an ideal form of education that would lead to social improvement and political stability.[31]

Peale's museum was something of a shrine to the natural world that laid the basis for republican governance. Peale sought to re-create the "world in miniature," complete with thousands of stuffed animals, animal skeletons, natural specimens, and a collection of fine art.[32] He hired natural scientists to help arrange and organize exhibits, ultimately settling on a Linnaean taxonomy that shaped the physical layout of the museum's exhibits.[33] Peale's undertaking also had deistic pretenses. Enlightenment science was, in some ways, an effort to understand and catalog God's creation, making Peale's museum a sort of temple, and its specimens the stripped-down reliquary of the natural world. Peale often quoted a remark uttered by the French philosopher Comte de Volney when he visited the museum in 1797, "This is the House of God! Here is nothing but truth spoken." Truth and access to a catalog of God's creation were the underlying purposes of the museum.[34]

In many ways Peale's museum was a nationalistic and institutional retort to the theories of the Comte de Buffon and others, who argued that the New World stood on inferior natural foundations. American species of wild animals and flora were inferior to those in Europe and other parts of the world, Buffon argued. Because the size and strength of natural flora and fauna served as a measurement of an environment's natural capacities, the American people—and, in turn, American government—were built on shaky natural foundations insufficient to build a great civilization. Thomas Jefferson was among those Americans that countered Buffon by turning to natural specimens to argue for the strength and integrity of the continent and its capacity to support a great nation.[35] Peale's museum—which embodied this Jeffersonian retort—included specimens gathered from Jefferson's renowned Lewis and Clark expedition. When mastodon bones were discovered in upstate New York in 1801—evidence that American nature had once supported massive, powerful species—Peale personally took over the excavation and later displayed the reconstructed skeleton as the centerpiece of his museum. In so doing, Peale was the curator of an institution that housed the natural evidence that the United States had the capacity for greatness.[36]

Animals native to North America, in particular, were a source of national pride and emerging identity. Over time, Peale's animal exhibitions developed thicker layers of scientific lacquer. Although early entries on bird species included unscientific descriptions—"striped black and white bird, chocolate colored bird with black head, tail and striped wings"—Peale's later displays carried the weight and language of scientific classification. A large 40-foot room was devoted entirely to stuffed bison, elk, a great anteater, a sloth, a grizzly bear, a llama, a musk ox, and 21 monkeys.[37] Animals were posed in "natural attitudes" with smaller animals in glass cases in front of painted landscapes. A larger room that measured 100 feet in length contained more than 1,000 birds in 140 cases. Despite efforts to exhibit nature in its purest forms, and to connect visitors to distant natural worlds, the human hand was everywhere: from the rigid organizational taxonomy, to the printed museum guides with animals listed by category, to the paintings of animals and images of famous scientists and explorers. The fossils exhibited in Peale's museum were not only part of a deistic temple but also served as the evidentiary basis for numerous scientific publications in Europe and North America.[38]

Essential to Peale's mission was the cultivation of a certain intellectual and emotional orientation toward animals and nature. Rather than emotional excitement, Peale's exhibits presented dead animals in a way that allowed for cool, rational examination of the natural world in ways living animals did not typically allow. In its appreciation and worship of nature and animals as well as its noble intention to cultivate higher forms of human engagement with nature, Peale would likely have cringed at the Animal Boat spectacle at Niagara Falls, and the variety of other entertainments that used animals to create intensely emotional or amusing experiences. For Peale, it was the observation and study of animals that cultivated humanity in its highest forms.

But Peale's vision of public engagement seemed to be floundering in the early 1800s. Whether he sought to create a form of popular entertainment remains debatable. Costly ticket prices and the museum's formal social environment would have served as serious barriers to entry for much of the public.[39] Even if they could afford a ticket, it remains unclear whether most families would have chosen to spend time in the stuffy museum: class stood as a division in early American cities as new political and cultural forms of democracy took root in the Early Republic.[40] By the early 1800s, Peale's museum was in financial ruin as attendance declined. Citing his value as an institution for the public good, Peale sought funding from the federal government in 1811. His request denied, Peale handed over control of the museum to his son, Rubens, who immediately made updates that he believed would improve attendance and put the museum on secure financial footing.

Rubens Peale sought to popularize the museum in the 1810s. He closed three rooms in the Philosophical Hall and gathered the entire collection in a single room. He added live entertainment in the evenings, which sometimes included animal tricks and shows. He installed gaslights in 1816 and replaced the Linnaean organization and catalogs with framed Bible verses. Most important, he brought out "natural curiosities" that his father had intentionally left in storage, including a two-headed cow and a specimen he claimed was a mermaid.[41] These were "curiosities" of the natural world, and not "representative species" of God's creation. These animals were the quirks, imperfections, and mistakes of God and Nature, and not their finest masterpieces. They were evidence of the possibility of natural disorder and confusion, not order and perfection. For years, Charles Willson Peale had deliberately hidden these curiosities from public view so as to create and preserve certain illusions about the natural world. Charles was resisting the tide of popular demand for animal curiosities. With the addition of these new forms of animal exhibits, Rubens started giving the people of Philadelphia glimpses of the animal shows that he believed they wanted to see, and not those Charles believed they needed to see.

Even with these new exhibits, the museum continued to struggle financially. Charles returned as manager in 1821, in an effort to revive the museum as an institution of republican virtue, and he hired prominent natural science professors to restore the museum's relevance as an educational institution. But his efforts did little to stop the financial hemorrhaging that stemmed from a fundamental disconnect with a public increasingly interested in animal "curiosities"—a public seeking a different emotional and intellectual orientation toward animals and nature than what Charles offered. Charles Willson Peale died in 1827, just a few months before the Animal Boat took its trip over Niagara Falls. The museum limped along until it went bankrupt in the failure of 1845. Its collections were sold at auction soon after.[42]

Blurring Lines and Crossing Species: P. T. Barnum and Popular Animal Entertainments

At auction, the largest portion of Peale's collection ended up in the hands of a young businessman from Connecticut named Phineas Taylor Barnum. In the years that followed, Barnum appropriated both the physical objects and some of the Enlightenment rhetoric of Peale's republican museum, but transformed the animal collection into something entirely new. In creating animal exhibits Barnum walked a line between civility and incivility, subversiveness and sobriety, often crossing back and forth into these seemingly opposed spaces. A Yankee farmer turned New York City businessman, Barnum understood the elements of public entertainment and celebrity as well as anyone in his generation. Barnum turned Peale's scientific specimens into iconic expressions of democratic popular entertainment.

Over time, Barnum's animal exhibitions showed little intellectual coherence and shifted constantly to reflect popular interests and consumerism, while adapting to new public policies and law enforcement around animal entertainments. Though Barnum remains somewhat inscrutable, he may also have adapted his animal exhibitions out of a change of heart. It is hard to know whether decisions about animal exhibits reflected Barnum's own beliefs and ideas, or, more likely, his pervasive desire to accommodate his customers. The sensationalistic animal exhibits of Barnum's early years as a showman—in the 1840s and 1850s— gradually gave way to reflecting a more moderated form of animal entertainment in the years after the Civil War, even as his circus became popular. Barnum argued that popular entertainment served a public good by easing the tensions and stresses of urban life, but also adapted his animal exhibits, in particular, to fit certain moral ideals and goals of reformers. He established a strict temperance policy at his museum and, over time, adapted many of his animal exhibits to meet evolving standards of decency—including those set forth by the ASPCA.[43] Although at first a nemesis to elitist social reformers and museum men like Charles Willson Peale, Barnum later showed signs he was becoming much like them.[44]

Long before Barnum was a showman, he understood animals as many Americans did: through labor.[45] He not only lived in New York when pigs still roamed the streets and dairy cows lived on many city blocks, but Barnum spent time with animals throughout his childhood growing up on a Connecticut farm. "I drove cows to and from the pasture, shelled corn, [and] weeded the garden," wrote Barnum in his autobiography—itself an artistic work of popular personal narrative. As a child—in one of his first profitable ventures—Barnum saved his money and purchased a lamb and a calf, which he presumably sold later for a profit.[46] When he grew older he "rode a horse for ploughing."[47] Barnum made his first trip to New York City at age twelve, in 1822, when he was hired to drive cattle from Bethel, Connecticut, to Manhattan, where he stayed for a week at the Bull's Head Tavern. Had it not been for the animal economy that connected Bethel and New York City in the early nineteenth century, Barnum might never have found his future in New York City as an entertainer.[48]

But it would be years before Barnum took up animal entertainments as a centerpiece of his public exhibitions. After his 1822 visit to New York, Barnum returned to Connecticut, where he continued to work on the farm. The very banality of the relationships he experienced on the farm stood in sharp contrast to those he and others would actively seek out in more exciting forms of animal entertainment. Barnum's childhood milking and herding of animals was the sort of work "I never really liked," he admitted. "As I grew older my settled aversion to manual labor, farm or other kind, was manifest in various ways," he wrote.[49] Farm work was tedious and dull. Animals were bred for consistency, profit, and predictability: their best traits were reproduced to create animal bodies that were most effective in turning out milk, meat, and skins; their temperament was bred for pliability and human control. In short, livestock offered humans little in the way of thrills or emotional excitement. An animal "curiosity" on the farm—most often a deformed calf, lamb, or pig—was not the stuff of entertainment so much as it was a potentially serious threat to a family's subsistence, or worse, a bad omen for the religious and superstitious.[50] Livestock bodies were, in many ways, the creation of Enlightenment values of science, rationality, predictability, and categorization. In the years that followed, the popular animal exhibitions that Barnum created would reflect a demarcation from this world of rational and predictable relationships with animals that had once anchored his and others' lives.[51]

Once the adornments of the "Jeffersonian deistic temple for the religion of humanity," Peale's collection of animals would be sold to Barnum and exhibited "beneath the gaze of working-class masses," in the 1840s. Here they made up an important part of P. T. Barnum's "Jacksonian theater of the absurd."[52] The transformation of the animal exhibits and the "vulgarization of the museum," marked a larger shift in American culture from "Jeffersonian republicanism to Jacksonian democracy."[53] But it was a transformation marked by contentious debates and conflict over the course of the century, as reformers pushed back.

Barnum's museum was not universally celebrated. To many, his exploitation of the natural world and science was "vulgar"—a crass commercialization that betrayed truth and virtue in favor of profits and public ignorance. The stodgy Henry Tappan called Barnum's museum a place for "stuffed birds and animals, for the exhibition of monsters, and for vulgar dramatic performances—a mere place of popular amusement."[54] Where Peale sought to display representative species and explain their place in God's creation, Barnum sought freakish exhibits of "missing links," mermaids, bearded ladies, and deformed dwarfs that defied categorization and reason, blurred scientific categories, and engaged audiences with excitement and intense emotions.

Designed primarily to entertain and make money, Barnum's animal exhibits often captured public attention by pressing at the very boundaries and categories that Peale and others in the scientific community had worked to establish. The transition from Peale's Museum to Barnum's was less a clean break and more a gradual and complicated transformation. Barnum needed Peale and his scientific cohort to create the categories of species that his popular exhibits picked apart and dismantled. Many of his most popular exhibitions were those that blurred species and other biological boundaries of gender and age—lines that held immense cultural and political meaning. In one room Barnum displayed the stuffed specimens arranged in scientific categories, while in another room he exhibited new specimens that deconstructed those very categories. "Curiosities," in many cases, were living creatures that did not fit neatly within existing scientific categories or rules. They defied human expectations and knowledge and pushed at the edges of the known and quantifiable world. These curiosities were among the most popular attractions at Barnum's museum.

The Fejee Mermaid was perhaps Barnum's most popular and controversial attraction in the 1840s. The mermaid Barnum exhibited was a shriveled-up specimen with the head and hands of a monkey and the body of a fish—"an ugly, dried-up, black-looking, and diminutive specimen, about three feet long," according to Barnum.[55] Adding to the curiosity and its exciting and emotional appeal, the creature's body and face were frozen in a position that gave it the appearance of "having died in great agony."[56] The existence of such an object implicitly posed numerous questions to viewers: What was it? How had it died? If it was a forgery, how had the hoax been created? If it was real, how did this animal fit into scientific and religious understandings of the world? How did the existence of a half-human or interspecies creature challenge prevailing explanations of the origins and existence of the world?[57]

If authentic, the Fejee Mermaid was an extraordinary discovery—"*the greatest Curiosity in the World*," according to Barnum.[58] At first, Barnum sought scientific authentication of the creature. When the first naturalist he approached privately declared the object a fake, Barnum nevertheless went ahead with the exhibit, perhaps knowing already that controversy would be good for business. When other scientists refused to authenticate the object, Barnum simply invented his own science. In 1842, in an elaborate hoax, Barnum hired an actor named Levi Lyman to play an English scientist named "Dr. Griffin." Griffin unveiled the specimen to the public for the first time, and gave lectures on its origins and meaning. He told audiences he had purchased the expensive specimen in China for the Lyceum of Natural History in London, and presented other species alongside the

FIGURE 6.1 The "Fejee Mermaid." This image appeared in the *Sunday Herald* in 1842, and was reprinted in P. T. Barnum's 1855 autobiography, *The Life of P. T. Barnum.*
Reproduced from P. T. Barnum, "The Life of P. T. Barnum: Written by Himself" (New York: Redfield), 1855.

Fejee Mermaid that he said proved the links in the Great Chain of Being theory of natural order. There was a species linking the seal and the duck, flying fishes that linked birds and fish, and a "Mud Iguana," which was part reptile and part fish.[59] In truth, Barnum had leased the mermaid from the Boston showman Moses Kimball. Kimball had purchased the specimen from an American seaman in 1842, who had procured it from Japanese sailors in Calcutta in 1817.[60] Its complicated and obscure origins shrouded the fact that it was, of course, a humbug.

As visitors flocked to his museum to see the mermaid, other scientists pushed back against Barnum and Lyman's absurd claims. The Reverend John Bachman, a colleague of John James Audubon, argued that Barnum's scientific claims of authenticity were baseless. But instead of debating Bachman, Barnum played on the widespread distrust of scientific expertise.[61] It was up to the people to decide, Barnum argued, and it was "submitted to the public for inspection."[62] Standing in sharp contrast to the scientific bent of some museums that came before, Barnum understood that certainty and "absolute conviction" in exhibits made them less profitable and less appealing to the public. In the weeks that followed, the mermaid exhibition drew crowds so large that Barnum tripled his receipts in the first four weeks alone.[63]

For many, however, blurring the divisions between humans and animals was a dangerous proposition that contradicted the Bible's explanation of separate human and animal creations and destabilized certain biological categories that were foundational to political and social order. The mermaid exhibit went on tour in 1843 to Charleston, South Carolina, where large crowds paid admission to see the curiosity. Many in Charleston were exhilarated by the show, including a writer for the *Charleston Courier* who defended the authenticity of the specimen, which he believed showed a "connection . . . between fish and women," and which also suggested a similar interconnection "that every body knows to exist between monkey and man." The same journalist went on to describe the emotional engagement with the exhibit: "It amuses the grave and heightens the gayety of the gay—and the delight it ministers to children is literally uproarious—and exhilarating to all who own a sympathy with the innocent enjoyments of childhood."[64] Others were not so pleased. Crowds in Charleston became so angry and raucous that Barnum demanded the item be returned to New York for fear it would be turned to "mince meat."[65]

Perhaps worried about public backlash, Barnum backed down. He considered suing Bachman, who had publicly debunked the exhibit, but decided that a lawsuit might subject the mermaid to greater scrutiny and would reveal its inauthenticity. Instead, he chose to retire the exhibit to a shelf in his personal office. When the mermaid was ultimately exposed as a fake, Barnum feigned contrition and wrote the "true story" of the Fejee Mermaid in his autobiography, thereby turning the incident into an opportunity for further profits. Writing years later, Barnum claimed he had only used the specimen to advance his more respectable exhibits, "of which, I confess, I am not proud."[66] It was the sort of comment from a man who, by that point, carried himself with the comportment of a Republican politician and social reformer. Years later Barnum often joked publicly about the Fejee Mermaid, which became an iconic humbug of its time.[67]

═══

Other exhibitions at Barnum's museum also blurred scientific categories of species, particularly distinctions between humans and animals. In the 1840s, Barnum exhibited an orangutan dressed in women's clothes named "Mademoiselle Fanny," who was presented as a "connecting link between man and brute creation."[68] Beginning in the 1880s, Barnum exhibited a "Dog-Faced Boy," a person with profuse facial hair on his forehead and nose.[69] But among Barnum's most popular exhibits was a long-standing show called "What Is It?" which was later sometimes billed as the "Missing Link." "What Is It" showed that the species boundary could be blurred from either direction. As the popular entertainments at Niagara suggest, earlier forms of entertainment in the United States often humanized animals as part of popular entertainments—"learned" dogs and pigs, clothed and civilized primates, and dancing bears. "What Is It?" blurred the species line from the opposite direction, presenting a man as existing somewhere between human and animal.

FIGURE 6.2 Matthew Brady photographed the actor who played "What Is It?" circa 1865. Meserve Collection, National Portrait Gallery, Smithsonian Institution, Washington, DC.

Over the years, Barnum would feature various iterations of "What Is It?" and "Missing Link" performances—later employing William Henry Johnson, who gained some notoriety for playing "Zip" in Barnum's traveling circus. But there appears to have been another actor who played "What Is It?" in the 1860s, and little is known about him. He was an African American man whose true name and identity seems lost to history. Some accounts suggest he was born to former slaves in the early 1840s, and found his way into the small-scale entertainment circuit for several years before joining Barnum's show in 1860. Barnum discovered what he called the "queer little crittur" in Philadelphia and "secured" him from a museum proprietor based in St. Louis.[70] The actor who played the

"What Is It?" in the 1860s was a distinctive looking man: small in stature, with a gently sloping forehead that may have indicated microcephaly.[71] When Matthew Brady photographed the actor in 1860, he captured his unambiguous humanity.

By all indications, the actor who played "What Is It?" did so as a carefully constructed performance. Whether or not he was intellectually disabled, he was able to play the role in ways that at once inspired awe at his mysterious and "nondescript" appearance, while also allaying crowds as disarming and gentle. In the museum show, the actor wore a furry bodysuit and engaged the audience in ways that evoked his supposed animal and human natures, often beginning the show by storming about the cage furiously and screeching when the curtain went up, only later to show subdued restraint and a capacity to learn.[72]

Fundamentally, the exhibit asked viewers to look closely and decide whether the living being on display was human, animal, or something in between. A Currier and Ives lithograph invited viewers to consider: "Is it a lower order of MAN? Or is it a higher order of MONKEY?" or "Perhaps it is a combination of both." Barnum's promotional literature helped the audience suspend disbelief through an invented story that the "What Is It?" was discovered living in a tree-dwelling community by a party of European naturalists searching for gorillas in Africa. As in Barnum's other animal exhibits, the "What Is It?" created a space for controlled forms of discomfort and uneasiness, but ultimately nothing radical. Barnum continually reassured his customers that everything was safe. The "What Is It?" was "intelligent, docile, active, sportive, and PLAYFUL AS A KITTEN," the lithograph suggested. An advertisement in the *New York Times* noted that there was "nothing repulsive to his appearance" and that those who saw him were "captivated, astonished, and delighted." The actor's portrayal of the "What Is It?" was meant to show not only the dual nature of his human and animal being—to confront the crowd with ambiguity and uneasiness—but, ultimately, to show the creature's capacity for learning and civilization.[73] The act was cleaned up to be made safe for middle-class New York culture.

The timing of Barnum's "What Is It?" exhibit was significant within a larger and interconnected political, cultural, and scientific moment in America. Politically, state and national governments struggled to define the status and rights of black Americans, in both the North and the South, converging in the controversial Dred Scott Supreme Court decision of 1857, which denied national citizenship and full legal personhood to people of the "negro race." Arguments that blacks were inferior to whites were not new to the nineteenth century or to the United States, but they did take on a new power, force, and scientific sheen amid rising movements of abolitionism and antislavery. Southerners, in particular,

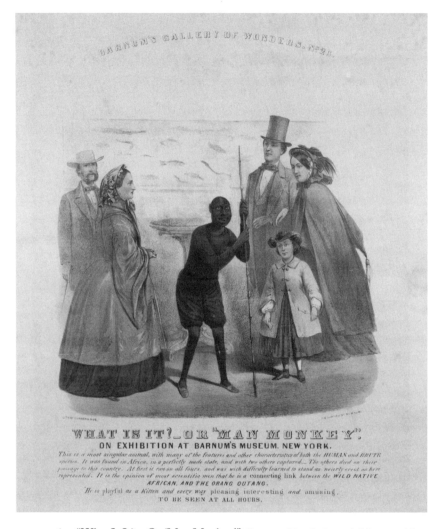

FIGURE 6.3 "What Is It?—Or, 'Man Monkey,'" Currier and Ives Lithograph, Museum of the City of New York, circa 1860.

pushed back against calls for equality and antislavery by justifying slavery on biological grounds, ushering in a new wave of scientists who sought to prove that races were biologically separate and unequal. The *Richmond Examiner* made the argument quite succinctly, noting that blacks should remain enslaved and should be denied "liberty and pursuit of happiness" because the negro "IS NOT A MAN!"[74]

A key way that white Americans sought to denigrate African Americans and justify black slavery was to compare "negroes" to animals. This, too, was nothing new, but the arguments emerged with notable zeal amid scientific and political discourses of the mid-nineteenth century that sought to differentiate blacks and whites as a way of justifying slavery.[75] American doctors and scientists such as Samuel Cartwright, Josiah Nott, and Samuel George Morton joined a larger global network of pseudoscientific researchers who looked closely at human and animal bodies to make arguments that races were inherently unequal, and that blacks were inferior in part because of their alleged likeness to "higher orders" of animals, particularly apes. Some even went so far as to argue that each race was a separate divine creation (polygenesis), which stirred controversy because it clashed with the Bible's description of a single human creation (monogenesis) in the Garden of Eden. Polygenists were suggesting that racial distinctions were effectively species distinctions—that different races of people came from different creations. Americans were prominent in this network of "ethnologists" across Europe and Britain who studied skulls, brains, bodies, and behaviors of humans to prove the inferiority of blacks in justification of racialized slavery. Whether a separate species or simply a "degraded" race, these scientists sought to animalize black Americans and Africans.[76]

Darwin complicated the circulating theories of race and species with his publication of *On the Origin of Species* in 1859. In fact, Barnum's exhibition of "What Is It?" began just four months after Darwin published the groundbreaking, controversial, and widely read volume, which suggested evolutionary connectivity between species—and, implicitly, between humans and animals.[77] The timing and popularity of the "What Is It?" exhibit suggests that ordinary Americans were grappling with these questions on their own terms—a sort of folk discourse that interacted with scientific, legal, and political conversations. Darwin blurred the boundaries of species, but had nothing explicit to say about racial differences among people. Nevertheless, his theories were easily and quickly co-opted into racist explanations for perceived racial differences. Scientific racism—whether monogenistic or polygenistic—adopted comparisons of certain races to animals, often to diminish the status of blacks. These theories emboldened the boundaries of race by blurring the boundaries of species. Whether one believed in a single human creation or evolutionary origin (monogenism), or a series of separate human creations or evolutionary paths (polygenism), it was still possible for scientific race theorists to denigrate blacks by arguing their likeness to animals.

Darwin's blurring the lines of species—combined with pervasive animalized racism in white American culture—had the capacity to do real harm to black Americans. Frederick Douglass vehemently resisted animalized racism, which had immense political, cultural, and social importance. At first, Douglass thought the debate beneath his dignity, asking, rhetorically, in his 1852 Fourth of July speech, "Must I undertake to prove that the slave is a man?" He did not want to dignify the debasing question. Douglass continued: "When the dogs in your streets, when the fowls of the air, when the cattle on your hills, when the fish of the sea, and the reptiles that crawl, shall be unable to distinguish the slave from a brute, then I will argue with you that the slave is a man!"[78]

But by 1854, Douglass felt he needed to address the festering question more directly in an address titled "The Claims of the Negro, Ethnologically Considered," delivered at Western Reserve College in Hudson, Ohio. Douglass openly disputed the emerging arguments of scientific racist theories that sought to denigrate blacks by comparing them to animals. "Man is distinguished from all other animals," he said in 1854, holding the line between humans and animals. Humans were "the only two-handed animal on the earth," he argued, and "the only one that laughs, and nearly the only one that weeps." Expressing his opposition to scientific and casual comparisons of blacks to apes, Douglass argued that "common sense itself is scarcely needed to detect the absence of manhood in a monkey, or to recognize its presence in a negro." Humanity, he continued, was not "a sort of sliding scale, making one extreme brother to the ourang-ou-tang, and the other to angels, and all the rest intermediaries."[79] Rather, people of all races were part of one "human family . . . descended from a common ancestry," and should see "mankind in one brotherhood."[80] "Away, therefore, with all the scientific moonshine that would connect men with monkeys," he concluded.[81] The possibility of blurring lines between humans and animals was a dangerous business in a dominant white culture with such deep prejudices against blacks. Douglass sought to hold the line of species, to keep humans separate from animals, to preserve the humanity of blacks, and to combat scientific racism that sought to animalize African Americans. He fought simply for the recognition that "the negro is a MAN."[82]

It was in this larger context that Barnum's "What Is It?" premiered in 1860 in New York City. The question of whether blacks were fully persons in both science and politics was an open wound that had serious consequences. Barnum picked at that open wound and turned serious questions of rights and dignity into popular entertainment and spectacle. At its core, Barnum's "What Is It?" encouraged white audiences to explore the possibility that there existed a "missing link" somewhere between an ape and a black man. Barnum's peddling of species brinkmanship was not merely mild entertainment, but came loaded with significant political, cultural, and social implications.

Besides creating a spectacle and attracting paying customers, Barnum's "What Is It?" did not have a single intended meaning or objective. But it no doubt inspired countless interpretations among visitors who sought a space to process important questions of race and species by peering into the cage of the "What Is It?". Most visitors—like George Templeton Strong—were amused and entertained, but not convinced. Strong described the "What Is It?" as "an idiotic negro dwarf," "fearfully simian," and "great fact for Darwin."[83] Reflecting the complexities of nineteenth-century racial thinking, Barnum and Strong were both antislavery Republicans, and yet seemed all too eager to promote ugly stereotypes of racial inequality by comparing blacks to "higher orders" of animals. It was possible to believe or peddle ideas of racial hierarchy and also to be opposed to slavery.[84] But many white visitors no doubt held their own private interpretations and reactions to the exhibit that likely reinforced ideas of black inferiority more than they disrupted those popular beliefs. "What Is It?" may have muddled those distinctions and boundaries of species, but it did so by degrading an African American as something closer to animal than those who filed through to look.[85]

Darwin's evolutionary theory was a two-edged sword for the status of both humans and animals in mid-nineteenth-century America. It may at once have elevated the status of certain animals and particular "higher orders" of species as part of the same creation and lineage as human beings, while also offering fodder for the degradation of certain groups of people as something closer to animal. The popularity of "What Is It?" "Missing Link," and other exhibits reflected broader concerns and tensions regarding natural categories that served as the basis of rights and social order. In a post-Darwinian world of connectivity between people and animals, the question of who deserved rights was thrown into question. If there were beings that occupied spaces in between men and women, humans and animals, maturity and immaturity, then what did those categories really mean? Bearded ladies, missing links, mermaids, "dog-faced" boys, and adults that resembled children confused and complicated these powerful distinctions. Through entertainment, spectators processed the contradictions of certain perceived biological categories that laid the foundation for their social and political order. Visitors to Barnum's exhibits looked hard to determine whether their categories and worldview still made sense. Often recognizing such shows as "humbug" even before walking through the doors of Barnum's museum, most returned home with their prior views intact.

Barnum and Bergh

As Barnum ascended the social ranks in New York and Connecticut, he actively sought to remake himself publicly as a man of refinement, honesty, and moderation.

Many of his exhibits developed stronger characteristics of social rectitude, science, and improvement beginning in the 1850s. He argued that his entertainments were essential to new ways of life in America, particularly in cities, and conducive to sobriety, social well-being, and enlightenment. He was a temperance reformer who abandoned the Democratic Party in the 1850s, taking with him Jacksonian populist ideas as a Republican. He actively proclaimed the virtues of his museum as a place that welcomed families and did not allow liquor or prostitutes, which purportedly plagued other leisure spaces in the city.[86]

Perhaps nowhere was the evolving refinement of Barnum and his animal exhibits more evident than in his public relationship with ASPCA founder and president, Henry Bergh. By the 1860s Barnum was a celebrity in New York City and increasingly across the United States. He built lavish and ostentatious estates in Bridgeport, Connecticut, where he spent most of his days. In the 1860s and 1870s Barnum served in the Connecticut state legislature, ran unsuccessfully as a Republican for the United States Congress, and eventually served one term as mayor of Bridgeport in 1875. He sought respectability through politics, but ultimately returned to business in the last decades of the nineteenth century when he reinvented the circus.[87]

Henry Bergh's ascension in New York's popular culture emerged at about the same time. The scion of the largest shipbuilding fortune in New York City, Bergh came from a privileged and refined world of upper-class New York—quite different than Barnum's upbringing on a Connecticut farm. After establishing the ASPCA in 1866, Bergh worked single-mindedly to protect the city's large and changing animal populations in the last decades of the nineteenth century. Bergh and Barnum became two of the most well-known men in New York City, and the separate subjects of countless cartoons and newspaper columns. Both pursued reform agendas that fit loosely within a Republican political ethos, but their frequent confrontations revealed deeper social and political tensions. Their contentious relationship early on eventually shifted to some degree of mutual agreement, respect, and understanding.[88]

Bergh and Barnum shared a remarkable savvy for engaging the public and attracting media attention. Both believed that public theater and controversy furthered their causes, and both enjoyed notoriety. Bergh was a veteran of the New York antebellum theater world, where he spent his early life as a struggling actor and playwright. Even after he gave up on his dreams of becoming a star, Bergh maintained an affinity for theater and, like Barnum, recognized the power of spectacle and controversy. Tall and impeccably dressed—complete with what became a signature top hat—Bergh's interventions on behalf of animals often took the form of highly staged theater on the streets of New York. Standing on street corners, Bergh stopped drivers of horse carriages and omnibuses to demand they offload cargo or passengers. In one notable performance on a busy street in front of City Hall, Bergh stopped a man transporting a cow and calf. The cow's udders were full with milk for the market, but the owner of the animals refused to let the hungry calf nurse. Bergh stopped the man on a busy street corner and forced him to allow the calf to drink from its mother's swollen udders. Crowds looked on as Bergh delivered a speech declaring that the milk belonged to "nature."[89] Numerous other cases revealed Bergh's appetite for public controversy and theater, including his raids of dog and rat fights at the moment they were about to begin, often tipping off the press in advance. These public demonstrations of SPCA power typically concluded with a speech to those in attendance, which often became part of the news story in the next day's papers. Bergh loved a good animal show as much as anyone. In going after Barnum and his museum, Bergh sought to beat the master of publicity and popular entertainment at his own game.

For Bergh and his cohort of humane reformers—many of whom emerged from the Republican and antebellum sisterhood of reform movements—improving the lives of animals was a central element in a broader agenda of social improvement. Reducing animal suffering and eliminating human violence toward animals, many believed, would lead to improvements in the way human beings treated one another. Within this ideology, childhood became a central site of social intervention—a time when children might be molded into upright and moral adults. "As the twig is bent, the tree's inclined," said Bergh, who believed it was essential that children learn to respect and "appreciate living creatures" to expand compassion to humanity more broadly.[90] As childhood became defined and demarcated in the Victorian Era, humane reformers saw this period of life as precisely the place to restrict or eliminate exposure to suffering and violence. Reformers also sought to foster positive and nurturing relationships with animals.[91]

Perhaps no institution in the city played as large a role in the imagination and lives of children as Barnum's American Museum. Barnum himself embraced this role and saw enormous profits in presenting his museum as a safe and uplifting space for children in particular. "To me there is no picture so beautiful as ten thousand smiling, bright-eyed, happy children; no music so sweet as their clear ringing laughter," wrote Barnum near the end of his life. "That I have had power, year after year, by providing innocent amusement for the little ones . . . is my proudest and happiest reflection."[92] The museum was a central place for both urban animal entertainment and children, making it fertile ground for Bergh and his Society. Here the ASPCA might pursue their two central and interconnected goals: preventing animal suffering, and cultivating sympathy and kindness among children.

For the ASPCA, Barnum's museum was low hanging fruit. In 1865—a year before the founding of the ASPCA—Barnum's museum burned to the ground. The memory of the fire was seared into the minds of New Yorkers. Crowds gathered on the street, where they heard the animals screeching and screaming from their confinements as smoke and flames engulfed the building. Nearly all the live animals were killed, including the two white whales, whose tanks were broken in a last ditch attempt to pour water on the fire. The "leviathan natives of Labrador," reported the *New York Times,* were last seen "floundering in mortal agony, to the inexpressible delight of the unfeeling boys, who demanded a share of the blubber."[93] It was precisely this sort of callousness—particularly among boys—that the ASPCA sought to reform. In short order Barnum rebuilt his museum at a great expense, and it reopened four months later at a new location. Within months, Bergh established the ASPCA headquarters a mere six blocks north of Barnum's New American Museum.

By 1866, Bergh's ASPCA and Barnum's New American Museum seemed set on a collision course. When Bergh visited the museum in 1866 he found few problems. It wasn't the cramped animal confinements that troubled the ASPCA president. Rather it was Barnum's snake exhibit. As in the case of the Walker dog machine, Bergh's actions originated with the complaints of friends and members of the ASPCA, who had written Bergh to ask that he intervene in the snake exhibit. Bergh saw an opportunity to challenge Barnum—perhaps knowing full well that the public dispute would serve as advertising for his new Society. But it was not the condition of the snakes that troubled Bergh and his members; it was the live mouse, rabbit, or pigeon that was often confined alongside the boa, poised to be devoured. One concerned spectator wrote Bergh to express his "intense terror" at seeing the "poor rabbit" that had been "thrust into the cage of a serpent." Its "pitiable helplessness made me sick."[94] Their concern was for the "pitiable" and helpless animals, but also for the people who were there to witness the degrading scene.

For Bergh and members of his Society, the sense of terror visitors experienced on seeing a harmless animal confined with the boa was a key part of the problem. In a series of letters Barnum would later leak to the *New York World,* Bergh demanded that Barnum change the exhibit. Confining and displaying animals "destined to be devoured while living," said Bergh, was nothing short of an "inhuman, and demoralizing spectacle."[95] Like the Animal Boat at Niagara Falls decades earlier, Barnum's exhibit offered visitors a spectacle that was emotionally thrilling and terrifying. Like the Animal Boat, it was some degree of human empathy for animals that roused these profound human emotions. But in 1860s New York City, these emotions were increasingly seen as dangerous to public well-being. Whereas a prior generation had indulged and celebrated feelings of terror, a new Victorian sensibility saw human and animal suffering, fear, and violence as destructive for individuals and society. Bergh saw Barnum's exhibition as morally corrosive—it was savagery at the center of the institution that would form children and families of New York City. "This is a barbarity which is unworthy of a people calling themselves civilized," said Bergh of Barnum's snake exhibit, adding that it "must be stopped."[96] Bergh warned Barnum sternly: if the "cruel exhibition" were to happen again "the Society will take legal measures to punish the perpetrators."[97]

Barnum was outraged by Bergh's aspersions and strong-arm tactics. The showman ridiculed the ASPCA president, calling him naive and saying that he knew nothing about the lives of animals and the practices of keeping snakes, which required feeding them live animals. Barnum solicited the supporting opinion of Louis Agassiz, the famous Harvard philosopher and scientist. This was not the first animal cruelty question Agassiz was asked to adjudicate. As one of the most authoritative public voices on animals in the 1860s, Bergh had solicited Agassiz's opinion earlier that year on the issue of whether the hundreds of thousands of turtles shipped yearly to New York City were capable of feeling pain. In that case, Agassiz supported Bergh's contention that turtles felt the pain of being strung together and kept alive in ship holds, flailing on their backs for days or weeks. Although Agassiz commended Bergh's work as a "praiseworthy object," this time he supported Barnum, saying, "I do not know of any way to induce snakes to eat their food otherwise than in their natural manner: that is alive." Although Agassiz's claim has since been disproved, his opinion nevertheless lent a respected scientific voice to the debate, which Barnum advertised as support for his position.[98]

This time Bergh was unconvinced by Agassiz's scientific opinion. Even more, the ongoing debate between Bergh and Barnum reflected a deeper divide in the way they understood God's creation. Echoing ideas prominent in the Second Great Awakening, Bergh saw the world as a place that could be made perfect and free of suffering.[99] It was this belief in human capacity to make the world perfect that led Bergh to distrust the assertions of Barnum and Agassiz that snakes would not eat animals that had been humanely killed. For Bergh, it was illogical that a creature was incapable of the sort of moral improvement he understood as central to God's designs and human work. It did not make sense that a creature would "allow itself to perish of hunger, with food before it, be the aliment dead or alive." The natural fact that an animal could only survive through cruelty toward another was beyond his own imagination of God's creation. If snakes could only survive through wanton cruelty, Bergh concluded, then they were beyond saving, and humans should "let them starve." Bergh continued to believe that the natural world—itself the creation of God—would ultimately yield to moral improvement. Failing that, those stubborn immoral relics of nature lay beyond the moral universe of man and God, and deserved to perish, "for, it is contrary to the merciful providence of God that wrong should be committed in order to accomplish a supposed right."[100] "If Yankee ingenuity cannot devise some other means of keeping these horrible creatures alive," said Bergh, "I am sure we are better without the sight of them."[101]

Barnum and Agassiz had another view of nature and animals—one that did not so easily conform to human morality and perfectionism. But Barnum also challenged Bergh on the facts, arguing that Bergh was naive and uninformed about the actual conditions of the animals on display. The story of the "trembling, fearful rabbit" was a "shallow hoax," said the master of humbug, arguing that Bergh had been duped. It was "simply a ridiculous Munchausenism," said Barnum that a "persistent, unwinking snake should be staring incessantly at his terrified little victim" for four straight days, as one of Bergh's constituents testified. Such premeditation and malice was not within the snake's capacity. "No naturalist will pretend for a moment, that the lazy, dull-eyed boa constrictor possesses any such power, or that any bird or animal placed in his cage has the slightest instinctive admonition that he is in danger." Pigeons hopped around the boa "as fearlessly as if he was the branch of a tree," said Barnum, and rabbits slept "among his folds with as much unconcern as if within their own burrows."[102] Premeditated animal cruelty—along with prolonged suffering and fear attributed to the prey— were figments of human imagination, according to Barnum. These animals were unthinking and unaware, and incapable of the morality and emotions that so gripped their human audiences.

But in some ways, whether or not animals felt pain and suffering was beside the point for the ASPCA. If people *believed* that animals felt pain, then they experienced a set of emotions that were socially degrading. Bergh's objections to Barnum's snake exhibits were, in many cases, as much about the human observation of suffering as they were about the objective conditions of the animals themselves. Although Bergh and other ASPCA members no doubt cared for the lives of animals, they also cared for the social effects of exhibitions of violence and suffering. Speaking for the popular support for his cause, Bergh warned Barnum that "parents and other guardians of the morals of the rising generation" would stop taking their children to "a mis-called museum, where the amusement chiefly consists in contemplating the prolonged torture of innocent, unresisting, dumb creatures."[103] Bergh believed that the tide of public opinion was shifting in his favor and would usher in an era of greater social kindness and compassion. Barnum seemed content to count his profits from ticket sales.

In the face of Barnum's resistance, Bergh took the offensive. The ASPCA president's powers to regulate the great showman of New York demonstrated the potent police and prosecutorial powers vested in him and his organization. Like many who came under regulation of SPCAs, Barnum expressed his frustration at the clout of Bergh and his Society, calling Bergh "unsufferable," "dictatorial," and full of "petty malice." Barnum believed that his museum had public virtue of its own—a "private enterprise" that provided a form of public good that governments could not. With initial investments to rebuild the museum exceeding $500,000, and yearly disbursements of $300,000, Barnum described his own work in lofty rhetoric of public benevolence that echoed Peale's words decades before. Barnum spoke of his work as "plac[ing] before the public a full representation of every department of natural history for a mere nominal sum—an enterprise never before attempted in any city in the world without governmental aid." It was simply "disgraceful," said Barnum, for Bergh to label his museum a mere "amusement" that peddled "the prolonged torture of innocent and unresisting dumb creatures."[104] The split between Barnum and Bergh was over the definition of public good itself.

Things got more contentious in early 1867, when Barnum threatened to publish the lengthy private correspondence if Bergh did not offer him a public apology. Believing that the public would take his side, Barnum told Bergh that his letters would "inevitably make you [Bergh] the laughing stock of every naturalist in Christendom."[105] Bergh refused to apologize, believing that public opinion would side with him. Barnum published the letters in the *New York World*.

The public appeared split in its opinion on the matter. One New York newspaper said that Bergh was "a trifle too sentimental," and Barnum "a good deal too impudent." Although the editorial applauded the work of the ASPCA, the author believed that Bergh "in the tenderness of his heart," had "probably overrated the nervous susceptibility of rabbits" and was falsely ascribing human emotions to animals. Barnum, on the other hand—according to the editorial—had engaged in his "usual offensive readiness to turn everything into an advertisement," and "employed language much too gross and self complacent to be addressed to a courteous, refined, and well-meaning gentleman." By March 1867, Barnum was beginning a campaign for a seat in the US House of Representatives. The same newspaper suggested that if Barnum were to win, he should bring the snake to the House Chamber, and "if the great snake should accidentally get loose and make rabbits of a few of his companions the country would assuredly be none the worse for it."[106] If the editorial were any indication of public senti-ment, many New Yorkers saw the conflict from a middle ground, somewhere be-tween Barnum and Bergh.

In debating and resolving the dispute, the lives and experiences of animals themselves seemed to fade. By one account, when Bergh first threatened legal action, Barnum's manager packed the serpents in suitcases and sent them to Hoboken, New Jersey, to feed—an area outside Bergh's police jurisdiction.[107] Bergh's eventual compromise again reinforced the centrality of human emotions in controversies over animal cruelty. Bergh agreed to allow Barnum to continue the live feedings as long as the act of predation was not part of the public exhibit. Snakes continued to "torture" and eat live animals, but now did so out of sight and mind of the public. Perhaps Bergh and Barnum came to accept— opportunistically or honestly—the other's arguments. Regardless, the outcome reflected a larger trend in SPCA regulations of the late nineteenth century: an-imal suffering that could not be easily eradicated was instead made invisible. Like the cattle and slaughterhouses that increasingly inhabited invisible spaces at the distant fringes of cities, the live mice that Barnum fed his snakes were also erased from the visible world of urban life downtown. Families no longer had to wit-ness the same level of suffering in city streets and public spaces. But in choosing to hide many of these relationships instead of materially confronting them, SPCAs helped sow seeds of a world in which children were increasingly free of the de-sensitizing scenes of animal violence and death, but nevertheless did not substan-tively change or eliminate animal suffering. By hiding these relationships, people living in cities became increasingly separated from natural processes of death and suffering that had long been a part of human life. For many living in cities, animal suffering and death took place increasingly in the realm of other spaces, attended to by other people.

———

The snake controversy was just the beginning of a long and complicated relation-ship between Bergh and Barnum that would last until Bergh's death in 1888. The relationship was sometimes friendly and sometimes contentious—and often public in a way that brought attention to both men and their prominent organ-izations. Barnum gave up his museum business after another fire destroyed a large part of his collections in 1868. He shifted his attention to his traveling circus, which achieved new levels of success after 1870, and became known as "The Greatest Show on Earth."[108] Barnum's relationship with Bergh remained rocky at times in the years that followed, with numerous public confrontations over

Barnum's use of animals—and others over Bergh's zealous use of his police powers. As Barnum and Bergh became iconic figures in New York and American popular culture, they also represented two wider popular movements in America that were at once overlapping and conflicting. Increasingly, it seemed that each needed the other to survive. Barnum likely understood that he needed Bergh's public approval to make his shows safe and acceptable for popular middle-class consumption in an era of growing humane interest among the public. Similarly, Bergh seemed to understand that making enemies with Barnum was bad for his cause, while also recognizing that popular animal entertainments had the capacity to engage the public with animals in new ways. Barnum and Bergh appeared to accommodate each other publicly, but often at the expense of the animals that were ostensibly at the center of their quarrels. When Barnum and Bergh were finished sparring, the lives of those animals were often little changed, except for the way they appeared to the public. The absence of suffering from public view was just another deception, like the Fejee Mermaid and the "What Is It?".

In two prominent cases in the 1880s, Bergh lent the ASPCA's stamp of approval to Barnum's animal entertainments. Barnum seemed adept at playing Bergh to his advantage—and, in at least one case, Barnum made Bergh and the ASPCA part of the show. In 1879, Bergh warned Barnum that his act involving a Fire Horse named Salamander was cruel and dangerous. Salamander leaped through flaming hoops to the astonishment and applause of crowds. In 1880, Bergh was poised to make another public spectacle by arresting Barnum if he performed the Fire Horse act again. Predictably, Barnum welcomed the controversy; he invited Bergh to attend the show in New York City and turned to newspapers to hype the impending clash. Bergh did not attend, but sent eight ASPCA officers and twenty additional police officers to arrest Barnum if he performed the Fire Horse act. Bergh was making a public show of his police powers. Barnum sold more tickets.[109]

The Fire Horse act came late in the show, and the packed crowd watched with growing anticipation over the looming confrontation. Midway through the show, Barnum moved to the center of the ring to introduce Salamander, the Fire Horse. But before he did, Barnum gave a speech ridiculing Bergh and his Society. He harkened back to his first encounter with Bergh over snakes at his museum, reading Bergh's letters to the crowd from the 1866 dispute. Barnum went further, mocking Bergh for having directed him to provide a water tank to his rhinoceros— a measure that would have "killed it," he said with derision. "I know more about the animals than he knows," declared Barnum, adding that he had long been a member of the Royal Society for the Prevention of Cruelty to Animals in England, and was a prominent member of the Bridgeport branch of the

Connecticut Humane Society. Barnum touted his membership in these Societies as evidence that he cared for the cause of animal welfare, and reassured the crowd that the animals performing for them had been "taught and governed only by kindness."[110]

When he finished his speech, Barnum commenced the Fire Horse act. Clowns leaped through the flaming hoops, then Salamander the horse, then Barnum himself. In one last triumph, Barnum invited the ASPCA's superintendent Hartfield to the ring, where he was directed by Barnum to walk through one of the flaming hoops, which he did to great applause. The flames were also a deception—relatively harmless to the people and animals. Hartfield concluded that there was no danger to the animals or the people in attendance, and made no arrests. One newspaper concluded that Bergh had "evidently made a mistake in the matter." In his autobiography, Barnum declared Bergh "vanquished."[111]

By the 1880s, Barnum seemed to have partially captured the ASPCA and Henry Bergh. Increasingly, Bergh appeared more as an ally than an adversary. Still, he was not entirely "vanquished." Barnum repeatedly made public concessions to Bergh and his ASPCA, showing a recognition that the humane movement was a powerful force in American culture and society—and a powerful political and legal actor that needed to be placated and disarmed. Barnum needed Bergh and continually showed a willingness to concede to the ASPCA at various points. When Bergh and the ASPCA protested the use of hot pokers to train elephants, Barnum changed his public position to abandonment of the practice, ostensibly embracing more positive training techniques.[112] But Barnum's trainers continued to use elephant goads—sharp hooks that many at the time saw as cruel, and that have remained controversial in the decades since. When Barnum was skewered in newspapers in 1885 for using goads, Bergh came to his defense and publicly backed the showman's false belief that the elephants did not feel the sharp hooks as significant pain. Bergh went further, publicly calling Barnum "one of the most humane and kind-hearted men living"—an endorsement that Barnum printed in his autobiography.[113] But Barnum showed a willingness to accommodate Bergh, and even at times feared Bergh's police powers. In 1883, Barnum spent hundreds of dollars to have a dead elephant chopped into pieces "to prevent Bergh's men from looking for wounds."[114]

By the 1880s, Bergh seemed to more fully embrace and enable Barnum. What had changed to allow Bergh to accept Barnum's animal shows? Perhaps it was Bergh's recognition that animal shows cultivated a positive and joyful experience with animals that fit with the larger goals of the humane movement. As with pets, Bergh shifted away from an early preoccupation with suffering to a broader desire to accommodate a public seeking interactions with animals defined by kindness and enjoyment. Perhaps Bergh saw the massive popularity of Barnum's entertainments and thought it wise to avoid meddling. On the other hand, perhaps Barnum truly believed in aspects of animal welfare. In 1880, Barnum and his wife became founding members of the Connecticut Humane Society, and Barnum began touting himself the "Bergh of Bridgeport."[115] Nancy Fish—or "Mrs. P.T. Barnum" as she was known in annual reports—would serve as vice president of the Connecticut Humane Society throughout the 1880s.[116]

But Bergh's acquiescence to Barnum might also have been financially motivated—a sort of corruption of the public-private dimensions of SPCA power. Perhaps Barnum understood that supporting the ASPCA and the humane movement was a sound financial investment. It would not only keep Bergh off his back but also assuage the humane concerns of his customers. As Bergh sought to put the ASPCA on firm financial footing in 1884, he wrote Barnum, praising the showman for "the vast amount of pleasure and instruction you have afforded the human family." Bergh then appealed to Barnum's morality: "I wonder whether Mr. Barnum has remembered in his will, the poor dumb animals from whom he has derived so large a share of his splendid fortune?"[117] When Barnum wrote his will in 1882, there was no mention of Henry Bergh, the ASPCA, or the Connecticut Humane Society. By 1889, however, Barnum had amended his will to include bequests to the ASPCA and the Connecticut Humane Society, along with funds to build a statue in honor of Henry Bergh in Bridgeport.[118]

Although Barnum's contributions to the humane movement have been hailed as a generous commitment to animal welfare, they were relatively meager. In his will, he scattered donations across dozens of organizations, and to distant relatives and friends. Bergh's ASPCA received $1,000, and so did the Connecticut Humane Society—the same amount Bergh bequeathed to the Bridgeport Protestant Widows' Society and a variety of other small charitable organizations.[119] Although $1,000 was a significant sum, Barnum's estate was valued at nearly $4.3 million when he died in 1891, making his combined contributions to the ASPCA and the Connecticut Humane Society a mere 0.04 percent of the value of the showman's estate.[120] For someone who paid $10,000 for a single elephant in 1882, his bequest of $2,000 to the humane movement was relatively parsimonious.[121] What was the monetary value that Barnum got in exchange for his alliance with Bergh? What fines and harassment did he evade? How many customers returned to Barnum's shows with their moral qualms allayed by Bergh and the ASPCA? By any calculation, Barnum's bequest of $2,000 was a profitable investment.

One of the more unusual parts of Barnum's will—added sometime between 1882 and 1889—was a contribution of $1,000 to the city of Bridgeport to help pay for a statue to honor Henry Bergh. After Barnum's death, the city dragged its feet on building the monument, but finally erected the statue in 1897. The monument did not feature a likeness of Bergh, however, but rather a plaster horse atop a large stone pillar, which had a two-level drinking fountain for large and small animals. In 1964, a car jumped the curb and crashed into the monument, damaging the base and toppling the horse.[122] The statue was repaired but not entirely restored, and still stands in Bridgeport. The brown horse now appears speckled with white markings, but it is the plaster and paint that is chipping away. Like most of the remnant horse water fountains of the era, the trough has been converted into a planter for flowers. Less than a half mile away, in the center of the park stands a massive bronze sculpture of Barnum. He sits in a chair and looks calmly out onto the Long Island Sound, his back to Bergh's crumbling memorial.

Barnum and Bergh's public feuds and implicit alliance served each man in the context of a broader social struggle to define the place and character of animals in entertainment in the nineteenth century—particularly in cities. Although Barnum continued to showcase nature as a menagerie of oddities and exotics, he adapted his animal shows to adhere, on some level, to evolving standards of decency and humane ideals—in part to appease Bergh's ASPCA and the wider humane movement. Barnum's gambit appears to have worked. In 1891, the *New York Recorder* said that no one had done more than Barnum "to preserve the circus from vulgarity, and to hold it to its proper province of instructing and edifying, while it amuses."[123] As part of Barnum's pursuit of respectability, he also bolstered the scientific elements of his animal shows in the last decades of the nineteenth century—even as the more boisterous animal acts of his circus persisted. Later in life, Bergh publicly endorsed Barnum for his kindness and humanity, and told the showman that he merited "all the happiness . . . in return for the pleasure you have given to the world."[124]

=====

After months of illness—"chronic bronchitis and enlargement of the heart"—Henry Bergh passed away on March 12, 1888, during the Great Blizzard that blanketed the city in more than fifty inches of snow. Traffic in New York came to a silent stillness, causing Bergh's doctor to be delayed. Bergh drew his last breath only fifteen minutes after his doctor finally arrived. When the funeral finally took place on March 17, the horses that carried the hearse and carriages of mourners labored with loud, heavy breaths, struggling in "soft snow up to the hubs." The "city's most prominent men" filled the pews of St. Mark's Church on Second Avenue, and Bergh's coffin was carried in by six officers of the ASPCA. The ceremonial procession of mourners included pallbearers Elbridge Gerry, Mayor

Abram Hewitt, the city's recorder, and other notable and wealthy New Yorkers. Family members and prominent SPCA leaders from around the Northeast followed the casket into the church. There in the procession was P. T. Barnum, whose lavish wreath was also draped prominently over Bergh's casket. Bergh's body would be laid to rest in Brooklyn's Green-Wood Cemetery several days later, but not before the streets could be cleared for the horses.[125]

Toward the end of his life, Barnum declared his own fondness for Bergh, saying—with typical ambiguity and perhaps some disdain—that he had great respect for the "well-meaning and tender-hearted gentleman."[126] In the wake of Bergh's death, Barnum called the ASPCA to "express his regret at the loss of one whom he considered among his oldest and most valued friends."[127] Barnum and Bergh had made amends by the late 1880s. But their reunion came at a price. The sufferings of entertainment animals did not cease. They went on ignored, excused, and increasingly undetected by consumers of Barnum's circus, Bergh's Society, and the larger public. Elephants were jabbed and prodded with sharp hooks to coerce them into doing tricks that resembled amusing play. Rabbits and birds spent their last moments in the grasp of boa constrictors, but out of sight of visitors. The appearances of joyful and lighthearted entertainment—"amusements" as they were increasingly called—obscured the underlying fear and discontent that many animals likely still experienced.

Barnum's commitment to Bergh's goals seemed to be largely opportunistic. Two months after Bergh's burial, Barnum advertised a show at Madison Square Garden, which promised "Big Snakes" feeding on "Live Guinea-Pigs, Rabbits, and Pigeons."[128]

Conclusion

Although not entirely cleansed of animal suffering, mainstream animal entertainments had undergone massive transformations over the course of the nineteenth century—not least of which were the ways in which animal shows roused particular human emotions. The humane movement and SPCAs had done much to remake public entertainment to be free of gratuitous and blatant forms of animal suffering that might upset the public. Eliminating such displays was an important component of this larger movement to reform social relationships among people. Whether animals suffered or not—and to what extent—was, and remains, a matter of great uncertainty and inscrutability. Perhaps reformers were more comfortable assessing and addressing human responses to such shows. In the face of such uncertainty and the absence of popular agreement, the solution to animal suffering was often invisibility rather than eradication. Animal exhibits and shows were being made safe for middle-class sensibilities, and remade to cultivate emotional states of joy and amusement without the disquieting emotions of pity, terror, and fear. By the 1880s, it was hard to imagine the sort of animal entertainment that drew massive crowds to Niagara Falls that September of 1827. When a circus owner arranged to have his trick horse walk a tightrope over Niagara Falls in 1886, the ASPCA intervened and stopped the show before it could begin.[129]

By the late 1800s, entertainers like Barnum had to adapt to a growing public opinion that increasingly found the sight of animal suffering objectionable. But these entertainers also had to abide by a wide array of new laws and powerful new law enforcement agencies of Humane Societies and SPCAs—both in New York and nationally. Something similar was happening in San Francisco, where popular animal entertainments and zoos were undergoing massive transformations in the last decades of the 1800s, marking a larger remaking of the visible and invisible worlds of animals in American life.

CHAPTER SEVEN

Domesticating the Wild

Woodward's Gardens and the
Making of the Modern Zoo

In the late 1870s or early 1880s, the poet Robert Frost—at the time a boy of less than eleven years old—visited Woodward's Gardens, the private pleasure grounds and zoological park in San Francisco that bloomed in last decades of the nineteenth century. After paying 10 cents for admission, Frost would have passed through the ostentatious gate on Mission Street, beneath the sculpted statues of grizzly bears and the goddess California. Once in the gardens, Frost would have seen, to his right, the thirty-seven–foot-tall bust of George Washington and, to his left, the two massive whale bones that formed an arch over the entrance to Woodward's natural history museum. Frost would have meandered through a series of winding paths, past the glass conservatory, the art museum, the Turkish-mosque-themed pavilion, the ethnological museum, the music hall, and the Italian Terrace. There was a playground (a "gymnasium"), a "balloon ascension," and a rotary boat. But the main attractions of Woodward's Gardens were the animal exhibits and zoo. Frost would have gazed expectantly into the animal enclosures: the seal pond, the fish hatchery, the fish pond, the indoor aquarium, the aquatic fowl enclosure, the great aviary, the bear pit, and the fenced and caged homes of dozens of animals, large and small.

Near the farthest end of the park, Frost came to the monkey house, which he remembered decades later when he wrote the poem "At Woodward's Gardens," in 1936. In the poem, Frost remembered the "two little monkeys in a cage," who suffered a "prisoners' ennui." Wanting to animate them, Frost teased and tormented the monkeys with the burning, concentrated light of a magnifying glass. The monkeys were puzzled, pained, and panicked by the "sting" of the light on their noses and hands. Then, with a "sudden flash of arm," one of the monkeys snatched the lens from the boy and retreated to the corner of his cage, inspecting the glass before stashing it in his "bedding straw." Frost looked into the cage, past a divide of comprehension, where "words are no good," but concluded: "Who said it mattered / What monkeys did or didn't understand? / They might not understand a burning-glass. / They might not understand the sun itself. / It's knowing what to do with things that counts."[1]

It was noteworthy that one of the most prominent twentieth-century writers on rural life and nature had his beginnings looking at—and bothering—animals in an urban zoo. But Frost's visit to the gardens—his descriptions of boys and of animals—was telling of larger issues in nineteenth-century animal entertainment and the development of urban zoos. The animals at the zoo were bored and listless, with a certain "ennui" recognizable in zoos today—an ennui that was also seen at the time as a loathsome condition of modern urban life.[2] Like many children, Frost was testing the rules of his physical environment—performing informal experiments of cause and effect by shining the burning light of a magnifying glass on the faces of monkeys. But Frost was also testing the rules of his social environment—performing an act he no doubt understood as transgressive. Young Robert was coming of age at a moment when humane education played a prominent role in the lives of children across the United States. The act of needlessly tormenting animals was considered an abomination by humane educators and reformers such as George Angell and Henry Bergh and members of organizations that constituted the humane movement. Humane education sought to remake children—and boys in particular—into kind and empathic adults. Growing up amid this wave of humane education, Frost likely knew that burning the noses of monkeys was a subversive act. It was the sort of rebellion that leaders of the humane movement most feared—the unfeeling and unreformed boy who would become the cruel and heartless man.[3]

The development of Woodward's Gardens in San Francisco, in the wake of the Civil War, marked an important moment in the development of American zoos and animal entertainments. The cultural and social conflicts exposed in Barnum and Bergh's public battles in New York were part of a larger national conversation about the nature of animal expositions in American cities. Similar questions and debates unfolded across the United States, including in San Francisco where Robert Woodward became known as the "P. T. Barnum of the West."[4] Animal exhibits in museums, zoos, and traveling shows grew with notable frequency and scale in the second half of the nineteenth century, particularly in cities.

Cities, therefore, became one of the central sites for observing "wild" animals—urban portals to distant nature. The rise of reform-minded entertainers such as Moses Kimball in Boston, Barnum in New York, and Woodward in San Francisco demonstrated widespread popular interest in animal entertainments and also powerful ideas that underlay such exhibits, which many believed could either improve or degrade cities and societies.

The characteristics of these animal exhibitions were often measures of civilization and progress more broadly. In the minds of those who created and supported them, zoos were civilizing institutions that sought to connect urban residents to an uplifting form of nature. "What our museums are doing for art and natural science, this Park and its fair botanical companion up the Bronx will do for Nature," said the prominent scientist William F. Osborn at the opening ceremony for the New York Zoological Park (now the Bronx Zoo) in 1899. Osborn saw the zoo as bringing the "wonders and beauties" of nature "within the reach of thousands and millions of all classes who cannot travel or explore."[5] The creators of zoos also promised civic pride and social cohesion. New York City's comptroller, Bird S. Coler, said that the New York zoo would "Add inestimably to the attractiveness of our City," "attract visitors," and "help to give our City the reputation it should possess among the great capitals of the world." The zoo, he said, would add "to the civic pride which is at the basis of good citizenship."[6] But the ideology that zoos were purveyors of urban nature and civic pride—so clearly articulated in 1899—had been in the making for decades in places like Woodward's Gardens in San Francisco.

Taming the Wild West

As San Francisco grew into a major city in the 1860s, reforming popular animal entertainments was central to many San Franciscans' quest for civility and civilization. Looking back on the nineteenth century, John Young—the antisocialist editor of the *San Francisco Chronicle*, and one of the five founders of the Commonwealth Club of California—depicted the changes in the city's relationships with entertainment animals as a mark of its development as a city.[7] Young spoke of the crude horse races, small-scale circuses, and bullfights that constituted a large share of the city's crass popular entertainments in the 1850s. "More amusement was derived from turning a bull and a bear into an enclosure to fight for the mastery," wrote Young of the mid-nineteenth–century city, from his perch in 1912.[8] In the city's early years, San Franciscans had enjoyed a modified form of bullfighting, which Young said was "not indigenous," and had origins in colonial

Mexican culture.[9] The city's efforts to regulate and eliminate bullfights in the decades that followed—including a large and effective push by the San Francisco SPCA—were part of a larger Anglocentric cultural and social reform agenda among city leaders.[10] Even horse racing, said Young, was vulgar in the 1850s—little more than a venue for degenerate gambling. Californians, he said, showed little care for the "improvement of the breed of horses."[11]

Men like Young marked human progress through the ways people related to animals. It followed that animal exhibits and relationships became a central site of active and deliberate reform. A key channel of that reform involved the development of places where people could passively and thoughtfully observe wild animals. But those places needed to be created and developed in San Francisco over time, following trends in other American and European cities. Creating zoos required large and sustained investments of capital, with uncertain possibilities of long-term profits and social improvements. In the 1860s, Robert Woodward became a key figure in the development of animal exhibits in San Francisco, seeking not merely profits, but also an agenda of social reform.

═══

The animal shows and exhibits in San Francisco in the 1850s bore little outward resemblance to the gardens and zoos that would emerge in the decades that followed. The Cobweb Palace—a waterfront bar on Powell Street—had a ragged collection of a few monkeys and parakeets in the 1850s.[12] The famous performer Grizzly Adams temporarily opened a museum downtown to showcase wild bears he had caught—the most famous of which he named Benjamin Franklin. Adams closed his museum shortly after it first opened, taking his show on the road to larger entertainment markets on the East Coast, including Barnum's museum and traveling circus. Adams used grizzlies as a way to sell a larger story of Western adventure to Eastern audiences—an entertainment that celebrated the wildness of the West and the taming of the frontier.[13] According to Barnum, Adams's show, at its largest, had more than thirty bears, which were accompanied by wolves, California mountain lions, tigers, buffalo, elk, and a sea lion named Old Neptune. These wild creatures had been trained to be "as docile as kittens," said Barnum, before going on to describe Adams's final moments in 1860, when he was mauled to death by one of his "pet" grizzlies.[14]

Despite these small-scale and impermanent animal exhibits in the 1850s, San Francisco's most prominent leisure spaces lacked a significant animal presence. Russ's Gardens and The Willows—two popular private city gardens—contained few, if any, animals. Russ's Gardens featured shows that were largely human-centered: acrobats, gymnasts, and other skilled performers who played to the working-class crowds, and also shooting competitions. People drank heavily and danced vigorously.[15] The Willows—founded in 1859, five years after Russ's Gardens—offered San Franciscans a "suburban retreat" from urban life downtown. It was the project of Francois Pioche, a wealthy capitalist born in France, who designed the private garden space on a gently sloping hill, with a small stream carving through a grassy hillside spotted with high-canopy willows. Pioche built an al fresco theater modeled after the one on the Champs Elysees, a shooting gallery, a small menagerie, grassy lawns, and spaces for picnics.[16] The menagerie featured a small number of "birds and beasts," including an emu from Australia, along with monkeys.[17] But the centerpieces of these gardens were the picnic grounds and the large pavilion where dances and dinners were held. Although Pioche was already a wealthy man by the time he established The Willows, his park may have been a scheme to increase ridership on the rail line that he had helped build.[18]

Mark Twain visited The Willows at least once in his twenties. But it was not until he visited Hawaii in the late 1860s that he thought to mention it. Twain contrasted The Willows—a place of aspiring natural beauty in the city—with what he saw as the authentic natural splendor he encountered on the Pacific islands. "In place of the dingy horrors of San Francisco's pleasure grove, the 'Willows,'" he said, "I saw huge-bodied, wide-spreading forest trees, with strange names and stranger appearance."[19] For Twain and others, The Willows was a "dingy" replica of a more authentic nature that existed in some distant place, far from the city. The Willows was not an especially compelling attraction; when the gardens flooded in 1861—only two years after opening—Pioche closed the doors permanently, perhaps realizing the land was becoming more valuable for residential development amid the city's population boom of the 1860s.[20]

Woodward's Gardens

The most popular leisure spaces that would replace these urban gardens would rely more heavily on animals to entertain and educate the masses. The development of Woodward's Gardens and Golden Gate Park in the 1860s and 1870s fulfilled a popular desire to interact with what many understood as a more dignified form of nature. A chief element of this new relationship was the observation of wild animals. Animals played a central and growing role in connecting urban populations with the nature they sought—and the nature that many civic leaders believed urban residents needed.[21] Woodward and others actively constructed, edited, and censored animal exhibits to fulfill an agenda of reform. The very bodies and behaviors of animals in these spaces held immense social and cultural significance.

Woodward's Gardens first opened its doors in 1866, and for more than two decades was an iconic attraction in San Francisco. It was primarily a zoo, but also included an art gallery, a collection of small museums, and a series of manicured gardens. Situated almost halfway between Russ's Gardens and The Willows, Woodward's Gardens occupied two blocks on the edge of residential San Francisco when it was first constructed. The trickling stream that ran through Woodward's Gardens drained into Mission Creek where, less than a mile downstream, it passed the cluster of slaughterhouses and hog ranches in Old Butchertown before emptying into the San Francisco Bay. If the winds were blowing just right, visitors might have smelled the miasmatic fumes from the slaughterhouses and hog ranches downstream. The arrival of Woodward's Gardens and the ensuing departure of the slaughterhouses, corrals, and hog ranches were, in many ways, connected phenomena; they were two essential developments in the Gilded Age city that reflected larger social changes that pushed and pulled particular animal populations and institutions across the urban landscape. In purchasing the land and building an amusement park, Woodward hoped that the area would become a place of refined residential and leisure space: filled with the sounds of laughing children, and not the squealing of hogs; the smell of popcorn, and not offal; a place of human health, happiness, and liveliness, and not a space of sickness and morbidity.

Born in Rhode Island in 1824, Woodward came to San Francisco in the gold rush. Like many successful pioneers who would become prominent business and civic leaders in San Francisco in the 1850s and 1860s, Woodward succeeded not by striking gold, but by provisioning fortune seekers. He opened the What Cheer House in 1852, a temperance hotel near the busy downtown waterfront, which was distinctive in that it did not have a saloon or gambling hall. The hotel provided a safe haven from the rough and inebriate crowds that were giving the city a reputation. The hotel admitted only men—in the bedrooms and also in the lobby and restaurant—presumably as a way to prevent prostitution and immoral cavorting. Advertisements for the What Cheer House highlighted the hotel's temperance characteristics, along with its civilizing baths and barbershop.[22]

Throughout his life, Woodward understood his businesses as doing something greater than making money and maximizing profit. In this popular view, modest profits and social progress could be complementary and not conflicting. Over the course of the 1850s, Woodward constructed a massive library in the What Cheer House—perhaps the largest and most distinguished library of its type on the

Pacific Coast. The library contained a large collection of books on natural history, which he hoped would educate and tame even the most disorderly of urban social environments. In 1860, Woodward added a museum to the hotel, which was accessible only by walking through the library. Reminiscent of Charles Willson Peale's American Museum, Woodward's collections contained a large number of stuffed animals and specimens from around the world—as many as 12,000 by one generous count. There were eggs, minerals, shells, butterflies, insects, animal horns, and some 600 birds and 25 stuffed mammals. Alongside these specimens were human artifacts from indigenous cultures in North America, South America, and the South Pacific—artifacts representing cultures Woodward likely saw as outside the realm of civilization, but nevertheless considered their presence central to his construction of civility.[23]

By the 1860s, Woodward had entered the upper echelon of San Francisco's social elite. He bought a house in San Francisco's fashionable Rincon Hill neighborhood and began constructing an elaborate mansion and private gardens on a large plot of land occupying two city blocks (between Mission and Valencia Streets, and Thirteenth and Fifteenth Streets), which would later be the site of Woodward's Gardens. Woodward traveled to Europe in 1861 and returned with paintings and sculptures he had purchased with the help of prominent landscape painters Albert Bierstadt and Virgil Williams.[24] Woodward's new "suburban villa" was classical Pompeian in style, complete with frescoed walls, painted floors, hand-carved furniture, chairs of original Greek design, and statues and busts of Michelangelo, Raphael, Petrarch, Dante, Ariasto, and Tasso. He ordered other pieces from Italy, and had live swans shipped from England and Australia.[25]

Woodward's home and gardens would remain private until 1866. In 1864, Woodward opened the gates to his estate as a fundraiser for the Union's Sanitary Fund during the Civil War—a model of fundraising popular in elite circles, including New York City where William Astor and August Belmont held similar events.[26] It would be another two years before Woodward would again open his doors to the public. In the meantime—in April 1866—Woodward was elected president of the Board of Directors of San Francisco's Omnibus Railroad Company, which ran lines across the city, including one that passed his estate, where he would eventually build the oversized gates to his gardens.[27] Less than three months after becoming president of the board, he opened his San Francisco estate to the public as Woodward's Gardens, charging visitors a nominal fee for entry.[28] The crowds that would gather at Woodward's Gardens came and went on the omnibus line he, in part, owned. In the years that followed, his gardens and rail lines serviced thousands of visitors each week. Woodward's investments were self-reinforcing: he made money on people coming and going, and on the entertainment and concessions they consumed in between.

Woodward's investments were also meant, ostensibly, to improve the lives of his customers and the city as a whole. To leading men like Woodward, families were foundational units for a civilized democracy. It was the work of institutions to cultivate and strengthen families in order to overpower the demimonde of single men, gamblers, drunks, and prostitutes. There was profit in providing San Francisco families with popular entertainments and culture that would also improve the city.[29] Woodward's project sought both reform and profit, though it was never clear that his gardens were actually profitable.

The museum at Woodward's Gardens offered a larger space to showcase the thousands of items Woodward had collected at the What Cheer House, which he added to and expanded in the years that followed. He also invested heavily in creating a sizable private zoo, a plant conservatory, a skating rink, a decorative mosque, a restaurant, and an amphitheater. Like the animals that were confined, human visitors were closely monitored and regulated. And, like Barnum's exhibition spaces, Woodward's Gardens did not allow "intoxicating liquors" of any kind—a fact that Woodward was proud to proclaim at every opportunity. Instead, visitors could drink freely from any of the twelve "drinking posts" scattered around the park, which flowed with "cool water."[30]

Central to this vision of social improvement was an interest in cultivating a safe urban space for children. Like Barnum, Woodward catered to children and saw them as building blocks of his larger project of social improvement and stability. When the gardens first opened in 1866, Woodward admitted school groups free of charge, and in the years that followed he opened his doors to numerous school groups, Sunday school classes, and charitable institutions at little or no cost.[31] Children always received discounted admission, just as they did at Barnum's museum and shows (10 cents, compared to 25 cents for adults). "When useful instruction can be combined with rational amusement," said one admirer of Woodward's Gardens in 1869, "one of the great ends of popular education is accomplished."[32] Woodward's Gardens was one of the few places parents could leave their children unattended, said Woodward, where "no chance is left for a child to get hurt."[33] In 1869, a group of eight hundred students took a steamboat from Vallejo to spend the afternoon in Woodward's Gardens. At the end of the day, only three children were left behind in the city.[34]

Woodward also offered preferential treatment for groups he saw as serving a greater public good—church groups and benevolent societies he deemed worthy of support. In 1870, Woodward distributed five thousand tickets at no charge to ten separate benevolent institutions in the city as part of an effort to help them

raise funds for their public-improvement projects.[35] Attendance and patron loyalty was high in the 1870s, with reported individual ticket sales often well above
five thousand on a single weekend day. Although he frequently ran ads in the
city's newspapers, Woodward also relied on these private organizers as part of an
informal marketing network.[36] Even when Woodward gave away tickets, he still
made money from the sales of concessions and streetcar fares. If visitors were
happy on their first free visit, they were more likely to return. But the fundraisers
were ultimately a form of social politics, favoring and supporting some groups in
the city over others. Going to the zoo was not merely a leisure activity, but a form
of piecemeal politics intended to promote certain social reforms, and a form of
politics that favored some political and social institutions over others. One writer
called Woodward's Gardens "a public benefit to the city, especially to children
and to the poorer classes, and to Mr. Woodward are due the hearty thanks of our
population."[37] Woodward's own advertisements proclaimed the gardens a "Resort for the People!" without saying which ones.[38]

Woodward's zoo was a carefully curated part of this larger social agenda, but also
appealed broadly to a public curious about animals. Woodard sought to establish
and develop his zoo as the finest on the West Coast, and frequently advertised his
animal attractions in city newspapers. One visitor in 1869 described the gardens
as "the most extensive collection of savage animals and rare birds in America—
camels, elks, grizzlies, black and cinnamon bears, a California lion, Bengal tiger,
female jaguar and whelps, male jaguar; red, gray, black and blue foxes; kangaroos,
leopards and wild cat, wallabies, emus, eagles, golden and silver pheasants, monkeys without end, and more than a hundred other living varieties, not necessary
to mention."[39] Over the years, the makeup of the zoo would change, but animals
remained central to the distinct appeal of Woodward's Gardens.

Tourists visiting San Francisco often put Woodward's Gardens at the top of
their itinerary. The other main attraction of the city was the Cliff House, a restaurant and hotel perched precariously on a rock over the Pacific Ocean with a
view of Seal Rock and its wild and noisy animal inhabitants.[40] When former president Ulysses Grant visited Woodward's Gardens in 1879, he was greeted with an
"enthusiastic ovation" by "not less than twenty-thousand youngsters."[41] Barnum
also visited Woodward's Gardens in 1870, and left wanting to purchase seals and
sea lions from Woodward for his own exhibitions.[42] In 1872, Louis Agassiz asked
Woodward for a private visit to the gardens, so he could study the "peculiarities
and habits of the seals and sea lions." One of the city's newspapers described

Agassiz's visit under the headline "Sea Lions to Be Interviewed."[43] For Agassiz, the seals in the cramped pond at Woodward's Gardens were not inauthentic forms of wildlife, uprooted from their natural habitats, but animals that maintained their essential characteristics and behaviors that he sought to observe as natural science.

Perhaps the most telling description of Woodward's Gardens came from Miriam Leslie—the ambitious and influential publisher and wife of New York socialite and newspaper owner Frank Leslie. Miriam Leslie visited San Francisco in 1877, noting the "fine collection of wild animals" at Woodward's Gardens, including "ferocious ones" that looked out from their cages appearing "languid and disgusted of [humans]."[44] A well-traveled woman who moved in elite circles in New York City, Leslie had likely seen many zoos around the world. She seemed impressed by Woodward's zoo. What struck her, in particular, were the spaces in which Woodward's animals were confined and exhibited. The animals were, she said, "more beautiful than we often see them, because they are at liberty within their fenced paddocks."[45] Although cramped and overbuilt by later standards, the enclosures at Woodward's Gardens were spacious and naturalistic for their time—features that supposedly improved the enjoyment and imagination of human visitors, as much as they improved the lives of animals themselves. As a member of the San Francisco SPCA, Woodward may have believed that the welfare of animals was intrinsically valuable. He certainly understood that the appearance of contented animals was valuable for advancing his reform agenda and creating a pleasing atmosphere for his customers.

As Leslie's observations suggest, the designs of Woodward's animal enclosures were deliberate attempts to change the ways in which people saw and experienced animals—to create a placid experience of observation, often purporting to emulate the conditions of a particular idea of nature. "One gets a better idea of an ostrich in seeing him upon a sunny hillside," said Leslie, than "in a cage six feet square with his beautiful plumes as broken and worn as an old feather duster." The "deer in their park," she continued, were "as free and graceful as in their native wilds."[46] The aquarium was, according to another observer, "a very good imitation of Nature," and the ponds and rocks were "made to look as much as possible like natural sea-work rocks."[47] Woodward's new park was a landscape project that sought to connect urban visitors with a curated form of nature. Animals were not only living creatures to be observed up close but also key set pieces in the construction of natural landscapes that were designed to comfort and elevate urban residents.

The landscaping of Woodward's Gardens was also an effort to channel animal behaviors to meet human expectations and to create a park that was safe and appealing for public consumption. Leslie found the bear pit to be "the most amusing feature of all," in large part because of the environment in which the bears were confined. At first glance, there was nothing particularly "natural" about the bear pit—no trees, no vegetation of any kind, just wood-planked decks and large vertical posts. But in the bear pit, it was "naturalistic" behavior that Woodward sought to exhibit. The architecture of the bear pit created pathways for bears to behave in ways that visitors desired. "Tall poles were erected in the middle with little platforms on top," wrote Leslie, such that "Bruin might pretend to himself that he was climbing a tree and resting in the branches."[48] What the bears thought remains inscrutable, but it seems likely that most of the pretending happened on the human side of the fence. The "tall poles" created an opportunity for people to imagine how a bear might have behaved in the wild, in some distant forest far from the din of urban life. In what was likely a form of misunderstanding, bears climbed the poles for reasons quite different than those ascribed by human onlookers—perhaps, even to escape the endless crowds that gathered below.

Although zoo exhibits like Woodward's supposedly sought to remove the human hand from the exhibition of animals, they were nevertheless quite controlling of animal behavior. The bear pit enclosure gave bears little choice in how to move and spend their energy. The tall poles were all they had. The built structures within the bear pit compelled animals to behave in certain ways to meet human expectations—which, in turn, reinforced those behaviors as natural in the eyes of visitors. Over time, the bear pit had black and grizzly bears—both capable of climbing trees, but neither particularly eager to do so in the wild. In Woodward's Gardens climbing "trees" was most of what they did. Woodward's display ostensibly stripped away human artifice from the exhibition of animals. There was "no attempt at deception or misrepresentation," noted one observer.[49] But the exhibits remained profoundly human constructions that manipulated animals into behaving in ways that met human expectations and desires.

Other prominent visitors were not nearly as impressed with Woodward's Gardens as Miriam Leslie. When Anthony Trollope visited California in 1875, he proclaimed that there was "nothing to see in San Francisco," and specifically cited the city's "inferior menagerie of wild beasts" as an example.[50] In 1879, Otto Finsch, the aptly named German ornithologist and ethnographer, visited San Francisco and compared Woodward's zoo to "some of the smaller gardens in Germany," while also complimenting Woodward for his collection that "contained some birds seen alive by me for the first time." It was true, Finsch said, that Woodward's Gardens were "intended more for pleasure and amusement than pure science," but he added that it was, nevertheless, "a most interesting institution, and just what

San Francisco and America generally require."[51] To European and British visitors, most American zoos—and Woodward's Gardens in particular—likely appeared to be second-rate attractions compared to the older and larger zoological parks that existed across the Atlantic during the same period.[52] A Europhile himself, Woodward understood these larger and older institutions as shining examples he wished to replicate in civilizing the gold rush city.

In many cases, the living animals were disappointing for audiences who wished to see wild and spirited animals. If modern zoos are any indication of how animals behaved at Woodward's Gardens, many of the creatures on display became languid and indolent in confinement. No amount of landscaping or architecture—islands of rocks for seals, wooden poles for bears, "pastures" for deer, concrete rocks for fish—could make up for fact the these were not the vivacious creatures that would link urban residents to a vital and distant nature.

When living animals would not behave in ways that pleased the crowds, Woodward and others invented ways to animate nature. Although largely disappointed with the living animals on display, Otto Finsch expressed a fascination with another animal exhibit in the gardens: a machine called the Zoographicon. An invention of Woodward's manager, Ferdinand Gruber, the Zoographicon was a rotating diorama with moving parts—which Finsch described as a "representation of the chief types of the different zoological centres of the globe"—including "the Arctic," "North America," "South America," "South Pacific Islands," "Australia," "Africa," "Europe," and "Asia." Crowded with artificial plants, trees, and moving animals, the Zoographicon was a stimulating attraction. Gruber also advertised it as the "Great Educator" because he believed it could teach zoology and ecology to the public. Visitors could marvel at the human elements that went into the exhibit—the scientific research and mechanical mastery—while also experiencing animal movement lacking in the living creatures only steps away. Woodward's catalog described in detail the "North American" scene, crammed with animals and natural features:

Passes a view of the Mississippi River. An alligator sitting on a log floating and dipping in the water. A coot exercises his diving skill; the teal his swimming powers. To the left on top of a tree, a large black woodpecker is hammering; underneath a drowsy owl is peeping out of her hiding place; while in a hole on the base of the tree a squirrel, frightened by a watchful fox, withdraws to its retreat. A weasel is seen to come out of a cave on the shore and disappear. A puma or cougar crouching on a precipitous rock seems to be ready to jump down upon a deer and fawn resting on the ground under a magnolia tree. A golden eagle carries off a white rabbit to a dense foliage. Bluejays, robins, meadow larks, blackbirds, tanagers and numerous

FIGURE 7.1 The "Australia" scene of the Zoographicon, a mechanized, animated tableau invented by Ferdinand Gruber and displayed at Woodward's Gardens in San Francisco. Photograph by O. V. Lange, stereograph. California History Room, California State Library, Sacramento, California.

other birds enliven this very beautiful scene, as if to observe the sunset on the Mississippi River.[53]

The chaotic and overcrowded mise-en-scène would have been impossible outside human construction. Yet Otto Finsch, a man of science, who spent much of his time studying dead birds, delighted at the Zoographicon: "The Woodpecker hammers; the Dipper dives; the Ducks swim, and so on," he said with apparent excitement, adding that it was "always crowded!" with spectators.[54] The Zoographicon provided visitors with animal motion and ecological context that the living zoo could not.

Woodward also offered an older form of animal display: stuffed and mounted animals. While some of these specimens were indoors and under glass, others were displayed around the gardens. Animals that had been stuffed and preserved allowed visitors to get close in ways that they could not with living creatures. In 1869, Woodward hired the English photographer Eadweard Muybridge to photograph his gardens. The commission came just a year after Muybridge had gained notoriety for his photographs of Yosemite Valley, but still years before he earned his greatest fame as a pioneer of motion pictures and studies on human and animal movement. While Muybridge's later work concerned animal movement, his photographs of Woodward's Gardens required the stillness of animals that were stuffed and mounted. Among the animals—human and nonhuman alike—only the languid sea lions seemed able to remain still long enough to be photographed clearly. Instead, Muybridge captured still images of the many stuffed animals on display, with people posed in various ways.[55]

If the handful of images Muybridge created were at all representative, Woodward's Gardens was the kind of place where women with dead birds on their hats went to see dead birds arranged in lifelike poses in naturalistic settings.[56] Multiple photographs show well-dressed women posing with large stuffed waterfowl arranged around a small artificial pond. In another photo, a woman kneels to stroke the head of a stuffed tiger as though it were a large dog—its teeth bared menacingly in perpetuity. Another photograph shows a young girl and her mother posing with an eclectic cluster of stuffed animals—a gazelle, a fawn, several rabbits, and a kangaroo—arranged carefully in front of a pine tree. In another photograph a woman is seated among stuffed deer, holding a fawn on her lap, with exotic-looking plants as a backdrop.

Although Woodward's Gardens was ostensibly about civilized entertainment and scientific education, Muybridge's photographs suggest that the gardens were organized to reflect and cultivate human emotions, rather than to achieve ecological or zoological coherence. In one photograph women sit beside a carefully arranged set of stuffed birds, their long beaks and thin legs reflecting a certain gendered refinement. In another photograph, monkeys and sloths are displayed together—animals that have little in common except, perhaps, their relative physical and facial resemblance to human beings. In another portrait of ecological incoherence, a leopard, a tiger, and a hyena appear to be sharing—or perhaps fighting over—a small species of deer; their common characteristics might have been their ferocity and capacity to evoke fear and awe in the minds of visitors. In another photograph, a group of peaceful and harmless creatures that hopped and grazed shared a single frame: a stuffed kangaroo, a gazelle, and several rabbits. Animals were stuffed and frozen into poses, becoming set pieces for a human play with wide-ranging emotional states, but ultimately safe for consumption.[57]

═══

The *Illustrated Guide and Catalogue* for Woodward's Gardens offered visitors another means of accessing the elusive lives of animals. In most years, the catalog ran to almost one hundred pages. It offered practical information for park visitors (such as where to find a water fountain) and details about the artistic, botanical, and zoological collections. But the largest share of the catalog was devoted to describing and depicting the living and stuffed animals on display. As they walked through the park—or sat at home remembering their trip to Woodward's Gardens—visitors could browse the catalog's sketches and scientific descriptions of animals that they had seen in one form or another. The catalog was another means of breathing life into animal exhibits that may have disappointed in the flesh. Sketches showed animals as they might have appeared in the wild, not as they appeared in the zoo—in motion, teeth bared, or surrounded by vibrant natural landscapes. The catalog helped visitors make the leap of imagination necessary to see animated wild animals in creatures that idled in cages and enclosures.[58]

The contents of the catalog changed over time, offering a glimpse into the evolving scientific and social purposes and characteristics of the gardens. By 1880, Woodward had added Latin genus and species names to each of the animal descriptions in an apparent effort to bolster the scientific credentials of the gardens. Coupled with the addition of the mechanical Zoographicon in 1878, Woodward's

FIGURE 7.2 "Aquatic Birds at Woodward's Gardens." Women and children pose with what appear to be stuffed birds. Original stereograph by Eadweard Muybridge (1869).
San Francisco History Center, San Francisco Public Library

FIGURE 7.3 A woman petting a stuffed tiger poses for a photograph at Woodward's Gardens. Eadweard Muybridge, "Animals at Woodward's Gardens," The Bancroft Library, Berkeley, California.

Gardens increased its emphasis on scientific and ecological education—an ideal that he likely understood as a higher and uplifting form of entertainment.

Numerous elements of Woodward's Gardens harkened back to Peale's museum of republican Enlightenment. Indeed, Woodward's efforts to show American landscapes alongside European ones echoed Jefferson's impassioned defense of American nature. Native North American species—bison, bears, deer, seals, and birds—shared physical space with creatures of world renown: emus, Bengal tigers, African lions, monkeys, and Asian water buffalo, among others. In his galleries, Woodward displayed paintings of California's Napa Valley alongside classical scenes of the Tiber River, the Alban Hills, and street scenes from Florence and Rome. In presenting American nature and culture alongside these formidable and classical examples from Europe, Woodward was trying to put California on the global map of civilization.[59] Through animals and nature, Californians told stories about themselves and their rising place in the world.

Catch and Display

But beneath the placid scenes of urban residents enjoying animals and nature in the Gilded Age city was a darker reality. Woodward's Gardens was part of larger project of zoo building that expanded nationally and internationally in the late nineteenth century. Between 1859 and 1910, forty-six public zoos were built in cities across the United States, to say nothing of the many large private zoos like Woodward's.[60] Nationally and internationally, demand for wild animals soared, forging vast regional and global networks to provision these first-generation zoos. Growing demand for zoo animals worldwide spawned an international trade in live animals that was often quite brutal. The German zookeeper Charles Hagenbeck and others assembled international networks of suppliers and buyers in the 1880s, risking the lives of men who hunted live animals, while subjecting animals themselves to violent capture, transport, and confinement.[61] Woodward's Gardens was a node in this growing trade network of zoo animals, and Woodward traded with dealers in New York and London—even becoming a global supplier of California sea lions, which were in high demand internationally.

The scenes of children and families gazing happily at the sea lions at Woodward's Gardens concealed a darker reality of capture and confinement. Trapping sea lions was perilous work. The first men to gather sea lions for Woodward's Gardens and other zoos worldwide worked the rough and rocky Channel Islands, off the coast of Santa Barbara, along with other islands along the California coast. When seasons, tides, and weather conditions were optimal, they landed their boats on the cliff-faced islands, and "three or four expert vacqueros" descended on the herds of beached sea lions. Picking the finest of the rookery—often weighing more than one- or two thousand pounds—they lassoed one sea lion at a time, at both the head and the tail. Once a sea lion was roped and immobilized, the hunters waited as the animal struggled to the point of exhaustion, which sometimes took more than an hour. Lips curled and tusks bared, the massive creature might charge the men, who clambered for safety on the slippery rocks on the edge of the roaring Pacific Ocean. Once the sea lion was exhausted, the trappers dropped a cage over the weary creature and towed it to shore.[62] After a dozen catches, the trappers shipped the animals by rail to San Francisco. The dangerous work was generously rewarded: whereas a bear cost Woodward about $10 on average, sea lions were worth $500 or more, depending on size.[63]

Once in captivity the brutality continued. Despite the best efforts of handlers and zookeepers to protect their expensive investments, sea lions died in captivity at alarming rates. Faced with the immense stresses of confinement, many sea lions did not eat for as many as ten or twenty days, dying of "self-imposed starvation." Of the eleven sea lions that Woodward purchased in a single shipment in 1874, seven died within two months, and one of the remaining four was "sick."[64] Some exhausted themselves by ceaselessly tracing the edges of their confinement, likely searching for an exit.[65] Visitors to Woodward's Gardens delighted in seeing animal activity. But what they were seeing was likely a distressed and desperate struggle to find an escape—or perhaps expressions of what are now called zoo stereotypies that may be an animal's attempt to self-soothe and cope with stresses of confinement.[66] Through animals, visitors searched desperately for an authentic connection to the natural world, perhaps imagining themselves on the shoals of the Channel Islands. Unbeknownst to many, a more authentic and desperate search for nature may have been happening right before their eyes.

The bifurcated world of consuming animals in zoos and producing those animals for exhibition reflected similar spatial and moral divisions in production and consumption in other working relationships with animals in cities. Slaughterhouses, hog ranches, and sea lion hunts shared a similar moral geography: they all required animal suffering and sacrifice in distant and invisible spaces that produced palatable and consumable products for urban residents. Woodward sought to construct a place of human refuge, pleasure, and civility, but it was built on a foundation of invisible and distant animal suffering. Indeed, had the violent capture of sea lions happened in the streets or on the piers of San Francisco, Woodward and most urban residents likely would have objected emphatically to the inhumane treatment.

The invisible brutality of creating Woodward's Gardens was part of a larger trend in the development of zoos in the last decades of the nineteenth century—and one that zookeepers actively sought to hide from visitors. Hagenbeck's trapping campaigns in Africa in the late nineteenth century were notoriously violent and destructive. In New York, William Hornaday, the famous zoologist who served as the first head of the New York Zoological Park, believed that the best zoo specimens were "those born in a wild state, or else in a game preserve so large that captivity has not necessarily resulted in degeneracy." Animals that were caught young and "reared in confinement" created the "best possible results in the stocking of a vivarium." It was, Hornaday noted, "impossible to capture adult animals of the larger types and induce them to become cheerfully resigned to captivity. In most cases they either kill themselves by struggling or die of melancholy."[67] The hardship of Woodward's sea lions was one that many zoo animals understood.

Capturing young animals was notably violent and bloody. "In order to catch the young, it is usually necessary to kill the mother," Hagenbeck wrote.[68] The pursuit of one or a few young animals could lead to outright massacres. In 1900, a Danish expedition to Greenland killed twenty-eight musk oxen to capture one young specimen for the Copenhagen Zoo.[69] By the turn of the twentieth century, Hornaday understood that the public would disapprove if they knew that their amusements were born of such violence and brutality. In 1902, Hornaday wrote to Hagenbeck to procure a rhino for the New York Zoo, but asked that Hornaday "keep very still about forty large Indian rhinoceroses being killed in capturing the four young ones." If the violence and brutality of capturing wild animals were to get into the newspapers, he continued, "there would be things published in condemnation of the whole business of capturing wild animals for exhibition." Hornaday complained of the "many cranks" who were "so terribly sentimental that they affect to believe that it is wrong to capture wild creatures and exhibit them,—even for the benefit of millions of people." For Hornaday, the work of zookeeping was heroic. It was better, he said, to bring wild animals from the re- mote corners of the earth to the urban centers of civilization, where they would be "of more benefit to the world" than they were "in the jungles of Nepal, and seen only at rare intervals by a few ignorant natives."[70] In both New York and San Francisco, the immeasurable sacrifices and sufferings of animals in distant places were largely invisible to urban customers who visited zoos.

While urban residents and visitors consumed wild animals at Woodward's Gar- dens and other zoos in various, mediated ways, a large number of Americans also became involved with zoos as suppliers and dealers of animals.[71] This was often far less formal than the organized professional expeditions led by Hagenbeck and other animal trappers and dealers. Although Woodward traded in the interna- tional market—and was in contact with Barnum and Hagenbeck—he also en- gaged extensively with individuals who wrote to him offering various animals for sale. Of the remaining letters addressed to Robert Woodward from the early 1870s, a vast majority came from ordinary Americans seeking to sell or donate living animals to his zoo. The geography of these letter writers suggests the expansive cultural and economic sphere of influence of Woodward's Gardens, whose repu- tation and influence ranged tens or hundreds—sometimes thousands—of miles beyond the city of San Francisco. Many rural Americans sought to contribute and stake a claim to Woodward's institution of civilized urban life. Others wished simply to make a buck.

Most of these rural letter writers imagined a more robust market for wild ani- mals than what actually existed. But imagination of the market nevertheless had real consequences for animals that were captured and confined, but never sold.

Many amateur trappers wrote Woodward to offer only a single animal for sale, which they often acquired incidentally and without much organization, planning, or knowledge of the market. Such writers offered a snake from Livermore, deer from Napa and Watsonville, two owls from Yolo County, a roadrunner from Calistoga, an albatross from Mendocino, a white swan from Oroville, and a hedgehog from Shasta County, to name just a few of the hundreds of submissions.[72] These trappers and hunters showed their inexperience by deferring to Woodward on the value of the animals they offered for sale.

Other letters suggested an expansive network of small-scale professional trappers and traders across California, the American West, and the United States, some of whom corresponded regularly with Woodward. The letters from these professionals read more like company inventories and stock listings, with sellers confidently stating their prices up front. They came from men who likely planned the capture or purchase of the animals in their possession, and had some knowledge of which species had real value in the zoo and entertainment markets. Many of these trappers sold animals that required skilled hunting and trapping—animals that were effective at avoiding human contact or ensnarement, or that posed physical danger to hunters. Some of these trappers were clearly part of a larger network of traders that had a vast geographic reach. Among these small-scale animal traders was a man from Santa Barbara selling an owl, a vulture, and a pelican.[73] A letter from Gilroy offered an anteater, a monkey, and a squirrel for sale.[74] A trapper from Cottonwood offered four foxes, bears, fisher cats, raccoons, and minks.[75] Others offered four mule deer from Modoc County; a cinnamon bear and foxes from Red Bluff; reindeer and caribou from British Columbia; wild cats from the Sierra Mountains near Marysville; prairie dogs from Wyoming Territory; seals from Santa Barbara; brown bears from Porterville; and a cinnamon bear cub from Mendocino, which, it was said, could be "handled quite easily."[76] Some sellers appeared to have small farms of wild animals, or unusual breeds of domesticated species, such as deer and partridge, which they sought to sell as wild rarities. Despite the professionalism of these small-scale hunters, trappers, and farmers, these were not the large-scale, global animal traders that were emerging at the same time to furnish the zoos of Europe, Britain, and the United States.[77]

The animals that Woodward predictably purchased were those that he had in short supply or those he knew held value in the larger global market. Woodward rarely turned down an opportunity to acquire precious species such as seals and sea lions. They held value to Woodward both in his gardens and in the international live animal market. Woodward also understood the challenges of domesticating wild animals for this wave of first-generation zoos, and often leaped at the opportunity to purchase young species of deer, bears, and wildcats. Raising those species in captivity was beneficial to Woodward and offered the possibility of raising offspring that were more docile and accustomed to confinement. For some species, Woodward had to renew his stock constantly because of their high rates of mortality. "As I have found pumas as well as all the Cat tribe short lived, yours will do to keep my stock good," he wrote to a man in Mendocino offering a puma that was "tame like a dog."[78]

The broad cultural and social significance of Woodward's Gardens was also apparent in the number of letters Woodward received offering to donate animals to his zoo. Without asking for compensation, a man from Watsonville sent Woodward a single fox—an animal Woodward usually refused when offered for sale by traders and trappers. "I make you a present of it," said the man from Watsonville, "I want you to put it in your Gardens and put on the cage who it was caught by. I do this just for the novelty of the thing. I have a great many friends that visit your gardens." Woodward accepted the gift.[79] A wealthy San Francisco banker, George Hickox, wrote to Woodward on his son's behalf, sending Woodward a "large Eagle" from the mountains of California that his son had received as a gift from a friend, but that had become an "'elephant' in our garden." Woodward typically refused to purchase eagles, but in this case accepted the bird. "My boy will be glad to add to his 'Savings Bk Deposit,'" added Hickox. Woodward paid the boy nothing, but sent him a free pass to the gardens that reflected the eagle's value as closer to a ten-cent admission.[80]

Perhaps more revealing than the animals Woodward accepted and purchased were those that he declined. These were species that were plentiful, easily trapped or farmed, or those that survived relatively well in captivity and rarely needed replacement. "I have a surplus of foxes," wrote Woodward, who rarely purchased new foxes.[81] "We have a good supply of hawks," he wrote on another occasion, and "plenty of eagles."[82] In Woodward's Gardens, many of the live birds were not caged, but instead chained to perches along a pathway leading to the art museum.

More importantly, Woodward declined acquisition of another set of animals because they did not fit the larger social reform agenda of his gardens. This was an approach he arrived at over time. Woodward's early catalogs featured several "freaks of nature." The 1873 catalog listed three- and six-legged sheep, a two-tailed horse, and a "wooly horse" purportedly born from a mule. In the Buffalo paddock, Woodward also kept "that extremely strange freak of nature, the five-legged calf," from one of the "southern counties" in California. "The fifth leg, which hangs from the top of the shoulders, has grown larger in proportion to its growth otherwise. It is also a hermaphrodite," noted the catalog.[83] Traveling shows that performed at Woodward's Gardens also exhibited animal deformities in the early years, including "The Living Headless Rooster," which was exhibited in 1868.[84]

FIGURE 7.4 Live birds were tethered to perches that lined the walkway to the museum at Woodward's Gardens. Eadweard Muybridge, "Entrance to the Museum at Woodward's Gardens," California History Room, California State Library, Sacramento, California.

Although animal deformities were acceptable to Woodward in his early years, they appeared always to be domesticated species—perhaps the product of overbreeding, as California farmers sought to rapidly build breeds and herds to fill the expanding pastures in the Central Valley and areas around San Francisco.[85] Perhaps the fact that these deformed species were human creations—errors of human meddling rather than originating from wild or divine creation—made their exhibition more acceptable. In exhibiting the deformities of human creation, there was an implicit misanthropy in Woodward's collection of animal oddities—a distaste for working relationships with animals—along with an implicit veneration of a purer, higher natural world of respectable wild animals. Farm animals only appeared in Woodward's Gardens when they demonstrated oddities or abnormalities. In later years, farm animals appeared almost not at all. In showing domestic animals only when freakish—and shifting his collection to exotic and wild animals—Woodward contributed to a growing invisibility and indifference to farm work, landscapes, and animals that fell in between the vaunted spaces of the civilized city and wild and distant nature. Domesticated livestock increasingly disappeared from Woodward's Gardens, as they did from San Francisco in general.[86]

In the early 1870s, Woodward showed a strong desire to remake his animal collection to reflect the higher ideals of his museum. The domesticated "freaks of nature" gave way to "representative species" of nature. In his correspondence, Woodward typically rejected offers of freaks of nature. An 1873 letter from Island County, Washington Territory, from a man who had visited Woodward's Gardens several times, offered Woodward a "freak in nature, devided [sic] between Human and Frog Families"—what was likely a person with severe physical deformities. Woodward was uninterested.[87] A letter to Woodward from Philadelphia offering an "educated pig"—a popular entertainment of an earlier generation—got no apparent response from Woodward, and was never listed in the catalog.[88] "It often happens that persons write to us about the 'greatest (?) curiosity,'" said Woodward, when in fact he saw these specimens as "no curiosity at all."[89] In the first years of the gardens, Woodward apparently displayed a fake mermaid, but showed little interest in acquiring other "curiosities" in the 1870s.[90] These creatures were not scientific specimens or representative species that Woodward increasingly understood as the cornerstone of his project. They were holdovers of animal "humbugs" and oddities of a prior generation, and did not fit the civilizing and scientific institution he sought to cultivate. They made a mockery of the nonhuman world and played on the basest human forms of engagement, rather than encouraging visitors to see animals as part of a more authentic and higher form of nature.

Rural letter writers continued to offer deformed livestock for sale in the 1870s, but Woodward became even more resolute in rejecting such offers. Woodward showed no interest in several of these curiosities: a "two-footed lamb" from Folsom that walked on his front legs; two-legged calves from Grand Island and Big Meadows; three-legged cows from San Marino, San Jose, and Linn County, Oregon; and a five-legged sheep from San Jose.[91] By every indication, Woodward refused to buy from these sellers. When a man tried to sell Woodward a goat from Nevada with "hind legs turn backward at the knee joint," Woodward responded, "Your curiosity is not of a pleasing nature and would create more sympathy than anything else and is therefore not very desirable."[92] In response to another undated letter offering a sheep that walked only on its front legs,

Woodward said he might be interested "if the sheep is comical and pleasing." But if its "deficiencies causes pity I would not want it."[93] A farmer in Oregon selling a three-legged calf got Woodward's blunt response: "Your calf does not warrant being placed on exhibition."[94]

Woodward was doing nothing short of reconstructing the visible world of animal exhibits in the late nineteenth century, shaping the ways visitors engaged with animals—what they saw and did not see—and how those animals activated certain human feelings and emotions. Woodward's own efforts to actively construct his zoo in opposition to the unscientific and crass freak shows of a previous generation were emblematic of a broader effort among many who imagined themselves as reformers of humans and animals alike. In New York, Hornaday echoed this perspective in 1900, arguing that "animals exhibited in the Zoological Park" should be "worthy representatives of the species they illustrate." To do that, "great care is exercised in their selection," he continued, and "imperfect specimens excluded."[95] In weeding out degenerate and "imperfect specimens," Woodward and Hornaday were perfecting and idealizing nature. Woodward was seeking to remake and control human emotional relationships with animals and nature—not as something that was terrifying or displeasing, but as a source of carefree pleasure, education, and spiritual fulfillment. By 1879, Woodward's *Illustrated Guide and Catalogue* no longer listed the deformed livestock that had once had a small presence at Woodward's Gardens. The new catalog added a scientific gloss to its animal descriptions, including Latin species names for all animals on display, living and dead.[96]

Even as Woodward carefully remade his exhibitions to present "representative species" and eliminate deformed animals, he seemed to care little about eliminating human oddities and freak shows from his gardens. In fact, it seems that human oddities increased in the 1870s and 1880s. Animals were made other and exotic by being "representative" species from far and distant places—often deemed "wild"—while human beings were made other by their physical or cultural anomalies. Over the course of two decades, Woodward's Gardens hosted a woman with no arms, a Chinese Giant, and an American Indian child who had supposedly never learned to walk upright.[97] A fire swallower, described as stout and "dark as any African we ever saw," drew large crowds in the 1870s.[98] Performers likely made decent money playing the roles of human "freaks," but probably had few other opportunities for gainful employment. In Woodward's civilizing project, animal irregularities were something to be pitied, whereas human irregularities were something to be monetized and gawked at.

Conclusion: "The Death of Art and Nature"

In the years that he operated his gardens, Woodward sought to significantly re-make the ways people interacted with animals. In many aspects, Woodward's as-pirations for social reform seemed to harmonize with the humane movement and the work of the San Francisco SPCA, which also sought to eliminate visible forms of suffering as a means of improving society. Indeed, the SFSPCA seemed largely indifferent to Woodward's Gardens. Robert Woodward was listed as a dues-paying member in 1879—and, despite being located only few blocks apart, the SFSPCA seemed to meddle little or not at all in Woodward's affairs. There are no records of SFSPCA prosecutions, and agents rarely mentioned Woodward's Gardens in the 1870s and 1880s.[99] Woodward's Gardens appeared only in passing in 1879, when the SFSPCA agent "shot an old horse in front of Woodward's Garden."[100] What went on inside the gates of Woodward's Gardens was appar-ently of little concern.

In some ways, Woodward's remaking of animal life in the city fit with the larger efforts to eliminate livestock from urban life. In rejecting the vulgar dis-plays of deformed livestock, Woodward also eliminated some of the last remnants of agricultural life from his urban museum. In choosing some animals over others, and carefully rejecting those that were not pleasing to the public, Woodward was presenting to the city a sanitized version of animals and nature—a small sliver of a broader set of animal types and human-animal relationships that existed in the wider world. Like the health reformers and humane reformers, Woodward's agenda prioritized human improvement through reform of human-animal inter-actions. His response to the farmer from Oregon—"Your calf does not warrant being placed on exhibition"—could have been applied to the new landscape of urban animal life more broadly: domesticated livestock and the unpleasant as-pects of those relationships deserved no visible or perceptible place in the civi-lized city.

In all cases, the process of creating a refined urban animal environment did not eliminate animal suffering and violence, but merely displaced and concealed them: snakes still fed on live rabbits and mice; sea lions were still captured and tormented; lambs and cows were still overbred to the point of disfigurement; and cattle and pigs were still pushed and prodded into pens, strung up, and slaugh-tered. But the commodities animals provided—meat, milk, leather, companion-ship, entertainment, and access to certain emotional states—were increasingly sanitized for urban residents. Although emerging zoos sought to strip away "humbug" and to present animals in ways that evoked their dignity and authentic place in nature, there was artifice in the authentic. What Woodward was doing informally through cultural institutions mirrored what the SPCA was doing in formal political circles: cleansing the city of certain unpleasant and degrading relationships with animals and fostering others that were deemed to have social benefits.

═

Despite its years as a leisure space at the center of refined and middle class culture in San Francisco, Woodward's Gardens began its decline into obsolescence in the late 1880s. Golden Gate Park and a growing set of new amusements in the western part of the city offered San Franciscans many of the same pleasures and benefits as Woodward's Gardens, but on a larger scale and in a more dramatic landscape. Perhaps the traveling circuses that emerged with notable popularity in the 1880s also undermined Woodward's space in San Francisco's entertainment industry. By the late 1880s, Golden Gate Park not only had the expansive natural spaces that overshadowed Woodward's relatively small gardens, but they had also built a small zoo. Once a large and attractive urban park, Woodward's Gardens seemed relatively cramped and dingy. The wild animals seemed less authentic than those now celebrated in the writings of John Muir and Jack London, who looked to a more distant nature as a place to consume wild animals and nature. Many came to see Woodward's Gardens as Mark Twain had seen The Willows in 1868, a place of "dingy horrors" and a poor replica of a truer, wilder nature.

Woodward's Gardens saw a rather precipitous decline in the 1880s. Robert Woodward died in 1879, leaving his estate, including Woodward's Gardens, to his three children. But problems soon emerged, and the park fell into obsolescence. Some residents looked at the decline of Woodward's Gardens as merely another step in the city's progress. Others wallowed in nostalgia at the decadence of the gardens' deterioration. It "reminds us of the past glories of this resort," said one San Franciscan in 1895, "and of the fact that there is nothing in the form of a private show to take its place as an attraction for rural visitors; but Golden Gate Park, which is free, is a greater show than this old resort ever was."[101]

Woodward's Gardens—with its large amphitheater—increasingly found a niche as a venue for human sports after Woodward's death. The Knights of Labor and other private organizations held annual meetings there, and sports such as Spanish sword fighting, boxing, and Greco-Roman wrestling served as the primary forms of entertainment in the late 1880s and early 1890s.[102] Woodward's Gardens lost much of its Victorian passivity in favor of activities that promoted a sense of human vitality through controlled violence and feats of manliness. Wealthier San Franciscans flocked to the gardens in Golden Gate Park—made to accommodate their fine-bred horses and elegant carriages. Many of the working-class residents, who lived disproportionately near Woodward's Gardens, continued to use the old pleasure grounds. In the 1880s and 1890s, the class melting pot of Woodward's Gardens seemed to be giving way to a more socially and spatially divided engagement with nature and public spaces, with wealthier residents accessing Golden Gate Park in greater numbers and Woodward's Gardens relegated to a working-class clientele.

As the park spiraled into a new iteration of itself after Woodward's death in 1879, his estate became the subject of a drawn-out legal dispute among his heirs. As the case made its way through the courts, a judge appointed a manager of the gardens who later said he was losing $1,000 per month feeding the animals amid declining attendance.[103] The animals were a form of property that needed to be kept alive to preserve the value of the estate, said the judge, despite the financial losses they seemed to be causing. In the late 1880s and early 1890s, the gardens fell into greater disrepair as attendance plummeted. Neighbors began complaining of Woodward's Gardens as a public nuisance in the 1880s, and health officers looked into doing something about the unpleasant smells. "The gardens have outlived their usefulness, and in a few years they will only be a memory among old inhabitants," said one premature obituary for the amusement park in 1893.[104]

After years in litigation, Woodward's Gardens' collection of animals and relics was finally put up for sale in the 1890s. But nobody wanted the animals. The heirs tried to donate the zoo in its entirety to the new zoo in Golden Gate Park, but the Park Commission refused, for unknown reasons. Other offers to donate the collection were also declined.[105] Once valuable, the living animals now appeared to be toxic assets. In February 1893, a California lion and two jaguars mysteriously died of poisoning in the gardens.[106] By then, the menagerie was a run-down collection of "pulmonary monkeys and rheumatic lions."[107]

Faced with the need to liquidate their assets, Woodward's heirs put the entire collection up for auction in 1893. The auction itself was a final attraction for visitors who wished to remember the Woodward's Gardens of their youth. "Men stood among the crowd whose memories turned time far backward in its flight," said the *San Francisco Call*. The disassembly and piecemeal auction of the gardens was "like the breaking up of some old ship that had carried them [the residents of San Francisco] safely from some faraway shore." Visitors and buyers arrived one last time to get a glimpse of their "boyish days, and the sweet faces of mothers and fathers long since dead." More than a thousand people came to the auction to see "an old landmark being dismantled," and people gathered to watch "what became of some of the favorites they knew so well."[108] The space of amusement had become a space of nostalgia and loss.

The animals and specimens sold at auction for paltry prices. It did not help that the auction took place as the Panic of 1893 was taking its heaviest tolls in California and across the country. The collection—which had taken decades and probably hundreds of thousands of dollars to create and maintain—sold in a matter of hours for a fraction of the original cost. A man from Salt Lake City purchased the jawbones of a mammoth whale that once stood over the entrance of the museum. He paid a mere 50 cents, which had been the price of admission for two adults. The massive bust of George Washington, thirty-seven feet tall, sold for a dollar. Sea lions and seals drew the "most lively" competition, selling for $250—about half what Woodward would have paid in the early 1870s. Other showmen and zookeepers from Denver and Salt Lake City purchased some of the more valuable and robust animals to add to their collections. Adolph Sutro—the wealthy capitalist and future mayor of the city who owned the Cliff House and was developing his own public pleasure gardens near Golden Gate Park—dressed in disguise and bid anonymously from the back corner of the crowd, purchasing most of the collection without anyone noticing until the whole ordeal was over.[109] Like Barnum's repurposing of Peale's American Museum, Sutro would appropriate some of Woodward's collections in a new and different form of entertainment.

In the days after the auction, horses uprooted and hauled away many of the finest trees that had been sold, leaving gaping holes in the ground that would soon be graded for new construction. The merry-go-round boat—a major attraction of the park—sat in a stagnant pond of "green slime" for some time before men with hatchets arrived to break it apart. Some of the aquarium tanks dried out, and others were still full of "stagnant water reeking with decomposed vegetable matter." Broken pieces of wood, ladders, and other debris were tossed into the vacant seal pond that had once been a centerpiece of the Woodward's Gardens. The whole of the scene was, according to one reporter, "the funerals of nature and art."[110]

What was most telling was the fate of some of the more "vicious" animals. A butcher purchased one of the brown bears for $34, presumably to make into steaks that were increasingly "a delicacy reserved for the rich."[111] The "little black bear" was shot for its skin, and a month after the auction the hyena could be seen in the window of a taxidermy shop on Kearny Street. A writer for the *San Francisco Call* speculated that the man who purchased the coyote planned to use the animal for "target practice." The free market in animals that Woodard had staved off for years now showed its true nature.[112]

As the market suggested, the collection of stuffed animals, skins, and mounted heads was reaching new popularity in the late nineteenth century with the craze of bourgeois hunting culture in North America, along with the consumption of wild game at the tables of wealthy urbanites. These were the commodities of a new culture of hunting and wilderness-seeking that gave rise to cultural hunting icons like Theodore Roosevelt, the Boone and Crocket Club, and others proclaiming the virtues of a rugged outdoor life far from cities. Roosevelt declared "hunting big game in the wilderness . . . a sport for a vigorous and masterful people," and a central part of the strenuous life that served a mythical antidote to the soft, flabby, sentimental, and overcivilized city life he and others knew firsthand. In their urban torpor, humans and zoo animals, it turned out, had something in common.[113]

The rise of hunting and the strenuous life was also a backlash against Victorian ideals of civility that had become embodied in the culture and policies of the SPCA and humane movement, along with the development of passive observation of animals at places like Woodward's Gardens and the zoos that spread widely in the last decades of the nineteenth century. These efforts to tame boys and men—to cultivate passive civility through animal relationships, including zoos and pets—may have been the cause of some of this backlash. For Roosevelt and the new purveyors of manliness, childhood was not merely a place to quash boyish impulses to hurt and torture animals and to cultivate kindness. It was, instead, an opportunity to channel and train those impulses toward vitality and national strength, with the help of rifles, fishing rods, and saddles. Killing animals was central to the creation of virile men in America and the fulfillment of a strenuous life, constructed in defiance of a generation of Americans that sought to control and mask cruelty and animal suffering.[114]

The symbols of this novel and prized masculine culture of hunting were the heads and skins of animals that were cleaned, stuffed, and turned into trophies—objects that soon became fetishized commodities separate from the original behaviors and actions that inspired their creation. These were the objects that filled the dens and offices of powerful men and became a language of their own.

It was the lion's fate at Woodward's Gardens that spoke most to these changing dynamics and tensions in the ways many Americans related to animals by 1893. The market was telling of the animal's true value. Days after the auction, the highest bidder arrived with a hired hand to bring home the big cat. When they arrived at the lion's enclosure the hired man pulled out a Winchester rifle, aimed carefully, and began firing shots into the cage. But the rifleman was stingy with the bullets, in his desire to take the skin with as few holes as possible. In the long seconds between each shot, the lion bounded from one end of the cage to the other, roaring furiously and leaping up against the bars, "shaking his shaggy mane as though it were a flag of defiance." Like the sea lions on the rocky shoals, the lion eventually weakened and withdrew into a corner, wailing as more shots continued to ring out. Blood ran between the bars of the cage and pooled along the walkway, where eager children and families once stood gazing in wonder. It took ten shots before the lion finally died.[115]

Born into captivity in the heyday of Woodward's Gardens, in 1881, the lion had been named after then-president James Garfield, who was killed by an assassin's bullet later that same year. Garfield's birth was celebrated by those who looked to the urban gardens as a place of civic pride, naturalistic retreat, civility, and amusement for children and families. In a matter of minutes, the lion was transformed from a living animal used for passive observation and the cultivation of society, into an inanimate object of status and manhood. "The sight was pitiful," said one newspaper—echoing Woodward's description of exhibitions that he sought to exclude.[116] Just as Peale's republican collection of scientific specimens became the foundation of Barnum's "Jacksonian theater of the absurd," only to be reinvented by Barnum again and again, so also were Woodward's living animals repurposed to fit powerful new human desires. Despite the resistance of the animals themselves—Garfield's "flag of defiance"—humans continued to use animals to access what they believed were essential parts of their selves, and of humanity. Concern for animals remained secondary, or even nonexistent. Seen today, the boat full of living animals launched at Niagara Falls in 1827 was an unconscionable act of cruelty. There, at least, most of the animals were unchained and given an improbable opportunity to escape.

Conclusion

Stampede

IN SAN FRANCISCO, things fell apart in 1906. On April 18, at 5:12 A.M., the ground shook violently for more than forty-five seconds, turning buildings into rubble and setting off an uncontrollable fire that swept across the city for the next four days. In the hours immediately after the massive quake the air grew thick with dust and smoke. Residents made their way into the streets, many stunned into silence. South of Market Street, a young patrolman named Harry Walsh surveyed the scenes of destruction. The first aftershock came as a quick jerk, he remembered years later, "like the pull-back in the snap of a cracking whip." When stillness returned it was broken by wails of anguish and the intermittent crashes of buildings as their weakened foundations gave way.

Then the rumbling returned. Residents might have braced themselves, expecting another aftershock. Instead, out of the smoke and dust, came something perhaps more terrifying: a stampede of "wild cattle," charging furiously through downtown. The animals had broken loose—likely in transit from the wharves to Butchertown—and now tore through city streets "with terror." As they ran down Mission Street, south of Market, a warehouse suddenly collapsed onto the street, killing and injuring some of the herd and sending the rest into greater agitation. Walsh had only a handful of bullets, but decided to use them to compassionately shoot some of the animals trapped and suffering beneath the rubble, leaving him with only "six shots." But there were "more cattle coming along," and Walsh braced himself for "big trouble."

Walsh went to get help. He summoned John Moller, the owner of a nearby saloon, and sent two men to get more ammunition. As they did, two of the cattle charged the men, one at Moller, the other at Walsh. As the steer bore down upon him, Walsh kept his hand and eye steady, waiting until the animal got close enough for him to fire off a fatal shot. Walsh's shot landed. The steer went down hard. But Moller was not so lucky. "Paralyzed with fear, [he] held out both hands as if beseeching the beast to go back." The steer lowered his horns, and with one swift motion "ripped him" up before Walsh could turn and shoot. Moller had survived one of the most deadly natural disasters in American history only to be killed by a runaway steer. Walsh finished off the "dozen or more of the wild cattle," with the help of a Texan with a rifle. "We probably killed fifty or sixty out of that herd," he remembered years later. It was likely the last time so many cattle ran in the streets—and died—in downtown San Francisco.[1]

The cattle stampede in downtown San Francisco highlighted how far the city had come in controlling its animal populations in the preceding four decades. For a brief moment after the earthquake, the man-made controls on livestock failed. Physical structures crumbled. The work of driving and managing animals was temporarily suspended. Laws and institutions broke down. But the brief collapse of San Francisco's collective separation from livestock proved short-lived. Vaqueros and slaughterhouse laborers returned to work. Pens, stables, and corrals were rebuilt. SPCA agents and police officers went back to patrolling the streets. Animal laws were rewritten, and the Two-Cow Limit expanded. Livestock returned to their circumscribed places, once again separated and largely concealed from life downtown. The cattle that ran down Mission Street would be the species' grand exit from downtown San Francisco.

San Francisco would be rebuilt, but not without further animal sacrifice. "Into the foundations of the new city is going the life-blood of fifteen thousand superb horses," wrote Rufus Steele in *Harper's Weekly*. Horses did work that automobiles and other machines simply could not. They could fit through narrow alleyways, traverse uneven surfaces, and pull debris from basements. For many tasks, "nothing has been able to replace the horses," wrote Steele.

But horses were suffering and dying at extraordinary rates in the reconstruction of San Francisco. Building contractors got bonuses for doing a job quickly. In turn, they drove their horses hard. "The contractor reaps the premium by driving his horses to death," wrote Steele. The animals died of exhaustion at extraordinary rates, and their dead bodies littered the streets downtown. "A half-hour's walk from Market and Kearny streets at any hour of the day will lead you to a dead horse—dead in the harness—worked to death," wrote Steele. He continued, "The vans that carry off carcasses are busier than the vans which carry drunk men to jail." Ranches

FIGURE C.I A herd of cattle ran wild on Mission Street after the 1906 earthquake, killing John Moller. Some cattle died from a building that fell into the street, and the rest were shot dead. California Historical Society.

from California to as far as Oregon, Nevada, and Montana tried to keep pace with the endless demand for horses in the city. The prices of horses and horse feed soared.[2] With the city's water pipes destroyed, many horses worked all day without water, leading the SFSPCA and the Drayman's Association to construct new water fountains for horses throughout the city.[3] Although horses rebuilt San Francisco, their presence in the city would decline sharply in the years that followed. Their work in rebuilding the city was "willful murder in a just cause," said Steele, "a deliberate sacrifice of five million dollars' worth of horseflesh."[4] Horses were laboring and dying to rebuild a city that would soon have little use for them.

═══

In 1906, the same year that cattle ran wild after the earthquake in San Francisco, a young Socialist muckraker named Upton Sinclair published *The Jungle*, setting off public outrage over the conditions of slaughterhouses in Chicago. Like the cattle on Mission Street, Sinclair's exposé collapsed a spatial and intellectual divide between urban residents and the invisible world of livestock and slaughter. It was a divide that had grown wider in the previous half century, in Chicago and across the United States.

As popular reaction to Sinclair's exposé would suggest, nineteenth-century urban residents found themselves at the forefront of an experiment now fully formed: people living apart from the animals they consumed as food, clothing, and other products—while increasingly embracing new relationships to animals as domestic companions and as new forms of entertainment. These changes marked a pivotal moment in human life more broadly. For thousands of years, most human lives contained a wide range of animal relationships. Humans constructed spiritual beliefs and rituals through animals, making sense of the world through the nonhuman creatures that inhabited their material and spiritual lives. They participated in killing, skinning, processing, wearing, and eating animals that they knew and understood in ways historians will never fully grasp.[5] In a few short decades, beginning in American cities, reformers narrowed the range of experiential relationships with animals to what were thought to be a palatable few. By the early twentieth century, most Americans experienced animals in profoundly different ways than even a generation before. By 1920, when the population of the United States shifted to majority urban, cities had been largely sanitized of flagrant animal suffering—scenes of animal pain and animal death—that had once been commonplace.

Most Americans today live in the shadow of this nineteenth-century moment. They interact with living animals on terms of kindness, affection, and passive observation. Most do not personally kill animals for food. Even those who hunt and fish typically do so in the limited context of recreation, and in places that are often spatially and psychically apart from everyday life. Only a tiny minority have seen or smelled the inside of a modern slaughterhouse—a fact that would have pleased and astonished many mid-nineteenth-century reformers and urban residents, who knew the sights and smells of slaughterhouses and animal businesses all too well. Most Americans do not know the work of confining and feeding animals in pens or cages, of killing them, and of turning their body parts into pieces of meat and consumable products. Most pay others to do that work, enabling the illusion of a kind, clean, and pleasurable world—a fiction that emerged with much deliberation among well-intentioned nineteenth-century urban reformers.

Despite their many shortcomings, most animal welfare reformers of the late nineteenth century cared sincerely for the animals and the people they sought to protect from the deep unkindness of the world—an unkindness that was laid bare in the most brutal and widespread war the nation had ever seen in the 1860s. These early efforts to reduce animal suffering and violence—and with it human suffering and human violence—were in some ways collective efforts to heal the gaping psychic wound of the Civil War. "Neither the churches nor the schools have saved us from a great civil war, and the political and financial corruptions growing out of it," wrote George Angell in 1869.[6] Others who joined Angell in the humane movement believed that remaking human relationships with animals would save humanity from future wars and prevent the sorts of catastrophe the nation had just experienced. Teach our children to love animals, they said, and they will learn to care for one another.

In some ways, reformers were right in thinking that promoting kindness and gentleness with animals would remake human life. The almost-complete absence of animal suffering and animal death in mainstream modern American life has enabled humans to imagine the world in new and distinctive ways. Though the evidence and causal relationship is elusive or wanting, there are some signs that interpersonal violence and murder rates may be lower in societies that have entered what Richard Bulliet calls "post-domesticity"—in which the vast majority of people in society no longer personally kill animals for food, and where most people in society are unacquainted with personal experiences of violence toward animals.[7] While it seems possible that interpersonal violence in these societies may be in decline, how do we measure invisible and impersonal violence and suffering? How do we measure the violence of distant and invisible wars, distant and invisible labor abuses—and also distant and invisible animal landscapes of cramped and foul feedlots, overstuffed cages, and windowless slaughterhouses? Post-domesticity societies may at times offer the appearances of diminished violence and suffering, but there is violence in the machinery.

Although there are advantages of living in a world where violence and suffering is imperceptible, what have modern Americans lost in the bargain? In separating themselves from the unpleasant realities of animal suffering and death, Americans have also lost a connection to essential processes of life. In separating animal killing, animal death, and animal sex, most Americans have become walled off from everyday reminders of their own animality and mortality. They have become alienated from the interdependence of life and death. Perhaps modern American life has created the conditions for greater sensitivity to suffering and violence, but it has also created modern landscapes of human and animal interactions that cause profound human distress when the invisible becomes visible—when the curtain is pulled back to reveal the realities of factory farming and the endless drone of the slaughterhouse. Like their late nineteenth-century forebears, children are taught kindness and affection through animals, only later to learn that the meat on their plates comes from the cows, pigs, and chickens that had kept them company in their earlier years as stuffed animals, cartoons, and film actors. The psychic human toll of these contradictions—and the immeasurable suffering of animals themselves—is unfathomable and vast.[8]

Americans are showing signs of wanting to confront these apparent contradictions in their treatment of animals. There are record levels of vegetarianism and veganism in the United States, along with a growing number of omnivores who pay attention to where their meat comes from.[9] A wave of popular articles, films, and bestselling books indicate a widespread interest in animal suffering and a popular desire to understand how animals are raised for food.[10] It remains to be seen whether these are meaningful calls to action or merely the latest iteration of the long and tortuous history of using animals as forms of entertainment. But the signs of another moment in animal politics are everywhere. Despite strong and well-funded campaigns in opposition, ballot measures to improve the welfare of farm animals have passed with large majorities in Massachusetts in 2016 (78 percent), California in 2008 and 2018 (64 percent and 63 percent, respectively), Ohio in 2009 (64 percent), and Arizona in 2006 (62 percent).[11] Recent polling suggests that support for animal welfare and even animal rights enjoys wide margins of support across age, race, gender, income, region, and political affiliation, although politicians rarely make animal protection a central campaign or governing issue.[12]

The longer history of the ways in which people understood and related to animals offers important context in thinking about contemporary political concerns. In some ways, the past reveals the very specificity—indeed oddness—of the present moment. Decisions made in the distant past continue to shape the present: from hunters and herders thousands of years ago, whose decisions and actions shaped human tastes and desires; to reformers of various kinds who forged new cultures and landscapes of modern human and animal interactions. Indeed, ideas about animals today are shaped and enabled by living in a world cleansed of many types of human-animal relationships that were once ordinary in the human experience.

Despite the profound reordering of animal life that emerged in the late nineteenth-century city, domesticated animals have not disappeared from urban life. New York City continues to debate the fate of the city's last equine residents that pull carriages through Central Park and remind visitors of the many "inconveniences" these creatures once posed. The romance of the horse-drawn carriage—like many nostalgic longings for the past—is most alluring from afar. Pet ownership in cities is probably higher than it has ever been. New York City has more than one million pets.[13] In San Francisco, dogs now outnumber children.[14] The Boston Common is full with the bustle of squirrels, rats, pigeons, and hawks—to say nothing of the often less numerous humans and dogs. In nearby urban and suburban landscapes turkey, deer, and coyote populations have boomed.[15] Animals are not gone from urban life, but their presence has been utterly remade over the course of two centuries.

Far from the Boston Common and other city centers, the massive populations of animals that support modern American life remain largely invisible. More than 30 million cattle and calves, 110 million pigs, 240 million turkeys, and 8 billion chickens are slaughtered each year in the United States for food.[16] On any given day, there are some 360 million egg-laying hens, 3.5 million wool-producing sheep, and 9.5 million milk-producing cows in the United States—to say nothing of international production and trade. In a sense, the concentrated populations of most farm animals are themselves types of "animal cities." Cattle feedlots often contain tens of thousands of animals, with some exceeding 100,000 bovine residents over several hundred acres.[17] Five Rivers Cattle Feeding—one of the largest feedlot companies in the world—has more than 950,000 head of cattle (and only 600 employees) across 11 feedlots in Colorado, Kansas, Oklahoma, Texas, Arizona, and Idaho. In 2018, the company was sold to Pinnacle Asset Management, whose offices are on Fifth Avenue in New York City, just south of Central Park.[18] Livestock remain a part of the city, even when their physical bodies are distant.

Uneasiness about the sheer scale of animal production is something that nineteenth-century animal reformers knew well. The work of policing nineteenth-century American cities was exhausting and overwhelming, Herculean in its intentions but Sisyphean in its reality. "Day after day . . . I am in slaughterhouses," said Henry Bergh, "or lying in wait at midnight with a squad of police near some dog pit; through the filthy markets and about the rotten docks; out into the crowded and dangerous streets; lifting a fallen horse to his feet, and perhaps sending the driver before a magistrate; penetrating dark and unwholesome buildings where I inspect collars and saddles for raw flesh; then lecturing in public schools to children, and again to adult Societies. Thus my whole life is spent."[19] George Angell suffered from insomnia and exhaustion, which seemed to be exacerbated by his work. "In founding of the Massachusetts Society for the Prevention of Cruelty to Animals," he wrote, "I had very little sleep for several months." It was, he said, "a heavy job," and one in which he faced critics and skeptics.[20]

For most workers, too, the vast scale of animal suffering and death was—and remains—overwhelming. The separation of livestock and slaughter has perhaps enabled greater abuses of animals and workers, who suffer out of sight and mind of the consumer and voting public. That deliberate separation was reaching completion as early as 1906, when Sinclair published *The Jungle* in the hopes of igniting public outrage over poor labor conditions—"aiming at the public's heart," and hitting them "in the stomach," as he later claimed.[21] It continues today in a livestock and slaughterhouse industry riddled with widespread and serious injuries and abuse to workers, and widespread suffering—both human and animal. Slaughterhouse work may well be one of the most dangerous jobs in the United States, and certainly one of the least tolerable and desirable based on its high rates of turnover.[22] "The worst thing, worse than the physical danger, is the emotional toll," said one slaughterhouse worker in Sioux City, Iowa.[23]

In the late nineteenth century, the individuals and Societies that sought to re-make human-animal relationships faced off against a behemoth of animal in-dustries. Unable to entirely police this massive set of animal industries of the late nineteenth century, urban animal reformers often settled for improving human life by separating and rendering invisible certain unpleasant relationships with animals from their more civilized human lives downtown. Humans were spared the sight of animal suffering, but the suffering continued. The benefits of living in the world those reformers created—with its selectively visible and invisible sites of animal relationships—carries with it an underworld we may choose to ignore. But the lives of billions of animals—and millions of workers—are at stake each year. Those invisible sites of human-animal relationships have undoubtedly shaped and enabled our modern world and helped forge many of the values many Amer-icans take for granted. It remains to be seen whether the people and animals who inhabit those invisible spaces will see the benefits of the world their absence and silence have helped to create.

NOTES

Introduction: Gentlemen Hogs

1. Charles Dickens, *American Notes for General Circulation* (Paris: Baudry's European Library, 1842), 99–102.
2. For the sake of readability I use the term "animals" to refer to nonhuman animals, with awareness that human beings are, of course, animals.
3. Dickens, *American Notes,* 106.
4. Dickens, *American Notes,* 106.
5. Dickens, *American Notes,* 109.
6. Etienne Derbec and Abraham Nasatir, eds., *A French Journalist in the California Gold Rush: The Letters of Etienne Derbec* (Georgetown, CA: Talisman Press, 1864), 170.
7. For the centrality of horses in late nineteenth-century urbanization, see Clay McShane and Joel Tarr, *The Horse in the City: Living Machines in the Nineteenth Century* (Baltimore: Johns Hopkins University Press, 2007); Clay McShane, "Gelded Age Boston," *New England Quarterly* 74, no. 2 (2001): 274–302; and Ann Norton Greene, *Horses at Work: Harnessing Power In Industrial America* (Cambridge, MA: Harvard University Press, 2008).
8. Jared Diamond, *Guns, Germs, and Steel: The Fates of Human Societies* (New York: W. W. Norton, 1997); Richard Bulliet, *Hunters, Herders, and Hamburgers: The Past and Future of Human-Animal Relationships* (New York: Columbia University Press, 2005).
9. For the centrality of livestock in colonial and early America, see Brian Donahue, *The Great Meadow: Farmers and the Land in Colonial Concord* (New Haven, CT: Yale

University Press, 2004); Virginia DeJohn Anderson, *Creatures of Empire: How Domestic Animals Transformed Early America* (New York: Oxford University Press, 2004).

10. "Sorting" is an effective concept for thinking about how humans remade urban animal populations, and something discussed extensively in Frederick Brown, *The City Is More Than Human: An Animal History of Seattle* (Seattle: University of Washington Press, 2016).

11. Michael Rawson, *Eden on the Charles: The Making of Boston* (Cambridge, MA: Harvard University Press, 2010).

12. See Chapter 3.

13. See Michael Rawson, *Eden on the Charles: The Making of Boston* (Cambridge, MA: Harvard University Press, 2010), chapter 1.

14. Catherine McNeur, *Taming Manhattan: Environmental Battles in the Antebellum City* (Cambridge, MA: Harvard University Press, 2014).

15. See Brown, *City Is More Than Human;* Catherine Brinkley and Domenic Vitiello, "From Farm to Nuisance: Animal Agriculture and the Rise of Planning Regulation," *Journal of Planning History* 13, no. 2: 113–135.

16. The large populations of cows in Mumbai and pigs in Cairo offer two compelling contemporary examples of modern-day cities that maintain significant livestock populations as part of urban life. The return of urban farming in the United States also suggests the possibility of the return of livestock populations in modern American cities. The growth of urban pet ownership in the United States is an urban domesticated animal population perhaps larger than almost any in history. See Jeremy Kahn, "Urban Cowboys Struggle with Sacred Strays," *New York Times,* November 5, 2008, A14; Marion Guenard, "Cairo Puts Its Faith in Ragpickers to Manage the City's Waste Problem," *Guardian Weekly,* November 9, 2013, accessed April 20, 2015, http://www.theguardian.com/world/2013/nov/19/cairo-ragpickers -zabaleen-egypt-recycling.

17. The relationship of city and country—both material and cultural—is central to this work. Urban reformers increasingly saw urban environments and animal life as antithetical, and remade urban and rural relationships in the new geographies they constructed. These ideas emerged out of a romantic impulse, and also out of new technological capacities. I draw on the influential works of Raymond Williams, *The Country and the City* (New York: Oxford University Press, 1973), and Leo Marx, *The Machine in the Garden: Technology and the Pastoral Ideal in America* (New York: Oxford University Press, 1964). The concept of a "dialogue" between city and hinterland comes from William Cronon, *Nature's Metropolis: Chicago and the Great West* (New York: W. W. Norton, 1991). See also Matthew Klingle, *Emerald City: An Environmental History of Seattle* (New Haven, CT: Yale University Press, 2007) and Rawson, *Eden On the Charles.* My skepticism on the effectiveness and efficiency of railroads comes in part from Richard White, *Railroaded: The Transcontinentals and the Making of Modern America* (New York: W. W. Norton, 2011).

18. For the development of the Humane Movement, see: Sydney H. Coleman, *Humane Society Leaders in America* (Albany, NY: American Humane Association,

1924); Susan Pearson, *The Rights of the Defenseless: Protecting Animals and Children in Gilded Age America* (Chicago: University of Chicago Press, 2011); Janet Davis, *The Gospel of Kindness: Animal Welfare and the Making of Modern America* (New York: Oxford University Press, 2016); Jessica Wang, "Dogs and the Making of the American State: Voluntary Association, State Power, and the Politics of Animal Control in New York City, 1850–1920," *Journal of American History* 98 (2012): 998–1024; and Diane Beers, *For the Prevention of Cruelty* (Athens: Swallow Press Ohio University Press, 2006).

19. See John Berger, "Why Look at Animals?" in *About Looking* (New York: Vintage, 1980): 3–28; Pearson, *Rights of the Defenseless;* Katherine Grier, *Pets in America: A History* (Chapel Hill: University of North Carolina Press, 2006); Beers, *For the Prevention of Cruelty.*

20. McShane and Tarr, *Horse in the City;* Greene, *Horses at Work: Harnessing Power in Industrial America* (Cambridge, MA: Harvard University Press, 2008).

21. The creation of animal regulations sheds light on urban political processes and class politics more broadly, building on works by Robin Einhorn, *Property Rules: Political Economy in Chicago, 1833–1872* (Chicago: University of Chicago Press, 1991), Philip Ethington, *The Public City: The Political Construction of Urban Life in San Francisco, 1850–1900* (Cambridge: Cambridge University Press, 1994), White, *Railroaded,* and Sven Beckert, *The Monied Metropolis: New York City and the Consolidation of the American Bourgeoisie, 1850–1896* (Cambridge: Cambridge University Press, 2001).

22. For zoning, see Michael Allan Wolff, *The Zoning of America: Euclid v. Amber* (Lawrence: University Press of Kansas, 2008) and Sonia A. Hirt, *Zoned in the USA: The Origins and Implications of American Land-Use Regulation* (Ithaca, NY: Cornell University Press, 2014).

23. For more on environmental change, urban development, and public health and policy, see: Theodore Steinberg, *Gotham Unbound: The Ecological History of Greater New York* (New York: Simon and Schuster, 2014); Martin Melosi, *The Sanitary City: Urban Infrastructure in America from Colonial Times to the Present* (Baltimore: Johns Hopkins University Press, 2000); Joel Tarr, *The Search for the Ultimate Sink: Urban Pollution in Historical Perspective* (Akron, OH: University of Akron Press, 1996); Linda Nash, *Inescapable Ecologies: A History of Environment, Disease, and Knowledge* (Berkeley: University of California Press, 2006); Conevery Bolton Valenčius, *The Health of the Country: How American Settlers Understood Themselves and Their Land* (New York: Basic Books, 2002); and Charles Rosenberg, *The Cholera Years: The United States In 1832, 1849, and 1866* (Chicago: University of Chicago Press, 1987). Concerns over animal bodies and animal-based health nuisances were constructed in time and place based on evolving ideas of health and sanitation. These concerns profoundly reordered the urban environment and shaped governmental development.

24. As a private corporation with vast public powers, the SPCA is a compelling example of a hybrid form of public-private governance—historically overlooked in studies of "state power." Scholars are paying more attention to these forms of power that shaped everyday life. See: William Novak, "The Myth of the 'Weak'

American State," *American Historical Review* 113, no. 3 (2008): 752–772; William Novak, *The People's Welfare: Law and Regulation in Nineteenth-Century America* (Chapel Hill: University of North Carolina Press, 1996); Daniel Carpenter, *The Forging of Bureaucratic Autonomy: Reputations, Networks, and Policy Innovation in Executive Agencies, 1862–1928* (Princeton, NJ: Princeton University Press, 2001); and Nicholas Parrillo, *Against the Profit Motive: The Salary Revolution in American Government, 1780–1940* (New Haven, CT: Yale University Press, 2013). Jessica Wang's article on the SPCA's dog policies in New York in the 1890s reinforced my inclination to see the SPCA as a powerful police power that fit into new ways of thinking about governmental power. See Wang, "Dogs and the Making of the American State."

25. For the larger legal and political context surrounding the *Slaughterhouse Cases,* see Ronald M. Labbé and Jonathan Lurie, *The Slaughterhouse Cases: Regulation, Reconstruction, and the Fourteenth Amendment* (Lawrence: University Press of Kansas, 2003).
26. Berger, "Why Look at Animals?" 3.
27. Bulliet, *Hunters, Herders and Hamburgers.*
28. Some early and influential works in what might be called a flowering field of "animal history" include Harriet Ritvo, *The Animal Estate: The English and Other Creatures in the Victorian Age* (Cambridge, MA: Harvard University Press, 1987), and *The Platypus and the Mermaid and Other Figments of the Classifying Imagination* (Cambridge, MA: Harvard University Press, 1997); McShane and Tarr, *Horse in the City;* Greene *Horses at Work;* Bulliet, *Hunters, Herders, and Hamburgers;* Jon Coleman, *Vicious: Wolves and Men in America* (New Haven, CT: Yale University Press, 2004); and Virginia DeJohn Anderson, *Creatures of Empire.*

1. Cow Town: New York City and the Urban Dairy Crisis, 1830–1860

1. "Report of the Committee on City Milk," in *The Transactions of the New York Academy of Medicine,* vol. 2 (New York: Balliere Brothers, 1863), 131–132.
2. Lemuel Shattuck and John Griscom both began accumulating data on infant mortality in Boston and New York, respectively. Their statistics show a spike in infant deaths as a percentage of total deaths in cities (the standard way of tabulating this sort data) during this period. The historian Richard Meckel points to their findings as supporting the growing notion at the time that "the social and environmental changes accompanying urbanization seemed to be taking their greatest toll among the young." See Richard Meckel, *Save the Babies: America's Public Health Reform and the Prevention of Infant Mortality, 1850–1929* (Baltimore: Johns Hopkins University Press, 1990), 18, 29.
3. Russell Thacher Trall, "Introduction," in *The Milk Trade in New York and Vicinity* (New York: Fowlers and Wells, 1853), v.
4. Robert M. Hartley, *An Historic, Scientific and Practical Essay on Milk as an Article of Human Sustenance with a Consideration of the Effects Consequent upon the Present Unnatural Methods of Producing It for the Supply of the Largest Cities* (New York: Jonathan Leavitt, 1842), 232.

5. In using the concept of a city-hinterland relationship as a "dialogue," I am using the language of William Cronon in *Nature's Metropolis: Chicago and the Great West* (New York: Norton, 1992), 8.

6. Conevery Bolton Valenčius argues that western settlers in this period engaged with the environment through powerful ideas and concepts of bodily health and land. While settlers experienced this environmental relationship directly, urban residents, especially reformers, also sought to connect with the "health of the country" through commodities such as milk. See Conevery Bolton Valenčius, *The Health of the Country: How American Settlers Understood Themselves and Their Land* (New York: Basic Books, 2002).

7. For more on the swill-milk crisis, see: Michael Egan, "Organizing Environmental Protest: Swill Milk and Social Activism in Nineteenth-Century New York City," in *Natural Protest: Essays on the History of American Environmentalism,* edited by Michael Egan and Jeff Crane (New York: Routledge, 2009), 39–63; John Duffy, *The Sanitarians: A History of American Public Health* (Urbana: University of Illinois Press, 1990); Melanie DuPuis, *Nature's Perfect Food: How Milk Became America's Drink* (New York: New York University Press, 2002); Jacqueline H. Wolf, *Don't Kill Your Baby: Public Health and the Decline of Breastfeeding in the Nineteenth and Twentieth Centuries* (Columbus: Ohio State University Press, 2001); and Norman Shaftel, "A History of the Purification of Milk in New York," in *Sickness and Health in America,* edited by Judith Walzer Leavitt and Ronald L. Numbers (Madison: University of Wisconsin Press, 1978), 275–291.

8. For animals in colonial New England life, see, in particular, Virginia DeJohn Anderson, *Creatures of Empire: How Domestic Animals Transformed Early America* (New York: Oxford University Press, 2004); William Cronon, *Changes in the Land: Indians, Colonists, and the Ecology of New England* (New York: Hill and Wang, 1983; Twentieth anniversary edition, 2003); and Brian Donahue, *The Great Meadow: Farmers and the Land In Colonial Concord* (New Haven, CT: Yale University Press, 2004).

9. Sarah McMahon, "A Comfortable Subsistence: The Changing Composition of Diet in Rural New England, 1620–1840," *William and Mary Quarterly* 42 (January 1985): 26–65, 38.

10. For the emergent "market economy" and the rise of cities in the eastern United States, there is an extensive literature. Daniel Walker Howe, *What Hath God Wrought?* (New York: Oxford, 2007); Sean Wilentz, *Chants Democratic: New York City and the Rise of the American Working Class, 1788–1850* (New York: Oxford University Press, 1984, 2004); and Charles Sellers, *The Market Revolution: Jacksonian America, 1815–1846* (New York: Oxford University Press, 1994).

11. Michael Rawson, *Eden on the Charles: The Making of Boston* (Cambridge, MA: Harvard University Press, 2010), 29–31.

12. Michael Rawson, *Eden on the Charles.* See also: Richard Bushman, *The Refinement of America* (New York: Vintage, 1993). Paul Johnson also describes these tensions over land use in developing mill towns in *Sam Patch: The Famous Jumper* (New York: Farrar, Strauss and Giroux, 2004).

13. Rawson, *Eden on the Charles,* 59–60.

14. Rawson, *Eden on the Charles,* 33. For numerous examples of this sort of dynamic, see Rawson, *Eden on the Charles,* Catherine McNeur, *Taming Manhattan: Environmental Battles in the Antebellum City* (Cambridge, MA: Harvard University Press, 2014), and Frederick Brown, *The City Is More Than Human: An Animal History of Seattle* (Seattle: University of Washington Press, 2016).

15. Hartley, *Essay,* 132.

16. DuPuis, *Nature's Perfect Food,* 5.

17. Sylvester Graham, "Lecture XX," in *Lectures on the Science of Human Life* (London: Horsell, Aldine Chambers, 1849), 225.

18. See Christine Stansell, *City of Women: Sex and Class in New York, 1789–1860* (New York: Knopf, 1986).

19. Jacqueline Wolf, *Public Health and the Decline of Breastfeeding in the Nineteenth and Twentieth Centuries* (Columbus: Ohio State University Press, 2001), 22.

20. Janet Golden, *A Social History of Wet Nursing in America: From Breast to Bottle* (Cambridge: Cambridge University Press, 1996), 6.

21. Hartley, *Essay,* 96. These ideas persisted long into the nineteenth century. Into the twentieth century, many still believed that a woman's mental state could affect the quality of her milk. "If the mother has been badly frightened or very angry or excited," said one Chicago health commissioner in 1897, "it is not safe to give the breast at all; it should be drawn and the milk thrown away." See Wolf, *Public Health,* 29–30.

22. Hartley, *Essay,* 205.

23. Hartley, *Essay,* 166.

24. Hartley, *Essay,* 232.

25. Oscar Anderson, *Refrigeration in America: A History of a New Technology and Its Impact* (Princeton, NJ: Published for the University of Cincinnati by Princeton University Press, 1953).

26. Sellers, *Market Revolution.*

27. Hartley, *Essay,* 252.

28. For discussions on seasonality, see Cronon, *Nature's Metropolis* and *Changes in the Land.*

29. See Ted Steinberg, "The Death of the Organic City" in *Down to Earth: Nature's Role in American History* (New York: Oxford University Press, 2002), 157–172 and McNeur, *Taming Manhattan.*

30. Hartley, *Essay,* 152–154.

31. Hartley, *Essay,* 144–145.

32. Hartley, *Essay,* 145.

33. Hartley, *Essay,* 134, 305.

34. Valerius, "Mysteries of Metropolitan Milk," *New York Observer and Chronicle,* January 24, 1846, 4; Hartley, *Essay,* 125; John Mullaly, *The Milk Trade in New York and Vicinity* (New York: Fowlers and Wells, 1853) 56.

35. Hartley, *Essay,* 198.

36. Hartley, *Essay,* 312; Mullaly, *Milk Trade,* 24. Despite the shocking range of additives, one might argue that among the most harmful components of the concoction was the water itself, particularly before the delivery of fresh water by the Croton Aqueduct in New York beginning in the 1840s.

37. Hartley, *Essay*, 133, 140; Valerius, "Mysteries of Metropolitan Milk," 4.

38. Hartley, *Essay*, 146.

39. Mullaly, *Milk Trade*, 48.

40. Shaftel, "A History of the Purification of Milk in New York," 278.

41. Hartley, *Essay*, 141; Mullaly, *Milk Trade*, 117. *Frank Leslie's Illustrated Newspaper* was relentless in publishing numerous articles on the swill-milk industry, including pieces that appeared in the issues of May 8, 1858, May 15, 1858, and July 17, 1858.

42. John Griscom's public health reforms reflected this emphasis on ventilation in tenements. Charles E. Rosenberg and Carroll Smith-Rosenberg, "Pietism and the Origins of the American Public Health Movement: A Note on John H. Griscom and Robert M. Hartley," in Leavitt and Numbers, *Sickness and Health in America*, 345–358. Dr. S. Rotton Percy also noted the importance of ventilation in creating healthy environments for poor people, particularly nursing mothers. See "Report of the Committee on City Milk," in *The Transactions of the New York Academy of Medicine*, vol. 2 (New York: Balliere Brothers, 1863), 122. For more on odor and public health, see Melanie A. Kiechle, *Smell Detectives: An Olfactory History of Nineteenth-Century Urban America* (Seattle: University of Washington Press, 2017).

43. Bee Wilson, *Swindled: The Dark History of Food Fraud, from Poisoned Candy to Counterfeit Coffee* (Princeton, NJ: Princeton University Press, 2008), 162. See also: Kendra Smith-Howard, *Pure and Modern Milk: An Environmental History since 1900* (New York: Oxford University Press, 2014); DuPuis, *Nature's Perfect Food*.

44. It was not until decades later that regulations and standard practices included pasteurization, homogenization, and industry grading of milk. Standardized milk was largely a development of the twentieth century. See DuPuis, *Nature's Perfect Food* and Smith-Howard, *Pure and Modern Milk*.

45. See Michael Pollan, *The Omnivore's Dilemma: A Natural History of Four Meals* (New York: Penguin Press, 2006) and Cronon, *Nature's Metropolis*.

46. Valerie Fildes, *Wet Nursing: A History from Antiquity to the Present* (Oxford: Basil Blackwell, 1988), 133–134.

47. There is no shortage of literature on the historical construction of the city as a place of degraded health and humanity, and the country as its supposed antidote. One classic text on this dichotomy is Raymond Williams, *The Country and the City* (Oxford: Oxford University Press, 1973).

48. Sylvester Graham, *A Treatise on Bread and Bread Making* (Boston: Light and Stearns, 1837), 34. For dietary reform as a key component of antebellum social reform, see Ronald Walters, *American Reformers, 1815–1860* (New York: Hill and Wang, 1978).

49. Graham, *Lectures*, 225.

50. Graham, *Lectures*, 226.

51. Valerie Fildes, *Breasts, Bottles and Babies: A History of Infant Feeding* (Edinburgh: Edinburgh University Press, 1986), 132.

52. Fildes, *Breasts, Bottles and Babies*, 132

53. Graham, *Lectures*, 225.

54. Although some historians have argued that social pressures came to dominate the relationships between mothers and wet nurses—encouraging women to hire locally, to consider a wet nurse's personal character above all else, and to carefully oversee a wet nurse's work and personal habits—the arguments of Graham and Hartley suggest that environments were also key to evaluating the health of wet nurses and their milk. Janet Golden argues that motherhood, child rearing, and nursing became more valued in the new republic, and that "the wet nurse became a potential threat as well as a possible savior." She goes on to say that direct supervision of wet nurses came to dominate the relationship between mothers and the women who fed their children, making the urban wet nurse popular despite environmental concerns. Wealthy women feared the moral deficiency of wet nurses and sought to oversee their activities. "Experts no longer advocated sending babies to the country, and middle- and upper-class families no longer did so. Good mothering, they believed, required that the nursery be closely watched." See Golden, *Social History of Wet Nursing*, 38–39.
55. Walters, *American Reformers*. Walters briefly mentions Hartley on pp. 181–182.
56. *Memorial of Robert Milham Hartley*, edited by Isaac Smithson Hartley (Utica, NY: Curtiss and Childs, 1882; Reprinted New York: Arno, 1976), 21–23.
57. *Memorial*, 27–28.
58. *Memorial*, 33.
59. *Memorial*, 34–35.
60. *Memorial*, 39.
61. *Memorial*, 65.
62. *Memorial*, 71.
63. *Memorial*, 78.
64. *Memorial*, 79.
65. *Memorial*, 92.
66. *Memorial*, 156.
67. Before his published volume on the swill-milk industry, Hartley published a variety of articles in the *New-York Evangelist*, which were reprinted in other newspapers.
68. Hartley, *Essay*, 123.
69. Hartley, *Essay*, 74, 124, 129.
70. Hartley, *Essay*, 128.
71. Letter from Doctor Charles Lee to Robert Hartley, in Hartley, *Essay*, 255.
72. Hartley discusses the concept of dominion in *Essay*, 35–40.
73. "Startling Exposure of the Milk Trade of New York and Brooklyn," *Frank Leslie's Illustrated Newspaper*, May 8, 1858. See other issues of *Frank Leslie's Illustrated Newspaper* for May 15, 1858 and July 17, 1858, "Assault by a Swill Milk Maid," *New York Times*, June 12, 1858.
74. Hartley, *Essay*, 308–309.
75. Hartley, *Essay*, 309.
76. Hartley, *Essay*, 112. See also, Mullaly, *Milk Trade*, 50.
77. Hartley, *Essay*, 113.
78. Dr. Charles Lee to Robert Hartley, in Hartley, *Essay*, 252.
79. Hartley, *Essay*, 192.

80. Mullaly and Graham also shared this sense that cows belonged, by natural and divine law, in the airy green pastures, and not in cities. See: Graham, *Lectures,* 226; and Mullaly, *Milk Trade,* 82.

81. For citations of "Dominion," see the Bible, Genesis 1:26. Hartley also assumes biblical dominion over animals, saying that man had "asserted that superiority over the brute creation which was originally conferred by the Sovereign Creator, who in giving him dominion over every living thing that moveth upon the earth, appointed him lord of this lower world." Hartley, *Essay,* 74.

82. Hartley, *Essay,* 142.

83. Hartley, *Essay,* 174.

84. Hartley, *Essay,* 147.

85. Hartley, *Essay,* 136, 167–168.

86. Mullaly, *Milk Trade,* 41–43.

87. Hartley, *Essay,* 143.

88. Hartley, *Essay,* 307.

89. See Lawrence B. Glickman, *Buying Power: A History of Consumer Activism in America* (Chicago: University of Chicago Press, 2009), and T. H. Breen, *The Marketplace of Revolution: How Consumer Politics Shaped American Independence* (New York: Oxford University Press, 2004).

90. Hartley, *Essay,* 74.

91. Hartley, *Essay,* 23, 205.

92. Graham, *Lectures,* 224–225.

93. Hartley, *Essay,* 141.

94. *Memorial,* 182.

95. "The Orange County Milk Business," *New-York Daily Tribune,* August 2, 1859, 3. See also *New-York Evangelist,* September 8, 1838, 2.

96. Hartley, *Essay,* 238.

97. Mullaly would go on to serve as Commissioner of Health, and helped establish the New York Park Association. See Mullaly, *Milk Trade.*

98. "The Orange County Milk Business," *New-York Daily Tribune,* August 2, 1859, 3.

99. "The Orange County Milk Business," *New-York Daily Tribune,* May 24, 1859, 3.

100. "The Orange County Milk Business," *New-York Daily Tribune,* August 2, 1859, 3.

101. "The Orange County Milk Business," *New-York Daily Tribune,* May 24, 1859, 3.

102. Like urban swill dairies, the "soiling" method of raising cows also allowed for easy collection of manure, which could be resold as a means of offsetting production costs.

103. "The Orange County Milk Business," *New-York Daily Tribune,* August 2, 1859, 3.

104. "The Orange County Milk Business," *New-York Daily Tribune,* June 13, 1859, 3.

105. "The Orange County Milk Business," *New-York Daily Tribune,* July 27, 1859, 3.

106. Kwang-Sun Lee, "Infant Mortality Decline in the Late 19th and Early 20th Centuries: The Role of Market Milk," *Perspectives in Biology and Medicine* 50, no.4 (Autumn 2007): 585–602.

107. Lee, "Infant Mortality." See also Smith-Howard, *Pure and Modern Milk.*

108. Mullaly, *Milk Trade,* 73; Hartley, *Essay,* 321; Charles Haswell, *Reminiscences of an Octogenarian of the City of New York* (New York: Harger and Brothers, 1896), 60–61.

109. "The Orange County Milk Business," *New-York Daily Tribune,* August 2, 1859, 3.

110. Some six thousand cows remained in Brooklyn through the early twentieth century. See Shaftel, "A History of the Purification of Milk in New York," 281.

111. "The Orange County Milk Business," *New-York Daily Tribune,* May 24, 1859, 3.

112. "The Orange County Milk Business," *New-York Daily Tribune,* May 24, 1859, 3.

113. Shaftel, "Purification of Milk in New York," 280.

114. See Egan, "Organizing Environmental Protest" and McNeur, *Taming Manhattan.*

115. DuPuis, *Nature's Perfect Food.*

2. "The War on Butchers": San Francisco and the Remaking of Animal Space, 1850–1870

1. "Instant cities" comes from Gunther Barth, *Instant Cities: Urbanization and the Rise of San Francisco and Denver* (New York: Oxford University Press, 1975). The final quotation is from Etienne Derbec and Abraham Nasatir, eds., *A French Journalist in the California Gold Rush: The Letters of Etienne Derbec* (Georgetown, CA: Talisman Press, 1864), 170. The population estimate comes from "San Francisco Population," San Francisco Genealogy, accessed March 1, 2019, http://www.sfgenealogy.com/sf/history/hgpop.htm.

2. Derbec and Nasatir, *French Journalist,* 170.

3. Population estimates come from various sources, including census data, combined in "San Francisco Population," San Francisco Genealogy website.

4. Jared Diamond, *Guns, Germs, and Steel: The Fates of Human Societies* (New York: W. W. Norton, 1997); Richard Bulliet, *Hunters, Herders, and Hamburgers: The Past and Future of Human-Animal Relationships* (New York: Columbia University Press, 2005).

5. Ronald Labbé and Jonathan Lurie, *The Slaughterhouse Cases: Regulation, Reconstruction, and the Fourteenth Amendment* (Lawrence: University Press of Kansas, 2003).

6. David Igler, *Industrial Cowboys: Miller & Lux and the Transformation of the Far West, 1850–1920* (Berkeley: University of California Press, 2001); Samuel Hayes, *Conservation and the Gospel of Efficiency: The Progressive Conservation Movement, 1890–1920* (Pittsburgh: University of Pittsburgh Press, 1959, 1999); James C. Scott, *Seeing Like a State: How Certain Schemes to Improve the Human Condition Have Failed* (New Haven, CT: Yale University Press, 1998); Nancy Langston, *Forest Dreams, Forest Nightmares* (Seattle: University of Washington Press, 1995); Richard White, *The Organic Machine* (New York: Hill and Wang, 1996); William Cronon, *Nature's Metropolis* (New York: Norton, 1991).

7. William Heath Davis, *Sixty Years in California* (San Francisco: AJ Leary, 1889), 376–377.

8. Philip Dreyfus, *Our Better Nature: Environment and the Making of San Francisco* (Norman: University of Oklahoma Press, 2008), 23–24. For another description of colonial conflict over domesticated animals, see Virginia DeJohn Anderson, *Creatures of Empire: How Domestic Animals Transformed Early America* (New York: Oxford University Press, 2004).

9. Davis, *Sixty Years in California,* 377.

10. Dreyfus, *Our Better Nature,* 35; William Issel and Robert W. Cherny, *San Francisco, 1865–1932: Politics, Power, and Urban Development* (Berkeley: University of California Press, 1986), 10.

11. Derbec and Nasatir, *French Journalist,* 173.

12. See Catherine McNeur, *Taming Manhattan: Environmental Battles in the Antebellum City* (Cambridge, MA: Harvard University Press, 2014), and Frederick Brown, *The City Is More Than Human: An Animal History of Seattle* (Seattle: University of Washington Press, 2016).

13. *Act of Incorporation and Ordinances of the City of San Francisco* (San Francisco: Printed at Offices of Evening Picayune, 1850), 11.

14. Novak convincingly argues that cities actively sought to establish "well regulated" societies under two common law maxims: *salus populi suprema lex est* (the welfare of the people is the supreme law), and *sic utere tuo ut alienum non laedas* (use your own so as not to injure another). William Novak, *The People's Welfare: Law and Regulation in Nineteenth-Century America* (Chapel Hill: University of North Carolina Press, 1996).

15. *Act of Incorporation and Ordinances.*

16. Novak, *People's Welfare.*

17. "Mayor's Message," delivered April 9, 1850, in *Act of Incorporation and Ordinances,* 17–24.

18. *Act of Incorporation and Ordinances,* 26. The full list of regulated materials: "All dirt, saw dust, soot, ashes, cinders, shavings, manure, waste water, or any animal or vegetable substance, rubbish or filth of any kind, in any house, cellar, yard, or other place which the mayor or city marshal shall deem it necessary for the health of the city to be removed," was to be "carried away" at "the expense of the owner or occupant."

19. "Trouble among the Butchers," *Daily Alta California,* April 3, 1852, 7; "Local Matters," *Daily Alta California,* March 28, 1852, 2. Part of the confusion stemmed from the way the law was written, leaving some question as to whether the area west of Larkin Street and north of Broadway was an allowable space for slaughter.

20. "City and County Advertisements—Ordinance," *Daily Alta California,* May 28, 1852, 4. For an exhaustive analysis of the development of urban infrastructure related to sewage, see Joel Tarr, *Search for the Ultimate Sink: Urban Pollution in Historical Perspective* (Akron: University of Akron Press, 1996), along with Martin Melosi, *The Sanitary City* (Pittsburgh: University of Pittsburgh Press, 2008) and Melosi, *Effluent America: Cities, Industry, Energy, and the Environment* (Pittsburgh: University of Pittsburgh Press, 2001).

21. "City and County Advertisements—Ordinance," *Daily Alta California,* May 28, 1852, 4.

22. "City License Law, 1854," *Daily Alta California,* January 3, 1854, 2; Ordinance 498, Section 19, in *Ordinances and Joint Resolutions of the City of San Francisco* (San Francisco: Monson & Valentine, 1854), 221. See "Mapping the Law," accessed May 7, 2019, https://web.stanford.edu/group/spatialhistory/cgi-bin/site/viz.php?id=409&project_id=0.

23. "Slaughter Houses," *Daily Alta California,* June 15, 1855, 1.
24. For more on health, bodies, and public order in nineteenth-century America, particularly cities, see Charles Rosenberg, *The Cholera Years* (Chicago: University of Chicago Press, 1987), 113; Melosi, *Sanitary City;* Conevery Bolton Valenčius, *The Health of the Country: How American Settlers Understood Themselves and Their Land* (New York: Basic Books, 2002); Jennifer Seltz, "Embodying Nature: Health, Place, and Identity in Nineteenth-Century America" (PhD diss., University of Washington, 2005); Nayan Shah, *Contagious Divides: Epidemics and Race in San Francisco's Chinatown* (Berkeley: University of California Press, 2001); Linda Nash, *Inescapable Ecologies: A History of Environment, Disease, and Knowledge* (Berkeley: University of California Press, 2006); Melanie Kiechle, *Smell Detectives: An Olfactory History of Nineteenth-Century Urban America* (Seattle: University of Washington Press, 2017).
25. "Nuisances—Powder Houses—Slaughter Houses," *Daily Alta California,* June 14, 1855, 2.
26. "Nuisances—Powder Houses—Slaughter Houses," *Daily Alta California,* June 14, 1855, 2.
27. "Nuisances—Powder Houses—Slaughter Houses," *Daily Alta California,* June 14, 1855, 2.
28. Susan Pearson, *The Rights of the Defenseless: Protecting Animals and Children in Gilded Age America* (Chicago: University of Chicago Press, 2010).
29. "Nuisances—Powder Houses—Slaughter Houses," *Daily Alta California,* June 14, 1855, 2.
30. The quote is from Issel and Cherny, *San Francisco, 1865–1932,* 19. See also Philip J. Ethington, *The Public City: The Political Construction of Urban Life in San Francisco, 1850–1900* (New York: Cambridge, 1994), 94–95, and William Issel and Robert Cherny, *San Francisco: Presidio, Port and Pacific Metropolis* (Sacramento: Boyd and Fraser, 1988), 18.
31. Mel Scott, *The San Francisco Bay Area: A Metropolis In Perspective,* 2nd ed. (Berkeley: University of California Press, 1985), 43; John Philip Young, *San Francisco: A History of the Pacific Coast Metropolis* (Chicago: S. J. Clarke, 1912), 311.
32. I have not found expenditures of the city 1856–1859. The figures from 1854 to 1856 come from Roger Lotchin, *San Francisco, 1846–1856: From Hamlet to City* (Urbana: University of Illinois Press, 1974, 1997). *San Francisco Municipal Reports: 1859–1860* (San Francisco: Towne and Bacon, 1860) provides statistics for 1859–1860. For tax rates, see Lotchin, *From Hamlet to City,* 245.
33. "Board of Supervisors," *Daily Alta California,* February 4, 1857, 2.
34. "California Legislature," *Sacramento Daily Union,* March 31, 1859, 1.
35. Ilza Hakenen, "Ephraim Willard Burr: A California Pioneer" (MA thesis, Humboldt State University, 2008). In the years that followed, Burr pushed for additional improvements in the city's water supply.
36. "California Legislature," *Sacramento Daily Union,* March 31, 1859, 1.
37. "California Legislature," *Sacramento Daily Union,* March 31, 1859, 1.
38. "California Legislature," *Sacramento Daily Union,* March 31, 1859, 1.
39. "California Legislature," *Sacramento Daily Union,* March 31, 1859, 1.
40. "California Legislature," *Sacramento Daily Union,* March 31, 1859, 1.

41. "California Legislature," *Sacramento Daily Union*, March 31, 1859, 1.
42. "California Legislature," *Sacramento Daily Union*, March 31, 1859, 1; "Laws of California," *Sacramento Daily Union*, April 9, 1859, 6.
43. Lux's statement is from "Butchertown: The Property-Owners Protesting against the Order Extending the Slaughtering Limits," *Daily Alta California*, February 24, 1878, 1; "California Legislature," *Sacramento Daily Union*, March 31, 1859, 1; "Laws of California," *Daily Alta California*, April 9, 1859, 6.
44. The area proposed for extending the limitations on slaughter was marked by Market Street, Ninth Street, Potrero Avenue, and Sixteenth Street—an area that included many slaughterhouses along Mission Creek. "California Legislature," *Sacramento Daily Union*, March 14, 1861, 1.
45. "City Items," *Daily Alta California*, October 25, 1859, 2.
46. "City Items," *Daily Alta California*, October 18, 1860, 1.
47. "City Items," *Daily Alta California*, November 29, 1860, 1.
48. "City Items," *Daily Alta California*, October 18, 1860, 1.
49. Ethington, *Public City*, 47.
50. Ethington, *Public City*, 47–48. See Issel and Cherny, *San Francisco, 1865–1932*. For more on the making of San Francisco's middle class, see Barbara Berglund, *Making San Francisco American: Cultural Frontiers in the Urban West, 1846–1906* (Lawrence: University Press of Kansas, 2007).
51. Dreyfus, *Our Better Nature*, 69.
52. Improvements in Lafayette and Alamo Squares are discussed in *San Francisco Municipal Reports for the Fiscal Year 1863–64* (San Francisco: William P. Harrison, 1864). Citations of municipal reports hereafter will use the abbreviation *SFMR* followed by the fiscal year volume.
53. Dreyfus, *Our Better Nature*, 80.
54. Dreyfus, *Our Better Nature*, 73; Christopher Pollock, "Golden Gate Park," online Encyclopedia of San Francisco, accessed March 1, 2019, http://www.sfhistoryencyclopedia.com/articles/g/goldenGate-park.html.
55. Tamara Venit-Shelton, "Unmaking Historic Spaces: Urban Progress and the San Francisco Cemetery Debate, 1895–1937," *California History* 85, no. 3 (2008): 26–47, 28.
56. Morse Scrapbook 1, Huntington Library, newspaper article clipping dated January 5, 1853. For changing ideas and rituals related to death and cemeteries, particularly around the Civil War, see Drew Gilpin Faust, *This Republic of Suffering: Death and the American Civil War* (New York: Vintage, 2008).
57. Venit-Shelton, "Unmaking Historic Spaces," 32. Today those bodies remain buried beneath the public golf course in Golden Gate Park.
58. Melosi, *Sanitary City*, 43.
59. Rosenberg, *Cholera Years*, 228.
60. Rosenberg, *Cholera Years*, 215.
61. Melosi, *Sanitary City*, 20–21.
62. "Health Officer's Report," *SFMR 1864–65*, 395.
63. Shah, *Contagious Divides*; Seltz, "Embodying Nature."
64. Charles Rosenberg argued that the New York Board of Health—established in part because of cholera—was unmatched as an entity: "No American city

possessed a board of health with powers even approximating those of the Metropolitan." While a detailed comparison is not within the scope of this analysis, it is certainly worth raising the question of why San Francisco had a permanent Board of Health one year earlier than New York, with expansive powers from its inception. See Rosenberg, *Cholera Years*, 211. Two important factors in San Francisco's development of a Board of Health may be its unmatched urban growth rate and the city's large immigrant (specifically, Chinese) population, which posed particular health risks according to many residents at the time. See Seltz, "Embodying Nature."

65. Seltz, "Embodying Nature," 14, 153–154,161.
66. Andrew Masich, *The Civil War in Arizona: The Story of the California Volunteers, 1861–1865* (Norman: University of Oklahoma Press, 2012).
67. See Faust, *This Republic of Suffering*, and Louis Menand, *The Metaphysical Club* (New York: Farrar, Straus and Giroux, 2001).
68. *SFMR, 1865–66*, 234–235.
69. For maps showing this development, see, for example: A. F. Rogers, "U.S. Coast Survey: City of San Francisco and Its Vicinity," (Washington, DC: U.S. Coast Survey, 1857); Benjamin Pierce, "San Francisco Peninsula, Benjamin Peirce, Superintendent (Washington, DC: U.S. Coast Survey, 1869). Both available through David Rumsey Map Collection (online), accessed May 7, 2019, www .davidrumsey.com.
70. "The Slaughter-House Nuisance," *Daily Alta California*, April 22, 1867, 2.
71. "The Slaughter-House Nuisance," *Daily Alta California*, December 31, 1864, 1.
72. "The Slaughter-Houses of San Francisco," *San Francisco Bulletin*, April 29, 1867.
73. "The Slaughter-House Nuisance," *Daily Alta California*, April 22, 1867, 2.
74. *SFMR 1867–68*, 284–285.
75. "Board of Supervisors," *Daily Alta California*, January 23, 1866, 1.
76. "The New Butchertown Project," *Daily Alta California*, December 7, 1867, 2.
77. See Chapter 1.
78. See Cronon, *Nature's Metropolis*, and Richard White, *Railroaded: The Transcontinentals and the Making of Modern America* (New York: Norton, 2011).
79. See essays in *Meat, Modernity, and the Rise of the Slaughterhouse*, edited by Paula Young Lee (Durham: University of New Hampshire Press, 2008). See also: Christine Meisner Rosen, "The Role of Pollution Regulation and Litigation in the Development of the U.S. Meatpacking Industry, 1865–1880," *Enterprise and Society* 8, no. 2 (2007): 297–347.
80. See Lee, *Meat, Modernity, and the Rise of the Slaughterhouse* and Scott, *San Francisco Bay Area*, 43.
81. Kyri Claflin, "La Villette: City of Blood (1867–1914)," in Lee, *Meat, Modernity, and the Rise of the Slaughterhouse*, 27–45, 28–29.
82. See Lee, *Meat, Modernity, and the Rise of the Slaughterhouse;* Louis Carroll Wade, *Chicago's Pride: The Stockyards, Packingtown, and Environs in the Nineteenth Century* (Urbana: University of Illinois Press, 1987); Dominic Pacyga, *Slaughterhouse: Chicago's Union Stockyard and the World It Made* (Chicago: University of Chicago Press, 2015).

83. Jeffrey Pilcher, "Abattoir or Packinghouse? A Bloody Industrial Dilemma in Mexico City, c. 1890," in Lee, *Meat, Modernity, and the Rise of the Slaughterhouse,* 216–236, 218.

84. See *First Annual Report of the State Board of Health of Massachusetts* (Boston: Wright & Potter, 1870); Labbé and Lurie, *Slaughterhouse Cases.*

85. See *First Annual Report of the State Board of Health of Massachusetts,* and Labbé and Lurie, *Slaughterhouse Cases.*

86. See Scott, *Seeing Like a State* and Cronon, *Nature's Metropolis.*

87. *SFMR* 1869–70.

88. See "Health Officer's Reports," in *SFMR,* for 1866–1872.

89. "Local Intelligence," *Daily Alta California,* October 21, 1867, 1.

90. *Ex Parte Shrader,* 33 Cal. 279, 1867 WL 694 (Cal.).

91. "Supreme Court Decisions," *Sacramento Daily Union,* November 13, 1867, 2–3.

92. See Novak, *People's Welfare.*

93. "Supreme Court Decisions," *Sacramento Daily Union,* November 13, 1867, 2–3.

94. *Ex Parte Shrader,* 33.

95. *Ex Parte Shrader,* 33.

96. For more on this important historical context as it relates to a historical revision of the meaning and significance of the Slaughterhouse Cases, see Labbé and Lurie, *Slaughterhouse Cases.*

97. "Pig Rancher Arrested," *Daily Alta California,* December 27, 1867, 1.

98. "The Butchertown War Resumed," *Daily Alta California,* June 4, 1868, 1.

99. "The Butchertown War Resumed," *Daily Alta California,* June 4, 1868, 1.

100. "Humbug Ordinances," *Daily Alta California,* January 8, 1869, 2.

101. "By State Telegraph," *Sacramento Daily Union,* June 10, 1870, 1.

102. "Board of Supervisors," *Daily Alta California,* June 21, 1870, 1.

103. "Removal of Butchers," *Daily Alta California,* October 16, 1870, 1.

104. Henry Miller, "Dictation of Henry Miller, Esq." Miller was interviewed for Hubert Bancroft's *Chronicles of the Builders of the Commonwealth.* Bancroft Library, MSS C–D 791.

105. Miller, "Dictation of Henry Miller, Esq." See also, the semifictional book by Edward Treadwell, *The Cattle King: A Dramatized Biography* (New York: Macmillan, 1931), 274–275.

106. "Notes by the Way," *Daily Alta California,* January 9, 1866, 1.

107. Igler, *Industrial Cowboys.*

108. See Gray Brechin, *Imperial San Francisco: Urban Power, Earthly Ruin* (Berkeley: University of California Press, 1999). For more on the concept of "dialogue" of the city and hinterland, see Cronon, *Nature's Metropolis.*

109. Igler, *Industrial Cowboys.*

110. *SFMR, 1869–70,* 234–235.

111. See Frederick Jackson Turner, *The Frontier In American History* (New York: H. Holt and Company, 1920).

112. Issel and Cherny, *San Francisco, 1865–1932.*

113. "Nuisances—Powder Houses—Slaughter Houses," *Daily Alta California,* June 14, 1855, 2.

3. Blood in the Water: The Butchers' Reservation
and the Reshaping of San Francisco

1. San Francisco Department of the Environment, "Tidal Energy," accessed March 1, 2019, http://www.sfenvironment.org/article/hydro/tidal-energy.

2. Joe Eaton and Ron Sullivan, "S.F. History Lesson Runs through Islais Creek," *San Francisco Chronicle,* January 14, 2009, accessed March 1, 2019, http://www.sfgate .com/homeandgarden/article/S-F-history-lesson-runs-through-Islais-Creek -3176646.php.

3. William Bright, *1500 California Place Names: Their Origin and Meaning* (Berkeley: University of California Press, 1998, 1949), 72. "Academy of Sciences," *Sacramento Daily Union,* May 21, 1868, 2.

4. Roger R. Olmsted, *Rincon de las Salinas y Potrero Viejo—The Vanished Corner: Historical Archaeological Program, Southeast Treatment Plant, 1978–1979: Report* (San Francisco: San Francisco Clean Water Program, 1981).

5. For more on the extensive practice of filling the bay, see Philip Dreyfus, *Our Better Nature: Environment and the Making of San Francisco* (Norman: University of Oklahoma Press, 2008). Filling tidelands was a national and international project in many cities at this time. See Boston's Back Bay, in particular: William A. Newman and Wilfred E. Holton, *Boston's Back Bay: The Story of America's Greatest Nineteenth-Century Landfill Project* (Boston: Northeastern University Press, 2006).

6. "City Items," *Daily Alta California,* April 21, 1864, 1; "Bay View Valley Sale," *Daily Alta California,* May 2, 1867, 1.

7. "The Growth of San Francisco," *Daily Alta California,* April 23, 1869, 2.

8. "A Homestead for All," *California Farmer,* June 6, 1862, 1; "Plan of the O'Neill and Haley Tracts" [map], L. H. Shortt, surveyor (San Francisco, January 31, 1867).

9. "Sale of Bay View Tide and Submerged Lands," *Daily Alta California,* May 6, 1869, 2.

10. "The Growth of San Francisco," *Daily Alta California,* April 23, 1869, 2.

11. *San Francisco Municipal Reports, 1869–70* (San Francisco: William P. Harrison, [various]), 234. Citations of municipal reports hereafter will use the abbreviation *SFMR* followed by the fiscal year volume.

12. "A Nose from South San Francisco," *Daily Alta California,* December 17, 1867, 1.

13. "The Slaughter-House Nuisance," *San Francisco Bulletin,* February 26, 1870.

14. "A Nose from South San Francisco," *Daily Alta California,* December 17, 1867, 1. This trans-Atlantic conversation may be an early iteration of what Daniel Rodgers has identified as a Trans-Atlantic set of policies and solutions that defined Progressive Era reforms. See Daniel Rodgers, *Atlantic Crossings: Social Politics in a Progressive Age* (Cambridge, MA: Belknap Press of Harvard University Press, 1998).

15. See Theodore Steinberg, *Gotham Unbound: The Ecological History of Greater New York* (New York: Simon and Schuster, 2014) and Steinberg, *Down to Earth: Nature's Role in American History* (New York: Oxford University Press, 2009), chapter 10.

16. See William Cronon, *Nature's Metropolis: Chicago and the Great West* (New York: W. W. Norton, 1991).

17. "A Nose from South San Francisco," *Daily Alta California,* December 17, 1867, 1. On guano, see Gregory Cushman, *Guano and the Opening of the Pacific World: A Global Ecological History* (Cambridge: Cambridge University Press, 2013).

18. "A Nose from South San Francisco," *Daily Alta California,* December 17, 1867, 1.

19. US Census Bureau, "Population of the 100 Largest Cities and Other Urban Places in the United States: 1790 to 1990," accessed March 1, 2019, https://www.census .gov/population/www/documentation/twps0027/twps0027.html.

20. David Igler, *Industrial Cowboys: Miller & Lux and the Transformation of the Far West, 1850–1920* (Berkeley: University of California Press, 2001).

21. "The Sewers," *Daily Alta California,* September 20, 1888, 1.

22. "From Our Own Correspondent: California Gossip," *New York Times,* October 27, 1874, 6.

23. "Butchertown," *San Francisco Bulletin,* November 13, 1876.

24. Matthew Booker, *Down by the Bay: San Francisco's History between the Tides* (Berkeley: University of California Press, 2013), 120–122.

25. *SFMR 1874–75,* 308–309.

26. See Igler, *Industrial Cowboys.*

27. For the centrality of horses in late nineteenth-century urbanization, see Clay McShane and Joel Tarr, *The Horse in the City: Living Machines in the Nineteenth Century* (Baltimore: Johns Hopkins University Press, 2007); Clay McShane, "Gelded Age Boston," *New England Quarterly* 74, no. 2 (2001): 274–302; and Ann Norton Greene, *Horses at Work: Harnessing Power in Industrial America* (Cambridge, MA: Harvard University Press, 2008).

28. Figures from *Crocker-Langley San Francisco Directory* for 1869, 1900, 1910, 1920, and other years, published in San Francisco by H. S. Crocker Company. The number of stables would reach 121 in 1910, then drop precipitously to a mere 22 in 1920, as automobiles rapidly replaced horses in the city. For more detailed treatment of the rise and decline of the urban horse, see Tarr and McShane, *Horse in the City* and Greene, *Horses at Work.*

29. "By the Vallejo Route," *Sacramento Daily Union,* October 26, 1869, 3.

30. See "Accidents Yesterday," *Daily Alta California,* January 30, 1870, 3, which told of a hunting accident that caused the shooting of a fourteen-year-old boy.

31. "Across the Bridge," *San Francisco Call,* June 24, 1890, 3.

32. "Below the Bridge," *San Francisco Call,* January 4, 1892, 4.

33. "A Hunter's Death," *San Francisco Call,* October 21, 1895, 7.

34. "Mr. Dockery Was on the Warpath," *San Francisco Chronicle,* December 9, 1895, 12.

35. "A Hunter's Death," *San Francisco Call,* October 21, 1895, 7.

36. This was happening as a culture of sport hunting was contributing to emerging wildlife conservation, emphasizing hunting as a way of engaging with a more distant and purer form of nature. See Louis Warren, *The Hunter's Game: Poachers and Conservationists in Twentieth-Century America* (New Haven, CT: Yale University Press, 1997); Karl Jacoby, *Crimes against Nature: Squatters, Poachers, Thieves, and the Hidden History of American Conservation.* (Berkeley: University of California Press, 2001); Mark Spence, *Dispossessing the Wilderness: Indian Removal and the Making of the National Parks* (New York: Oxford University Press, 1999);

John Reiger, *American Sportsmen and the Origins of Conservation*, 3rd ed., rev. and expanded (Corvallis: Oregon State University Press, 2001); and Jennifer Price, *Flight Maps: Adventures with Nature in Modern America* (New York: Basic Books, 1999).

37. "South San Francisco," *San Francisco Call*, March 16, 1892, 7.

38. "Butchertown," *Daily Alta California*, February 7, 1881, 1.

39. "Flesh and Fish: An Early Morning Ride to Butchertown," *San Francisco Call*, December 12, 1892, 2.

40. "A Few Words about Ducks," *Pacific Rural Press*, July 14, 1888, 22.

41. *San Francisco Bulletin*, April 6, 1877, as quoted in Olmsted, *Rincon de las Salinas*, 116

42. "A Few Words about Ducks," *Pacific Rural Press*, July 14, 1888, 22.

43. See Nayan Shah, *Contagious Divides: Epidemics and Race in San Francisco's Chinatown* (Berkeley: University of California Press, 2001).

44. "Orders Slaughter Houses Destroyed," *San Francisco Call*, February 29, 1908, 7. See also Shah, *Contagious Divides*.

45. "Butchertown," *Daily Alta California*, February 7, 1881, 1.

46. "Butchertown," *San Francisco Chronicle*, February 21, 1870, 3.

47. "Butchertown," *Daily Alta California*, February 7, 1881, 1.

48. The area just north of Butchertown is today known as "Dogpatch," though it remains unclear when that name first emerged or why. It may have origins in the heyday of Butchertown, though there is little clear evidence to support it.

49. "Butchertown," *San Francisco Chronicle*, February 21, 1870, 3.

50. "Rodent-Killing," *Daily Alta California*, May 5, 1884, 1.

51. See "Rodent Killing," *Daily Alta California*, May 5 1884, 1; "In the Pit," *Daily Alta California*, May 9, 1888, 1; "In a Rat Pit," *Daily Alta California*, June 16, 1887, 4.

52. "Rodent-Killing," *Daily Alta California*, May 5, 1884, 1.

53. "Rodent-Killing," *Daily Alta California*, May 5, 1884, 1; "Dick, the Rat," *New York Times*, January 30, 1876, 10.

54. "Rodent-Killing," *Daily Alta California*, May 5, 1884, 1; "In the Pit," *Daily Alta California*, 1; "In a Rat Pit," *Daily Alta California*, June 16, 1887, 4.

55. "In a Rat Pit," *Daily Alta California*, June 16, 1887, 4.

56. "Dick, the Rat," *New York Times*, January 30, 1876, 10.

57. "Ratters Raided," *San Francisco Call*, July 20, 1893, 10.

58. Joanna Dyl, "The War on Rats versus the Right to Keep Chickens: Plague and the Paving of San Francisco, 1907–1908," in *The Nature of Cities: Culture, Landscape and Urban Space*, edited by Andrew C. Isenberg (Rochester, NY: University of Rochester Press, 2006), 38–61, 38.

59. Dyl, "War on Rats," 41.

60. Dyl, "War on Rats," 44–46.

61. Frank F. Latta Collection: Miller & Lux Papers, Huntington Library, San Marino, California. See, in particular, Box 6, volume on "Animal Care and Operations." Some of Miller & Lux's hogs were raised in Gilroy, according to shipping receipts from the late 1860s and early 1870s.

62. "Butchertown," *Daily Alta California* February 7, 1881, 1.

63. "Infectious Meats," *Daily Alta California*, October 19 1888, 1.
64. "Report of the Veterinary Inspector," *Pacific Rural Press* 36, no. 17 (October 27, 1888): 351.
65. "Hogs Must Be Removed," *Daily Alta California*, November 21, 1888, 2.
66. "An Unsavory Spot," *Sacramento Daily Union*, November 16, 1888, 1.
67. "A Filthy Locality," *Daily Alta California*, August 14, 1889, 8.
68. "Where Cattle Are Killed," *San Francisco Call*, October 9, 1895, 7.
69. Large parts of this route would become Highway 101.
70. "Death Is Hidden in the Swamp," *San Francisco Call*, October 16, 1897, 14.
71. Arthur McEvoy, *The Fisherman's Problem: Ecology and Law In the California Fisheries, 1850–1980* (Cambridge: Cambridge University Press, 1986), 76.
72. "Chinese Shrimpers," *San Francisco Morning Call*, October 26, 1891, 2.
73. McEvoy, *Fisherman's Problem*, 96.
74. "Fish Commissioners," *Sacramento Daily Union*, January 9, 1885, 4.
75. "Chinese Fishermen," *Daily Alta California*, May 11, 1888, 1.
76. McEvoy, *Fisherman's Problem*, 101.
77. "Butchertown Shrimps Not Germ-Ridden," *San Francisco Call*, May 2, 1900, 7.
78. See Kendra Smith-Howard, *Pure and Modern Milk: An Environmental History since 1900* (New York: Oxford University Press, 2014) and Melanie DuPuis, *Nature's Perfect Food: How Milk Became America's Drink* (New York: New York University Press, 2002).
79. "Need the New Officials," *San Francisco Call*, September 30, 1895, 12.
80. "Need the New Officials," *San Francisco Call*, September 30, 1895, 12.
81. "Need the New Officials," *San Francisco Call*, September 30, 1895, 12.
82. "Need the New Officials," *San Francisco Call*, September 30, 1895, 12.
83. "Sickness Lurks in Water Tanks," *San Francisco Chronicle*, September 28, 1895, 16.
84. "Miscellaneous," *Daily Alta California*, April 7, 1891. At the time of his appointment Dockery was employed selling personal insurance—a novel and booming industry that was also a popular symbol of progress. For the growth of the personal insurance industry, see Jonathan Levy, *Freaks of Fortune: The Emerging World of Capitalism and Risk in America* (Cambridge, MA: Harvard University Press, 2012).
85. "James Dockery Is Dead," *San Francisco Call*, July 24, 1913, 13.
86. "Victory for Dockery" in *San Francisco Call*, November 1, 1895, 7; "Dockery as a Drover," *San Francisco Call*, December 10, 1895, 9.
87. "Dockery as a Drover," *San Francisco Call*, December 10, 1895, 9.
88. "Crusade against Unwholesome Milk," *San Francisco Chronicle*, November 28, 1895, 8.
89. "Mr. Dockery Was on the Warpath," *San Francisco Chronicle*, December 9, 1895, 12.
90. The SPCA became something of an animal police force, seeking arrests and prosecutions for violators of a variety of animal laws not necessarily connected to cruelty. For example, they were known to enforce the "Fish Law" on several occasions, and also took charge of the city pound in the 1890s. More on the specific role of the SPCA can be found in Chapters 4 and 5.

91. The functions of these various departments are detailed in bits and pieces in sources too expansive to numerate here. The city's *Municipal Reports*, from 1860 to 1910, detail many of the activities of most of these departments, including statistics on animals impounded.
92. "Crusade against Unwholesome Milk," *San Francisco Chronicle*, November 28, 1895, 8.
93. "Crusade against Unwholesome Milk," *San Francisco Chronicle*, November 28, 1895, 8.
94. "Mr. Dockery Was on the Warpath," *San Francisco Chronicle*, December 9, 1895, 12.
95. For more on the ways in which relationships with animals informed and reflected social tension, see: Virginia DeJohn Anderson, *Creatures of Empire: How Domestic Animals Transformed Early America* (New York: Oxford University Press, 2004); Catherine McNeur, *Taming Manhattan: Environmental Battles in the Antebellum City* (Cambridge, MA: Harvard University Press, 2014); Warren, *Hunter's Game*; Jacoby, *Crimes against Nature*.
96. *History of San Mateo County, California* (San Francisco: BF Alley, 1883), 253–255.
97. R. G. Sneath, "History of Jersey Dairy Farm" (San Francisco: G. Spaulding & Co., publication date unprinted, marked as 1880, Bancroft Library, Berkeley, California).
98. Sneath, "History of Jersey Dairy Farm."
99. Sneath, "History of Jersey Dairy Farm."
100. Sneath, "History of Jersey Dairy Farm." See also: *History of San Mateo County*, 246–248. For more on late-nineteenth century efforts to improve the efficiency of natural production, see: Donald Worster, *Nature's Economy: A History of Ecological Ideas*, 2nd ed. (Cambridge: Cambridge University Press, 1994); Joseph Taylor, *Making Salmon: An Environmental History of the Northwest Fisheries Crisis* (Seattle: University of Washington Press, 1999); Samuel Hays, *Conservation and the Gospel of Efficiency: The Progressive Conservation Movement, 1890–1920* (Cambridge, MA: Harvard University Press, 1959). Aspects of this spatial reach of San Francisco's urban capital and markets appears in Gray Brechin, *Imperial San Francisco: Urban Power, Earthly Ruin* (Berkeley: University of California Press, 1999). See also Richard Walker, *The Country in the City: The Greening of the San Francisco Bay Area* (Seattle: University of Washington Press, 2007).
101. Dockery dumped a load of milk from the Jersey Dairy Farm, according to "After the Milkmen," *San Francisco Call*, June 12 1896, 8.
102. "Mr. Dockery Was on the Warpath," *San Francisco Chronicle*, December 9, 1895, 12.
103. "Death Is Hidden in the Swamp," *San Francisco Call*, October 16, 1897, 14.
104. "Milk Prices Advanced," *Pacific Rural Press* 50, no. 20 (November 16, 1895), 306.
105. "Two Men with Pistols," *San Francisco Call*, October 2, 1897, 9; "Dockery Uses His Revolver," *San Francisco Chronicle*, October 1, 1897, 12; "City News in Brief," *San Francisco Call*, March 17, 1896, 7; "Seized Four Cows," *San Francisco Call*, March 17, 1896, 7; "Board of Health" *San Francisco Post*, June 24, 1896 (Morse Scrapbook 11, Huntington Library); "Death Is Hidden in the Swamp," *San Francisco Call*, October 16, 1897, 14.

106. See Crocker-Langley San Francisco City Directories for these years. See also: Liz Fenje, Mark Sanchez, Jake Coolidge, Erik Steiner, and Andrew Robichaud, "Animal City" visualization, Stanford Spatial History Project, Center for Spatial and Textual analysis, accessed March 1, 2019, https://web.stanford.edu/group /spatialhistory/cgi-bin/site/viz.php?id=397&project_id=0.

107. "Dockery's Head to Drop into Burns' Basket," *San Francisco Call*, April 9, 1899, 7; "Governor Gage's Appointments," *San Francisco Call*, April 12, 1899, 6.

108. "The Board of Health Scandal," *San Francisco Call*, June 30, 1896, 6.

109. "Will Use Ashes to Rebuild City," *Los Angeles Herald*, May 5, 1906, 1.

110. "Eleven Milkmen Have Water in their Milk," *San Francisco Call*, November 27, 1910, 29.

111. "War Waged on Poor Milk," *San Francisco Call*, January 22, 1912, 7.

112. "James Dockery Is Dead," *San Francisco Call*, July 24, 1913, 13.

113. See Cronon, *Nature's Metropolis*.

114. Clifford Rechtschaffen, "Fighting Back against a Power Plant: Some Lessons from the Legal and Organizing Efforts of the Bayview-Hunters Point Community," *Hastings West-Northwest Journal of Environmental Law & Policy* 537 (2008): 536–572; Teresa Garcia, "Hunters Point Power Plant Demolished," ABC News, San Francisco, September 19, 2008, accessed March 1, 2018, http://abc7news.com /archive/6401882/.

115. Cynthia Dizikes and Michael Cabanatuan, "SF Shipyard Activists Frustrated by Naval Officials on Alleged Soil Test Fraud," *San Francisco Chronicle*, April 12, 2018.

116. Lindsey Dillon, "Redevelopment and the Politics of Place in Bayview-Hunters Point," The Institute for the Study of Social Change, University of California, Berkeley, August, 2, 2011, accessed March 1, 2019, https://escholarship.org/uc/item /9s15b9r2#page-20.

117. James Baldwin, *Take This Hammer* (San Francisco: KQED, 1963), San Francisco Bay Area Television Archives, accessed March 1, 2019, https://diva.sfsu.edu /collections/sfbatv/bundles/216518.

118. "Bayview Revitalization Comes with Huge Price to Black Residents," *San Francisco Chronicle*, January 14, 2008.

4. How to Kill a Horse: SPCAs, Urban Order, and State Power, 1866–1910

1. For the centrality of horses in late nineteenth-century cities, see Clay McShane and Joel Tarr, *The Horse in the City: Living Machines in the Nineteenth Century* (Baltimore: Johns Hopkins University Press, 2007); Clay McShane, "Gelded Age Boston," *New England Quarterly* 74, no. 2 (2001): 274–302; and Ann Norton Greene, *Horses at Work: Harnessing Power in Industrial America* (Cambridge, MA: Harvard University Press, 2008).

2. For more biographical information on Captain Burns and the Sumner Light Guard, see: "The Apache War," *Daily Alta California*, January 11, 1873, 1; "Sumner

Light Guard," *Daily Alta California,* May 31, 1873, 1; "Rifle Shooting," *Daily Alta California,* July 21, 1874, 1; "Shocking Accident," *Daily Alta California,* April 19, 1876, 1. The Sumner Light Guard is also mentioned in Benjamin Lloyd, *Lights and Shades in San Francisco* (San Francisco: Bancroft, 1876), 126–130.

3. "Shocking Accident," *Daily Alta California,* April 19, 1876, 1.

4. William Novak, "The Myth of the 'Weak' American State," *American Historical Review* 113 (2008): 752–772.

5. Jessica Wang has made this case, in part, in her analysis of the ASPCA in New York City. See "Dogs and the Making of the American State: Voluntary Association, State Power, and the Politics of Animal Control in New York City, 1850–1920," *Journal of American History* 98 (2012): 998–1024. My understanding of these public-private forms of power comes, primarily, from: Novak, "Myth of the 'Weak' American State"; William Novak, "Public-Private Governance: A Historical Introduction," in *Government by Contract: Outsourcing and American Democracy,* edited by Jody Freeman and Martha Minow (Cambridge, MA: Harvard University Press 2009), 23–40; William Novak, *The People's Welfare: Law and Regulation In Nineteenth-Century America* (Chapel Hill: University of North Carolina Press, 1996); Hendrik Hartog, *Public Property and Private Power: The Corporation of the City of New York in American Law, 1730–1870* (Chapel Hill: University of North Carolina Press); Daniel P. Carpenter, *The Forging of Bureaucratic Autonomy: Reputations, Networks, and Policy Innovation in Executive Agencies, 1862–1928* (Princeton, NJ: Princeton University Press, 2001); Susan Pearson, *The Rights of the Defenseless: Protecting Animals and Children in Gilded Age America* (Chicago: University of Chicago Press, 2011); Brian Balogh, *A Government out of Sight: The Mystery of National Authority in Nineteenth-Century America* (Cambridge: Cambridge University Press, 2009).

6. Novak, *People's Welfare.* My understanding of the development of corporations and corporate governance in nineteenth-century America is also shaped by Jonathan Levy's talk, "Corporate Personality Revisited," Stanford University, January 23, 2014.

7. George Orwell, *Animal Farm* (New York: Houghton Mifflin Harcourt, 2009), 192.

8. "Protecting Animals from Needless Cruelty," *Daily Alta California,* October 29, 1867, 1.

9. I discuss these ideas and aspirations at more length in Chapter 5, which considers the ASPCA and the regulation of dogs. This understanding of animal protection and human improvement is widespread in the literature of the time, from SPCA annual reports to newspaper articles. For one example, see "Editorial Notes," *Daily Alta California,* February 19, 1868, 2. See also Pearson, *Rights of the Defenseless* and Janet Davis, *The Gospel of Kindness: Animal Welfare and the Making of Modern America* (New York: Oxford University Press, 2016).

10. "California Legislature," *Sacramento Daily Union,* February 27, 1868, 1. For more on this see legislative reports printed in the *Sacramento Daily Union* for February and March 1868.

11. "Society for the Prevention of Cruelty to Animals," *Daily Alta California,* May 23, 1868, 1.

12. "California Legislature," *Sacramento Daily Union*, March 5, 1868, 1.
13. Roswell McCrea, *The Humane Movement* (New York: Columbia University Press, 1910), 34.
14. "Laws of California," *Sacramento Daily Union*, April 20, 1868, 1; "Local Intelligence," *Daily Alta California*, June 1, 1868, 1.
15. "Laws of California," *Sacramento Daily Union*, April 20, 1868, 1; "Local Intelligence," *Daily Alta California*, June 1 1868, 1.
16. "Laws of California," *Sacramento Daily Union* April 20, 1868, 1; "Local Intelligence," *Daily Alta California*, June 1 1868, 1.
17. "Laws of California," *Sacramento Daily Union* April 20, 1868, 1; "Local Intelligence," *Daily Alta California*, June 1 1868, 1; San Francisco Society for the Prevention of Cruelty to Animals, *Tenth Annual Report: 1877* (San Francisco), 22.
18. "Laws of California," *Sacramento Daily Union* April 20, 1868, 1; "Local Intelligence," *Daily Alta California*, June 1 1868, 1.
19. For the centrality of courts in governance, see Michael Willrich, *City of Courts: Socializing Justice in Progressive Era Chicago* (Cambridge: Cambridge University Press, 2003).
20. "Laws of California," *Sacramento Daily Union* April 20, 1868, 1; "Local Intelligence," *Daily Alta California*, June 1, 1868, 1. This sort of funding stream was not unusual as a way of financing nineteenth-century services and law enforcement. See Nicholas Parrillo, *Against the Profit Motive: The Salary Revolution in American Government, 1780–1940* (New Haven, CT: Yale University Press, 2013).
21. "Filed," *Sacramento Daily Union*, April 24, 1868, 2; "Secretary of State's Office," *Daily Alta California*, April 25, 1868, 1.
22. The sources used in investigating the lives of SFPSCA trustees are too numerous to list here. Two notable sources are Oscar Tully Shuck, *Representative and Leading Men of the Pacific* (San Francisco: Bacon and Company, 1870) and San Francisco Journal of Commerce, *The Builders of a Great City: San Francisco's Representative Men, the City, Its History and Commerce* (San Francisco, 1891). For Henry Gibbons, see Gibbons, *Fifty Years Ago* (San Francisco: Bancroft and Company, 1878). For August Helbing, see "A Jew in Charity," *Overland Monthly* 148 (April 1895): 386.
23. "Robert Swain," in Shuck, *Representative and Leading Men*, 615–624.
24. Sven Beckert discusses some of these struggles and contemporaneous efforts to run city hall as a sort of shareholder organization, controlled by the wealthiest taxpayers based on their share of tax contributions, which emerged as a proposal in New York City in 1867. This echoes other shareholder-model forms in governance in the late nineteenth century. See Sven Beckert, *The Monied Metropolis: New York City and the Consolidation of the American Bourgeoisie, 1850–1896* (Cambridge: Cambridge University Press, 2001).
25. For membership records mentioned here, see San Francisco SPCA Annual Reports for years ending in 1879, 1880, 1886, California History Room, San Francisco Public Library (SFPL).
26. "Editorial Notes," *Daily Alta California*, February 19, 1868, 2.
27. "Local Intelligence," *Daily Alta California*, June 1, 1868, 1; "Meeting of the Society for the Prevention of Cruelty to Animals" *Daily Alta California*, July 27, 1869, 1.

28. "California Legislature," *Sacramento Daily Union,* January 12, 1870, 1.
29. Terence Young, *Building San Francisco's Parks, 1850–1930* (Baltimore: Johns Hopkins University Press, 2004), 224.
30. "Local Intelligence," *Daily Alta California,* June 1, 1868, 1.
31. In this regard, the SFSPCA resembled the Massachusetts SPCA, which sought cultural and social influence above police power. In New York, on the other hand, the ASPCA eagerly and actively embraced their police and prosecutorial roles, reflecting a deeper set of divisions within SPCAs over preferred uses and sources of power. I examine these divisions further in Chapter 5. These quotations suggest that San Francisco appeared to mimic Massachusetts in its early efforts to downplay its hard power in favor of social, cultural, and intellectual interventions.
32. "Society for the Prevention of Cruelty to Animals," *Daily Alta California,* July 19, 1870, 1.
33. Winans's biographical information comes from several sources: Oscar T. Shuck, *History of the Bench and Bar of California* (Los Angeles: Commercial Printing House, 1901); Shuck, *Representative and Leading Men,* 249–254; "Memorial of the Late Regent Winans," in *Annual Report of Secretary to the Regents of the University of California* (Sacramento: State Office, 1887), 5–9.
34. "Cruelty to Animals," *Daily Alta California,* July 19, 1876, 1.
35. "Cruelty to Animals," *Daily Alta California,* July 19, 1876, 1; SFSPCA, *Tenth Annual Report: 1877.*
36. See Annual Reports of the San Francisco Society for the Prevention of Cruelty to Animals for fiscal years ending in 1877, 1879, 1880, 1886, 1890, 1898, 1902, and 1907, California History Room, SFPL.
37. SFSPCA, *Twelfth Annual Report: 1880.*
38. Susan Craddock, *City of Plagues: Disease, Poverty, and Deviance in San Francisco* (Minneapolis: University of Minnesota Press, 2000), 70.
39. For membership statistics, see: "Meeting of the Society for the Prevention of Cruelty to Animals," *Daily Alta California,* July 27, 1869, 1; "Anniversary Exercises," *Daily Alta California,* April 9, 1872, 1; "Cruelty to Animals," *Daily Alta California,* July 19, 1876, 1; SFSPCA *Annual Reports: 1877, 1879.*
40. "Address of the President," in SFSPCA, *Twelfth Annual Report: 1879* (San Francisco: Spaulding & Williams, 1879), 5.
41. See David Igler, *Industrial Cowboys: Miller & Lux and the Transformation of the Far West, 1850–1920* (Berkeley: University of California Press, 2001) and William Cronon, *Nature's Metropolis: Chicago and the Great West* (New York: W. W. Norton, 1991).
42. "The Bay Shore and Dumbarton Cut-Offs of the Southern Pacific," *Railroad Gazette* 42, no. 11 (March 15, 1907): 328–331.
43. San Francisco ordinance 1587, passed in 1880, restricted many forms of animal keeping in the city, and also carved a single path for driving cattle from the Second Street Wharf to Butchertown: "But it is lawful to drive cattle from the landing at the foot of second street along King Street to Third Street, then to Berry, then to 6th street, then along sixth to Townsend, along Townsend to Seventh Street, then to Brannan, then to Ninth Street." The path led out to parts of town where

keeping cattle was legal, and specifically to Butchertown. *General Orders of the Board of Supervisors Providing Regulations for the Government of the City and County of San Francisco* (San Francisco: P. J. Thomas, 1884), 25.

44. News clipping marked "San Francisco Chronicle," April 19, 1878, in Agent Diary, 1877–1879, SFSPCA Collection, SFPL.

45. Agent Diary, 1877–1879, SFSPCA Collection, SFP.

46. See Agent Diary, 1877–1890, SFSPCA Collection, SFPL.

47. Agent Diary, 1877–1879, SFSPCA Collection, SFPL.

48. See entry for May 9, 1878, in Agent Diary, 1877–1879, SFSPCA Collection, SFPL.

49. "The Prevention of Cruelty," *San Francisco Call*, August 16, 1878, news clipping in Agent Diary, 1877–1879, SFSPCA Collection, SFPL.

50. See "Record of Prosecutions," SFSPCA Collection, SFPL.

51. Richard White, *Railroaded: The Transcontinentals and the Making of Modern America* (New York: W. W. Norton, 2011); Cronon, *Nature's Metropolis;* Igler, *Industrial Cowboys.*

52. For the transformation of livestock shipping, see: White, *Railroaded;* Igler, *Industrial Cowboys;* and Cronon, *Nature's Metropolis.* Much emphasis has been put on the centrality of domesticated animals such as horses and pets in the ideology of SPCA activism. Burns's ineffective efforts to regulate livestock suggest that there was at least significant interest in livestock, but that laws and legal powers were not favorable to such interventions. See Jennifer Mason, *Civilized Creatures: Urban Animals, Sentimental Culture, and American Literature, 1850–1900* (Baltimore: Johns Hopkins University Press, 2005) and Susan Pearson, *The Rights of the Defenseless: Protecting Animals and Children in Gilded Age America* (Chicago: University of Chicago Press, 2011).

53. See entry for October 6, 1878, in Agent Diary, 1877–1879, SFPSCA Collection, SFPL.

54. See entry for March 18, 1878, in Agent Diary, 1877–1879, SFSPCA Collection, SFPL.

55. For more on "spatial politics" of railroads, see White, *Railroaded.*

56. Diane Beers, *For the Prevention of Cruelty: The History and Legacy of Animal Rights Activism in the United States* (Athens: Swallow Press / Ohio University Press, 2006), 67–69.

57. There are countless examples of SFSPCA officers ordering that livestock be shot in the early years of enforcement. Large numbers of horses were shot throughout the last decades of the nineteenth century. For examples of SFSPCA officers ordering livestock destruction see Agent Diary, 1877–1879, SFSPCA Collection, SFPL.

58. For SFSPCA leadership and membership, see SFSPCA Annual Reports, California History Room, SFPL.

59. Beers, *For the Prevention of Cruelty,* 70.

60. Levi Doty to Ferd. W Peck, October 24, 1885, Illinois Humane Society Collection, Box 12, "Letters, 1883–1888," Abraham Lincoln Library, Springfield, Illinois.

61. Levi Doty to Ferd. W Peck, October 24, 1885, Illinois Humane Society Collection, Box 12, "Letters, 1883–1888," Abraham Lincoln Library; Nelson Morris to William Shortall, February 10, 1890, Illinois Humane Society Collection, Box 12, Abraham Lincoln Library; Mitchell to Shortall, July 20, 1890, Box 12, Abraham Lincoln Library; Swift to IHS, May 25, 1893, Illinois Humane Society Collection, Box 29, "William Mitchell—Union Stock Yards," Abraham Lincoln Library.

62. Cases of the SFSPCA agent investigating resident and member complaints are numerous. See Agent Diaries and Annual Reports, SFSPCA Collection, SFPL.

63. "Local Intelligence," *Daily Alta California*, June 1, 1868, 1.

64. "Local Intelligence," *Daily Alta California*, June 1, 1868, 1.

65. SFSPCA *Annual Report: 1877*, 7–8.

66. Other SPCA's, including the ASPCA in New York, shared this expansive and disperse police power. See C. C. Buel, "Bergh and His Work," *Scribner's Monthly* 7, no. 6 (April 1879): 872–884, 884; Wang, "Dogs and the Making of the American State."

67. For 1869, see: "Meeting of the Society for the Prevention of Cruelty to Animals," *Daily Alta California*, July 27, 1869, 1; for 1872, see "Anniversary Exercises," *Daily Alta California*, April 9, 1872, 1; for other years see SFSPCA Annual Reports for 1877, 1902, and 1907.

68. Beers, *For the Prevention of Cruelty*, 88–89.

69. "Does It Pay?" 1897 pamphlet, San Francisco SPCA, San Francisco Bands of Mercy, xF869.S3C47.v.2:7, San Francisco Charities, Pamphlets, vol. 2, no. 7., Bancroft Library, University of California, Berkeley. *Our Dumb Animals*, May 1888 (Boston: MSPCA, 1888).

70. *Our Dumb Animals*.

71. "Yellow Dog Safe on Tehama Street," *San Francisco Call*, May 31, 1896, 18.

72. "Children as Detectives," *San Francisco Call*, February 11, 1900, 32.

73. "Does It Pay?" 1897 pamphlet, San Francisco SPCA, San Francisco Bands of Mercy, xF869.S3C47.v.2:7, San Francisco Charities, Pamphlets, vol. 2, no. 7., Bancroft Library, University of California, Berkeley.

74. "Does It Pay?" 1897 pamphlet, San Francisco SPCA, San Francisco Bands of Mercy, xF869.S3C47.v.2:7, San Francisco Charities, Pamphlets, vol. 2, no. 7., The Bancroft Library, University of California, Berkeley.

75. "Record of Prosecutions," SFSPCA Collection, SFPL.

76. The Agent Diaries show the ways in which power was used beyond mere prosecution and arrest. Only a small fraction of interventions ended in arrest or prosecution. Most ended in warnings and orders to abate abuse, with the threat of arrest and fine. Nevertheless, the SFSPCA's interest in livestock in appears to wane in the last decades of the nineteenth century.

77. Agent Diary, 1877–1879, SFSPCA Collection, SFPL.

78. "Cruelty to Animals," *San Francisco Bulletin*, June 3, 1878, newspaper clipping from Agent Diary, 1877–1879, SFSPCA Collection, SFPL.

79. "Record of Prosecutions," SFSPCA Collection, SFPL. This fact perhaps gets at another question, which is whether corporations or executives could be charged with misdemeanors and under what circumstances.

80. This is based on a systematic review of the Agent Diaries from the 1880s and 1890s in the SFSPCA Collection, SFPL.

81. Many SPCAs and Humane Societies expanded into operating city pounds in the 1890s. Caroline Earle White, founder of the Pennsylvania SPCA and the Women's SPCA in Philadelphia, began to contract pound work as early as 1869. By the 1890s, many SPCAs were doing such work for cities. See Sydney H. Coleman, *Humane Society Leaders in America* (Albany, NY: American Humane Association, 1924), 63, 181; Wang, "Dogs and the Making of the American State"; Beers, *For the Prevention of Cruelty,* 94–95.

82. "Record of Prosecutions," SFSPCA Collection, SFPL.

83. D. D. Slade, *How to Kill Animals Humanely* (Boston: MSPCA, date unknown), Boston Public Library.

84. SFSPCA Annual Reports for 1898 and 1902.

85. As quoted in Coleman, *Humane Society Leaders,* 53.

86. October 21, 1878, Agent Diary, 1877–1879, SFSPCA Collection, SFPL.

87. October 28, 1878, Agent Diary, 1877–1879, SFSPCA Collection, SFPL.

88. John Shortall to "Several Societies Constituent," January 23, 1894, Illinois Humane Society Collection, Abraham Lincoln Library.

89. Upton Sinclair, *The Jungle* (1906; reprint, New York: Penguin, 2006), 38.

90. October 21, 1878, Agent Diary, 1877–1879, SFSPCA Collection, SFPL.

5. That Doggy in the Window: The SPCA and the Making of Pets in America

1. Bergh's testimony is recorded in "The People vs. Charles W. Walker," *Supreme Court, The East New York & Jamaica Railroad Company* (New York: E. Hoyt & Co., 1874).

2. The calculation of labor equivalency of $25 is imprecise, but arguably serves as a better measure of cost than a mere dollar conversion (see www.measuringworth .com). A shoemaker in New York City made roughly $2.36 a day in 1874. Unskilled workers in similar labor markets earned about $1.75 per day in 1873. See "Housing," Tenement Museum, accessed March 17, 2015, http://www .tenement.org/encyclopedia/housing_rent.htm.

3. For the variety of roles dogs played in America, beginning with the colonial period, see Mark Derr, *A Dog's History of America: How Our Best Friends Explored, Conquered, and Settled a Continent* (New York: North Point Press, 2004), 153–155.

4. For early mentions of dog power, see: *Connecticut Courier,* September 18, 1822, 3; *Evening Post* (New York), January 24, 1825, 3; "Variety," *Macon Telegraph,* January 14, 1828, 5. The article from the *Macon Telegraph* described Dutch New Yorkers using dog power to churn butter.

5. *Friend* 1, no. 23 (March 22, 1828): 183.

6. *Kaleidescope* 10, no. 478 (August 25, 1829): 64.

7. Alexis de Tocqueville, *Democracy in America: Part the Second, The Social Influence of Democracy* (New York: Langley, 1840), 45.

8. "American Farming as Seen by an Englishman," *Genesee Farmer* 23, no. 1 (January 1862): 20.

9. *Friend* 1, no. 23 (March 22, 1828): 183; "Dog-Mill," *Commercial Advertiser*, March 18, 1828, 1.

10. F. W. Shelton, *Up the River* (New York: Scribner, 1853), 34–36.

11. Olmstead actually believed that sheep were the best power source for small machines. Many advertisements for dog churns also noted that sheep could be used to power the machines. See Hiram Olmstead, "The Dairy: Practical Farming as Connected with the Manufacture of Butter," in *Transactions of the N.Y. State Agriculture Society, XIX—1859* (Albany: Charles Van Benthuysen, 1860), 101–112.

12. Olmstead, "Dairy," 101–112.

13. "Dog Power," *American Railroad Journal* 3, no. 20 (May 24, 1834): 310.

14. Dog power was also ostensibly used to power laundry machines. See "A Home Made Dog-Power Churn," *Ohio Cultivator (1845–1866)* 8, no. 22 (November 15, 1852): 339. The same article was reprinted in the *Indiana Farmer* on December 1, 1852. Others have noted the longer history of "turnspit dogs," especially in England where, going back to the sixteenth century, dogs turned cooking spits. This is widely noted. See Jeanne Schinto, "The Clockwork Roasting Jack, or How Technology Entered the Kitchen," *Gastronomica*, February 1, 2004, 33–40; and Charles McFarlane, "A Dog's Life: A Brief History of the Turnspit Dog," *Modern Farmer*, June 13, 2014, accessed March 1, 2019, http://modernfarmer.com/2014/06/turnspit/.

15. For middle-class culture, see Laurel Thatcher Ulrich, *The Age of Homespun: Objects and Stories in the Creation of an American Myth* (New York: Alfred A. Knopf, 2001), and Mary Ryan, *Cradle of the Middle Class: The Family in Oneida County, New York, 1790–1865* (Cambridge: Cambridge University Press, 1981).

16. "Dog-power for Churns," *Cultivator* 13, no. 5 (May 1865): 157.

17. *Southern Cultivator* 10, no. 10 (October 1852): 304.

18. Olmstead, "Dairy," 105.

19. Olmstead, "Dairy," 105.

20. John Burroughs, "Real and Sham Natural History," *Atlantic Monthly* 91 (March 1903): 298–309.

21. Clara Barrus, *John Burroughs: Boy and Man* (New York: Doubleday, Page & Co., 1920), 67–68.

22. *American Agriculturist* 2, no. 9 (November 1843): 272.

23. Shelton, *Up the River*, 34–36.

24. "Rotary Knitting Machine," *New-York Daily Tribune*, March 13, 1843, 2.

25. *New England Farmer* 14, no. 7 (July 1862): 334.

26. "The Rag-Picker," *Harper's Weekly* 14, no. 697 (May 7, 1870), 301.

27. "Walks among the New York Poor," *New York Times*, January 22, 1853, 2.

28. "The Rag Pickers and Bone Gatherers in New York," from the *New York Journal of Commerce*, as printed in *National Aegis*, April 13, 1853, and reprinted in Rev. E. J. Stearns, *Notes on Uncle Tom's Cabin* (Philadelphia: Lippincott, Grambo & Co., 1853), 288–290. For an account of ragpickers in the 1870s, see "The Rag-Pickers at Home," *Harper's Weekly* 18, no. 899 (March 21, 1874), 253–54.

29. "Walks among the New York Poor," *New York Times*, January 22, 1853, 2; "The Rag-Picker," *Harper's Weekly* 14, no. 697 (May 7, 1870), 301.

30. "Tenement Life in New York," *Harper's Weekly* 23, no. 1162 (April 5, 1879), 265–267.

31. *Report of the Select Committee appointed to examine into the condition of tenant houses in New-York and Brooklyn*, vol. 3, no. 145–211 (Albany: C. Van Benthuysen, 1857), 18–21.

32. "New York Tenant Houses," *New York Herald*, July 6, 1856, 5.

33. *Report of the Select Committee . . . to examine . . . tenant houses*, 18–21.

34. "Rag and Bone-Pickers' Paradise," *New-York Daily Tribune*, June 10, 1857, 7.

35. Henry Guernsey presented a paper before the New York Sanitary Association, which was printed in Appendix A (pp. 24–26) of the "Report of the Committee on the Incorporation of Cities and Villages, on the bill entitled 'An act concerning the Public Health of the counties of New York, Kings, and Richmond," in *Documents of the Assembly of the State of New York, Eighty-Third Session—1860* IV, nos. 104 to 180 (Albany).

36. "Rag-Pickers of New York," *American Phrenological Journal* 26, no. 4 (October 1857): 84.

37. "Dog Power," *New England Farmer* 14, no. 7 (July 1862): 334.

38. "Rag-Pickers of New York," *American Phrenological Journal* 26, no. 4 (October, 1857), 84.

39. See Sydney Coleman, *Humane Society Leaders in America: With a Sketch of the Early History of the Humane Movement in England* (Albany, NY: The American Humane Association, 1924).

40. These numbers are based on data in the *American Society for the Prevention of Cruelty to Animals: Thirty-Fourth Annual Report for the Year Ending December 31, 1899* (New York: ASPCA, 1900), and include Humane Societies, which were closely aligned with SPCAs and often included protection of children and animals under the same umbrella organization.

41. ASPCA, *Seventh Annual Report* (New York, 1873).

42. C. C. Buel, "Bergh and His Work," *Scribner's Monthly* 7, no. 6 (April 1879): 872–884, 872.

43. These descriptions from Bergh come from a wide range of sources, but especially Zulma Steele, *Angel in Top Hat* (New York: Harper & Brothers, 1942) and Coleman, *Humane Society Leaders*, 57–58. For American culture and death rituals in the mid- and late nineteenth century, see Drew Gilpin Faust, *This Republic of Suffering: Death and the American Civil War* (New York: Vintage, 2008).

44. ASPCA, *First Annual Report: 1867* (New York, 1867), 5.

45. See earlier chapters of this book on San Francisco, especially Chapters 3 and 4.

46. See Clay McShane and Joel Tarr, *The Horse in the City: Living Machines in the Nineteenth Century* (Baltimore: Johns Hopkins University Press, 2007) and Ann Norton Greene, *Horses at Work: Harnessing Power in Industrial America* (Cambridge, MA: Harvard University Press, 2008).

47. See ASPCA Annual Reports for years ending 1867–1869.

48. Steele, *Angel in Top Hat*, 128–129.

49. Clara Morris, "Riddle of the Nineteenth Century: Mr. Henry Bergh," *McClure's Magazine,* 18, no. 5 (March 1902): 418.

50. "The Boston Bergh," *New York Times,* November 4, 1870, 5; George Angell, *Autobiographical Sketches and Personal Recollections* (Boston: Franklin Press, 1884), 8–9.

51. "The Boston Bergh," *New York Times,* November 4, 1870, 5; Angell, *Autobiographical Sketches,* 8–9.

52. See San Francisco Society for the Prevention of Cruelty to Animals, *OurAnimals* (San Francisco: April, 1943), 6–7.

53. Katherine Grier, *Pets in America: A History* (Chapel Hill: University of North Carolina Press, 2006), 28; Jake Page, *Dogs: A Natural History* (New York: Smithsonian Books / Collins, 2007), 81–82.

54. Grier, *Pets in America,* 28–30.

55. Grier, *Pets in America,* 74; Susan Pearson, *The Rights of the Defenseless: Protecting Animals and Children in Gilded Age America* (Chicago: University of Chicago Press, 2011).

56. *Our Dumb Animals* 1, no. 4 (September 4, 1868), 1.

57. *Our Dumb Animals* 1, no. 4 (September 4, 1868), 1. See also Pearson, *Rights of the Defenseless* and Janet Davis, *The Gospel of Kindness: Animal Welfare and the Making of Modern America* (New York: Oxford University Press, 2016).

58. "The Boston Bergh," *New York Times,* November 4, 1870, 5.

59. "The Boston Bergh," *New York Times,* November 4, 1870, 5.

60. George Angell, "Congress of Nations," *Our Dumb Animals* 2, no. 6 (November 2, 1869): 59, also quoted in Angell, *Autobiographical Sketches,* 26–27.

61. "The Boston Bergh," *New York Times,* November 4, 1870, 5.

62. Angell, "Congress of Nations," 59, also quoted in Angell, *Autobiographical Sketches,* 26–27.

63. "The Boston Bergh," *New York Times,* November 4, 1870, 5.

64. "The Boston Bergh," *New York Times,* November 4, 1870, 5.

65. Coleman, *Humane Society Leaders,* 178.

66. Angell, *Autobiographical Sketches,* 33.

67. See "Charter," in ASPCA, *First Annual Report* (1867).

68. See "An Act," in ASPCA, *First Annual Report* (1867), 61–62.

69. ASPCA, *First Annual Report: 1867,* 64.

70. "The Chiffonniers in Convention," *Harper's Weekly* 11, no. 549 (July 6, 1867): 427, 430.

71. "Midsummer Nights among City Tenements," *Harper's Weekly* 27, no. 1384 (June 30, 1883): 410; *London Society* 30, no. 180 (December 1876): 545–553.

72. "Tenement Life in New York," *Harper's Weekly* 23, no. 1162 (April 5, 1879), 265–267.

73. Joshua Lawrence, "The Italians of New York," *Ballou's Monthly Magazine* 59, no. 5 (May 1884): 451.

74. H. C. Bunner, "Shantytown," *Scribner's Monthly* 20, no. 6 (October, 1880): 855–869, 865–866.

75. Bunner, "Shantytown," 855.

76. See also "Improved Dog Cart," *Scientific American* 47, no. 19 (November 4, 1882): 297.

77. "The New York Dog Pound," *Daily Intelligencer,* August 15, 1853, 2.

78. "The Dog Crusade in New York," *Express,* June 7, 1859, reprinted in *Norwich Aurora,* June 18, 1859, 1.

79. ASPCA, *Annual Report* for the year ending 1876.

80. Angell, *Autobiographical Sketches,* 52.

81. "The People vs. Charles W. Walker," 15–16.

82. "The People vs. Charles W. Walker," 35.

83. "The People vs. Charles W. Walker," 39–40.

84. "The Recordership," *New York Times,* January 12, 1866, 2; "John K. Hackett's Death," *New York Times,* December 27, 1879, 1–2.

85. "Sporting Reminiscences," *Forest and Stream* 60, no. 6 (February 7, 1903): 103.

86. L. Blanchard Evans, "Trap Shooting," *Brentano's Monthly* 3, no. 2 (May 1880): 168.

87. Henry Lauren Clinton, *Celebrated Trials* (New York: Harper and Bros., 1897), 292; *Officers, Members, Constitution and Rules of the South Side Sportsmen's Club of Long Island* (New York: Burnet & Co., 1907); "Sporting Reminiscences," *Forest and Stream* 60, no. 6, (February 7, 1903): 103.

88. "The South Side Sportsmen's Club," *New York Herald,* October 20, 1889, 11; "Recorder Hackett Dead," *New York Herald-Tribune,* December 27, 1879, 2; "John K. Hackett's Death," 1–2.

89. "The People vs. Charles W. Walker," 26.

90. "The People vs. Charles W. Walker," 27. See Richard White, "Are You an Environmentalist or Do You Work for a Living?" in *Uncommon Ground: Toward Reinventing Nature,* edited by William Cronon (New York: W. W. Norton, 1995), 171–185.

91. See Derr, *Dog's History of America.*

92. George Shields, *The American Book of the Dog* (Chicago: Rand, McNally, 1891), 623.

93. For a larger discussion, see Page, *Dogs,* 83.

94. "Old Grouse," *Forest and Stream* 5, no. 23 (January 13, 1876): 357.

95. "Old Grouse," *Forest and Stream* 5, no. 23 (January 13, 1876): 357. See also "Dogs for Sale," *Spirit of the Times* 31, no. 8 (March 30, 1861): 125.

96. "Old Grouse," *Forest and Stream* 5, no. 23 (January 13, 1876), 357.

97. Marshall Saunders, *Beautiful Joe: An Autobiography* (Philadelphia: C. H. Banes, 1893). See also: Gerald Carson, *Men, Beasts, and Gods: A History of Cruelty and Kindness to Animals* (New York: Scribner, 1972), 111; and Frank Ascione, *Children and Animals: Exploring the Roots of Kindness and Cruelty* (West Lafayette, IN: Purdue University Press, 2005), 25–26.

98. "The People vs. Charles W. Walker," 32–33.

99. "The People vs. Charles W. Walker," 32–33.

100. "The People vs. Charles W. Walker," 33.

101. "The People vs. Charles W. Walker," 55–56.

102. Amy Dru Stanley, *From Bondage to Contract: Wage Labor, Marriage, and the Market in the Age of Slave Emancipation* (Cambridge: Cambridge University Press, 1998); Eric Foner, *The Story of American Freedom* (New York: W. W. Norton, 1999).

103. "The People vs. Charles W. Walker," 70.

104. "The People vs. Charles W. Walker," 63.

105. "The People vs. Charles W. Walker," 49–50.

106. "The People vs. Charles W. Walker," 52.

107. For a greater understanding of how slave owners justified their practices based on a concept of paternalism, see Walter Johnson, *Soul by Soul: Life inside the Antebellum Slave Market* (Cambridge, MA: Harvard University Press, 1999).

108. "The People vs. Charles W. Walker," 68.

109. "The People vs. Charles W. Walker," 74–78.

110. "The People vs. Charles W. Walker," 30.

111. "The People vs. Charles W. Walker," 30.

112. See David S. Favre and Vivien Tsang, "The Development of Anti-Cruelty Laws during the 1800s," *Detroit College of Law Review* (Spring 1993): 1–35.

113. "The People ex. rel. Charles W. Walker v. The Court of Special Sessions of the City and County of New York," in *Reports of Cases Heard and Determined in the Supreme Court of the State of New York*, vol. 11 (New York: Banks & Brothers, 1875), 441; "The Dog Treadmill Case," *Central Law Journal* (St. Louis, MO) 2, no. 21 (May 21, 1875): 325.

114. "Cruelty to a Dog," *New York Times*, January 8, 1875, 10.

115. "Jefferson Market Police Court," *New York Herald*, February 13, 1875, 11.

116. "One of Mr. Bergh's Officers in Trouble," *New York Times*, February 13, 1875, 3.

117. "One of Mr. Bergh's Officers in Trouble," *New York Times*, February 13, 1875, 3; "Jefferson Market Police Court," *New York Herald*, February 13, 1875, 11; "The Tombs Police Court: The Apple-Grinding Dog," *New York Times*, January 10, 1875, 12; "Cruelty to a Dog," *New York Times*, January 1, 1875, 10.

118. "Bergh Again on the Rampage," *New York Herald*, October 19, 1875, 13.

119. "A Boy-Slave's Treadmill," *New York Herald*, August 13, 1874, 8.

120. See Pearson, *Rights of the Defenseless*.

121. "Human vs. Dog Life—Where's Bergh?" *New York Herald*, June 30, 1874, 8.

122. Coleman, *Humane Society Leaders*, 73–75. See also Pearson, *Rights of the Defenseless*.

123. Jack London, *Call of the Wild* (1903, reprint London: Puffing Books, 2008), 42. Cases of dog labor in San Francisco appear in several newspaper articles, including "Industrial Topics: A Dog-Power Device for Pumping," *San Francisco Chronicle*, August 24, 1888, 5; *San Francisco Chronicle*, October 3, 1893, 9; "The Dog as a Motor," *San Francisco Chronicle*, July 30, 1891, 6.

124. See T. J. Jackson Lears, *No Place of Grace: Antimoderism and the Transformation of American Culture, 1880–1920* (New York: Pantheon Books, 1981); and William Cronon, "The Trouble With Wilderness," in *Uncommon Ground: Rethinking the Human Place in Nature*, edited by William Cronon (New York: W. W. Norton, 1996): 69–90.

125. Ambrose Bierce, "Dog," in *The Collected Works of Ambrose Bierce, Volume XI* (New York: Neale Publishing Company, 1912), 310–327, 320.

6. Captivating Spectacles: Public Battles over
Animal Entertainment

1. "Passage of Niagara by the Schooner Michigan," *Ariel* 1, no. 12 (October 6, 1827): 92; "Descent of the Michigan over Niagara Falls," *Baltimore Gazette,* September 17, 1827, 2 (reprinted article from the *Rochester Telegraph*).

2. "Descent of the Michigan," *Cleveland Weekly Herald,* September 14, 1827, 3; "Descent of the Michigan over Niagara Falls," *Baltimore Gazette,* September 17, 1827, 2.

3. "Descent of the Michigan," *Cleveland Weekly Herald,* September 14, 1827, 3.

4. "Descent of the Michigan over Niagara Falls," *Baltimore Gazette,* September 17, 1827, 2.

5. For estimates of crowd sizes I have relied on several sources. For the Animal Boat at Niagara: Samuel De Veaux, *The Falls of Niagara* (Buffalo: William B. Hayden, 1839), 70–71, which estimated a crowd of 15,000 to 20,000; The *Buffalo Emporium* estimated a crowd of 10,000 to 12,000 (see the issue of September 10, 1827); *Ariel* estimated between 15,000 and 30,000, see "Passage of Niagara by the Schooner Michigan," *Ariel* 1, no. 12 (October 6, 1827): 92. Paul Johnson puts the crowd size at somewhere between 10,000 and 50,000, see Johnson, *Sam Patch: The Famous Jumper* (New York: Hill and Wang, 2003), 107. For the crowds at Jackson's inauguration, Margaret Bayard Smith estimated around 20,000 people, though she, herself, questioned that number as a bit "exaggerated." Others have put the number gathered that day closer to 10,000 people. See Robert Remini, *Andrew Jackson: The Course of American Freedom, 1822–1832* (New York: Harper and Row, 1981), 74–76. Estimates for the Cane Ridge Revival are between 12,000 and 40,000, but the largest at any one time was probably no more than 20,000. See Samuel Hill, *Religion in the Southern States: A Historical Study* (Macon, GA: Mercer University Press, 1983), 104; William Wallis Woodward, *Surprising Accounts of the Revival of Religion in the United States of America* (Philadelphia: William W. Woodward, 1802), 107.

6. The crowds might have been larger had the event not been scheduled for the end of the season. One journalist, writing for the *Buffalo Emporium,* believed that if the "voyage" were postponed until June, "thousands would flock from Europe to witness it." See *Buffalo Emporium,* July 23, 1827.

7. The histories of animal entertainment and popular culture in the nineteenth century are too extensive to list in full. See in particular: Janet M. Davis, *The Circus Age: Culture & Society under the American Big Top* (Chapel Hill: University of North Carolina Press, 2002); Susan Nance, *Entertaining Elephants: Animal Agency and the Business of the American Circus* (Baltimore: Johns Hopkins University Press, 2013); James W. Cook, *The Arts of Deception: Playing with Fraud in the Age of Barnum* (Cambridge, MA: Harvard University Press, 2001); along with the numerous works on P. T. Barnum cited throughout.

8. Elizabeth McKinsey, *Niagara Falls: Icon of the American Sublime* (Cambridge: University of Cambridge Press, 1985), 148.

9. "Descent of the Michigan over Niagara Falls," *Baltimore Gazette,* September 17, 1827, 2.

10. William Lyon Mackenzie, *Sketches of Canada and the United States* (London: E. Wilson, 1833), 94.

11. McKinsey, *Niagara Falls,* 148.

12. For my understanding of the "sublime," I rely on: McKinsey, *Niagara Falls;* Barbara Novak, *Nature and Culture: American Landscape and Painting, 1825–1875,* 3rd ed. (Oxford: Oxford University Press, 2007); and William Cronon, "The Trouble with Wilderness," in *Uncommon Ground: Rethinking the Human Place in Nature,* edited by William Cronon (New York: Norton, 1995), 69–90.

13. Ginger Strand, *Inventing Niagara: Beauty, Power, and Lies* (New York: Simon and Schuster, 2008), 65; and Donald Braider, *The Niagara* (New York: Holt, Rinehart and Winston, 1972), 246.

14. "Descent of the Michigan," *Cleveland Weekly Herald,* September 14, 1827, 3; John W. Hall, *Marine Disasters of the Great Lakes* (Detroit: Free Press Book and Job Printing, 1872), 4; Johnson, *Sam Patch.*

15. "Niagara Falls," *Cleveland Weekly Herald,* August 10, 1827, 3.

16. *Essex Register,* September 17, 1827, 3.

17. Strand, *Inventing Niagara,* 65.

18. For the Cartesian understanding of animals, see: Roderick Nash, *The Rights of Nature: A History of Environmental Ethics* (Madison: University of Wisconsin Press, 1989), 18; Marion Lane and Stephen Zawistowski, *Heritage of Care: The American Society for the Prevention of Cruelty to Animals* (Westport, CT: Praeger, 2008), 12.

19. "Descent of the Michigan over Niagara Falls," *Baltimore Gazette,* September 17, 1827, 2.

20. "Grand Descent over the Falls of Niagara," *Eastern Argus,* August 10, 1827, 1; "Descent of the Michigan," *Cleveland Weekly Herald,* September 14, 1827, 3; "Descent of the Michigan over Niagara Falls," *National Aegis,* September 26, 1827, 1; "The Passage of the Niagara, by the Schooner Michigan," *Kaleidoscope* 8, no. 381 (October 16, 1827): 127–128.

21. "Passage of Niagara by the Schooner Michigan," *Ariel* 1, no. 12 (October 6, 1827), 92.

22. "Passage of Niagara by the Schooner Michigan," *Ariel* 1, no. 12 (October 6, 1827), 92; *Essex Register,* September 17, 1827, 3.

23. *Essex Register,* September 17, 1827, 3.

24. "Grand Descent over the Falls of Niagara," *Eastern Argus,* August 10, 1827, 1.

25. *Essex Register,* September 17, 1827, 3.

26. "Grand Descent over the Falls of Niagara," *Eastern Argus,* August 10, 1827, 1.

27. De Veaux, *Falls of Niagara,* 70.

28. Jon T. Coleman, *Vicious: Wolves and Men In America* (New Haven, CT: Yale University Press, 2004); Katherine C. Grier, *Pets in America: A History* (Chapel Hill: University of North Carolina Press, 2006).

29. Robert Buford, *Description of a View of the Falls of Niagara* (Boston: Perkins and Marvin, 1837), 9; De Veaux, *Falls of Niagara,* 71.

30. Vernon Kisling Jr., "The Origin and Development of American Zoological Parks to 1899," in *New Worlds, New Animals: From Menagerie to Zoological Park in the*

Nineteenth Century, edited by R. J. Hoage and William A. Deiss (Baltimore: Johns Hopkins University Press, 1996), 109–125, 110–111.

31. See Mark Fiege, *The Republic of Nature* (Seattle: University of Washington Press, 2012).

32. Robert Schofield, "The Science Education of an Enlightened Entrepreneur: Charles Willson Peale and His Philadelphia Museum, 1784–1827," *American Studies* 30, no. 2 (Fall 1989): 21–40, 25.

33. Peale's use of Linnaean taxonomy was significant. Linnaeus was among the more conservative theorists at the time, arguing that species were immutable, distinct, and separate. Evidencing his scientific "turn," Peale shifted the naming pattern of his sons from famous painters (Raphael, Rembrandt, Titian, Rubens, Vandyke) in the 1770s and 1780s to famous scientists (Charles Linnaeus, Benjamin Franklin) in the 1790s. Sally Gregory Kohlstedt, "Entrepreneurs and Intellectuals: Natural History in Early American Museums," in *Mermaids Mummies and Mastodons: The Emergence of the American Museum,* edited by William T. Anderson (Washington, DC: American Association of Museums, 1992), 24.

34. Schofield, "Science Education of an Enlightened Entrepreneur," 37.

35. See Thomas Jefferson, *Notes on the State of Virginia* (London: Stockdale, 1787); Lee Alan Dugatkin, *Mr. Jefferson and the Giant Moose: Natural History In Early America* (Chicago: University of Chicago Press, 2009).

36. Edward Alexander, "Mermaids, Mummies, and Mastodons," in Anderson, *Mermaids, Mummies, and Mastodons.*

37. Schofield, "Science Education of an Enlightened Entrepreneur," 30.

38. Schofield, "Science Education of an Enlightened Entrepreneur," 33.

39. David R. Brigham, "Social Class and Participation in Peale's Philadelphia Museum," in Anderson, *Mummies, Mermaids and Mastodons,* 84.

40. For more on these tensions, see: Seth Rockman, *Scraping By: Wage Labor, Slavery, and Survival in Early Baltimore* (Baltimore: Johns Hopkins University Press, 2009); Sean Wilentz, *The Rise of American Democracy: Jefferson to Lincoln* (New York: Norton, 2006); and Johnson, *Sam Patch.*

41. Schofield, "The Science Education of an Entrepreneur," 31.

42. Schofield, "The Science Education of an Entrepreneur," 32.

43. Neil Harris, *Humbug: The Art of P. T. Barnum* (Boston: Little, Brown, 1973), 108.

44. For Barnum, I have relied on numerous secondary sources: Harris, *Humbug;* A. H. Saxon, *P. T. Barnum: The Legend and the Man* (New York: Columbia University Press, 1989); John Richards Betts, "P. T. Barnum and the Popularization of Natural History," *Journal of the History of Ideas* 20, no. 3 (June–September 1959): 353–368; James Cook, *The Arts of Deception: Playing with Fraud in the Age of Barnum* (Cambridge, MA: Harvard University Press, 2001); and M. R. Werner, *Barnum* (New York: Harcourt Brace, 1923), among others. These works have complemented Barnum's own writings, including *Struggles and Triumphs* (Buffalo, N.Y.: Warren, Johnson & Co., 1873), which was revised and republished over the course of the late nineteenth century, along with P. T. Barnum and A. H. Saxon, *Selected Letters of P. T. Barnum* (New York: Columbia University Press, 1983).

45. For more on the importance of labor in environmental history and in evolving human-animal relationships, see Richard White, "Animals and Enterprise," in *The Oxford History of the American West,* edited by Clyde Milner, Carol A. O'Connor, and Martha A. Sandweiss (New York: Oxford University Press, 1994), 237–274; and Richard White, "'Are You an Environmentalist or Do You Work for a Living?': Work and Nature," in Cronon, *Uncommon Ground,* 171–185.

46. Werner mentions that Barnum owned a sheep and a calf of his own as a child. See Werner, *Barnum,* 5.

47. Barnum, *Struggles and Triumphs* (1873), 25

48. Barnum, *Struggles and Triumphs* (1873), 27.

49. Barnum, *Struggles and Triumphs* (1873), 32–33.

50. As David Hall notes, deformed animals were often understood in Puritan New England as spiritual signs and symbols. See David Hall, *Worlds of Wonder, Days of Judgment: Popular Religious Belief in Early New England* (Cambridge, MA: Harvard University Press, 1990). See also John Murrin, "'Things Fearful to Name': Bestiality in Early America," in *The Animal-Human Boundary: Historical Perspectives,* edited by Angela N. H. Creager and William Chester Jordan (Rochester, NY: University of Rochester Press, 2002), 115–156.

51. Playing on these distinctions and tensions, Barnum later hired a man to wear "Oriental costume" and plow at his Bridgeport estate using an elephant. The performance was synchronized with train schedules to draw the attention of passengers. This generated quite a bit of media attention and free advertising in the 1850s. See Barnum, *Struggles and Triumphs* (1873), 357.

52. Schofield, "Science Education of an Enlightened Entrepreneur," 22.

53. Harris, *Humbug,* 33.

54. Harris, *Humbug,* 33.

55. Phineas Taylor Barnum, *The Yankee Showman and Prince of Humbugs* (London: Piper, Stephenson and Spence, 1855), 88.

56. Barnum, *Yankee Showman and Prince of Humbugs,* 88.

57. For pervasive questions of popular and scientific understandings of classification of species, particularly in nineteenth-century Britain, see Harriet Ritvo, *The Platypus and the Mermaid: And Other Figments of the Classifying Imagination* (Cambridge, MA: Harvard University Press, 1997), and Jan Bondeson, *The Feejee Mermaid and Other Essays in Natural and Unnatural History* (Ithaca, NY: Cornell University Press, 1999).

58. Harris, *Humbug,* 65–66.

59. Harris, *Humbug,* 64; Barnum, *Life of P. T. Barnum* (London: Sampson Low, Son & Co., 1855), 238.

60. Harris, *Humbug,* 62, Barnum, *Struggles and Triumphs* (1873), 71, Barnum, *Life of P. T. Barnum* (1855), 231.

61. For distrust of experts in this period, see Ronald Walters, *American Reformers, 1815–1860* (New York: Hill and Wang, 1995, 1978), and Charles Rosenberg, *The Cholera Years: The United States in 1832, 1849, and 1856* (Chicago: University of Chicago Press, 1962, 1987).

62. Saxon, *Barnum*, 122.

63. Harris, *Humbug*, 89.

64. "The Exhibition at the Masonic Hall," *Charleston Courier,* January 21, 1843, 2.

65. Saxon, *Barnum*, 121.

66. Barnum, *Struggles and Triumphs* (1873), 130.

67. Saxon, *Barnum*, 122–123.

68. Saxon, *Barnum*, 98.

69. Phil B. Kunhardt Jr., Philip B. Kunhardt, and Peter W. Kunhardt, *P. T. Barnum: America's Greatest Showman* (New York: Knopf, 1995), 290–291.

70. P. T. Barnum to "My dear Uncle Sol," letter 86, in Barnum and Saxon, *Selected Letters of P. T. Barnum,* 104.

71. Cook, *Arts of Deception,* 129.

72. Cook, *Arts of Deception,* chapter 3, "Describing the Nondescript," 119–162; Saxon, *P. T. Barnum,* 98–99; Harris, *Humbug,* 167.

73. See "Amusements," *New York Times,* March 1, 1860, 12 and March 2, 1860, 7. See also Cook, *Arts of Deception,* chapter 3.

74. As quoted in Frederick Douglass, *The Claims of the Negro, Ethnologically Considered: An Address before the Literary Societies of Western Reserve College, at Commencement, July 12, 1854* (Rochester: Lee, Mann & Company, 1854), 6–7.

75. Agassiz's mentor, the influential French scientist Georges Cuvier, argued that Africans were "the most degraded of human races, whose form approaches that of the beast and whose intelligence is nowhere great enough to arrive at regular government." As quoted in Randall Fuller, *The Book That Changed America: How Darwin's Theory of Evolution Ignited a Nation* (New York: Viking, 2017), 113.

76. For more on science and biological racism, see Ann Fabian, *The Skull Collectors: Race, Science, and America's Unburied Dead* (Chicago: University of Chicago Press, 2010); George Frederickson, *Racism: A Short History* (Princeton, NJ: Princeton University Press, 2002); George M. Frederickson, *The Black Image in the White Mind: The Debate on Afro-American Character and Destiny, 1817–1914* (Middletown, CT: Wesleyan University Press, 1987); Matthew Karp, *This Vast Southern Empire: Slaveholders at the Helm of American Foreign Policy* (Cambridge, MA: Harvard University Press, 2016), 164–165; Fuller, *The Book That Changed America,* 88–90.

77. P. T. Barnum to "My dear Uncle Sol," 104.

78. Frederick Douglass, "What to the Slave Is the Fourth of July?" in *My Bondage and My Freedom* (New York: Miller, Orton & Co., 1857), 443.

79. Douglass, *Claims of the Negro,* 8.

80. Douglass, *Claims of the Negro,* 10.

81. Douglass, *Claims of the Negro,* 8.

82. Douglass, *Claims of the Negro,* 8.

83. Allan Nevins and Milton Halsey Thomas, eds., *The Diary of George Templeton Strong: The Civil War, 1860–1865* (New York: Macmillan, 1952), 12. See also: Saxon, *Barnum,* 99, and Cook, *Arts of Deception,* 139.

84. David Roediger, *The Wages of Whiteness: Race and the Making of the American Working Class* (London: Verso, 1991), 133.

85. Harris, *Humbug,* 167. For further discussion of "What Is It?" in the scientific and cultural context of mid-nineteenth–century America, see Cook, *Arts of Deception,* and Fuller, *Book That Changed America.*

86. Harris, *Humbug,* 108.

87. Harris, *Humbug,* 186, 189–192, 196–200.

88. Zulma Steele, *Angel in Top Hat* (New York: Harper Brothers, 1942).

89. ASPCA Annual Report for the Year Ending 1870, 43; C. C. Buel, "Henry Bergh and His Work," *Scribner's Monthly* 7, no. 6 (April 1879): 872–884.

90. Steele, *Angel in Top Hat,* 169.

91. See Susan Pearson, *The Rights of the Defenseless: Protecting Animals and Children in Gilded Age America* (Chicago: University of Chicago Press, 2011).

92. P. T. Barnum, *The Life of P. T. Barnum, Brought Up to 1888* (Buffalo: Courier Company, 1888), 346.

93. "Disastrous Fire," *New York Times,* July 14, 1865, 1; Barnum, *Life of P. T. Barnum* (1888), 241–246.

94. Henry Bergh to P. T. Barnum, March 7, 1867, vol. 7, ASPCA Private Collection, New York City (henceforth cited as ASPCA Collection)

95. Henry Bergh to John Row, July 25, 1866, vol. 7, ASPCA Collection.

96. Henry Bergh to John Row, July 25, 1866, vol. 7, ASPCA Collection.

97. Letter from Henry Bergh to the Managers of Barnum's Museum, December 11, 1866, New York Historical Society digital collection, accessed December 21, 2018, http://digitalcollections.nyhistory.org/islandora/object/islandora%3A103373.

98. Louis Agassiz to P. T. Barnum, February 28, 1867, vol. 7, ASPCA Collection, and also transcribed online, "Letters between P. T. Barnum and Henry Bergh of the ASCPA," accessed December 21, 2018, https://lostmuseum.cuny.edu/archive/letters-between-p-t-barnum-and-henry-bergh-of. For the question of feeding snakes live animals see Lane and Zawistowski, *Heritage of Care,* 24.

99. For more on this, see Daniel Walker Howe, *What Hath God Wrought: The Transformation of America, 1815–1848* (Oxford: Oxford University Press, 2007).

100. Letter from Henry Bergh to the Managers of Barnum's Museum, December 11, 1866, New York Historical Society digital collection, accessed December 21, 2018, http://digitalcollections.nyhistory.org/islandora/object/islandora%3A103373.

101. Henry Bergh to P. T. Barnum, March 7, 1867, transcribed online, accessed December 21, 2018, http://digitalcollections.nyhistory.org/islandora/object/islandora%3A103373.

102. P. T. Barnum to Henry Bergh, March 11, 1867, transcribed online, accessed December 21, 2018, http://digitalcollections.nyhistory.org/islandora/object/islandora%3A103373.

103. Henry Bergh to P. T. Barnum, March 7, 1867, vol. 7, ASPCA Collection, also transcribed online, accessed December 21, 2018, http://digitalcollections.nyhistory.org/islandora/object/islandora%3A103373.

104. Letter from P. T. Barnum to Henry Bergh, March 11, 1867, ASPCA Collection, also transcribed online, accessed December 21, 2018, http://digitalcollections.nyhistory.org/islandora/object/islandora%3A103373.

105. Letter from P. T. Barnum to Henry Bergh, March 11, 1867.

106. "Mr. Bergh, Mr. Barnum, and the Boa," *Round Table: A Saturday Review of Politics, Finance, Literature, Society and Art* 5, no. 112 (March 30, 1867): 196–197.

107. Steele, *Angel in Top Hat,* 237; Gerald Carson, "The Great Meddler," *American Heritage* 19, no. 1 (December 1967), accessed May 15, 2019, https://www.americanheritage.com/great-meddler.

108. Although SPCA organizations across the United States monitored circuses and traveling shows, the itinerancy of these animal exhibits likely made them harder to regulate.

109. Barnum, *Life of P. T. Barnum* (1888), 322–323.

110. Barnum, *Life of P. T. Barnum* (1888), 323–324.

111. Barnum, *Life of P. T. Barnum* (1888), 323–324.

112. A larger development of a rhetoric of humane elephant training techniques emerged in the last decades of the 1800s. See Davis, *Circus Age,* 159–160. See also Nance, *Entertaining Elephants,* 132–133. For the wider use of positive training techniques in the late nineteenth century, see Pearson, *Rights of the Defenseless,* 44–50.

113. The original letter from Bergh likely appeared in the *Democratic Times,* a New York newspaper, as quoted in Steel, *Angel in Top Hat,* 245. Barnum used the quote in later versions of his autobiography, see Barnum, *Life of P. T. Barnum* (1888), 351.

114. P. T. Barnum to Spencer Baird, April 11, 1883, in Barnum and Saxon, *Selected Letters of P. T. Barnum,* 233.

115. ASPCA Collection, folder "The Fire-Horse Salamander," newspaper clipping, *The Herald,* April 14, 1880. "Mrs. P. T. Barnum" is listed as the sole vice president from Bridgeport in *The Connecticut Humane Society: First Annual Report, 1880–1881* (Hartford: Case, Lockwood, and Brainard, 1881), 3.

116. Saxon, *Barnum,* 238; Connecticut Humane Society Annual Reports for the years 1881–1882, 1895.

117. Henry Bergh to P. T. Barnum, March 22, 1884, Connecticut Digital Archive, accessed May 15, 2019, https://collections.ctdigitalarchive.org/islandora/object/110002:5397.

118. *Will & Codicils of Phineas Taylor Barnum,* Barnum Museum Collections, Connecticut Digital Archive, accessed November 7, 2018, https://collections.ctdigitalarchive.org/islandora/object/60002%3A3118. See pages 26, 46–47.

119. *Will & Codicils of Phineas Taylor Barnum,* Barnum Museum Collections, Connecticut Digital Archive, accessed November 7, 2018, https://collections.ctdigitalarchive.org/islandora/object/60002%3A3118. See pages 26, 46–47.

120. Barnum's estate was appraised at total value of $4,278,532. "P. T. Barnum's Estate," *New York Times,* June 9, 1891, 4.

121. Barnum, *Life of P. T. Barnum* (1888), 330.

122. Carson, "Great Meddler." See also: "Barnum's Will Not Respected," *New York Times,* August 2, 1894, 5.

123. Harris, *Humbug,* 280.

124. Steel, *Angel in Top Hat,* 245.

125. "Henry Bergh's Funeral," *New York Times,* March 17, 1888, 8; "Death of Henry Bergh," *New York Times,* March 13, 1888, 8.

126. Steel, *Angel in Top Hat*, 246.

127. "Henry Bergh's Funeral," *New York Times*, March 17, 1888, 8.

128. Steele, *Angel in Top Hat*, 248.

129. "Mr. Bergh Interferes," *New York Times*, August 26, 1886, 8; Steele, *Angel in Top Hat*, 246.

7. Domesticating the Wild: Woodward's Gardens and the Making of the Modern Zoo

1. Robert Frost, "At Woodward's Gardens," *Poetry: A Magazine of Verse*, edited by Harriet Monroe, 18, no. 1 (April 1936): 2–3.

2. My understanding of the backlash to modern urban life—particularly in gendered terms—is most influenced by T. J. Jackson Lears, *No Place of Grace: Antimoderism and the Transformation of American Culture, 1880–1920* (New York: Pantheon Books, 1981) and Lears, *Rebirth of a Nation: The Making of Modern America, 1877–1920* (New York: Harper, 2010); Gail Bederman, *Manliness & Civilization: A Cultural History of Gender and Race in the United States, 1880–1917* (Chicago: University of Chicago Press, 1995), and Anthony Rotundo, *American Manhood: Transformations in Masculinity from the Revolution to the Modern Era* (New York: Basic Books, 1993).

3. See Chapters 4–6 in this volume, Susan J. Pearson, *The Rights of the Defenseless: Protecting Animals and Children in Gilded Age America* (Chicago: University of Chicago Press, 2011), and Janet M. Davis, *The Gospel of Kindness: Animal Welfare and the Making of Modern America* (New York: Oxford University Press, 2016).

4. Barbara Berglund, *Making San Francisco American: Cultural Frontiers in the Urban West, 1846–1906* (Lawrence: University Press of Kansas, 2007), 77, 242.

5. *Fourth Annual Report of the New York Zoological Society* (New York: Office of the Society, 1900), 76.

6. *Fourth Annual Report of the New York Zoological Society*, 79.

7. "Editor John P. Young Talks to Socialists," *San Francisco Call*, April 15, 1907, 2.

8. John P. Young, *San Francisco, a History of the Pacific Coast Metropolis, Vol. 1* (Chicago: S. J. Clarke, 1912), 59.

9. Young, *San Francisco*, 58.

10. For SFSPCA efforts to modify and curb bullfighting, see: "Sunday Sport," *San Francisco Chronicle*, November 12, 1877, 3; "Spoiled a Bull Fight," *San Francisco Call*, July 8, 1895, 10; "Humane Society Reviews Its Work: Will Take Immediate Steps to Prevent the Bull Fight," *San Francisco Chronicle*, July 22, 1902, 7; "'Humane' Bull Fight Held Despite Ministers," *San Francisco Call*, August 15, 1904, 3.

11. Young, *San Francisco*, 58.

12. "The Cobweb Palace, San Francisco," *Overland Monthly* 72, no. 6 (December 1918): 582–585. James R. Smith, *San Francisco's Lost Landmarks* (Sanger, CA: World Dancer Press, 2005), 56.

13. See P. T. Barnum, *Struggles and Triumphs* (Buffalo, NY: Warren, Johnson & Co., 1873) 529–542; Theodore Hittell, *The Adventures of James Capen Adams* (Boston: Crosby, Nichols, Lee and Company, 1860).

14. Barnum, *Struggles and Triumphs,* 531. See also Jon T. Colman, "The Shoemaker's Circus: Grizzly Adams and Nineteenth-Century Animal Entertainment," *Environmental History* 20, no. 4, (October 1, 2015): 593–618.

15. Terence Young, *Building San Francisco's Parks, 1850–1930* (Baltimore: Johns Hopkins University Press, 2004), 37–42; R. A. Burchell, *The San Francisco Irish, 1848–1880* (Berkeley: University of California Press, 1980), 31; Philip Dreyfus, *Our Better Nature: Environment and the Making of San Francisco* (Norman: University of Oklahoma Press, 2008), 91, 94.

16. Charles Warren Stoddard, *In the Footprints of the Padres* (San Francisco: A. M. Robertson, 1901, 1911), 100; Dreyfus, *Our Better Nature,* 94.

17. Stoddard, *In the Footprints,* 100.

18. Dreyfus, *Our Better Nature,* 93–94.

19. Mark Twain, *The Innocents Abroad, Roughing It* (New York: Library of America, 1984), 870.

20. Stoddard, *In the Footprints,* 110; Nancy Olmsted, *Vanished Waters: A History of San Francisco's Mission Bay* (San Francisco: Mission Creek Conservancy, 2010), 35; Nancy Olmsted, "Early Development around Mission Bay, 1850–1857," Found SF, accessed April 10, 2015, http://foundsf.org/index.php?title=Early_Development _Around_Mission_Bay,_1850-1857.

21. For nature and urban reform, see Young, *Building San Francisco's Parks*; Michael Rawson, *Eden on the Charles: The Making of Boston* (Cambridge, MA: Harvard University Press, 2010); Catherine McNeur, *Taming Manhattan: Environmental Battles in the Antebellum City* (Cambridge, MA: Harvard University Press, 2014); Roy Rosenzweig and Elizabeth Blackmar, *The Park and the People: A History of Central Park* (Ithaca, NY: Cornell University Press, 1992); Frederick Law Olmsted and S. B. Sutton, *Civilizing American Cities: Writings on City Landscapes* (New York: Da Capo Press, 1997); Colin Fisher, "Nature in the City: Urban Environmental History and Central Park," *OAH Magazine of History* 25, no. 4 (October 1, 2011): 27–31.

22. "R. B. Woodward," *Daily Alta California,* August 23, 1879, 1; Gary Kurutz, "A Library of Libraries: The Formation of the Adolph Sutro Collection and the Library of Woodward's Gardens," *California State Library Foundation Bulletin,* no. 57 (October 1996): 9–14; Berglund, *Making San Francisco American;* Dreyfus, *Our Better Nature.*

23. Kurutz, "Library of Libraries," 11.

24. "City Items," *Daily Alta California,* July 31, 1862, 1.

25. "Improvements at the Mission," *California Farmer and Journal of Useful Sciences,* August 19, 1864, 1; "City Items," *Daily Alta California,* November 13, 1864, 1. See also Caroline Winterer, *The Culture of Classicism: Ancient Greece and Rome in American Intellectual Life 1780–1910* (Baltimore: Johns Hopkins University Press, 2002).

26. "City Items," *Daily Alta California,* November 13, 1864, 1.

27. "City Items," *Daily Alta California,* April 25, 1866, 1.

28. Classified advertisements for Woodward's Gardens first appear in July 1866. See *Daily Dramatic Chronicle,* July 3, 1866, 3.

29. See Berglund, *Making San Francisco American.*

30. *Illustrated Guide and Catalogue of Woodward's Gardens* (San Francisco: Francis, Valentine & Co., 1880), 3–4.

31. "Woodward's Gardens!" *Daily Alta California,* August 7, 1866.

32. "Sunday Recreations," *Daily Alta California,* August 21, 1869, 2.

33. *Illustrated Guide and Catalogue of Woodward's Gardens* (1880), 4.

34. "May Day Excursion of Vallejo School Children," *Daily Alta California,* May 2, 1869, 1.

35. The ten organizations were the San Francisco Benevolent Association, the Protestant Orphan Asylum, Catholic Orphan Asylum, Ladies Protection and Relief Society, British Benevolent Society, French Benevolent Society, German Benevolent Society, Italian Benevolent Society, Eureka Benevolent Society, and the San Francisco Lying-in Hospital. See "Generous," *Sacramento Daily Union,* December 7, 1870, 3. For more on church groups, see the Woodward's Gardens Collection, California State Library, Box 2842, folder 24.

36. See *Daily Alta California,* October 15, 1871, 4. In 1871, Woodward's Gardens served as the centerpiece attraction in a fundraiser for victims of the Chicago Fire.

37. "One of Our Parks," *Pacific Rural Press,* January 7, 1871, 13.

38. "The Resort for the People!" *Daily Alta California,* January 10, 1879, 4.

39. "Sunday Recreations," *Daily Alta California,* August 21, 1869, 2.

40. For one of many examples, see "Pacific Coast News," *Los Angeles Herald,* September 8, 1878, 2.

41. Loomis T. Palmer, *The Life of General U.S. Grant: His Early Life, Military Achievements, and History of His Civil Administration, His Sickness and Death, Together with His Tour around the World* (Hartford, CT: Park, 1885), 570.

42. "Wants Two Sea Lions," *Daily Alta California,* January 9 1871, 1. Woodard and Barnum also corresponded in the early 1870s. See Box 2842, folders 18, 38, Woodward's Gardens Collection, California State Library.

43. "Sea Lions to Be Interviewed," *Daily Alta California,* September 26, 1872, 1.

44. Mrs. Frank Leslie, *California: A Pleasure Trip from Gotham to the Golden Gate* (New York: Carleton & Co., 1877), 176.

45. Leslie, *California,* 176.

46. Leslie, *California,* 176.

47. "A Visit to Woodward's Gardens," *Elevator,* October 26, 1872, 1.

48. Leslie, *California,* 176.

49. "The Central Park of the Pacific," *Pacific Rural Press* 15, no. 10 (March 9, 1878): 153.

50. Anthony Trollope, "Nothing to See in San Francisco," in *San Francisco Stories,* edited by John Miller (San Francisco: Chronicle Books, 1990), 25–30.

51. Otto Finsch, "Ornithological Letters from the Pacific," *Ibis* 4, no. 13 (July 28, 1879): 75–76.

52. See Nigel Rothfels, *Savages and Beasts: The Birth of the Modern Zoo* (Baltimore: Johns Hopkins University Press, 2002) and R. J. Hoage and William A Deiss, eds., *New Worlds, New Animals: From Menagerie to Zoological Park in the Nineteenth Century* (Baltimore: Johns Hopkins University Press, 1996).

53. *Illustrated Guide and Catalogue of Woodward's Gardens* (1880), 64.

54. Finsch, "Ornithological Letters," 75–76.

55. The images discussed here are available through the Online Archive of California and Calisphere, University of California at Berkeley. Stereographs of the West from the Bancroft Library Pictorial Collection. For Muybridge, see Rebecca Solnit, *River of Shadows: Eadweard Muybridge and the Technological Wild West* (New York: Viking, 2003).

56. For birds on hats, see Jennifer Price, *Flight Maps: Adventures with Nature in Modern America* (New York: Basic Books, 1999).

57. For the history of animal taxonomy and classification in, particularly in nineteenth-century Britain, see Harriet Ritvo, *The Platypus and the Mermaid: And Other Figments of the Classifying Imagination* (Cambridge, MA: Harvard University Press, 1997). Ritvo notes that "the classification of animals, like that of any group of significant objects, is apt to tell as much about the classifiers as about the classified" (xii).

58. Based on access to *Illustrated Guide and Catalogue of Woodward's Gardens* published in 1869, 1873, 1875, 1879, 1880, and 1893.

59. See *Illustrated Guide and Catalogue of Woodward's Gardens* (1880).

60. See Vernon Kisling, ed., *Zoo and Aquarium History: Ancient Animal Collections to Zoological Gardens* (Boca Raton, FL: CRC Press, 2001), 375–376.

61. See Hoage and Deiss, *New Worlds, New Animals,* and Rothfels, *Savages and Beasts.*

62. "How to Catch Sea Lions," *Los Angeles Herald,* July 4, 1879, 1. "The Men Who Take Sealions Alive," *San Francisco Call,* July 21, 1907, 1.

63. The sea lions were usually priced by the pound, at about 50 cents per pound, sometimes 25 cents. See Woodward's Gardens Collection, Box 2842, folder 33; Box 2845, folders 11, 32, 46, and 78.

64. Woodward's Gardens Collection, Box 2842, folder 18, containing a letter from Barnum's Museum to Robert Woodward, March 24, 1874.

65. "Fur Seals Die in Captivity," *San Francisco Call,* November 29, 1909, 4; "Letters from the People," *San Francisco Call,* December 14, 1909, 6.

66. For zoo stereotypies, see G. J. Mason and J. Rushen, eds., *Stereotypic Animal Behaviour: Fundamentals and Applications to Welfare,* 2nd ed. (Wallingford, UK: CAB International, 2006).

67. *Fourth Annual Report of the New York Zoological Society,* 50.

68. Rothfels, *Savages and Beasts,* 75–76.

69. Rothfels, *Savages and Beasts,* 70.

70. As quoted in Rothfels, *Savages and Beasts,* 67.

71. Neil Harris, *Humbug: The Art of P. T. Barnum* (Boston: Little, Brown, 1973), 179.

72. For these examples, see Woodward's Gardens Collection, Box 2842, folder 51; Box 2843, folders 1, 18, 64, and 69; Box 2844, folders 6 and 9.

73. Woodward's Gardens Collection, Box 2842, folder 37.

74. Woodward's Gardens Collection, Box 2842, folder 84.

75. Woodward's Gardens Collection, Box 2843, folder 9.

76. For these examples see (in order), Woodward's Gardens Collection: Box 2842, folder 86; Box 2843, folder 12; Box 2844, folder 7; Box 2842, folder 41; Box 2842,

folder 12; Box 2842, folder 34; Box 2842, folder 53. For seals and sea lions from Santa Barbara, see: Box 2842, folders 33 and 81; Box 2844, folders 28 and 54; Box 2845, folders 11, 32, and 46.

77. See Rothfels, *Savages and Beasts*, especially chapter 2; Eric Ames, *Carl Hagenbeck's Empire of Entertainments* (Seattle: University of Washington Press, 2008); Elizabeth Hanson, *Animal Attractions: Nature on Display in American Zoos* (Princeton, NJ: Princeton University Press, 2002).

78. Woodward's Gardens Collection, Box 2843, folder 73.

79. Woodward's Gardens Collection, Box 2843, folder 14.

80. Woodward's Gardens Collection, Box 2843, folder 31.

81. Woodward's Gardens Collection, Box 2842, folder 58.

82. Woodward's Gardens Collection, Box 2843, folder 70.

83. *Illustrated Guide and Catalogue of Woodward's Gardens* (1873).

84. "Amusements, Etc.," *Daily Alta California*, March 18, 1868, 1.

85. See David Igler, *Industrial Cowboys: Miller & Lux and the Transformation of the Far West, 1850–1920* (Berkeley: University of California Press, 2001).

86. See Chapters 2 and 3 in this volume for discussions of livestock removal from San Francisco. For ideas of distinctions between country and city, see William Cronon, "The Trouble with Wilderness," in *Uncommon Ground: Toward Reinventing Nature*, edited by William Cronon (New York: W. W. Norton, 1995), 69–90, and Raymond Williams, *The Country and the City* (New York: Oxford University Press, 1973).

87. Woodward's Gardens Collection, Box 2843, folder 57.

88. Woodward's Gardens Collection, Box 2842, folder 15.

89. Woodward's Gardens Collection, Box 2842, folder 35.

90. Woodward's Gardens Collection, Box 2842, folder 47; Box 2845, folder 32.

91. Woodward's Gardens Collection, Box 2842, folder 64; Box 2842, folder 76; Box 2843, folder 61; Box 2843, folder 8; Box 2843, folder 33; Box 2844, folder 15; Box 2843, folder 63.

92. Woodward's Gardens Collection, Box 2842, folder 79.

93. Woodward's Gardens Collection, Box 2843, folder 4.

94. Woodward's Gardens Collection, Box 2843, folder 63.

95. *Fourth Annual Report of the New York Zoological Society*, 50.

96. See *Illustrated Guide and Catalogue of Woodward's Gardens* (1879).

97. Woodward's Gardens Collection, Box 2843, folder 62. A "Chinese Giant" and his wife were on display as early as 1870, see: "Brief Items," *Sacramento Daily Union*, July 7, 1870, 2. For the "Bear Indian Child," who could not walk upright or speak, but who "grunts like a bear," see Woodward's Gardens Collection, Box 2843, folder 23.

98. "A Visit to Woodward's Gardens," *Elevator*, October 26, 1872, 1. The article described the African "Fire King"—a stout man, "dark as any African we ever saw" who walked on coals, drank boiling oil, and put melted lead in his mouth.

99. See Twelfth Annual Report of the San Francisco Society for the Prevention of Cruelty to Animals (San Francisco: Office of the Society, 1879), 21. The absence of Woodward in the SFSPCA enforcement records is based on an index search of

agent diaries and prosecution records. See agent diary volumes available only for the years 1877–1879, 1879–1880, 1881–1882, 1882–1883, 1883–1884, 1884–1885, 1885–1886. See also "Record of Prosecutions," in SFPL Special Collections, unprocessed SFSPCA collection.

100. See Agent Diary for 1877–1879, SFPL Special Collections, unprocessed SFSPCA collection.

101. *San Francisco Call*, May 7, 1895, 6.

102. "Woodward's Gardens," *Daily Alta California*, May 15, 1886, 8; "A Day of Sports," *Daily Alta California*, July 5, 1887, 8.

103. "The Woodward's Gardens," *San Francisco Call*, August 24, 1892, 3.

104. "A Use for the Surplus," *San Francisco Call*, April 7, 1893.

105. "Starvation at Our Doors," *San Francisco Call*, August 25, 1892, 4.

106. "Work of a Miscreant," *San Francisco Call*, February 5, 1893, 8.

107. "Starvation at Our Doors," *San Francisco Call*, August 25, 1892, 4.

108. "Birds for Curios," *San Francisco Call*, April 7, 1893, 8; "And Bruin Wept," *San Francisco Call*, April 8, 1893, 8.

109. "Birds for Curios," 8.

110. "Gardens of Woe," *San Francisco Call*, May 4, 1893, 3.

111. "Bear Meat for the San Francisco Market," *San Francisco Chronicle*, January 24, 1897, 9. This article discusses bear hunting for urban meat markets, along with the emerging practice of raising bears on farms for urban meat markets, noting that "a stall-fed bear designed for the market is treated in about the same way as a hog."

112. "And Bruin Wept," *San Francisco Call*, April 8, 1893, 8; "Gardens of Woe," *San Francisco Call*, May 4, 1893, 3.

113. See Roderick Nash, *Wilderness and the American Mind*, 4th ed. (New Haven, CT: Yale University Press, 2001), 152.

114. The parallel transformations in manliness and hunting culture are notable in the last decades of the nineteenth century. Tina Loo, "Of Moose and Men: Hunting for Masculinities in British Columbia, 1880–1939," *Western Historical Quarterly* 32, no. 3 (Autumn 2001): 296–319. For manliness in this period, see Bederman, *Manliness & Civilization*, and Rotundo, *American Manhood*. For the place of animals and hunting in the new and pervasive culture of manliness, see Nash, *Wilderness and the American Mind*, 138–139 and 150–153. For the rise of sport hunting in this period and its popularity among urban elites, see John F. Reiger, *American Sportsmen and the Origins of Conservation* (New York: Winchester Press, 1975), Karl Jacoby, *Crimes against Nature* (Berkeley: University of California Press, 2001), Louis Warren, *The Hunter's Game: Poachers and Conservationists in Twentieth-Century America* (New Haven, CT: Yale University Press, 1997), and Lisa Mighetto, *Wild Animals and American Environmental Ethics* (Tucson: University of Arizona Press, 1991).

115. "The Lion's Fate," *San Francisco Call*, April 13, 1893, 2.

116. "The Lion's Fate," *San Francisco Call*, April 13, 1893, 2.

Conclusion: Stampede

1. Harry F. Walsh, "Cattle Stampede at Mission and Fremont," in *Three Fearful Days: San Francisco Memoirs of the 1906 Earthquake & Fire*, edited by Malcom E. Barker (San Francisco: Londonborn, 1998), 97–99. Walsh's account originally appeared in *Argonaut* (San Francisco), May 15, 1926.

2. Rufus M. Steele, "Killing an Army of Horses to Rebuild San Francisco," *Harper's Weekly* 51, no. 2626 (April 20, 1907): 580–581.

3. SFSPCA Annual Report: 1907, 8–9.

4. Steele, "Killing an Army of Horses."

5. Richard Bulliet, *Hunters, Herders and Hamburgers: The Past and Future of Human-Animal Relationships* (New York: Columbia University Press, 2005); Richard White, in *The Oxford History of the American West*, edited by Clyde Milner, Carol A. O'Connor, and Martha A Sandweiss (New York: Oxford University Press, 1994), 237–274; John Berger, "Why Look at Animals?" in *About Looking* (New York: Vintage, 1980): 3–28.

6. George Angell, *Autobiographical Sketches and Personal Recollections* (Boston: Franklin Press, 1884), appendix, 7–8.

7. See Bulliet, *Hunters, Herders, and Hamburgers*; Steven Pinker, *The Better Angels of Our Nature: Why Violence Has Declined* (New York: Viking, 2011); Rank Ascione, *Children and Animals: Exploring the Roots of Kindness and Cruelty* (West Lafayette, IN: Purdue University Press, 2005); Frank Ascione and Phil Arkow, *Child Abuse, Domestic Violence, and Animal Abuse: Linking the Circles of Compassion for Prevention and Intervention* (West Lafayette, IN: Purdue University Press, 1999).

8. Those struggles are revealed in the spate of literature on animal rights and animal welfare, including some works that have influenced this project: Peter Singer, *Animal Liberation: A New Ethics for Our Treatment of Animals* (New York: Random House, 1975) and Singer, *In Defense of Animals: The Second Wave* (Malden, MA: Blackwell, 2006), Cass R. Sunstein and Martha C. Nussbaum, eds., *Animal Rights: Current Debates and New Directions* (New York: Oxford University Press, 2004), Michael Pollan, *The Omnivore's Dilemma: A Natural History of Four Meals* (New York: Penguin Press, 2006), Tom Regan, *The Case for Animal Rights*, updated with a new preface (Berkeley: University of California Press, 2004), and Gary Francione, *Rain without Thunder: The Ideology of the Animal Rights Movement* (Philadelphia: Temple University Press, 1996).

9. Pinker, *Better Angels of Our Nature*, 471.

10. Some notable examples include: Pollan, *Omnivore's Dilemma*; Eric Schlosser, *Fast Food Nation: The Dark Side of the All-American Meal* (Boston: Houghton Mifflin, 2001); Jonathan Safran Foer, *Eating Animals* (New York: Little, Brown, 2009); and various films including the adaptation of *Fast Food Nation* (2007), *Food, Inc.* (2009), and *Death on a Factory Farm* (2009).

11. See "Treatment of Animals on the Ballot," Ballotopedia, accessed May 15, 2019, https://ballotopedia.org/Treatment_of_animals_on_the_ballot#By_year.

12. See Peter Moore, "Majority Endorse Animal Rights," and underlying polling data from YouGov, April 2015, accessed May 15, 2019, https://today.yougov.com/topics

/lifestyle/articles-reports/2015/04/29/majority-endorse-animal-rights. See also Lake Research Partners Memo, June 28, 2016, via ASPCA, accessed May 15, 2019, https://www.aspca.org/sites/default/files/publicmemo_aspca_labeling_fi _rev1_0629716.pdf.

13. "New York City's Pet Population," New York City Economic Development Corporation, accessed May 15, 2019, https://www.nycedc.com/blog-entry/new -york-city-s-pet-population.

14. Lisa Pickoff-White and Ryan Levi, "Are There Really More Dogs Than Children in S.F.?" KQED News, May 24, 2018, accessed May 15, 2019, https://www.kqed .org/news/11669269/are-there-really-more-dogs-than-children-in-s-f.

15. See Jim Sterba, *Nature Wars: The Incredible Story of How Wildlife Comebacks Turned Backyards into Battlegrounds* (New York: Broadway Books, 2012).

16. USDA, "Overview of U.S. Livestock, Poultry, and Aquaculture Production in 2017," accessed February 11, 2019, https://www.aphis.usda.gov/animal_health /nahms/downloads/Demographics2017.pdf.

17. See Pollan, *Omnivore's Dilemma* and "Power Steer," *New York Times Magazine,* March 31, 2002.

18. Esther Honig, "JBS Sells U.S.-Based Cattle-Feedlot Business for $200 Million after Brazilian Scandals," Harvest Public Media, March 20, 2018; Wyatt Bechtel, "JBS to Sell Five Rivers Cattle Feeding for $200 Million," *Drovers,* January 17, 2018.

19. Zulma Steele, *Angel in Top Hat* (New York: Harper Brothers, 1942), 6. This quote has appeared elsewhere, too, though the absence of footnotes in Steele's work—and the unavailability of archival sources available to her—has obscured its origins.

20. Angell, *Autobiographical Sketches,* 88, appendix, 6.

21. Upton Sinclair, *Autobiography of Upton Sinclair* (New York: Harcourt, Brace and World, 1962), 126.

22. US Government Accounting Office, "Workplace Safety and Health: Safety in the Meat and Poultry Industry, while Improving, Could Be Further Strengthened," GAO-05-96, January 12, 2005, accessed March 1, 2018, http://www.gao.gov /products/A15498. See also: Schlosser, *Fast Food Nation*; Timothy Pachirat, *Every Twelve Seconds: Industrialized Slaughter and the Politics of Sight* (New Haven, CT: Yale University Press, 2011); and Jennifer Dillard, "A Slaughterhouse Nightmare: Psychological Harm Suffered by Slaughterhouse Employees and the Possibility of Redress through Legal Reform," *Georgetown Journal on Poverty Law & Policy* 15, no. 2 (Summer 2008): 391–408.

23. Gail A. Eisnitz, *Slaughterhouse: The Shocking Story of Greed, Neglect, and Inhumane Treatment inside the U.S. Meat Industry* (Amherst, NY: Prometheus Books, 2007), 87.

ACKNOWLEDGMENTS

In writing a book, one accrues debts too great to list in only a few pages. This is an effort—no doubt incomplete—to acknowledge the colleagues, friends, and institutions that made this book possible through financial, intellectual, and emotional support. I am grateful for all the help I have had along the way, especially to those mentioned here.

This project began at Stanford University, where I was supported generously with fellowships from the History Department, the Bill Lane Center for the American West, and the Stanford Humanities Center—along with various travel and research grants from the History Department and the School of Humanities and Sciences.

My generous institutional support has continued at Boston University, which backed this project in many ways, including a junior faculty fellowship and teaching leave that allowed me to finish the manuscript. The B.U. Center for the Humanities provided an additional fellowship and award that gave me time and resources to finish this project and begin the next one. I am deeply grateful for B.U.'s commitment to developing teachers and scholars.

Intellectually, this project has roots in countless communities. My love of history was cultivated through remarkable social studies teachers at all levels of public schools in Concord, Massachusetts. At Brandeis University, I encountered exceptional history professors and small seminars that fostered my love of history. It was at Brandeis that Brian Donahue introduced me to environmental history, and where I became enchanted by the poetic lectures of David Hackett Fischer.

At Stanford, my development as a historian was shaped by Bart Bernstein, Matthew Booker, Al Camarillo, Jim Campbell, Gordon Chang, Zephyr Frank, Estelle Freedman, Allyson Hobbs, Amalia Kessler, Jack Rakove, Richard White, Kären Wigen, and Caroline Winterer. Any and all shortcomings of this book are mine alone.

I am also grateful for my graduate student community at Stanford—in particular the regular meetings of the U.S. History Workshop with Branden Adams, Jon Christensen, Andy Hammann, Destin Jenkins, Natalie Johnson, Kevin Kim, Beth Lew-Williams, Nicole Martin, Maria Ponomarenko, Julie Prieto, Claire Rydell, Scott Spillman, Alex Stern, Chris Suh, and Tim Tomlinson. At Stanford and beyond, I have had wonderful friends and colleagues who have been supportive in countless ways. I am especially grateful for the encouragement and friendship of Cameron Blevins, Lori Flores, Andy Gerhart, Cassie Good, Annelise Heinz, Ben Hoy, Ethan Hutt, Gabriel Lee, Julia Mansfield, Natalie Marine-Street, Katherine Marino, Lindsey Martin, Catherine McNeur, Alexis Peri, Kelly Richter, Nicholas Viles, and Adam Visconti. Thank you.

Although it appears now as a printed book, this project was very much shaped by work in the digital humanities—a sort of work that is truly collaborative in nature. The Animal City project (which remains online) enjoyed financial support from the Stanford Spatial History Project and the Stanford Center for Spatial and Textual Analysis. I am deeply grateful for the research assistance of Liz Fenje and Mark Sanchez, who worked tirelessly to collect and refine data that led to key findings that appear in this book. Their excitement and willingness to take on new challenges injected lifeblood into the project at numerous points. Jake Coolidge and Erik Steiner spent days—and probably some weekends—working through digital aspects of this project that were far beyond my expertise. My gratitude to Erik Steiner runs even deeper, as he created many of the maps and visualizations that appear in this book.

Over the past four years, I've been fortunate to be a part of a supportive and deeply engaged department at Boston University. I have grown from formal and informal conversations with my U.S. history colleagues: Brooke Blower, Daniel Bluestone, Charles Capper, Lou Ferleger, Brendan McConville, Will Moore, Sarah Phillips, Jon Roberts, Ed Russell, and Nina Silber. I could not ask for a more generous mentor, colleague, and friend than Bruce Schulman, who also read and commented on parts of the manuscript. I am grateful to be a part of a community of such dedicated scholars, teachers, and colleagues at B.U.

Over the years, I've enjoyed presenting pieces of this book at various venues, particularly the annual meeting of the American Society for Environmental History and Massachusetts Historical Society's seminar series. Sean Kheraj, Matt Klingle, Catherine McNeur, and Strother Roberts organized conference panels and conversations that ended up being immensely helpful. I am grateful to the Urban History Association, which generously advanced this project toward publication by conferring the Michael Katz award for my work. I am also grateful to Harriet Ritvo and Ed Russell, who generously read and commented on individual chapters of the manuscript.

There have been numerous archivists and research gatekeepers who were instrumental in helping me research this project. Susan Goldstein and Dee Dee Kramer at the San Francisco Public Library allowed me access to the San Francisco SPCA collection before it had been formally catalogued and sorted. This project would not have been possible without access to those records. Steven Zawistowski at the American Society for the Prevention of Cruelty to Animals in New York City and Jan Holmquist at the Massachusetts SPCA were beyond generous in their time and in sharing resources.

The final making of this book was a team effort with Harvard University Press. From our first conversation, Andrew Kinney believed in this book and effectively advanced the manuscript at every stage of publication. I am grateful for his thoughtful engagement and advocacy. Olivia Woods and Stephanie Vyce held my hand as I navigated the process of producing a book for the first time. The two anonymous reviewers engaged honestly and deeply with the manuscript and offered immensely helpful comments and support. Finally, the timely publication of this book would not have been possible without the help of Patrick Browne at Boston University, who organized and prepared images for publication. I am deeply grateful for his work.

My greatest debt of gratitude for this book—and for my development as a historian—is to Richard White, who has patiently supported and challenged me for more than a decade now. Richard's dedication as an advisor is unmatched in our profession, and I will always cherish having had the opportunity to work with someone of such astounding intellect, dedication, generosity, and kindness. As I have begun mentoring graduate students, I strive to pay forward the support I received from Richard. It is a tall order.

There are many who have lived closely alongside this project and deserve thanks simply for being there. I am grateful for the companionship of Lauren Meldonian and Karsten Barde, who shared a house in San Francisco's Bernal Heights, where most of the words in this volume were written. Many days of writing were hazy from sleep deprivation caused by an ambitious terrier named Harry, who lived next door and barked at raccoons by night and another neighbor's chickens by day. In San Francisco, the modern animal city was all too real.

Finally, I am grateful to family and friends for their love and support. Researching and writing a book can sometimes take a toll on relationships of all kinds. My extended family has been immensely supportive, as were Dan Garrelick, Andrew Guy, and Jonah Hall, who were always quick to return a call and to offer a humorous reprieve or words of encouragement. Bob Kagan has been a mentor, a family member, and a friend for almost two decades, and offered moral support and detailed comments on numerous chapters. My brother and sister-in-law, Carl Robichaud and Elsie Kagan, offered immeasurable moral support and encouragement, along with joyful diversions that included my nephews and niece: Jasper, Alexan, and Willa.

Throughout this project, I have been lifted and sustained by the unconditional love and support of my parents, William and Sandra Robichaud. I am grateful beyond words. Liz Beers bounded into my life as the end of this project was coming into sight. That was five years ago. Her love, patience, and unwavering support have helped me to finish these chapters and to begin the next ones together. It is to my mother, my father, and to Liz that I dedicate this work with deepest love and appreciation.

INDEX

The letter *f* following a page number denotes a figure.